THE PROCESS OF RECREATION PROGRAMMING
Theory and Technique
Third Edition

The Process of
Recreation Programming
Theory and Technique
Third Edition

Patricia Farrell
The Pennsylvania State University

Herberta M. Lundegren
The Pennsylvania State University

Venture Publishing, Inc.
1999 Cato Avenue
State College, PA 16801

Cover Design by Sandra Sikorski
Editorial Assistance by Michele Barbin
Production by Bonnie Godbey
Library of Congress Catalog Number 91-65114
ISBN 0-910251-40-1

To our students, families and friends.

To our students, families, and friends.

PREFACE

Good programming does not just happen; it is carefully planned for, thought about, and learned. Such skill cannot be picked up at the local department store, ready made and tailored to fit all situations. In this book we will take the programmer through the *process of programming*—addressing program classification systems, the setting of goals and objectives, and the evaluation of those objectives at the end of a class, a performance, a tournament, a club's season, or at the year's end. A close look at the participant and his or her life cycle and needs is provided. A program activity model consisting of five planning steps is proposed. The basic program areas are presented in terms of *how to program* the activities and experience rather than *how to do* the activity; for example, the reader will *not* learn how to shoot an arrow, play the guitar, chop down a tree, or make jewelry, but these are discussed in terms of how to "program" these activities or experiences in a step-by-step process. Motivations, leisure satisfaction and diversity of clientele are considered in terms of program needs of the participant.

We are fully aware that the beginning programmer's needs for specific skills and tools in the process are at different levels from those of the more advanced programmer, and the dilemma we faced was how to present material so that it would encompass that range successfully to allow *all* individuals to find something at a stage where they are best prepared to handle it. You will see the scope of the audience touched by recreation programming, and be introduced to the various ways of classifying activities in terms of facilities needed, age-group focus, and time the activity takes. We might ask the question, what is the effect on programming of participant-expected outcomes, and how can an area that is clearly designated for one specific outcome (e.g., golf course) be utilized to achieve other outcomes? What are the characteristics of the people of all ages who are going to use that facility and participate in that program, and how do their characteristics affect program planning? Last, but not least, is the question of approaches to programming. Do you place every activity you can think of before your participants and let them chose what they want, or do you set some objectives and plan programs to meet those objectives? What about needs? Should we be concerned with what the potential program participant thinks he or she wants? Programmers at all levels must consider these questions. We suggest you begin getting acquainted with the idea of needs, realizing that you should always know why you offered an activity and whether or not the goals you set were met in the activity. For example, if you offered an exercise program because your constituents wanted to improve their fitness, you should ask, "Did the program have enough vigorous activity in it for participants to improve fitness levels?" Some of the concepts presented may be difficult to grasp at first, but setting objectives is definitely desirable and, once you have mastered the technique, subsequent evaluation will be an easy task. Activity analysis, cluster analysis, and evaluation are techniques a programmer should master.

Chapters Four to Six are the meat of the programming process and take the programmer through all the processes needed to design programs and put them into operation under what we call the Five-Format Structure Model. This model includes (1) self-improvement, (2) competition, (3) social, (4) participant spectator, and (5) self-directing.

Format refers to the basic purpose for which a program is designed. Each format is explored in terms of how the program could be administered under that format, fee structure, budget, offerings under eight program areas for each format, types of leadership, and characteristics of participants who are drawn to each format. The important concept of scheduling is discussed here, and complete sample programs for such areas as ice rinks, swimming pools, and nature centers are presented, as are methods of inviting the public to join your programs. We believe that everyone, regardless of level of experience in programming, should read these three chapters carefully. Chapter Six is basically directed to the upper-level undergraduate, the graduate student, and the more experienced programmer. Although some evaluation should be conducted by everyone, the beginner must start with a brief questionnaire regarding participant satisfaction, conduct some observations of the program leader's on-the-job behavior, or check on whether a given program met the objectives set for it.

This book is directed to the programmer-in-training, to the student in a programming course, and to the experienced programmer who has been administering successful programs for years but now, contrary to earlier practice, has been told that (1) all programs will be planned on the basis of performance objectives, (2) interest inventories will be developed by the department personnel and administered on a regular basis, (3) since interest inventories show that environmental programs are high on the list, new environmental programs must be offered, or (4) financial constraints within the agency now require a greater demand for revenue-producing programs. Each teacher has a preference for how programming out to be taught. We encourage creative use of this textbook in hopes that we have been facilitators in this process.

In this third edition, we have added material that expands the programmers' understanding of the diversity of participants and their readiness for activity. We have considered leisure education, the use of volunteers, marketing of programs and qualitative approaches to evaluation. Those who are familiar with the first edition will welcome a reprise of data analysis presented here in Chapter Eight. We are excited about this revision and eager for you to use it and share our new ideas.

Programming is hard work but it is rewarding and, because it is, it is fun to do. Won't you join us and let us take you through the *process*?

Pat Farrell
Herberta Lundegren
January 1991

viii

CONTENTS

Preface

CHAPTER ONE

INTRODUCTION TO RECREATION ACTIVITY PROGRAMMING

SCOPE OF THE AUDIENCE

Recreation activity programming is a process. It is essentially a five-step process that includes all the critical planning elements. This book is focused on each of these steps with suggested techniques and pointers to aid the recreation programmer. This process is applicable to any agency that provides recreation program services to its constituents, and regardless of which agency is sponsoring the recreation program, the process is similar and employs the same procedural steps. In this book all areas of recreation activity planning and operations are covered. Regardless of agency sponsorship, the process for organizing the delivery of recreation services is essentially the same. There are some fundamental philosophical differences regarding the purpose for providing service; yet the process, planning and management techniques remain the same.

The authors intend the word recreation to mean the activity itself. Therefore, a recreation manager, leader, supervisor or director is that professional who handles the program activity within the recreation enterprise or recreation department. As a result of this understanding of the word recreation, the reader is encouraged to see the breadth of activity as significantly wide, challenging, limited by only the programmer's imagination, and an incredibly exciting opportunity to bring the concept of "the pursuit of happiness" into the center of the programmer's job.

There are some fundamental considerations that must be addressed when tackling the programming job. A decision must be clear throughout the organization regarding the purpose for which the program is offered. Knowing the purpose for doing anything is just good common sense; but knowing what is expected of the programmer in terms of service, profit, progress toward rehabilitation, gains in knowledge, etc. dramatically impacts on choices that must be made by the program manager. It is to these issues that this book is directed. The process used in programming is similar, but the setting in which the program takes place and the purposes guiding that enterprise are the differences that are addressed in this text.

There are many agencies whose major function is the provision of recreation activity experiences for their clientele. These agencies are found in both the public and private sectors of society. Some governmental agencies are mandated by law to provide recreation services to the taxpaying public acknowledging that the provision for leisure services stands on a par with other government functions. In the private sector, businesses may decide to provide recreation services for employees (and many times families of these employees) as a part of the benefits offered by the employer, again on a par with the view that leisure services are considered just as essential to good employee relations as are hospital plans, retirement and health care benefits.

There are many recreation agencies who serve in a semi-private or quasi-public mode in our society. These agencies are funded in a variety of ways that makes classifying them difficult. Some agencies are membership oriented such as the YM/WCAs, scout groups for both boys and girls, 4-H, etc. These are the recreation groups that generally are affiliated with United Way agencies.

A substantial segment of the lives of people institutionalized for physical or mental health disorders or incarcerated as the result of court actions are spent in some type of recreational activity.

The 1980s saw a significant growth in the amount of leisure services delivered through private sector sponsorship. The for-profit industry invested heavily in the leisure market and the recreation professional was identified as providing the appropriate talent bank of leadership for this field.

In order to provide program services, agencies employ professional recreation program administrators to manage a delivery system of facilities and activity experiences.

Throughout this book the word program should be understood to encompass (1) the activity in which people participate, (2) the facility that enables the activity experience to take place, and (3) the leadership that has been responsible for facilitating this experience. This broad concept is intentional. It is not realistic to think of activity existing in unidentified space; nor is it valid to omit the role of the leader or the administrator who has had a critical part in making the activity experience happen.

SPONSORING AGENCIES

The scope of agencies involved in recreation activity services is broad. There is almost no organization existing in our society in which at some time a recreation program activity was not a part of the annual agenda. Therefore, it is not necessary to quarrel with whether or not an organization has as its total purpose or part of its purpose providing for recreation activity services. It is critical to the student who is preparing for a professional career in the field of recreation and parks to (1) be knowledgeable regarding the scope of career opportunities and the agencies likely to sponsor recreation, (2) be alert to all recreation services within one's own local area, (3) be looking for ways to share programming responsibilities between agencies, thereby avoiding overlapping, (4) recognize the potential of other professional colleagues within the geographical area, and (5) become a part of truly regional recreation service to people, rather than a single entity with little or no knowledge of what others in the same service area are providing, and (6) be a participant in recreation activities personally. Your own behavior demonstrates a commitment to the product you are attempting to sell. Be a knowledgeable and experientially informed professional.

It is possible to identify the categories of agencies who are potential employers of the professional recreation programmer. Six broadly oriented functional units or clusters can be described.

Church and Religious-Oriented Agencies

This cluster typically includes many of the voluntary youth-serving agencies. Hanson and Carlson (1972) have prepared a thorough review of these agencies from the general posture of the involvement of younger people and the reader is referred to that book for details beyond the scope of this book. Some of the following agencies have larger combined national memberships than do others, but all are nationally chartered with central offices and accompanying organizational structures.

1. All Protestant denominational youth groups.
2. American Youth Foundation.
3. B'nai B'rith Youth Organization.
   (a) National Federation of Temple Youth (NFTY).
   (b) United Synagogue Youth (USY).
   (c) National Council of Youth/Israel (NCYI).
4. Christian Service Brigade.
5. Catholic Youth Organization (CYO).
6. Junior Missionary Volunteers (JMV Pathfinders).
7. Mutual Improvement Association (MIA) Church of Jesus Christ of Latter Day Saints.
8. National Jewish Welfare Board.
9. Pioneer Girls.
10. Salvation Army.
11. United Boys' Brigade.
12. United Services Organization (USO).
13. Young Life.
14. Youth for Christ.
15. Young Men's Christian Association–YMCA of the USA (Y-Indian Guides; Gra-Y or Hi-Y).
16. Young Women's Christian Association–YWCA of the USA (Tri-Gra-Y; Tri-Hi-Y; or Y-teens).

Private Voluntary Agencies

This cluster, together with the previous agency grouping, includes the other youth-serving agencies. In many cases, the United Fund has provided heavy financial support to these agencies, who lean for leadership on the use of volunteer staff under the direction of small state or regional professional staff. These agencies include:

1. American Legion.
2. American Red Cross.
3. American Youth Hostels, Inc.
4. Big Brothers of America.
5. Boy Scouts of America.
6. Boys Clubs of America.
7. Camp Fire, Inc.
8. Girl Scouts of the United States.
9. Girls Clubs of America, Inc.
10. Police Athletic League (PAL).
11. Settlement houses (specific to funding source).
12. Woodcraft Rangers.
13. Youth Organization United.

Each recreation serving agency has it own charter, function, and purpose. Resource materials, program standards, and suggested program tools and techniques are available through most agency systems. For instance: (1) scout manuals include badge and activity program requirements and suggestions; (2) there are regular periodicals in which program ideas and practical technique suggestions are shared; (3) use is made of research findings or established practices within the system; or (4) national standards exist for satisfactory levels of program service. Some of these materials are available through commercial outlet stores, while all materials could of course be traced through central home offices or headquarters. Youth serving agencies such as the Scouts may have specific program requirements for participants in their organization. Other agencies offering recreation program activity utilize the lifetime programming–a method in which a variety of offerings is made in hope that a broad spectrum of program interest will be served.

Government Agencies

One of the most functionally diverse clusters includes the group of agencies that operate totally or in part from tax based funding. Most of the following operate at many different governmental levels. Local, county (parish), state, and federal service systems are not uncommon, particularly in public recreation and park systems, correctional institutions, and resource based agencies. The local agency is more closely related to direct program services for the participant, while levels up the vertical system tend to be oriented toward the functions of facility management funding, revenue sharing, development of standards for planning, evaluation, and performance.

1. Armed forces or individual military base recreation.
2. Bureau of Land Management.
3. Corps of Engineers.
4. County Recreation Services.

5. Extension Service–through the Federal Department of Agriculture.
6. Fish and Wildlife Services.
7. General or specific disability homes, institutions, hospitals (mental retardation, psychiatric, physical disability, addiction, etc.).
8. National and state forest services.
9. National Park Service.
10. Natural resource or conservation departments.
11. Park districts or regional recreation/parks authorities.
12. Penal system agencies–corrective/rehabilitation.
13. Public recreation and parks departments–all levels.
14. State recreation bureaus/departments.
15. Tourist and convention services–federal and state.
16. Youth bureaus.

School and Education Agencies

Some of the agencies listed below are funded through tax monies, yet differ from the strictly governmental arena as was described in the previous section. Almost every public and private school, college, and university supports an extracurricular activity program. These activities are structured generally through varsity, intramural, and club programs.

1. Future Farmers of America (FFA).
2. Future Homemakers of America (FHA).
3. Intramural Department.
4. Job Corps.
5. Junior Achievement.
6. National Audubon Society.
7. National Grange.
8. School recreation districts.
9. Schools' performance groups, debate club, varsity sports, bands, etc.
10. Special interest extracurricular club programs.
11. Student union boards (Association of College Unions).

Industrial and Commercial Agencies

The growth of industry-sponsored programs exclusively for employees and their immediate families has increased steadily since the end of World War II. Recreation programs and facilities were believed to decrease employee turnover, boredom, and accident rates, while increasing company loyalty, fitness, and the general quality of life. Each company involved in recreation services to its employees administers activities in a variety of ways. The National Employee Services and Recreation Association is the central clearinghouse for companies wishing to affiliate and exchange professional methods and materials. Communication in this regard is carried through a monthly periodical called *Employee Services Management*. Commercial recreation and for profit leisure services have seen a tremendous growth in the 1980's. Small recreation enterprises have become popular as well as an important growth area in resort, theme parks, and convention services as a part of the tourism industry. Early evidences of this growth industry were the fitness program interests of the early eighties, while the later part of the decade witnessed increased attention to tourist services at many destination facilities where programs were designed specifically for visitor participation.

Commercially oriented agencies are numerous and perhaps the most varied. Listed below are some typical facilities and special program-targeted areas that are likely to be found available. In each of these agencies the participant actively uses the area. There are, of course, many commercial facilities that are designed to amuse and entertain the spectator participant, and these are not included here simply because there is so much variety. Professional preparation in a baccalaureate recreation and parks program has been helpful but not an advantage for employment in these types of businesses or industries:

1. Campgrounds.
2. Casinos, bars, and taverns.
3. Eating and dancing cafes/clubs.
4. Fishing ponds and other activity-specific sport and athletic areas such as golf courses, bowling lanes, aquatic centers, indoor/outdoor tennis facilities, billiard and pool centers, electronic playlands, amusement parks and centers, skating rinks, ski and winter sport areas.
5. Private camps.
6. Resort areas.
7. Retirement facilities (homes, developments, communities).
8. Theme parks.
9. Outdoor recreation facilities that provide rafting, trail riding, hiking trails, hang gliding areas, etc.

Since land tends to be central to many commercial enterprises and the government tends to be an important land holder, the provision of recreation activities is often a contracted service through leases with the land holding agency.

There are many organizations and agencies that have not been included in the preceding pages, since this listing has not been designed to be complete; instead, it is an attempt to note some of the more obvious agencies in which one might expect to find recreation program services provided.

PROGRAM CLASSIFICATION SYSTEMS

In order to handle the task of programming for any constituency within an agency, attention must be given to working from a fundamental understanding of the range, breadth, and variety of program opportunities that are potentially available. This requires the recreation staff to design a system that makes sense for its agency and a system consistent with its goals and purposes. Why? The tremendous variety of what is considered to be "leisure time activity" or recreation is so vast that the task must be disaggregated or broken down into manageable parts; thus giving the programmers some simple and uncomplicated ways to think about their jobs and the provision of a professional program of recreation activity.

There are a number of ways of attempting to disaggregate the programmer's task. To be an effective manager of the program requires the staff to classify activity into sensible units that are realistic for the agency. There is a popular way to code activity that has been used in preparing this textbook. Turn back to the table of contents and notice that chapter six is a presentation of program areas. This is a traditional system for classifying activity and we will call the categories of art, dance, sport, etc.–the functional program areas.

There are other ways to classify program activities. It is possible to look at this concept from the following views: (1) facilities required, (2) number of people required to do the activity or social interaction, (3) age-groups, (4) time availability, (5) motives and interests, and (6) expected outcomes.

Why is classification of activity given attention? In order to get a full look at the variety and balance of any program, the administrator of the program must be able to use some measuring stick. Any system to measure variety in programming will be a useful tool to the program evaluator. In the process of making an internal or external review of the program, some notion of breadth, variety, and scope will be of interest to the reviewer. Although a classification of programs is only one component of this review, it is an important one. Therefore, the more discrete a program activity classification system is the more useful that system becomes to the review and evaluation process.

Although utilizing the functional program areas has been a popular method for classifying activity, the challenge to the recreation profession is to go beyond this system and be prepared to codify activity in various other ways. This process demands that activity be more fully understood than simply knowing the name, rules, and equipment needs of an activity. It is important to know what possibilities exist for an area that on paper has been designed as a tennis court, a basketball floor, or a soccer field. The facility planners must not be the only ones to determine how an area should be used, and here we are including facility planners beyond the park and recreation planners. Shopping malls and parking lots, city streets, reservoirs, and natural wilderness areas, to mention a few, all have secondary functional uses which could be attractive to the recreation programmer. With an eye for innovation and creative use of space, each of these areas in its own way could facilitate additional programs. The shopping mall can be used to handle sidewalk art, walking area for indoor exercisers and puppet shows; parking lots are the skate board classroom and mobile van site; the reservoir and city street are the base facility for the kite contest and orienteering location; and the natural wilderness area carries the annual skijoring contest and cross-country skiing trails.

There are strengths and weaknesses inherent in all classification systems. Criteria for a strong system are that it:

1. Be discrete among units. This means that any given element in the group of "things" to be classified should be able to be placed into the same category no matter who was doing the classification. The units need to be clear and distinct. Think about the task of sorting solid-colored marbles. In order to do a correct job of sorting these marbles into categories; first, there need to be enough categories to accommodate all the colors of the marbles. Secondly, the names of the units have to be clear such that everyone sorting those marbles would put each marble in the same appropriate category. The units should be clearly identified, i.e. discrete, distinct, unique.

2. Cover all possible elements within the total construct. Continuing with the marbles example, there needs to be a unit for every marble. The sorter should not be left with a small handful of marbles not knowing where they fit or be unable to place them into some category.

3. Categorize components in approximately equal units. This criterion asks that when units or categories are being envisioned, that some size balance be considered. In essence, it is a question of how refined do the units need to be? Are two units better than eight? In our marble example, would it help to sort by a system of red and not red? Or would it be more helpful to sort by red, black, green, blue, white, etc.? Again, establishing the categories is a staff job. The number of units/categories must be compatible with the work and functions of the work to be done.

4. Relate all elements to one another. This guideline simply reminds us to sort like items. When the task is sorting marbles, do not have a category for baseball cards. They are not related in this classification system.

5. Avoid value judgements about the components. This relates back to criterion number one. It is always a stronger position in sorting, if the units are clearly defined such that no guessing on the part of the sorter ever occurs.

Any strong classification system should be able to withstand the test of all of the above criteria. For each criterion that is not met the system is weakened proportionately.

The programmer can look at classification, utilizing the above criteria. In the following four sections, a few of the systems that one might use to classify the recreation program are provided. Each system reflects a different approach in looking at program activity. The four systems are programming classification by (1) areas and facilities, (2) social interaction, (3) participant-expected outcomes, and (4) non-traditional activities of leisure education. The functional program area classification system referred to earlier is a first-order system, and it is expected that the programmer will go beyond this to a more complex, or secondary classification system in which not only the program area, for example, music, is considered, but additional factors such as social interaction will form the basis for further classification.

Classification by Areas and Facilities

In the previous section a few creative uses of established areas for recreation activities were suggested. It would be possible to list the variety of areas and types of facilities used by an agency and then note what activities could be planned in and on each facility. This listing of areas and facilities is a common process used for activity classifications in many agencies. A map may be posted in the main office with center building locations and parks designated. For agencies whose activities are building-centered, a list of open rooms is available.

To classify activity by a system that focuses on areas and facilities, the map or room chart should include mutations of activities that are possible within each of the areas shown. Almost every agency administrator is able to talk about the facilities in terms of acreage, number of ball diamonds, seating capacities, and square footage, yet it has been an almost neglected notion to talk about all the activities that people can do at these places. Therefore, to classify activity by areas and facilities, one needs to list all agency facilities and areas, and note the possible activities for which it could be used. This classification system would look as follows:

TABLE 1.1 Areas and Facilities Classification Example

Areas	Program Activities	
Golf course	Golf play	Sledding, tobogganing
	Golf driving range	Orienteering
	Cross-country running and skiing	Summer concerts
		Bird watching
	Jogging trail	Stargazing, fireworks
	Frisbee	viewing and firing range
	Arboretum	Site for planetarium
Tennis courts	Tennis play	Special events
	Dances	Talent show
	Skating	Band concerts
	New games site	Wheelchair games
	Bicycle skill contest	Skateboarding contests

An areas and facilities system has both advantages and disadvantages as a method for the classification of recreational activity. The first step is to test it against the criteria for judging a sound classification system. Go back to that section. Analyze this classification system against all criteria. Obvious weaknesses appear in the comparison, such as failing to meet criteria 1 and 3. It does meet the other requirements. Perhaps the biggest asset to the use of this system is that it assists others in addition to the program administrator in looking at a facility beyond its primary use and in exploring all the secondary uses for that area. This requires some trade-offs among personnel and departments regarding how the facility is to be used. For example, what if the best place to hold the summer concert series was on the steep slope of hole number twelve of the local golf course? Would closing that nine holes to play for six nights out of the season disrupt the golfers less in proportion to the trade-offs to the hundreds who might benefit from the music? Would that use for the concert ruin the course for the golfers? Traditionally, golf courses have been delicate facilities used for only one purpose. Can we continue to afford these luxuries? For those in the snow regions, golf courses have served important winter activities at minimal sacrifice to the game of golf. Again, this facility use requires a commitment to multiple use and innovative programming with the full knowledge that additional costs are going to be incurred. These costs are certainly not in proportion to that of building a band shell for hundreds of thousands of dollars, perhaps in a location with less aesthetic appeal and natural beauty. The possibilities are endless, yet traditional thinking and past practices are powerful counter forces when changes in use of facilities are proposed.

Managers of state and federal land operations are being asked to consider a Recreation Opportunity Spectrum system, which is another way of identifying potential uses of the land beyond a single purpose. The federal agencies (especially the U. S. Forest Service) are being deluged with users who seek a widening use of the environment. Greer (1990) has proposed a classification system that suggests some creative thinking on this topic. With continued refinement of the taxonomy presented in Table 1.2, the future work on this theme should be exciting to read.

Classification by Number of People Required to Do Activity-Social Interaction

A classification system using social interaction as its foundation can be simplistically devised. Working on a continuum from participation in an activity by a single individual to participation by a large crowd would be an acceptable approach to this system. In fact, this system might well be incorporated into any substantive evaluation process that is focused on program review, since this matter of numbers is implied in the program guideline that alludes to balance, variety, and diversity. This classification system would be organized as follows:

TABLE 1.2
Environmental Resources Habitat Classification Example

Category	Habitat
Extra-terrestrial	Microgravity environment
Open atmosphere	Thermals Clean, calm air Stormy or moving air
Land surface	Playing fields or arenas Tracks (established routes for races) Roads and trails Western wilderness Eastern wilderness Vertical climbing rock Desert Forest Range land and grasslands Beaches Rocky coasts
Ice and snow	Manicured snow Glaciers and mountain terrain Floating ice (ocean or sea, arctic) Floating ice (impounded as in lake shore or pond) Prepared ice (rink) Level or nearly level snow as in arctic expanses
Underground	Wet cave Dry cave Sea grotto Underground streams, rivers Mines
Water surface	Natural lakes Impounded, open reservoirs Ocean or sea Rivers and streams Wetlands
Underwater	Tropical reefs Deep open ocean or sea Rivers and streams Lakes and reserviors Deep pits, tubes, sinks

TABLE 1.3
Social Interaction Classification Example

Social Interaction	Activity
Alone/Single	Monologues, solo music (vocal or instrumental), sports—golf, swimming, hiking, fishing, hunting, cycling, sailing, track and field events, orienteering, archery, boating, bowling, bird-watching, nature walks, painting, sculpting, drawing, etc.
Alone/Together	Duets (vocal and instrumental), tennis, badminton, racket sports, board and table games, etc.
Small group (3-6)	Ensemble music, plays and skits, doubles in most racket sports, card games, etc.
Medium group (7-25)	Most team sports, small music groups (dance bands, madrigal singing groups, choristers), creative dramatics, parties, camping activities (cabin or unit), special interest clubs, etc.
Large group (26-100)	Choirs, orchestras, bands, most competitive team sports, theatre productions, classes in art, dance and crafts, etc.
Crowd mass (over 100)	Art festivals, sports events, special events (parades, celebrations, fairs, etc.), dance festivals, Octoberfests, and the like.

In the test of this classification system, it is again obvious that the first criterion—discreteness, is not met. One must be cautioned to keep the system free from judgmental aspects when viewing the alone/single area. It is tempting to suggest that many of these activities would be "more fun" if done with or in the presence of others, yet to be true to the classification system, this would be an inappropriate judgment to make. The obvious overlap tends to confound this system of classification yet, by virtue of activity format, the overlap is necessary. For example, let us consider figure skating on ice. Skating is an obvious example of overlap; in fact, it could appear in every category of this system. It is incumbent upon the program administrator to serve all these activity experiences in figure skating. From solo use of the ice to mass recreational skating times, all of these experiences need to be scheduled at the ice arena. The highly skilled skater needs time in the arena alone, when no other skaters are on the ice, since in perfecting the free-skating routine, the skater uses the entire rink. Also, pair skaters need ice time such that the two of them are present on the ice alone together. Small groups preparing for an ice show as a subgroup within the Silver Skaters Club will require rehearsal time, unhindered by other skaters. Perhaps the club apportions its time into 15-minute blocks for club members' use. In addition, the entire skating club may wish ice time for club skating, figure patchwork sessions, and general instruction work. Large groups, seeking mass instruction, will be an important programming element in the use of ice time. Finally, open recreational skating for all ages is necessary, for time for family groups is a must in an ice-skating program.

As has been discussed, it is not the activity that is the focus of this system, but rather the number of people required to do the activity. Some recreational agencies have traditionally been focusing service to large groups or crowd/mass populations, hoping that the small groups have been adequately served by the voluntary youth-serving agencies or through other leisure delivery systems. In times of tight money and intricate cost-benefit analyses, it has been difficult to justify facility development and programming efforts that serve a limited number of participants, especially when the organizational effort is similar regardless of how many people are served.

The professional recreation group that seems to come closest to working effectively with small and alone/together groups consists of those in the therapeutic agencies. The small group in these instances may be a part of the normalization process, and working with medium or large groups would be counterproductive. One caution should be noted here. The emphasis with some disability areas–psychiatric clients, for example, should not be in the single/alone area, since perhaps it is this aspect that is part of an individual's problem and a program requiring a group would be more appropriate.

The important point to note here is that even though agencies have developed traditional roles in terms of participant numbers in programs, it remains the creative challenge to any program administrator to work out other options and opportunities. Is it impossible to imagine permitting an eight-level or bronze-level skater the use of the ice between 2:00 and 3:00 AM in the morning? Could he/she be given a key and shown where the lights and tape decks are? Does the agency really need to have a supervisor on duty for this specialized type of use? Perhaps there are ways to extend use/time in the facilities to trusted members of the constituency without detracting from the mass use time slots. Our highly skilled participants will be willing to use facilities at unusual time periods. The general user will not find unusual hours attractive. Perhaps there are ways to serve small numbers, but this will take extra arranging and organizational efforts on the part of many people and especially on the part of the program administrator.

Classification by Expected Outcomes from the Activity Experience

Perhaps one of the most intriguing ideas concerning the classification of a recreation activity is exploring the meaning that an activity experience holds for each participant in the recreation program. We can then translate these findings into data on which to base program planning. A recurring and fascinating question seems to challenge the programmer: Why do people participate? Perhaps there are as many answers as there are people who are asked. The dilemma is most surely on the shoulders of the programmer. He or she designs a program with certain objectives and in many ways assumes that these same intents are held by the participant. Through some successful, and at times unsuccessful, trial and error periods, a common understanding between participant and leader is reached regarding what one can expect from various activity experiences. This process is clumsy, costly, and circumstantial. One is left with the thought that there ought to be a better way. A need exists for more research efforts to contribute to the solution to this problem. If we knew what people expected out of a program, how much more accurate our program planning could be and the programmer could be assured that participant needs were being met. Research currently being done in this area may produce findings of significance to the programmer.

This system of classification by expected outcomes is as refined as the program administrator wishes it to be and any number of categories could be used. A few are noted below and the reader will certainly want to add to the list:

Make friends.
Belong to a group.
Experience competition.
Learn a new skill.
Share a talent.
Have a night out.
Gain prestige.
Get in shape.

Almost any activity has the potential to serve these categories.

If this system is tested, it is shown to be lacking in criterion two–cover all possible elements–simply because there appears to be no limit to the totality of what constitutes expectations. It is tempting to look for some guarantees of results as far as an experience is concerned, but that is neither practical nor realistic. However, the study of program classification systems is an exciting area for further investigation and exploration.

If one were to examine any agency's recreation program, the findings would show certain patterns. These patterns would reflect an emphasis on similar types of activities. It is not unusual to find emphasis on sports programming and on medium- to large-size group activities. As you review any agency program, look for variety among some of the ideas presented in the secondary-level classification systems we have previously discussed. Do you find program variety among the functional program areas as you review various ongoing programs? Begin to ask not only what is the scope of the program, but also why it is as it is. What system has been used to establish program offerings, and is that system one that permits true variety from all sectors of the target population?

Non-traditional Activities of Leisure Education

Leisure education is a process by which people are taught to prepare for leisure (Farrell, 1989) much as they are prepared for work. Leisure education was originally thought to be under the purview of the school systems, and the recreation programs were where people would engage in activity because they were educated for leisure. The growth of adult education and the establishment of community educators brought to the programs themselves the need to develop value systems that included positive attitudes toward the use of leisure. Leaders find themselves teaching the public about program participation and providing them with the opportunity to develop the skills needed to take part in the planned programs or to pursue things on their own. The fact that young and middle aged adults found themselves with increased free time, the number of retirees is growing every year, and the philosophical approach to the disabled includes educating them for meaningful leisure experiences have combined to increase the attention being given to teach people about what is available for them to do and skills they need to be able to participate in various activities and events. Planning leisure for life has gained in importance as people live longer and are healthier. Research on leisure behavior shows that early life participation influences later life choices and attitudes. Further, the economic situation where the increase of the commercial profit-making aspects of the leisure industry and the growth in tourism where the audiences are moving away from the community, and the desire to increase quality of life have changed the picture some and caused concern over the status of education for leisure and who should be doing it. The bottom line seems to be that all programmers of leisure experiences and deliverers of leisure services are sharing the responsibility for the education for leisure of their particular clientele. It is not the only source of learning, but it is a key source.

What are the goals of leisure education? Let us take a look at those of a few exemplary programs. Mundy and Odum (1979) stated five goals for leisure education:

1. To develop an awareness of oneself.
2. To develop an awareness of the potential and significance of leisure in one's life and society.
3. To increase skills used during leisure time (activity skills).
4. To enhance one's social interaction skills.
5. To develop the decision-making and implementation skills necessary to enable the individual to the purposeful action.

Joswiak (1989) in a leisure education program for the developmentally disabled set three goals for the participant:

1. To demonstrate awareness of the meaning of play and leisure.
2. To demonstrate awareness of leisure resources in the home.
3. To demonstrate awareness of leisure resources in the community (p. 3).

Farrell (1989) suggests that the therapeutic recreation practitioners are doing more than any other group in employing leisure education with their clientele. This involvement is exemplified by Peterson and Gunn's (1984) Leisure Education Content Model which is conceptualized as being composed of four components: (1) Leisure awareness: knowledge of leisure, self-awareness, leisure and play attitudes and related participatory and decision-making skills; (2) Social Interaction Skills: dual, small group and large group; (3) Leisure Resources: activity opportunities, personal resources, family and home resources, community resources and state and national resources; and (4) Leisure Activity Skills: traditional and nontraditional. An expansion of these components may be found in Peterson and Gunn (1984).

Programmers must address the question of leisure education and what their role should be in delivering it in their agencies and communities.

PROGRAM APPROACHES WITH GUIDELINES

Being responsible for designing and managing the program offerings for an agency or any recreation enterprise is a significant responsibility in the organization. The program often represents the constituency's idea of the entire organization. If the program is weak, inappropriate or dull the user develops a negative opinion of the department or the total enterprise. When the program of activities is fresh, alive and exciting, clearly meeting the interests of the constituency, the opportunity to attract return visitors and participants as well as new users is greatly enhanced.

Thus, the program staff have a crucial role in making decisions about what actual activities should be made available to the potential customer. It is the strategy used in determining how to design the program that staff must address with professional wisdom. In addition, programming principles or guidelines are used to support various program approaches. Programmers must approach their task with some clear direction. The following principles are offered as possible guides whenever the program administrator begins the program design task.

It would be useful for the programming staff to have a clear vision of what the program activities were to accomplish–both philosophically and in articulation with the goals and purposes of the department. These should not just be "understood," but rather, should be written statements available to all staff and reminders to everyone in the organization. In this book, these statements are referred to as guidelines. These will be the guides against which every program will be compared to test the value of the proposed activity. Guidelines become the credo of the organization. In a well administered organization, every unit has its own particular set of guidelines whether it be budget, maintenance, personnel, etc., it must be clear in all areas what the nature of their service is to not only the rest of the organization but also to the constituency that the organization hopes to serve.

Guidelines relate to the intended quality of the program. Items such as safety, non-discrimination, variety in levels of skill, excellence in activity leadership become the areas where the program staff announce their intentions.

In the following pages, guidelines are indicated by solid dots and give examples not only of how these guidelines might be phrased, but how the guidelines themselves are related to specific program approaches.

Considerable attention has been directed toward solving the question of how program activities can be best delivered to the constituency. What is the best process to determine what programs will attract participants? How would one know, before investing large amounts of money into facility development, what the people want? There is perhaps no question of more single importance to the recreation programmer than that of what activities should be offered. There are many ways of resolving this question and perhaps this is a part of the programmer's dilemma.

The answer involves assumptions one must make about the potential participant. If the programmer believes that participants are unable to identify what they are interested in doing and are simply waiting to be told what to do, one style of program design will be used as an approach. If, however, the client is clearly able to articulate needs and specific activities to satisfy those needs, quite a different approach will be required. On the other hand, if funding opportunities appear to be possible because a program has met certain requirements, an entirely different approach may be taken. In addition, program staff serving for profit agencies are responsible for certain profit margins and must be sensitive to the user's willingness to pay for a program. This forces the program staff to weigh innovation against the tried and true successes of the past.

In the following section a variety of approaches to these questions are proposed such that each recreation programmer could operationalize within any given system. It is unreasonable to believe that any single approach will be the only one needed; thus, the reader should be looking ahead in terms of selecting one that is consistent with his or her leadership style. On the contrary, each approach will probably be found appropriate at various times in the programmer's career, and therefore each must be studied for its own value and be available for use when the occasion arises.

Programming by Objectives

Perhaps the most contemporary of all approaches, this tack of planning by objectives is one in which the programmer must clearly be able to chart some directions prior to the start of an activity. Inherent in selecting this approach are some assumptions:

1. The programmer is able to conceptualize the activity process. (This process is the program planning process.)
2. The programmer is skilled in writing performance objectives.
3. The objectives so stated are consistent with the objectives of the participants in the activity.
4. The program's success or failure will be evaluated fairly by whether the program has or has not realized its objectives.

We have chosen to begin with the objectives approach for many reasons. First, a sophisticated process is needed in the design of recreation programming. Second, well-written objectives provide a measurement opportunity by which accountability can be assessed and positions taken on whether or not to retain certain program activities. Third, the ability to put programs on a system of objectivity announces to others that professionals are at work. There is little question that almost anyone can run recreation programs; but it takes a person with professional preparation and know-how to use a programming approach with clear objectives. Finally, this approach is placed first because it is believed to be the most professionally sound system.

The approach itself should be based on solid planning principles. These include:
• The needs of the participants–recreation activity should be designed to meet the anticipated needs of the participants.
• Life enhancement–recreation programs should enhance educational and life-quality richness.
• Evaluation–recreation programs should be formally and regularly evaluated in terms of their planned purpose.
• Participant readiness–recreation programs should be related to participant readiness and abilities.

The programmer must be clear on the assumptions made and the principles that guide his or her efforts. The process of this programming approach is a simple one to discuss, yet a complex one to conceptualize and organize.

Programming by Desires of the Participants

This approach to programming is a most popular one to write about and discuss. To be opposed to this approach is a bit like disliking apple pie or not honoring motherhood. Again there are important assumptions to be considered when using this approach:

1. Desires of the participant groups can be ascertained.
2. Recreation programs are an important need-reduction milieu.
3. Programmers are able to understand which activities meet which desires in most individuals.
4. Programmers are able to know when desires have been met or satisfied.

As can be seen, these assumptions encompass a frightening amount of knowledge. The recreation profession is still unsophisticated when it comes to recognizing the meaning each experience has for the participant. We assume that people who continue to return to activities and programs must be having some important needs met, although we are not entirely clear what those needs are or what particular experiences within the activity are the meaningful ones to the participant. Therefore, in using this approach, the programmer must be willing to walk out on the proverbial limb and announce what desires are being met by the variety of activities in the overall program plan.

It is reasonable to suggest that after a fair amount of experience, programmers could develop a sensitivity to what meaning for the participant is inherent in specific activities.

Such a system of program development would demand long-term, on-the-job skill enhancement through constant assessment of activity value to the participant by the professional. The beginning programmer is mostly in the dark when it comes to being comfortable with this approach. If one is able to succeed in gaining this sensitivity, perhaps it is also possible for others to fail in this skill. Until the profession matures to the point of being able to ascribe certain happenings in certain activities that will satisfy certain desires, we are on uncertain ground in using this approach to programming and being able to defend the effects it has on the participants.

When we employ this approach there are planning principles that can be met:

- Needs and interest–recreation programs should be designed to meet the needs and interests of the participant.
- Variety and balance–recreation programs should encompass variety and balance both in substance and organizational patterns. This variety and diversity should encompass skill levels, in both sexes, noncompetitive to highly competitive activity, various financial arrangements–free to special costs, time offering, and format for participating in terms of size of activity groups. They should provide for social interaction.
- Health and safety–recreation programs should be set in an environment of safety and a healthy atmosphere.

Although the professionals seem to indicate the necessity for utilizing a programming approach based on desire, it is judged to be one of the most difficult to administer and certainly defend. This approach is addressed to satisfying interests that have been expressed to or felt by the programmer.

An evaluation of a program founded on this organizational approach must, of necessity, handle the behavioral changes that have occurred among the participants. Objectives must be set regarding what desires will be satisfied by the various activities. As stated previously, this requires knowledge that is generally unknown at that time in a planning sequence. Those studying the recreation field must approach this entire area with new research methodology.

Programming by Perceived Needs of the Participant

Of all the approaches to programming, this one is the most tempting to use and perhaps the easiest to design. In this approach the programmer makes some assumptions:

1. Because the programmer is a professional in the recreation field, he or she knows and understands what others will want.
2. The programmer is in a better position to know what others want than anyone else.
3. Participants are unable to identify program-activity desires.
4. Participants are anxious to be told what they are interested in.
5. Generally people are much the same, and time and money are saved by avoiding an expensive input system while the programmer designs what he or she thinks will be satisfactory.

Although the above assumptions tend to carry negative connotations, the programmer is often caught in a situation where no other alternative choice is possible, and efficiency or speed immediately become the criteria for the planning process. The programmer with a conscience agonizes over the use of this method, but recognizes the political stymie of the situation. There are times when it is difficult or impossible to seek guidance from the potential participant, and crucial decisions must be made by the programmer in isolation. However, the chances for misfiring are high and, since objectives are written with final evaluation in mind, the chances for program failure remain high.

Some programming principles can be attained while this approach is used:
- Available resources–recreation programs should be designed to utilize creatively all facilities and areas available.
- Planning–recreation programming should be efficiently organized and planned so that maximum participation is possible.
- Nondiscriminatory–the recreation program should be nondiscriminatory; in other words, it should be available to all people without regard to race, sex, creed, age, physical or mental capacities, religion, or national origin.
- Leadership–recreation programs should be staffed by top-quality leaders who understand and accept their role in the leisure service milieu.
- Skill levels–recreation programs should have an interrelationship and progress from one skill level to another. They should provide varied components of risk, intellectual aspects, and social interaction.

Certainly this approach lends itself to a quick and tidy design stage. The programmer need only review the most current ideas and infuse them into the activity-delivery system. If the choice can be correct it can also be incorrect; therefore, accepting these 50/50 odds for possible programming success, decisions are made. Perhaps it is unfair to suggest that there is only a 50 percent chance of success. Arguments could be made that the usual and familiar pattern for life in America today is to do very little asking and simply package the goods for the consumer. It then becomes the choice of the consumer to buy or pass on the activity-experience product. Then if a program fails, we go back to the packaging and advertising steps to reshape and resell. Next time we are hopeful that the customer will buy and be satisfied. This Madison Avenue model can have high rewards. In fact, some programmers believe that the nature of the activity has very little to do with satisfaction for the participant; but the surrounding trappings make it a satisfying experience–quality of leadership, activity's extrinsic reward system, location, expensive equipment, and so on. Therefore, the real skills needed in the recreation programmer are effective techniques for attracting potential participants. Once the invitation style becomes successful, can we fault the approach? Again, those holding the pocketbooks are interested in results, and the programmer will need to demonstrate some kind of evaluative design that ascertains the quality of these results.

It is not usual in this approach to set participant numbers as a measure of program success. This counting method is used mostly because other approaches to evaluation would be unrealistic in a given situation. Therefore, the programmer in that situation must set goals regarding how many participants will be necessary in order for staff to suggest that the program be noted as successful and perhaps continued the following year. This is a weak approach to evaluation.

Programming by Cafeteria Style

The cafeteria approach to recreation programming is similar to the previous approach, but much less risky. Assumptions surrounding this approach are:

1. Participant interests are constantly changing, and the least expensive way to satisfy these interests is to offer a wide variety of programs and let individuals indicate their preferences by their own selection. The recreation professional programmer cannot know every possible interest area. This smorgasbord is a fair device to uncover interests in a participant group.
2. Guiding principles of recreation programming can be met by offering a diverse program through which any potential participant can find at least one attractive activity.
3. Since people often do not know what they want and the programmer is unsure, this approach provides a happy compromise.

In considering the use of this approach, the programmer must be concerned with the area of facility development. Being responsive to the fickle interests of the constituency tends to put long-range planning in a difficult frame of reference. If the programmer is consistently unable to settle on some track of program stability, it complicates facility development. On the other hand, to use fad program activities as the base for capital area and facility development can be just as unsound in planning and development.

Perhaps this cafeteria approach to programming is most successful when used with structured classes, workshops, clinics, and other educational activities. If the required number fail to register, little is lost beyond the administrative costs and some disappointed customers. For activities requiring a large capital investment, the program administrator should base decisions on solid feasibility planning and not sheer guesswork. Guiding principles for recreation programming are possible with this approach:

- Available resources–recreation programs should tap the total possible resources within the area of their jurisdiction.
- Adventure–recreation programs should provide an opportunity for adventure, risk, and new and creative experiences at varied skill levels.
- Compatibility–recreation programs should be compatible with the economic, social, and physical abilities of the potential participants.

As we have noted before, this approach is safe and has the potential for a high degree of success. Of course, there will be some fallout, yet with practice and experience this can be reduced to negligible amounts. This system is a compromise between the desires approach and the perceived needs approach to programming. As such, it becomes an attractive style for the programmer who has difficulty in systematizing an input and feedback system, and yet is not willing to risk everything based on his or her judgment alone.

The key to this system is the design, offering not only activity variety, but format variety as well. The ice rink can be a cafeteria in itself with activities including patch sessions, beginning figure skating, stunt skating, hockey leagues, and an ice show. Included in this approach also will be tryouts, rehearsals, recreational skating, goal keeping clinics, and so on. The real challenge to the programmer, then, is to be the idea stimulus and the organizer par excellence. Exposure of the constituency to a large variety of choices will soon have people requesting time and offering their own suggestions and ideas.

One difficulty with this approach is the amount of time invested in what might become wasted efforts. Some portion of the programmer's time will be spent making administrative arrangements for programs that simply will not be popular. Yet this time can be justified. Knowing that people are not interested in some activities is often a valuable piece of information to be stored away for the present and be reintroduced at some later time. Another difficulty with this approach to programming is in setting criteria by which the programmer can measure success. With this shotgun approach the programmer may have to acknowledge an expected percent of misfire, never able to be confident about what portion will be successful and what will not. Therefore, setting the criteria becomes an educated guess with some intriguing results. If the program has been 100 percent successful, that is, everything offered has had high participation, was the design truly a cafeteria approach? If there was a dramatically low percent of success, should we blame or praise the programmer for his or her brave and avant-garde endeavor to help people realize some exciting and new program activities? Those are perhaps questions to be debated in the classroom and to be risked by the recreation programmer. The axiom, "nothing ventured nothing gained" ought to be of some help in the discussion.

Programming by External Requirements

For almost every system of social services, there exists some external assessment tool for measuring the effectiveness of the service. In the recreation and parks profession, as well as in others, the external assessment tools are called standards. Here we are considering programs standards, which if met by an agency, would indicate that the recreation program is good. The assumptions inherent in the programmer utilizing this approach are fairly obvious:

1. If the external standard is met, the program is good, that is, satisfying to the constituency.
2. Those persons involved in setting the standards (the experts) are able to make quality judgements about the local situation.
3. Standards generally represent minimums; therefore, to exceed the standard would indicate higher quality in the program experience.

Sociologist Roland Warren (1963) presented some important ideas regarding the use of this approach. He suggests that the programmer sits at the intersection of a vertical system joining or linking to a horizontal system. In this thesis, he suggested that the programmer probably has a better feel for what might be a more successful recreation activity program at the local level than any other professional who works at the county, regional, state, national, or district level. Yet it is not uncommon to have standards for programming generated from some level of this vertical ladder.

To present this concept more graphically let us consider the scouting model. At the closest level to the participant, we recognize the small troop with a volunteer leader. Available to these people are many resources, symbols, history, help guides, awards, etc. Scouting has traditionally been operated through a vertical model of programming. Badges and patches are earned by accomplishing steps in a performance and learning process that is standardized internationally. Regardless of what might be meaningful at the local troop or even council level, national standards are the guidelines for these young people's groups. Programs that vary from the accomplishment of these external awards are not encouraged and, in some instances, are disapproved of and are not permitted to carry the scout name.

The past decades have placed a great deal of emphasis on human-service delivery systems qualifying for association, state, or federal grants. In order to qualify, an agency must either have or plan to initiate certain elements that would satisfy the requirements of the funding agency. Nowhere has the responsiveness to the vertical system been more obvious than in these instances, that is, head start programs, model cities recreational aspects, Quaker Oats fitness, Ford's punt, pass, and kick, etc. In a sense, the programmer has indicated to the constituency that, by having this prescribed program, they will have a program that someone else thinks is good; therefore, it must be good for us (and we can get some financial help as well)!

The responsiveness of the programmer to the vertical system has been encouraged and expected. If one rejects the vertical system, one is sure to be censured, termed a failure, or certainly lose out on future opportunities and this loss would, in the long run, hurt the agency's participants. Community recreation departments have available to them a self-study guide in which evaluative criteria are noted for many different aspects of total department operation. Program criteria and standards are listed, against which each department can evaluate itself (van der Smissen, 1972). Those who rate high in this self-evaluation can feel some confidence that the program is sound. These standards will be discussed more carefully in the final unit, but the point here is to understand that frequently the evaluation of success of programs at the local (horizontal) level is measured by instruments designed somewhere in the external (vertical) level.

Programming by external requirements is a style through which some program principles can be realized:

- Diversity–recreation programs should have diversity and internal balance.
- Standards–program planning should adhere to carefully developed standards for both design and administration.
- Leadership–recreation programs should be delivered through a system of highly qualified leadership.
- Available resources–recreation programs should utilize the full resources available to the planning agency.

We tend to reject this particular approach to programming. Our personal philosophies reflect a sincere reluctance to adopt anything because of an external reward system, in either dollars or prestige; we share a belief that the local agency is more in touch with people and how best to serve them. Or perhaps in the true Mertonian sense, the programmers must be localites at heart.

There are many variations on the above themes for program approaches. Programmers are always interested in what is new and hot. Attending conferences or calling a colleague in a similar organization for ideas that are popular in their schedule are common planning strategies. The critical element in selecting any approach, even one that is not here discussed, is to recognize that consideration of a specific choice is advisable and then give some thoughtful analysis to *why* you have made that choice. Edginton et al., (1980, pp. 43-47) have presented a thorough articulation of these choices for consideration of what approach to designing the program might be taken.

To reiterate a point in conclusion of this section, the choice of which program approach to use will vary with different situations and varying pressure points. The skillful programmer will weigh the alternatives and assumptions present in each choice. Although each carries both negative and positive elements, there are possible situations in which any one of the approaches may be appropriate. The point here is not to believe that only one approach to programming is the correct one for you, but instead to master each and have a full range of answers in your programming skill bank.

PROGRAM MODEL

We began the chapter by describing programming as a process. Consider this process as a system that can be represented by a model. The model is used to describe pictorially the separate steps of the programming process. The program staff member will be more prone to successful programming if the steps of this model become automatic as the planning task proceeds. To avoid or neglect any step is to take some potentially dangerous shortcuts. In Figure 1.1 the recreation program activity model is drawn.

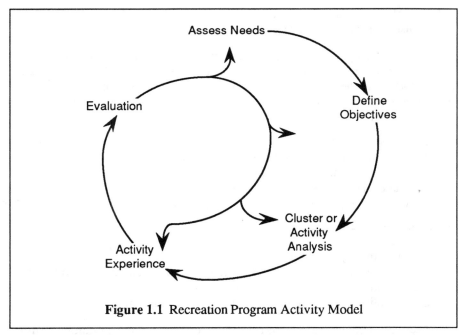

Figure 1.1 Recreation Program Activity Model

The process progresses from assessment of participant needs to writing objectives for program activities to meet those needs; to consideration of grouping and classifying all potential activity that might meet the objectives and perhaps goals; to leading the participant to the activity itself; and finally to some type of evaluation. This evaluation may lead the programmer back to any step in the model shown to need revision. The following chapters of this book will explore each of the steps in this model. Theory and techniques will be presented in as much detail as it seems may be helpful.

SUMMARY

Programming is a process. The principles on which this process is based apply to any agency that provides recreation program services to its constituents. The scope of the audience is extensive and embraces both the public and private sectors of society. In order to provide these services, agencies employ professional program administrators to manage this delivery system.

The word program, itself, refers in sum to (1) the activity in which people participate, (2) the facility in which the activity takes place, and (3) the leadership that is responsible for facilitating the experience.

Sponsoring agencies for recreation are numerous and can be identified in the following broad categories:

Church and religious agencies.
Private voluntary agencies
Government agencies.
School and education agencies.
Industrial and commercial agencies.

There are many ways to classify a program and a popular system for doing this is by functional program areas such as drama, crafts, dance, and so on. There are many others, and the more discrete a program activity classification system is, the more useful that system becomes to the review and evaluation process. Criteria for a strong system are that it:

1. Be discrete among units.
2. Cover all possible elements within the larger concept.
3. Categorize components in approximately equal units.
4. Relate all elements to one another.
5. Avoid value judgments about the components.

Other classification systems suggested are:

Classification by areas and facilities.
Classification by number of people required to do an activity-social interaction.
Classification by expected outcomes from the activity experience.
Classification by non-traditional leisure education system.

There are many approaches that a programmer could put into operation within any given system. No single one works for all situations or for all programmers' styles. Each approach should be studied for its own value and be available for use when the occasion arises. These approaches are:

1. Programming by objectives
2. Programming by desires of the participants.
3. Programming by perceived needs of the participant.
4. Programming by cafeteria style.
5. Programming by external requirements.
6. A program activity model is proposed that urges the programmer to follow five planning steps starting with needs assessment, stating objectives, clustering activity, enabling the actual activity experience, and finalizing the process with some type of evaluation.

BIBLIOGRAPHY

Anderson, J. M. (1955). *Industrial recreation.* New York, NY: McGraw Hill Book Company, Inc.

Carlson, R. E., Deppe, T. R., and MacLean, J. R. (1979). *Recreation and leisure: The changing scene* (3rd edition). Belmont, CA: Wadsworth.

Edginton, C. R., Compton, D.M. & Hanson, C. J. (1980). *Recreation and Leisure Programming.* Philadelphia, PA: Saunders College.

Farrell, P. (1989). Leisure Education: Where is it now? *Pennsylvania Recreation and Parks* 20:4 pp. 9-11 Spring.

Greer, J.D. (1990). Recreation habitats: A concept for study and management, Paper presented at the Outdoor Recreation Symposium III, Indianapolis, IN.

Hanson, R. F. and Carlson, R. E. (1972). *Organizations for children and youth.* Englewood Cliffs, NJ: Prentice-Hall.

Joswiak, K. F. (1989). *Leisure education: Program materials for persons with developmental disabilities.* State College, PA: Venture Publishing, Inc.

Kraus, R. (1978). *Recreation and leisure in modern society.* Santa Monica, CA: Goodyear Publishing Company Inc.

Miller, N. P. and Robinson, D. M. (1963). *The leisure age.* Belmont, CA: Wadsworth.

Mundy, J. and Odum, L. (1979). *Leisure education: Theory and practice.* New York, NY: John Wiley and Sons.

Peterson, C. A. and Gunn, S.L. (1984). *Therapeutic Recreation Program Design: Principles and Procedures*. Englewood Cliffs, NJ: Prentice-Hall, Inc.

Smith, M. (editor). (1973). *Leisure and society in Britain*. Thetford, Norfolk, VA: Love and Brydone (Printers) Ltd.

van der Smissen, B. (1972). *Evaluation and self-study of public recreation and park agencies* (revised edition). Arlington, VA: NRPA.

Vannier, M. H. (1977). *Methods and materials in recreation leadership* (2nd edition). Philadelphia, PA: W. B. Saunders Co.

Warren, R. L. (1963). *The community in America*. Chicago, IL: Rand McNally.

Yukic, T. S. (1970). *Fundamentals of recreation* (2nd edition). New York, NY: Harper & Row.

CHAPTER TWO

LIFE STAGES AND DEVELOPMENTAL AND PSYCHOSOCIAL THEORY

Theorists and researchers of leisure behavior promote the understanding of psychosocial theory and its application in helping program participants to pursue leisure satisfaction. Newman and Newman (1987) suggest that psychosocial theory deals with growth across the lifespan and they suggest further that people can direct their own development and integrate, organize and conceptualize their own experiences to achieve this growth.

> The theory takes into consideration the active contribution
> of culture in shaping the direction of an individual's growth.
> At each life stage, cultural aspirations, expectations, require-
> ments, and opportunities are assumed to have an impact on
> individual development. (p. 25)

Development is considered by these theorists to be on-going through all life stages with all the appropriate functions appearing sequentially and being integrated within a person by the end of the life span and not until the end is reached. Life stages may not be discrete in all cases, and often overlap, making it difficult to put inflexible boundaries on each stage. However, in all leisure service areas, the program designer will find the developmental stage approach invaluable.

Newman and Newman (1987) stated that the following assumptions underlie this developmental approach to life stages from a psychosocial perspective.

1. Growth occurs at every period of life, from conception through old age.
2. Individual lives show continuity and change as they progress through time.
3. There is a need to understand the whole person, because we function in an integrated manner on a day-to-day basis.
4. Every person's behavior must be analyzed in the context of relevant settings and personal relationships. Human beings are highly skilled at adapting to their environment. The meaning of a given behavior pattern or change must be interpreted in light of the significant physical and social environments in which it occurs. (p. 4)

The authors see that from a psychosocial perspective, human development is a product of individual needs and abilities, societal expectations and demands. Research has shown that early life stage participation in an activity influences later activity choice (Iso-Ahola, 1980; Riley and Lundegren, 1981; Kelly, 1974). These findings indicate that nature and nurture both play a part in what activities a person becomes skillful enough in doing that he or she wants to continue doing it. Therefore, it becomes necessary for programmers to find out what their older clients did in their earlier days and to try to influence the younger people to do *something* for those who do nothing are less apt to participate in activities when they get older. It behooves us, as programmers, then, to take a close look at life stage theory. In order to serve individuals or groups of people, some system of classifying them is necessary to assure the programmer that certain age or developmental levels have not been overlooked. Just as possible program opportunities can be classified into various groupings with different characteristics, so do participants differ, and it is important to understand and classify the various clientele with whom the programmer works. Knowing that all individuals differ, we focus on gaining an understanding of similarities in the many stages of people's lives. Sociologists as well as psychologists use a variety of terms to broaden the concept of grouping people by age—life cycles, life stages and stage of human life.

Previous authors have suggested that an appropriate way to group people for the purpose of recreation activity planning is by age. Four to seven such age groups have been identified by various authors in the recreation and leisure studies field. In any consideration of life stages or cycles there is a hint of age grouping. For our purposes, it seems more precise to look at the many life stages and the potential that the understanding of them have for the activity programmer.

A discussion of the life stages of human beings is at best a generalization and open to challenges of those examples that do not fit the norm. Nevertheless, the intention is to highlight the similarities with the understanding that there are differences. An average fictitious individual is presented by most authorities as representing a life-stage group and, since the activity needs of people fluctuate, it is difficult to apply one model to all for any set span of time.

Nesselroade and Baltes (1974) make a strong point in advising avoidance of the use of age for grouping children, indicating that in their view, age, per se, is not a very relevant variable. Developmental change is more influenced by cultural moment than by age sequences.

However, grouping people by age is a familiar pattern when working with children, especially to those who are accustomed to such a system in school. The key then is to use age-groups for program activity only when it makes sense to do so, thus capturing the Nesselroade and Baltes' concept. Some activities easily accommodate a broad range of ages—particularly programs in theater, art, music, and dance. On the other hand, a general rule of thumb for most physical activities is to avoid formal, organized groups with an age span greater than two or three years, particularly with people under 18.

LIFE STAGES

Erik H. Erikson (1963), the noted developmental psychologist, identified eight life cycles and labeled each as a psychosocial crisis:

Infancy	Basic trust versus basic mistrust
Early childhood	Autonomy versus shame, doubt
Play age	Initiative versus guilt
School age	Industry versus infinity
Adolescence	Identity versus confusion
Young adulthood	Intimacy versus isolation
Adulthood	Generalitivity versus stagnation
Old age	Integrity versus despair

Crises are not viewed in a negative sense so much as a developmental step, as one moves from a position of security into a new less secure zone. Erikson emphasized the early years as six of his eight cycles involve the first 25 years, leaving only two cycles to account for changes in one's remaining years.

A discussion of adult cycles was presented by Huberman (1974) who designated six cycles. Huberman's purpose was to align interests in adult continuing education with changes in age. He also designated age with each specific cycle as follows:

TABLE 2.1 Huberman's Life Cycle Categories

Cycle	Age
Focusing oneself	18 - 30
Collecting oneself	30 - 40
Exerting and assuring	40 - 50
Maintaining	50 - 60
Disengagement decision	60 - 70
Disengaging	70 - 80

A more recent presentation of the stages as an off-shoot of Erikson's work is that of Newman and Newman (1987) who added three new stages. People change and grow in a systematic direction, enhancing their potential for carrying their own and succeeding generations forward. (p. 76)

The authors' eleven stages of the lifespan are (p. 29):

TABLE 2.2 Newman and Newman's Life Stage Categories

Life Stage	Age
Prenatal	Conception to birth
Infancy	Birth to 2 years
Toddlerhood	2 to 4 years
Early school age	4 to 6 years
Middle school age	6 to 12 years
Early adolescence	12 to 18 years
Later adolescence	18 to 22 years
Early adulthood	22 to 34 years
Middle adulthood	34 to 60 years
Later adulthood	60 to 75 years
Very old age	75 until death

Again, the blocks of ten-year periods may be viewed as arbitrary. Huberman traced adults' interests in home, marriage and children; civic and social activities; professional and vocational work; and interpretive and aesthetic experiences. He emphasized the need for interpretive/aesthetic experiences blossoming in cycles 3 and 4 and, in doing this, supports those researchers who are disclaiming the myth that adults are too old to learn. As the elderly population becomes a larger percent of the human resources in America, we find less and less satisfaction with the idea of disengagement, first described by Cummings and Henry (1961). To dismiss the programming potential for the elderly would be a serious error and Huberman would probably revise his concept today.

Keeping these few examples in mind for the purposes of this text, the following classification system for life stages with specific characteristics of each is accepted. The younger years tend to follow the general school-grouping patterns, while the later years are traced by family involvements. In order to appreciate the framework in which this system exists, it is important to recognize the philosophy on which it is built.

One engages in recreational activity during discretionary time. It is crucial for the recreation programmer to recognize that time to play may well be one of the more crucial factors in people's selection of recreational activities. Major constraints on time are one's responsibilities to work and to family, both as a child to one's parents and as parents to children. Therefore, to look at an individual's personal activity pattern, it is possible to note various "time for recreation" constraints on the participation pattern. Although time-budget research reporting is not the intent of this book, the reader is advised to follow some of the work being done in this area–notably that of Robinson (1977).

Based on some of the work quoted earlier in this section, for the purposes of this book we can divide the life stages generally into these parts knowing the exact labeling or inclusive years may differ some from one author to another.

Preschool
Early childhood
Late elementary
Youth
Teenage
Young adult–no children responsibilities
Middle adulthood–child responsibilities
Maturity
Later old age

If this classification system is used to establish units for programming, there will be some clearly defined groups of people to serve and ample opportunity for overlap when it is desirable. Available free time for recreation activity is perhaps the most critical determination the programmer must make to ensure participation of the target population.

In today's society many forms of family life-styles are found in the adult population. There are single parent units where family members are blood relations, single men or women caring for adopted children, and multiple arrangements of men, women, and children sharing a single family unit relationship. The attitudes concerning the tidy nuclear family unit of the 1940s and 1950s changed considerably in the 1980s and it is expected that this outlook will continue into the following decades.

Activity Preferences by Life Cycles

A great deal has been written about the activity preferences of people as they move from one life stage to another. For an in-depth coverage of this topic, consult developmental psychology texts as well as works in human development, sociology, and gerontology. Only a brief overview of characteristic behavior for each age group will be provided here in hopes that elaboration and amplification will be gathered from the textbooks noted in the bibliography at the end of this unit.

Preschool
Side-by-side play but not interaction between and among–self-centered.
Dependent on supervision for structured play.
Short (5-10 minutes) attention span.
Perhaps the highest readiness for learning stage–motor skills, sharing, creativity.
Big muscle development needs–movement, voice, etc.
Awareness of flaws–self-doubt.
Low knowledge but high curiosity.
Language development.
Immediate gratification needs.
Needs for activity in which praise can be received.

Impatient for new challenges and varied activities.
Observant but lacks verbal skills.
Reduction of the ego.
Beginnings of being controlled by others and the environment.
Fantasy years.
Social attachment.
Primitive causality.
Emotional development.
Object permanence.

Early Childhood

Period of steady growth–physical, intellectual, and emotional.
Testing of independence.
Still a limited attention span (15-20 minutes).
Fantasy turning to relatives and truths–subjective to objective.
Security needs and familiarity are high–no alterations.
Individualism moves toward peer relationships.
General lack of fear of the now familiar.
Easily bored.
Needs to repeat activities that are well known and mastered.
Frustration comes quickly.
Fear of the unfamiliar and activities needed to conquer fear.
The beginning of valuing.
Group play.
Self-control.

Late Elementary

Solid moves toward groups of friends.
Idolization of significant others–hero worship.
Highly impressionable.
Willingness to seek risk and adventure.
Play has become filled with rules, team cooperation, etc.
Values and fair play begging to emerge.
Competition among group members has been clearly stylized.
Beginning to accept responsibility for self and others.
Attention span has lengthened (30-40 minutes).
High needs for skill development.
Eager learners and quick understanding of ideas and concepts.
Independence from adults begins.
Willing to work for external rewards.

Youth

Seeking self-identity.

Enormous capacity to perform new tasks, try new adventures.

High range of ability to carry responsibility.

Testing of boy-girl relationships.

Gender identification and alienation from other sex and family.

Concrete operations.

Maturation through puberty–body sex development.

Future orientation beginnings.

Interest in social intercourse–exploration of other sex.

Further refinement of independence needs.

Stable relationships begin to develop–same sex and other sex.

Group affiliation important.

Teenage

Full development of physique and physical powers.

Emotional development–giving incentives.

Capacity for total independence from family.

Strong aggressive drives.

Potential for high alienation from family, adults, society.

Continuance of drives beyond need reduction.

Part-time jobs become a familiar pattern.

Formal operations.

Team or group allegiance important.

Maturation begins in self-identity.

Strong needs to be alone, free from having to interact with others.

Uncertainty about others–to trust, to understand.

Begins to discern the difference between the real and ideal world.

Tends to view the organized world as a system of constraints.

Hero worship.

Young Adult

Major responsibilities for self (perhaps others).

Autonomy from parents.

Serious concern for support, work, and caring requirements.

Usually mobile.

Life-style experimentation and solidification.

Career choice.

Generally active, energetic, and flexible.

Needs for belonging.

Internalize morality.

Nonwork activities become important for success element.

Learning to become resourceful and adaptable.

Strong economic motivation for living.

Full physical and mental growth have been attained.

High needs for adventure–hazardous activities.

Needs for everything to happen immediately–no future.

High needs to do, not to learn or know, but simply do.

Strong ambitions to satisfy as if a lifetime were in the "permanent present."

Superior physical condition of well-being or has come to grips with state of health.

Vigorous recreation.

Attracted to outdoors.

Establishing family.

The period of strongest aggressive drives.

Middle Adulthood

Begins to set goals for a lifetime objectivity.

Nurturing marriage.

Managing career.

Awareness of own strengths and abilities.

Final phase in the development of values.

Security needs high–efforts devoted to assuring this status.

Committed to being a part of society.

Loss of individual independence where family is concerned.

Acceptance of obligations to community or neighborhood unit.

Novelty and variety are important.

Ability to plan and see long-range need fulfillments.

Lengthy attention span–able to see work through to completion.

Formal education has ended, yet as such novelty and variety important.

Has come to grips with society and culture.

Women homemakers return to work.

More spectator leisure.

Volunteering as leisure.

Oriented to clubs.

Maturity

Has reached full potential in efforts to meet personal needs.

Life-style is mostly objective–set rewards for efforts.

The threat of the permanent present–dull,boring.

The apex of life–security of position, occupation, associations.

Has a clear view of the past and beginnings of a realistic future view.

At the height of external respect and perceived contribution.

Developing new post-retirement roles.

Economic comfort not known before.

Enjoyment of life's comforts–no needs to rough it.
Enjoys being a member of a group–this is important.
Group of friends is large and varied–not yet too selective.
High leadership is asked of this group.
Behavior is constant and consistent in the healthy person.
Reduction in some drives to satisfy basic needs.
Lessening of aggressive feelings.
Fear of failing in many performance areas and activities.
Definite physical slowdown as well as energy needed to perform usual activities
     is harder to stimulate.
Desires full participation in society.
Experience oriented.

Later Old Age

Tends to exhibit similar activity patterns of previous life cycle.
Generally a lessening of activity and doing.
Danger of boredom, little is worth bothering about.
Inevitable physical deterioration is impossible to escape.
Often an unhealthy change in social position.
Less interest in material things, a clinging to the abstract.
Being loved, having emotional and economic security are important.
The past is an important reference point.
Health concerns are of paramount importance.
One moves back into subjectivity–not fact.
Progressive detachment from outside activities–disengagement.
Retirement from paid employment.
Caution is an important notion in all experiences.
Energies focused on intensifying a limited number of activities rather than
     touching many lightly.
Interested in sustaining a good life for self and others.
Begins to find others making one dependent–through receiving.
Tendency toward passive living.
The negatives appear to outweigh the positives.
Life tends to be self centered and self serving.
Increasing physical infirmity.
Painful loneliness and a sense of isolation.
Great decreases in power and participation.
Large amounts of unobligated time available.
Well-established patterns.
Travel.
Socializing and relaxing activities predominate for the well and able.

As life styles become more flexible, the attempts to share group activity based on the life stage model suggested may become outmoded. Single-parent families and cohabiting couples with children or no children are more prevalent. Regardless of family circumstance, the individual has certain needs for activity. The process of packaging these activity programs becomes the real challenges to the recreation professional. (Bloom, 1980; Osgood and Howe, 1984; Newman and Newman, 1987) Before looking at activity packaging as an outgrowth of the satisfaction of participant needs, it might be useful to address more thoroughly what the participant is like in a behavioral sense.

DEVELOPMENTAL AND PSYCHOSOCIAL THEORY

The preceding discussion on life stages and life span development is useful in understanding the diversity of the individual. The programmer finds that a means of classifying participants as individuals or as parts of groups is essential to being able to characterize the clientele one is serving. However, a closer look at the social and psychological aspects of the client is warranted, with one emphasis on self-concept and its link to leisure behavior and eventually to programming. This linkage becomes particularly important if programming is not done based on age groups, but on other, more compelling factors. These factors may be self-efficacy, assertiveness, emotional maturity, developmental change, social stability, risk taking, motivation, gender related expectations and self-esteem.

Iso-Ahola (1980) promoted the idea that every programmer must be aware of what the participants in their programs are like, what their needs are, and what satisfies them emotionally. Particularly important is knowledge of how the behaviors of one person influence the behaviors and feelings of others during the time that they are engaged in activities together. This study is in the field of social psychology of leisure. Until recently, professionals in this area of psychology dealt almost exclusively with play behavior, as it related to development rather than with interest in its social aspects. Social psychologists of leisure on the other hand are interested in attitudes, group affiliations, interpersonal relations and self-concept.

Acting from this perspective, Iso-Ahola (1980) defined the social psychology of leisure as:

> . . .that branch of scientific leisure studies which examines how the feelings, cognitions (thoughts or beliefs) and behaviors of one individual are influenced by the feelings, cognitions and behaviors of others during a period of time subjectively designated as unobligated, free, or leisure. (p. 18)

Before considering the implication of leisure behavior for the programmer and its influence on the quality of life of the clientele, it is useful to review the diversity of the participants and how their leisure choices are shaped by their self-concepts, motivations and needs. To interpret this knowledge adequately calls for an understanding of self-concept and selected variables associated with it.

Self-Concept

The ideas we hold about ourselves, the way we see ourselves, who we are and what we are comprise the self-concept (Ross, 1987) and these ideas wield a strong influence on all that we do. Although they can change, they do not do so rapidly and they tend to be fairly stable (Ross, 1987). People strive to achieve their ideal selves while at the same time being reconciled to their real selves (Rogers, 1961). When this reconciliation occurs, people are most apt to be content; when they constantly strive to be their ideal and fall short, they are likely to doubt themselves and experience a low self-concept. It is important for the programmer to provide activities that allow people to make the choices affecting their behavior that are consistent with their self-concepts and which maintain these self-concepts as the people involved see themselves. To be satisfying, roles that people take must be consistent with their self-concepts.

Early researchers in this area of personality study were exploring work roles but the same theory applies to nonwork roles. We look for leisure time activities that will be consistent with our view of self and reinforce it, not cast doubt on it. For example, if people see themselves as leaders, then they will be drawn to team sports, will be organizers of camping trips, attracted to being the captain, the first violinist, the director on wherever their talents take them where leadership is also needed. If the choice does not contribute to self-enhancement, then the person is unlikely to make that choice. The skilled soccer player is not likely to play with beginners long, or the well-skilled violinist to take happily the fourth chair in the second row. In understanding the importance of self-concept to behavior, we must recognize that although relatively stable, the self-concept is also somewhat situationally dependent, and behavior usually expected from a person with a certain recognized concept of self may be different in reaction to the constraints of a changing situation. This behavior can be confusing to the observer if the potential for this kind of reaction to change is not recognized. The programmer responding to this fact applies the knowledge by making sure the demands of a situation are supportive of the expectations of the participants in order to contribute to the successful outcome of the planned program.

Self-Efficacy

As noted, how one feels about oneself influences how one acts and how one views one's capabilities. This latter refers to self-efficacy and that [self-efficacy] affects how one meets challenges. How one feels about challenges, in turn, affects what one chooses to do for both work and recreation. If one does not like to meet challenges, this reflects a low self-efficacy and vice-versa. Low self-efficacy eventually reflects low self-concept (Ross, 1987; Bandura, 1977). People with low self-efficacy are not known for sticking to things for long, they set low goals, give up easily and are defeated by failure. Recreation activities for this type of person must be carefully chosen to avoid these things happening if possible. Otherwise, motivation also becomes a problem, and even the most brilliant programs will be difficult to deliver to the satisfaction of such a client. All of this is related to locus of control, or how strongly you believe that what you do influences what happens to you in life. Internal locus of control means that you believe you control what happens; external locus of control means that outside factors (luck, other people) control what happens to you. (Iso-Ahola, 1980) Locus of control is also related to motivation with the internal person more highly and easily motivated. (The reader is referred to Appendix E for a list of instruments which assess these and other personality traits.) All of which leads to a consideration of motivation, its meaning and its importance as an influence in recreation programming.

Motivation

It is important to a programmer to know why a person chooses to do a certain activity and what they expect to gain or receive from participation in it. If they are keyed to external rewards (e.g., trophies), then the format of the activity is likely to be different from what it would be if they were doing it for its own sake (e.g., singing in a group that never performs for the public).

A motive can be said to be something that makes a person do something or is the goal of an action. Motivation is an inner state that moves that person toward that goal (Ross, 1987). Some motives are innate and we share them with others, like physiological needs; and others are acquired in the course of our lives as we move through the life cycle. It is acquired motivation that the programmer concentrates on and uses to guide planning. Another way we can think of motivation is as intrinsic, contained within the activity, or extrinsic, originating outside of the individual. If a participant is motivated by risk-taking sensations, activity choices will be quite different from those of a person who is happiest when inside by a fire, reading. If need achievement is a strong motive, researchers have indicated that the person with this need is ambitious, competitive and persistent and that such a person responds well to striving for excellence. Maslow's hierarchy of needs is referred to frequently by leisure professionals (discussed in the next section of this Chapter). The ingenuity of the programmer is applied when the activities that might satisfy the motivations of a person are not essentially available (e.g., no musical group in town).

The relevance of querying motivation for a programmer is illustrated by a research study conducted by Iso-Ahola and Allen (1982) on the effects of outcomes of participation in competitive events on leisure needs. The authors showed that winning and losing had different psychological effects on males and females and that competitive and recreational leagues served different functions for males and females because the two leagues were expected to fulfill different leisure needs. Data such as these should impact program planners as they structure activity units for differing clientele.

Iso-Ahola (1980) believes intrinsic motivation is important in leisure activity selection and reflects perceived competence and self-determination. Since motives and needs are so closely linked as to have some authors view them as one, we are led to consideration of human needs themselves.

Human Needs

Human beings have certain physiological needs that are intrinsic to their makeup and are satisfied in a variety of identifiable, definable ways (Maslow, 1970). These needs are well documented and are illustrated by such things as need for food, air, and water. They are internally, or viscerally, induced and are satisfied in an organic or physical way. These are Murray's (1938) viscerogenic or primary needs. Along with these needs are others that psychologists have labeled as the psychogenic (Murray, 1938) or psychological needs, which are characterized by lack of focus or dependence on the organic system, are categorized as secondary, and are not satisfied by physical means. Examples of these are needs for achievement, dominance, and autonomy (Hall and Lindzey, 1978). Some needs are evident and can be readily seen and identified by a casual observer (overt) and others are essentially kept hidden (invert) and restrained (Hall and Lindzey, 1978). Hall and Lindzey proposed that overt needs typically express themselves in motor behavior, and invert needs are confined more to expression in the realm of fantasy. In some cases needs are specifically object-focused and in others are generalized and diffuse. Concern comes if there is an obsession developed regarding focus on a need object, or if there is failure to develop any need focus at all. Needs are also engendered from within a person, initiated by them and others, and are characterized by a response or a reaction to something from without or in the environment. There are those people with needs to perform an activity for the sake of the activity itself. Others have needs to perform for the excellence of the product of that performance, and it becomes necessary to reach that quality of performance, if the participation is to be satisfying. It is important to identify clearly the things to which needs refer and to the context in which they are to be assessed. Needs are separate from want and demand (McKillip, 1987).

The fact that needs do not exist in isolation from one another is agreed upon by most theorists. A person's body and mind (physical and psychological selves) interact, share dependence, and yield priority position to one another. The latter occurs particularly when conflicting need stimuli arrive at the same time and the individual must choose one to be satisfied first. Murray (1938) proposed that in this case, the preponent or predominant need, which cannot wait to be satisfied, takes precedence.

This discussion leads to consideration of the theory supporting the existence of a need hierarchy, as proposed historically by Maslow (1968, 1970), in which needs are seen to be a relative strength, with one preponent (as with Murray) over the other and, given a situation or deprivation of more than one type of need, one of these would clearly be attended to first. For example, in considering needs for love and water, water holds a hierarchically higher position. Maslow theorized that there are basic needs such as hunger, affection, security, and self-esteem, and meta-needs such as justice, goodness, beauty, and order, all subsumed under the rubric of self-actualization—the ultimate goal. The self-actualized person is the healthy person who has realized his or her potential to the fullest. Self-actualization implies actualization of latent capacities, full functioning and acceptance of the inner core of self (Maslow, 1968). It is a growth philosophy; it does not transcend human problems, but it equips one to deal with them. A self-actualized person has been characterized as being (1) realistic, independent, spontaneous, creative, and democratic; (2) problem-centered rather than self-centered; (3) a private person, somewhat detached; (4) resistant to conformity; (5) not superficial or stereotyped; and (6) one who does not confuse means with ends (Hall and Lindzey, 1978). Self-actualized people have had many peak experiences or moments of highest happiness or fulfillment (Maslow, 1968) when they feel most whole, most healthy, most creative–people who are aware of the meta-needs and are satisfying them.

Satisfaction of Needs

Maslow (1968) also implied that needs cease to play an active role as soon as they are gratified. This leads to the consideration of the satisfaction of needs.

> Satisfaction concerns the outcome of an event between a person and
> his environment. It refers to the internal state of a person who has
> obtained what he is seeking and is synonymous with getting and
> fulfilling. Because satisfaction involves interaction with the person's
> environment, its assessment (for both the person and the researcher)
> hinges in part on the objective nature of a person's external world.
> Satisfaction depends both upon the way the world 'actually' is and
> how this reality is perceived by the person. (Alderfer, 1972, p. 7)

Lewin (1951) suggested that every need carries with it the possibility of being in one of three stages: (1) hunger, (2) satiation, and (3) oversatiation. In stage one, a person is seeking the satisfaction or means to achieve it; in stage two he or she has found it; and in stage three a state of surfeit resulting in a turning against the satisfaction has occurred. One also sees that satisfaction at the lower levels of need is a prerequisite to satisfaction at higher levels of need. If satisfaction is not achieved, frustration then becomes the antithesis of satisfaction and relief from it becomes a motivating force. An example might be the golfer who longs all winter for the season to start and when it does for three months plays 18 holes every day, but in the fall when asked to join a foursome on Tuesday morning declares, "Not today, thanks. I've had enough." By March, however, the same longing gaze is directed outside–the urge to play builds up again.

Other theorists have a very different point of view from that of Maslow. One theory, which may speak strongly to a theory that a recreator sells a product related to the potential satisfaction of needs, suggests that human needs are plastic, flexible, and expanding; not static, with one size and shape, and satisfied by a single answer (Dichter, 1971). The American public is finding that it has more and more freedom, more and more leisure, and more disposable income. These facts, coupled with greater awareness of the potential for need satisfaction in the public domain, have created a trend toward the development of what can be termed perceived needs over and above the basic or even the growth needs. This theory suggests that years from now, new needs will exist and new services and new products will have to be created to meet the demands they create (Dichter, 1971).

Let us consider the position of recreation in terms of need satisfaction. One can, perhaps, consider it of great significance, almost a raison d'etre for the profession. If there were no needs, there would be little demand for specialists whose product promotes participation in activities leading to the achievement of self-actualization. On the contrary, as suggested by Danford and Shirley (1970) people are constantly seeking situations in which they can perceive themselves as adequate, or in which they can achieve self-realization, and this search for adequacy covers areas such as activity, mental health, recognition, acceptance and adventure. This is true for *all* people, even if they are limited in a physical or mental way–the need to feel adequate exists (Frye and Peters, 1972). That is, the program should also be flexible enough to allow for a sudden change in perceived leisure needs. Iso-Ahola (1980) posits that leisure needs are dynamic and subject to change. For example, they may change from one life stage to another, from one environment to another, both in respect to difference in people and in the situation. "Successful recreation programs not only consider people's stable leisure needs, but also provide opportunities for them to satisfy improvised leisure needs." (p. 245). What a fertile area for the recreator-programmer!

Having agreed with or at least perceived the viability of the concept of the existence of needs, the form they take, the road to adequacy, and the goal of self-actualization, how does a programmer proceed? The first step is to identify the perceived needs as well as indicators of needs such as social, economic and resource indicators for any given population.

Need assessment and the procedures relevant to it are presented in the next section. Once having identified or targeted these needs, the next step is to prepare objectives, the achievement of which will mean the satisfaction of the needs involved for the participant in any given program.

Need Assessment

There are times when the program evaluator desires to have direct expression of program interests from both participants and nonparticipants. In order to assess this interest a survey questionnaire can be designed. This can take many forms and, although it has many uses, it does have limitations. How well the participant needs are identified is closely related to how well the survey instrument is designed. The programmer is given this initial warning: surveys are expensive methods of data collection, usually slower than other methods, and can be complicated and cumbersome. The steps to use in designing a survey instrument are presented in Chapter Seven.

There are generally five types of need assessment techniques in recreation programming. First is the collection of activity interests or participation records. In this technique, the survey provides a long list of activities and the respondent is encouraged to check all those in which he or she has interest or has been a participant. It is not unusual to find these data collected at entrances to park areas and beaches, survey instruments distributed through schools, placed as a mail-in form in the local newspaper, or handled by an on-the-street interviewer. Although the results from such a survey are relatively easy to handle, the data itself may be spurious. It is difficult for respondents to show interest in activities to which they have had no exposure, and conversely it is easy to check many items that one might like to do, but probably would not do if something better were available. Thus the programmer is often caught in a difficult situation and may begin to feel that the survey has not been all that helpful.

Second, the programmer could survey general, descriptive data about the users already participating in the program. Responses to such items as age, hours of participation per week, income level, and distance of residence from the specific recreation facility can be collected. This method of survey focuses on the participant for whom the program has appeal. These data would be most helpful as a cross tabulation with general area data. Are the participants a good cross-sample of the constituency as a whole, or is the program neighborhood or income level specific? These data will be valuable to the program administrator during an evaluation of all programs regarding who is and who is not being served.

A third type of survey is to solicit evaluation of services and programs, that is, crowdedness, safety, satisfaction, and so on. The survey will then be focused on answers to items that ask the respondent to make a value judgement or state an awareness viewpoint. The respondent is typically given, for each survey question, four or five value-type statements. This is the Likert-type scale and is discussed in Chapter Seven.

An effort to assess the nonuser can set the stage for the fourth type of survey. An instrument could be designed to seek data on dissatisfaction or nonuse. The survey is typically designed with lead questions and multiple reasons as possible choice answers for the respondent. Different styles of answering–check all that apply, rank answers from main reason to third reason, circle the five that most describe your feelings–can be used. The more reasons provided on the survey to assist the respondent in completing it, the more helpful the answers will be to the programmer.

A fifth possible way to survey needs would be to use the instrument to assess constituency attitudes toward proposed services or opinions on priorities. There are times when the programmer may need reactions to proposed plans. Structuring a survey instrument to put the available choices in front of the constituency can accomplish a feedback loop as well as public involvement in the decision-making process.

Surveying assessment of participant needs is more successful when the respondent is able to share opinions and attitudes rather than make checks in a long list of activities. Needs assessment should reflect the psychosocial context of leisure behavior (Howe and Qui, 1988). If the program administrator wants a reading on the program needs of his or her constituents, measures must be made that reflect the quality of that experience. (Samples of instruments used in need assessment are in Appendix A.)

Remember that need implies that something of value is sought by someone or some group. In targeting that need the person has an expectation that the solution can be found that will result in need satisfaction. The programmer is in a position to meet that expectation. A caution is extended here to look carefully at needs assessed by a survey and to make an effort to sort needs from wants, the latter being what some people are willing to pay or put their own resources into. Consider also demands, which usually originate with the participant and not with the agency (McKillip, 1987).

McKillip (1987) proposes some interesting additional ways of looking at needs assessment that agencies might well consider. The author suggests that there are basically three ways of approaching needs assessment: (1) the discrepancy model (familiar to recreation service evaluators) in which goals and performance are compared and the gap or discrepancy between the two is assessed and labeled need; (2) the marketing model in which the needs assessment becomes a feedback process, needs are wants and the programmer identifies services for which target populations are willing to trade something of value with the agency; and (3) the decision-making model in which the multiple options confronting the decision-maker are listed and multiple attributes, or the sources of information used for need identification are considered for each option. This system results in a weighting in which the value of each need is considered and the decision-maker does not use just a rank ordering as in the other systems. The process uses values, which helps the decision-maker in deciding which trade-offs (costs/satisfaction) are acceptable in the decision. The reader interested in using this system is referred to McKillip (1987). It is obviously more complex than the other models.

Leisure Behavior

All of the factors discussed under diversity of the client are contributors to leisure behavior; a concept of paramount importance to recreation programmers whose goal it is to attract clients to their agencies as participants in the activities offered. The decision to offer these programs is based on analysis of how these potential participants behave or wish they could behave during leisure. What people experience as leisure behavior as individuals reflects their self-concepts, their self-efficacy, their motivations, their perceived needs, and most significantly, the stage each is in the life cycle.

Peterson and Gunn (1984) define leisure behavior as: ". . .the wide range of human expressions that are engaged in, voluntarily possess the element of freedom of choice, . . .are intrinsically motivated, and display characteristics of being enjoyable and meaningful to the individual." (p. 23). Carpenter and Howe (1985) characterize leisure behavior as what people actually do within the context of leisure.

Iso-Ahola (1980) presents a model of causality of leisure behavior that incorporates situational psychological, environmental, and biological factors all as contributors to leisure needs (p. 228). In this model, the author posits that biological dispositions and early socialization lay the groundwork for leisure behavior. One learns to respond to optimal arousal and incongruity with satisfying leisure activities. Intrinsic motivation also plays a key role in defining what represents each individual's leisure needs. Iso-Ahola concludes that leisure behavior is comprised of both hidden and observable reasons for participating. When one seeks to identify leisure needs of any group both of these components of causality must be explored.

Researchers in the area of leisure behavior explore reasons for leisure satisfaction and motivation for participating. Some typical results of these studies of interest to a programmer are presented here, although an in-depth exploration is not intended. It is useful for the programmer to consider the variations of preferences represented by typical potential clientele. Such consideration can point the way to factors which should be included in a needs assessment.

Ragheb (1988) studied leisure needs specifically as they relate to program planning. The author, reflecting the opinions of other theorists (Iso-Ahola, 1980) in the psychosocial foundations of leisure behavior, believes that researching this area has not been adequately applied to program development. Too often the results of studies are never used in the practice. Ragheb's findings are preliminary, but if they hold up in subsequent studies, programmers will find them useful. Ragheb's study indicated:

> . . .some interesting trends to be considered in program planning. For example, females seek more intellectual leisure than males, and males want their leisure and recreation to involve more competence/mastery of physiological aspects than females. Moreover, as a person gets older, social reasons to engage in leisure decrease. Married and separated individuals have fewer social leisure needs. Finally, those in lower income levels have stronger intellectual, social and competence/mastery needs than those in higher income levels. (p. 28)

The programmer who uses these data, of course, needs to be able to provide selections of activities in the social, competence/mastery and intellectual realms. A successful programmer must consider the influences of demographics on program choice as well as the influences of life style variables on program choice (Edginton, Compton, and Hanson, 1980). Rossman (1988) also emphasizes the importance of the elements of social interaction in the leisure experience (p. 10). The programmer is also advised to look at the constraints to leisure, which are key influences on behavior.

This point of view about the importance of social interaction is shared by Tinsley, Barrett and Kass (1977) whose research showed that in terms of need satisfaction, demographics that reflected the most differences in activity choice were sex, catharsis, independence, understanding, getting along with others, and affiliation. Such findings, if they are to serve the practitioners, mean that they must gather data on these variables as part of their needs assessment.

Landan, Crandall and Fitzgibbons (1977) added a dimension to the theory and its application to programming by showing that clientele viewed leisure activity in terms of the need dimensions of: "...Liking, Feedback and Positive Interpersonal Involvement," (p. 260). These authors advise that when one is looking for psychosocial meaning as an influencing factor in activity choice that the activities themselves, the needs they satisfy, and individual differences in perception of activities and their need satisfying properties all be considered. Need satisfaction is inextricably tied to leisure behavior.

SUMMARY

Theorists and researchers of leisure behavior promote the understanding of psycosocial theory and its application in helping program participants to pursue leisure satisfaction. This theory deals with growth across the lifespan. People can direct their own development and organize their experiences in order to achieve this growth. This is called a developmental approach to life stages. Pertinent to the programmer is that early life stage participation influences later life involvement. Programmers should take a close look at life stage theory and activity preferences by the life cycle and incorporate it in their planning.

Diversity of clientele is of prime consideration in classifying participants. The ability to classify them involves taking a closer look at the psychosocial aspects of the client including self-concept, self-efficacy and motivation. Further, human needs and their satisfaction are key factors in planning. Assessment of all these areas must be addressed and carried out since all of these factors contribute to leisure behavior.

The ideas we hold about ourselves will have a strong influence on all that we do. People strive to achieve their ideal selves while being reconciled with their real selves. Roles that people take must be consistent with their self-concepts. The programmer responding to these factors makes sure the demands of the program situation are supportive of the expectations of the participants in order to contribute to the successful outcome of the program.

How participants view their capabilities (self-efficacy) and their locus of control over situations also influence their choices of work and recreation. The people who view themselves as in control (internal locus) are usually more highly motivated than those who believe that outside forces are in control (external locus). A motive here is something that makes a person act. Motivation is an inner state that moves a person toward a goal. Some motives are innate (physiological needs) and others are acquired as people move through the life cycle. Intrinsic motivation is important in leisure activity selection. Motives and needs are clearly linked. Needs are presented as physiological or primary needs and psychological or secondary. Some of each are invert and overt. Needs are separate from want and demand. Various theories exist related to these variables.

The programmer is in the business of facilitating need satisfaction and must realize that needs change from one life cycle to another–they are dynamic and a program should be flexible enough to allow for a sudden change in perceived leisure needs from the clientele.

There are generally five types of need assessment techniques in recreation programming:

1. Collection of activity interests or participation records.
2. Survey of general descriptive data about current users.
3. Evaluation of services and programs by users.
4. Survey the non-users.
5. Survey constituency attitudes toward proposed services or opinions on priorities–get reactions to proposed plans.

All of the factors discussed under diverstiy of the client contribute to leisure behavior. Researchers in the area of leisure behavior explore reasons for leisure satisfaction and motivation for participating. Both demographics and constraints influence leisure participation. Need satisfaction is inextricably tied to leisure behavior.

BIBLIOGRAPHY

Alderfer, C. P. (1972). *Existence, relatedness, and growth.* New York, NY: The Free Press.

Bandura, A. (1977). "Self-efficacy: Toward a unifying theory of behavioral change," *Psychological Review, 84*: 191-215.

Bloom, M. (1980). *Life span development.* New York, NY: Macmillan Publishing Co. Inc.

Carpenter, G.M. and Howe, C.Z. (1985). *Programming leisure experiences* Englewood Cliffs, NJ: Prentice-Hall, Inc.

Cummings, E. and Henry, W. E. (1961). *Growing old: The process of disengagement.* New York, NY: Basic Books.

Danford, H. G. and Shirley, M. (1970). *Creative leadership in recreation* (2nd ed.). Boston, MA: Allyn and Bacon.

Dichter, E. (1971). *Motivating human behavior.* New York, NY: McGraw-Hill Book Co.

Edginton, C.R., Compton, D.M. and Hanson, C.J. (1980). *Recreation and leisure programming: A guide for the professional.* Philadelphia, PA: Saunders.

Erikson, E. (1963). "Eight ages of man," in *Childhood and society,* 2nd edition. New York, NY: Norton.

Frye, E. and Peters, M. (1972). *Therapeutic recreation.* Harrisburg, PA: The Stackpole Company.

Hall, C. S. and Lindzey, G. (1978). *Theories of personality* (3rd ed.). New York, NY: John Wiley & Sons.

Hawes, D. K. (1979). Satisfactions derived from leisure-time pursuits: An exploratory nationwide survey. *Journal of Leisure Research, 10*(4): 247-264.

Howe, C. Z. and Qui, Y. (1988). The programming process revisited: Assumptions underlying the needs based models. *Journal of Park and Recreation Administration, 6:* 4: 14-27.

Huberman, M. (1974) Looking at adult education from the prospective of the adult life cycle, *International Review of Education, 20:* 2:117-135.

Iso-Ahola, S.E. (1980). *The social psychology of leisure and recreation.* Dubuque, IA: William. C. Brown.

Iso-Ahola, S.E. and Allen, J. R. (1982). The dynamics of leisure motivation: The effects of outcome on leisure needs, *Research Quarterly for Exercise and Sport, 53*(2): 141-149.

Kelly, J.R. (1974). Socialization toward leisure: A developmental approach, *Journal of Leisure Research, 6* (3): 181-193.

Landan, M., Crandall, R. and Fitzgibbons, D. (1977). The psychological structure of leisure: Activities, needs, people, *Journal of Leisure Research, 9*(4): 252-263.

Lewin, K. (1951). *Field theory in social sciences: Selected theoretical papers.* D. Cartwright, Ed. New York, NY: Harper & Row.

Maslow, A. H. (1968). *Toward a psychology of being* (2nd ed.). New York, NY: Van Nostrand Reinhold Co.

Maslow, A. H. (1970). *Motivation and personality* (2nd ed.). New York, NY: Harper & Row.

McKillip, J. (1987). *Need analysis.* Newbury Park, CA: Sage Publications.

McTeer, W. (1972). *The scope of motivation*. Monterey, CA: Brooks/Cole Publishing Company

Murray, H. A. (1938). *Explorations in personality*. New York, NY: Oxford University Press.

Newman, B.M. and Newman, P.R. (1987). *Development through life: a psychosocial approach*. Chicago, IL: The Dorsey Press.

Nesselroade, J. R. and Baltes, P. B. (1974). *Adolescent personality development and historical change, 1970-1972*. Chicago, IL: University of Chicago Press.

Osgood, N.J. and Howe, C.Z. (1984). Psychological aspects of leisure: A life cycle developmental perspective, *Society and Leisure*, 7:1: 175-195.

Peterson, C. A. and Gunn, S. L. (1984). *Therapeutic recreation program design* (2nd ed.). Englewood Cliffs, NJ: Prentice-Hall.

Ragheb, M.G. (1988). Leisure and recreation needs or motivations as a basis for program planning, *Journal of Park and Recreation Administration*. 6:4: 28-40.

Riley, R. and Lundegren, H.M. (1981). Earlier recreation directs leisure in retirement, *Pennsylvania Recreation and Parks*. *13*:2: p.10-11.

Robinson, J. P. (1977). *How Americans use time*. New York, NY: Praeger.

Rogers, C. (1961). *On becoming a person*. Boston, MA: Houghton Mifflin.

Ross, A.O. (1987). *Personality*. New York, NY: Holt, Rhinehart and Winston.

Rossman, J. R. (1988). Development of a leisure programming theory, *Journal of Park and Recreation Administration, 64*: 1-13.

Tinsley, H. E. A., Barrett, T. C., and Kass, R. A. (1977). Leisure activities and need satisfaction, *Journal of Leisure Research, 9*(2): 110-120.

Zaichkowsky, L. D., Zaichkowsky, L. B. and Martinek, T. J. (1980). *Growth and development*. St. Louis, MO: Mosby.

CHAPTER THREE

GOALS AND OBJECTIVES

The goal of need assessment is to facilitate effective program planning; it is, in fact, the first step in the process that will culminate in an on-site program operation. Building in a hierarchical manner from this step leads to the consideration of goals and objectives and establishment of these objectives for the program in general, as well as for the various aspects of its subdivisions. It also leads to consideration of the question, "Whose objectives–the sponsoring agencies, the program administrators, the program leaders, or the participants?" Can they all be met by the same objectives or does each group perceive a different need to be met? Must they be specific or will general ones suffice? These questions are not considered necessarily in terms of what the objectives are, but how they are established and utilized in planning, in evaluation, and in accountability. More and more agencies are demanding the presentation of program objectives and a report on how they have been met. Objectives are no longer something that appear only in a classroom teacher's lesson plan, and recreation practitioners are expected to know what they are and how to present and interpret them to their sponsors. Therapeutic recreators and outdoor educational program leaders are especially responsive to this demand.

GOALS AND OBJECTIVES

Once the needs of the program participants have been assessed, the programmer is able to determine the goals of the program that are directed to the provision of means to satisfy those needs. After the general goals are set, the overall program objectives themselves are formulated, and finally, the specific objectives of the program are established!

Goals are related to the purposes of the organization and are concerned with ultimate outcomes and are general and global in nature. Goals are such things as "to provide creative programming for senior citizens" or "to appreciate music."

Objectives are less global and more immediate and they define performance of participants that together contribute to the goal. An example would be: "to recognize and discriminate between various musical forms and works."

Performance or behavioral objectives follow. They are stated at a level of greatest specificity and include a measurement that will indicate if the objective has been met.

The programmer should be aware that it takes training and practice to establish objectives and write objectives so that they will express accurately what you mean, but be understandable to the leader and participant alike, and also be attainable. In the next sections, ways and means of doing this are presented with examples. This part of the programming process is not easy, especially in the affective area, but it is essential to a good product and, with practice, becomes more satisfying. The writer must make sure that the objectives are written in such a way that the flexibility and the freshness of the program are preserved as the programmers strive to meet these objectives.

Instructional Objectives, Performance Objectives, Behavioral Objectives, or Learning Outcomes

Possibly the first step in the establishment of objectives is to recognize the proliferation of terminology in this field and realize that several terms may describe the same step in the procedure and that the variance is in how each person looks at what is done in this step. Is the person performing, behaving, learning, or receiving instruction? The overlap in intent is evident, and the implication for choice by the programmer on the basis of personal preference is clear, Mager said, "An objective is a description of a performance you want learners to be able to exhibit before you consider them competent. An objective describes an intended *result* of instruction, rather than the process of instruction itself" (1975, p.5). All of the components mentioned earlier-- behavior, performance, learning, and instruction--are in this definition. Whatever terminology is selected, it is clear that in the process, the participant and the leader have a similar understanding of the goal, and it understood that there are clear, definable criteria on which to base assessment of the learner's progress. What is it that learners can do at the end of the program, and how will one know they have done it? One of the ways that objectives can be stated is in terms of what the leader is going to do:

> To demonstrate the flutter kick.
> To lead the group in singing "Amazing Grace."
> To teach "Red River Valley."

This may satisfy the leader and indicate the scope of the task ahead in presenting material to the clientele, but it does not focus on the learner. By inference we may conclude that if those things are presented, then they will be learned, but in no way does this give any feeling for the extent of the learning expected, nor of its quality. If these things are to be evident and accountability for learning assigned to the leader, then expected outcomes must appear within the stated objective. The objective should encompass the behaviors to be demonstrated by the learner, showing that some mastery has taken place. Just what is expected of the participant after the flutter kick is demonstrated? The same objectives, then, stated from the participant's point of view, would read as follows:

1. Each participant in the swimming class, having been shown a demonstration of the flutter kick, will be able to swim a width of the pool without stopping, utilizing that kick with the aid of the flutter board for support. The form of the kick shall be adequate as judged by a qualified swimming instructor, based on Red Cross standards.
2. Each group member will demonstrate, in cooperation with three other members of the group that he or she knows the words and tune of "Amazing Grace" by singing it through once without error as judged by the leader.
3. Each couple in the group will demonstrate that they know the sequence and form of the dance, "Red River Valley," by dancing it in a regular square dance formation in which each couple leads out once. Couples will be judged as a unit and must do the dance without error as judged by the leader.

An in-depth look at the process is indicated.

Writing Instructional Objectives

What are the step-by-step procedures to be followed in preparing learner-focused objectives? Again, there are as many possibilities of ways to go about doing this as there are books on the market on the subject. However, agreement is found on the general progression to be followed, and the parameters of the problem are the same whatever the source.

The first step is to specify the task the learner is confronted with, the second step is to identify what action the learner is supposed to take and under what conditions it is to occur, and the final step is to set criteria that spell out specifically what the minimal level of acceptable performance is for that task. A time frame within which the behavior must be demonstrated must be set (Mager, 1975; Esbensen, ND). An example of this procedure follows.

Task: Given four trials at splitting logs with the appropriate equipment (*The student will . . .*)
Action: Split at least three logs correctly. (*Using . . .*).
Criteria: *Boy Scout Field Book.*

As Mager said, "A usefully stated objective is one that succeeds in communicating an instructional intent to the leader. It is useful to the extent that it conveys to others a picture of what a successful learner will be like that is *identical to the picture the objective writer had in mind*" (1975, p. 19). Specific references for writing objectives, giving greater detail than has been attempted here, are in the bibliography at the end of the chapter.

Before the recreator is ready to write specific behavioral objectives for a program or subunits of it, the content must be classified in terms of both the importance and the appropriateness of the material. Is the content related to thinking, to feeling or to action? Is one of these factors more important than the other in terms of desired program outcomes? That is, should one area get more emphasis than the others? What are the behaviors we most want to develop or change? The classic reference and the most well known presentation of all this from which all others are adopted is *The Taxonomy of Educational Objectives* (Bloom, 1956; Krathwohl et al., 1964) in which a classification system is presented that allows assignment of objectives into the cognitive (thinking), affective (feeling), and psychomotor (action) domains. The system also allows one to assign high or low importance to the objective so classified. One can proceed from the knowledge level of learning through comprehension, application, and analysis to synthesis and evaluation. (Further illustrations of the behavioral terms used to define objectives may be found in Tables 1-3 in Appendix B.) Recreation programs encompass all of these levels, as well as the three domains. These domains are further defined as follows:

1.   Cognitive: Objectives which emphasize remembering or reproducing something which has presumably been learned, as well as objectives which involve the solving of some intellectual task for which the individual has to determine the essential problem, and then reorder given material or combine it with ideas, methods, or procedures previously learned. Cognitive objectives vary from simple recall of material learned to highly original and creative ways of combining and synthesizing new ideas and materials (Krathwohl et al., 1964, p.6).

Some examples in recreation are to plan a budget, identify a scarlet tananger, and define paraplegia. See Table B.1 in Appendix B for some words and phrases to use in the cognitive domain.

2.   Affective: Objectives which emphasize a feeling tone, an emotion, or a degree of acceptance or rejection. Affective objectives vary from simple attention to selected phenomena to complex but internally consistent qualities of character and conscience (1964, p.7).

Some examples for recreation are to show sensitivity to disabled children, practice cooperation with other departments, share ideas with co-workers, and enjoy music. See Table B.2 in the Appendix B for sample words and phrases to use in the affective domain.

3.   Psychomotor: Objectives which emphasize some muscular or motor skill, some manipulation of material and objectives, or some act which requires a neuromuscular coordination (1964, p.7).

Some examples in recreation are to make a papier-maché ball, walk a balance beam, or put up a tent. See Table B.3 in Appendix B for some words and phrases to use in the psychomotor domain.

An expansion of these levels of behavior as defined for each of the domains is in order here. The use of these levels allows the programmer to order the objectives in terms of relative value in assessing to what extent the program reaches the higher values as defined by the classification system. This capability is especially valuable to the therapeutic activities specialist who is called upon by the medical staff to indicate how the clients are meeting remedial goals in their activity participation. This system further allows the ordering of objectives from simple to complex, which is an invaluable tool in evaluation of general contribution of the overall program to the participant. For example, if one surveys the objectives of a given program and finds all of the cognitive domain at the knowledge level, all of the affective domain at the receiving level, and all of the psychomotor domain at the imitation level, the conclusion would be that the program was in trouble. A description of the levels for each domain follows (Bloom, 1956; Krathwohl, et al., 1964; Gronlund, 1970; Armstrong, et al., 1970).

A. Cognitive

1. *Knowledge.* This category involved recall-of-facts, processes, methods, anything that has been learned and just needs to be brought out of the memory and used. *In recreation this would involve knowing the rules of a game.*

2. *Comprehension.* This category involves understanding or being able to determine the meaning of material. *An example in recreation would be demonstration of the ability to read music.*

3. *Application.* This category includes the ability to apply learnings to a new situation other than the one in which the original material was learned or the ability to use abstractions in concrete situations. *The recreation programmer can see this in the swimming instructor who suggests a swimmer attempt to float with the head back and the arms under the water over the head, thus applying the abstract principle of buoyancy in a real life situation.*

4. *Analysis.* This category involves the breakdown of more complex items into their component parts so that the relationship among the parts is made clear. *The ability to make a presentation of the department budget request to the Board would be an example of this level of cognition.*

5. *Synthesis.* This category involves the ability to join elements together to make a new whole which was not there before the process of synthesizing started. *Producing a play is a good example of a recreation specialist achieving synthesis.*

6. *Evaluation.* This category refers to the ability to make value judgements and to ascertain whether objectives are met. Judgments are made both internally and externally. *A crafts project winning first prize in the annual arts festival would be an example of evaluation.*

B. Affective

1. *Receiving.* This category involves awareness of stimuli or a sensitization of input and a willingness to receive it. *We see this level of behavior in the group listening to the introductory remarks of the ranger at the start of a nature walk.*

2.   *Responding.* In this category the participant goes beyond just attending to the input to responding actively to it and gains satisfaction from having responded. *An example of this is the choral singer who enjoys singing in a group and feels personally enriched by it.*

3.   *Valuing.* This category denotes believing in a thing as having worth and extends to attitudes toward an object. Behavior here is guided not just by compliance, but by commitment. *The Scout leader who devotes much time to the troop because of commitment to instilling the ideals of scouting into young people is operating at this level.*

4.   *Organization.* This category focuses on the bringing together of values into an organized system in which the subset values demonstrate an ordered relationship to one another. *The development of a philosophy of leisure would satisfy this category of behavior.*

5.   *Characterization.* At this level the participant demonstrates total life style behaviors which are consistent with the organization of values established in level 4. *The participant here shows commitment to the leisure ethic by regular involvement in recreation during discretionary time.*

C. Psychomotor

1.   *Imitation.* This level of behavior involves the participant imitating an action which has been demonstrated. *The games leader throws the ball overhand at the wall, the preschooler watches, then takes the ball and throws it toward the wall, with no real coordination, stepping forward on the same foot using both hands to hold the ball, which may not, in fact, reach the wall.*

2.   *Manipulation.* At this level the participant can follow instructions and perform the act with some understanding of it. The resultant action becomes stablized through practice. *An example would be performing a tennis forehand to contact a ball pitched by an automatic ball-boy.*

3.   *Precision.* In this category the participant surpasses manipulation to reach higher levels of skill, precision, and accuracy. *At this level the performer serves the ball accurately into the service court with regularity.*

4.   *Articulation.* Here the participant performs a series of acts with coordination, speed, and accuracy with some consistency. *For example, a child in a perceptual-motor program will be able, in meeting this objective, to run an obstacle course accurately under x number of seconds three days in a row.*

5.   *Naturalization.* This category includes the automatization of a single act so that it is performed correctly, smoothly and perfectly with no cognition necessary. It represents the highest level of perceptual-motor response so that the stimuli automatically triggers the correct response. *The basketball player who shoots 25 free throws without a miss is illustrating behavior in this category.*

SAMPLE PROGRAMS WITH SPECIFIED OBJECTIVES

The following section contains complete program segments that were actually conducted by practitioners in the field with the populations indicated. These programs are presented here complete with behavioral objectives either written by or augmented by the present authors. Different presentation styles are used. Programs to be presented were chosen because they were unique or different from the traditional sports program for which every recreation specialist knows the progression. The main focus here is in the form of the behavioral objectives and not on the session content.

Program I: A Bicycling Program for Institutionalized Adult Psychiatric Patients (David Caporale)

This program is designed at a beginning level for adults who are physically capable of riding bicycles, but who may be functioning at a child's level in many ways and, although they may have once ridden, appear to have little or no ability to reproduce the skill. There is an additional element of encouragement of socialization in these lessons, which, although not always planned for, is often a vital part of working with regressed psychiatric patients. All lessons are one hour in length. There is one bicycle for each participant. Group size is six.

Session One. The general purpose of the first lesson is to assess the functional ability of the participants to handle a bicycle by mounting, pedaling, braking, and dismounting a stationary bicycle, followed by an attempt being made by the participants to repeat these actions with a regular pedal-brake bicycle. The lesson then proceeds with an instruction group and a riding group.

A. Behavioral Objectives

1. Participants will demonstrate their confidence and abilities in handling a bicycle by:
    (a) Mounting, pedaling, braking, and dismounting a stationary bicycle three times.
    (b) Mounting, pedaling, braking, and dismounting a regular pedal-brake bike three times. (If they seem to have had previous experience with a bicycle.)
2. Participants will become acquainted with the bicycle by holding the bicycle by the handlebars and walking it back and forth for a space of 25 feet each way four times.
3. Participants will demonstrate ability to mount, sit on the seat, balance, and dismount three times with assistance from the instructor or another participant.
4. Participants will interact with another participant at least once by:
    (a) Assisting someone else with the bicycle activities. (Socialization)
    (b) Conversing with another person at some time during the lesson.

B. Planned Activities

1. Demonstrate mounting, pedaling, braking, and dismounting both on a stationary and a free-wheeling bicycle.
2. Have participants try both of the above activities, repeating them several times.
3. After removing the bicycles from the storage area, walk them around the yard area.
4. Redemonstrate mounting, sitting on, balancing, and dismounting from the regular bike. Have each participant try it with assistance. Encourage the participants to help each other. Repeat several times.
5. Let those who have experience ride around in a small area.
6. Walk bicycles back to storage area and store them properly. Demonstrate use of the bicycle stand or storage rack (dependent on storage facility for the latter).

Session Two. The general purpose of this session is to present the bicycle safety regulations code that will be enforced during the program and to instruct in the basic bicycling skills of mounting, pedaling, braking, and dismounting a bicycle. Participants will be divided into the riding group (those with experience) and the instruction group (novice riders) for practical purposes.

A. Behavioral Objectives

1. Participants will show they know the safety regulations by reciting them correctly when asked.
2. Participants will show they understand the safety regulations by demonstrating proper use of those appropriate to the situation while riding a bicycle.
3. Participants will demonstrate that they understand the regulations regarding bicycle maintenance by checking the seat and handlebars to see that they are not loose. (Other adjustment items may be substituted for these.)
4. In the riding group, participants will show that they have reinforced the bicycle skills by: (a) demonstrating the following sequence twice, which includes the ability to mount the bicycle, pedal it in a large circle without losing balance, brake and dismount it without losing control of the bicycle, and leave it stationary on its stand, and (b) by participating in the riding tour.
5. In the instruction group each participant will show development of bicycle riding skills by (a) mounting, balancing, and dismounting a bicycle three times with assistance and (b) mounting, pedaling, braking, and dismounting a bicycle twice with assistance.
6. Each participant will demonstrate the ability to interact with another person by assisting another person with the bicycle skills once or by conversing with another person once. (Socialization)

B. Planned Activities

1. In a presentation of the bicycling safety regulations code, which is as follows, the safe rider will:
   (a) Ride in a single file.
   (b) Ride with traffic on the right-hand side of the road.
   (c) Stop at all stop signs and traffic lights.
   (d) Use proper hand signals for turning either right or left or when stopping.
   (e) Dismount from the bicycle and walk it across any heavy traffic.
   (f) Obey all traffic regulations.
   (g) Keep a lookout for other bicycles and cars.
   (h) Make sure the seat and handlebars are adjusted properly and that they are not loose.

2. Progression for the riding group:
   (a) Walk bicycles from storage area to starting area.
   (b) Review safety regulations.
   (c) Check bicycles for proper seat and handlebar adjustment.
   (d) Practice mounting, pedaling in a large circle, braking, and dismounting. (Check off each one.)
   (e) Participate in a bicycle tour of the institution's campus with frequent rest stops.
   (f) Return bikes to storage area.

3. Progression for the instructions group:
   (a) Walk bicycles from storage to grassy area.
   (b) Review safety regulations.
   (c) Check adjustment of seat and handlebars.
   (d) Demonstrate mounting, balancing, and dismounting.
   (e) With assistance each participant will practice mounting, balancing, and dismounting several times.
   (f) With assistance, each will attempt pedaling and braking (in addition to instructions) several times.
   (g) Return bikes to the storage area.

Session Three. The general plan of this session is to review and reinforce the learnings of the previous meetings. The behavioral objectives and planned activities are the same as for Session 2, with the addition of demonstrating interaction with another person once during a rest break.

Session Four. The general plan of this session is to review and practice bicycle skills and safety regulations, for the riding group to plan a bike hike for the instructional group to take later, and for the instructional group to achieve the ability to handle the bike alone.

A. Behavioral Objectives

   1. Repeat objectives 2 and 3 of Session 2.
   2. Each member of the instruction group will demonstrate twice the ability to mount, pedal in a big circle, brake, and dismount without assistance and without falling (check off).
   3. The members of the riding group will demonstrate the ability to plan an appropriate bike hike for the instruction group to tour the hospital campus with the appropriateness of the plan judged by the recreation worker.
   4. Members of the riding group will test the appropriateness of the tour by taking it themselves once.
   5. Members of the instruction group will demonstrate interactions with others by assisting another in bicycle skills once and conversing during rest break at least once. (Socialization)

B. Planned Activities

   1. Progression for the riding group:
     (a) Review safety regulations.
     (b) Check bike for safety adjustments.
     (c) Plan a bike hike for the instruction group. Check it with the recreation worker.
     (d) Take the bike hike course just planned and follow safety regulations while doing it. (Encourage interaction on the rest breaks.)
     (e) Return bikes to storage area.
     (f) Invite the instruction group for a hike next week.
   2. Progression for the instruction group:
     (a) Repeat instruction a through f of Session 2.
     (b) Without assistance (or with little assistance the first time) mount, pedal the bike in a large circle, brake, and dismount. Repeat for check off.
     (c) Return bikes to storage area.

Session Five. The general focus of this session is on the completion of the bike hike by both groups.

A. Behavioral Objectives

   1. Members of the total group will demonstrate knowledge and understanding of the safety regulations by checking their bikes before leaving on the hike and following the correct regulations during the ride, as the situation demands, as judged by the recreation worker.
   2. The members of the riding group will demonstrate the ability to lead the other group and bike hike through the hospital grounds, starting at the storage area and completing it there successfully, as judged by the recreation worker.

3. The members of the instructional group will demonstrate mastery of basic bicycling skills by completing the course once without falling.
4. Group members will demonstrate interaction with others by:
   (a) Assisting at least one other group member during the bicycling activities.
   (b) Verbally encouraging another person during the bike hike.
   (c) Conversing with another group member twice during the rest break. (Socialization)

B. Planned Activities

1. The riding group will take the instruction group on the bike hike they planned in Session 4.
2. The riding group will evaluate the success of the hike at its conclusion with the help of the recreation worker.

Session Six. The focus of this lesson is to review all previous skills, to repeat the bike hike of Session 5 with fewer general rest stops, and to add a visit to the canteen for a snack. Proper care of a bicycle will be demonstrated.

A. Behavioral Objectives

1. Objectives of Session 5 will apply to this lesson.
2. The group members will demonstrate their understanding or proper care of a bicycle by dusting it off, checking for any loose parts and tightening them if possible, polishing the reflector, and putting oil in the chain before putting the bike in the storage area. Performance of these steps will be judged as correct by the recreation worker.

B. Planned Activities

1. Repeat the bike hike from Session 5. During the hike repeat safety rules as necessary and review skills as needed. Reduce the number of rest breaks.
2. Stop at the canteen for a snack before returning to the storage area.
3. Present the following basic rules for care of the bike and have the participants check each one out on the bike they are riding. (Provide rags, oil, and a screwdriver.)
   (a) Keep bike free from dust or mud.
   (b) Keep reflectors polished.
   (c) Keep the chain well oiled.
   (d) Keep the seat and handlebars tightened.
   (e) Keep air in the tires.

Program II: A Process-Oriented Art Activity Program for Alcoholics in a Treatment Center (Diane Knight)

These lessons were planned for 11 alcoholic adults in a treatment center where the therapeutic plan encourages communication about the drinking problem in a group setting. Art is being used as a therapeutic tool to assist in getting in touch with oneself and one's problems and communicating feelings to others. No previous art experience was required. Groups met for 10 one-hour sessions.

Session One

A. Content

1. Conduct automatic drawing activities.
    (a) Make free lines or scribbles on paper with eyes closed and with eyes open.
    (b) Draw with the nondominant hand.
    (c) Draw by not taking the hand off the paper until the picture is complete.
2. Develop media and color exploration activities.
    (a) Make blobs and dribbles on wet paper with watercolor.
    (b) Make blobs and dribbles on paper with ink.
    (c) Make a free-form design with pastels.
    (d) Make a free-form design with crayons.
    (e) Make a design using two different types of media.

B. Behavioral Objectives

Participants will:

1. Express themselves spontaneously by drawing on paper with various art media.
2. Become acquainted (or reacquainted) with art materials by using four different types of media in some way.
3. Explore the use of these media in making lines, symbols, and forms by making a design using at least two different media.

Session Two

A. Content

1. Explore conversational drawing activities.
    (a) An object, event, or feeling (which is related to alcoholism in some way) is drawn by the leader.
    (b) The drawing is passed to each person for additions and he or she communicates a specific meaning with shapes, lines, and colors.

2. Organize group discussions.

   When this drawn dialogue is complete, the group discusses what has taken place.

B. Behavioral Objectives

Participants will:
1. Express and face their feelings at least once during the session by painting or drawing lines, symbols, or forms that represent the way they feel.
2. Express at least once nonverbally to the group something related to their drinking problem.

Session Three

A. Content

1. Participate in figure drawing activity.
   (a) Draw a person–a "phenomenal" figure.
   (b) Draw yourself as you would really like to be (ideal self).
   (c) Draw yourself as you believe you really are (real self).
2. Share drawing of phenomenal figure with someone else.

B. Behavioral Objectives

Participants will:
1. Become more aware of body image or self-concept by drawing themselves and other human figures.
2. Interact with others by verbally interpreting their drawing of a person to *one* other person in the art group.

Session Four

A. Content

1. Make a drawing that expresses your innermost feelings.
   (a) Draw or paint how you feel at the moment by using color, shapes, and lines.
   (b) Draw or paint your mood of the moment.

B. Behavioral Objectives

Participants will:
1. Express and face their feelings by painting or drawing lines and shapes to represent at least one aspect of how they feel.
2. Express one feeling or mood using at least one color other than black or white.

Session Five

A. Content

    1. Do the road of life activity as follows:
        (a) Draw or paint the "road" or "path" you have been traveling in your life.
        (b) Put yourself in historical perspective and try to be aware of your feelings at certain points along this road.
        (c) Include in this work or in another drawing or painting the road you hope to or expect to travel in the future.
    2. Join with another person and attempt to interpret one of these "road" drawings with him or her.

B. Behavioral Objectives

Participants will:
1. Verbally interpret one drawing to one other person.
2. Interact with one other person by attempting to express one idea that the other's drawing means to them.
3. Demonstrate their ability to convey at least one idea or meaning through an art media.

Session Six

A. Content

    1. Draw yourself as an animal.
        (a) Draw yourself as the animal you would most like to be.
        (b) Draw yourself as the animal you would least like to be.
    2. Discuss your drawing with the group.

B. Behavioral Objectives

Participants should:
1. Demonstrate an ability to interpret their drawing to the group by doing so.
2. Become aware of ideas and meanings that can be expressed in symbols in art, and demonstrate their understanding of this by using an animal form to express things about themselves.

Session Seven

A. Content

 1. Affective words activity.
    (a) Write words connoting feelings on small pieces of paper, fold them, and place them in a box for the whole group.
    (b) Shake the box and have each member of the group pull out a piece of paper.
    (c) Draw or paint what the chosen word means to you without verbalizing the word to the others in the group.
    (d) Post a list of the words used by the group.
 2. In a group discussion, attempt to match the words with the pictures.
 3. Match the correct words with the pictures.

B. Behavioral Objectives

 Participants will:
 1. Demonstrate ability to express at least one word nonverbally in an art form.
 2. Demonstrate ability to interpret another person's painting or drawing and express that to group.
 3. Share themselves with others by participating in a group task.

Session Eight

A. Content

 1. Explore the three wishes activity.
    (a) Draw or paint three wishes expressing what you want most out of life.
    (b) In groups of three, share with each other the meaning of the picture to you and ask questions about the others' pictures. Explore areas of commonality and difference.
 2. In the total group, share the things you had in common. Did they relate to alcoholism in any way?

B. Behavioral Objectives

 Participants will:
 1. Show ability to share some feelings about themselves with at least two other people through the medium of an art form.
 2. Share interest in the feelings of at least two other people by asking at least one question of each about his or her drawing or painting.

Session Nine

A. Content

1. Choose an immediate states activity.
    (a) Select one of the following phrases to paint: "I am," "I feel," "I have," or "I do."
    (b) Discuss the painting with a partner. Exchange impressions about each other's feelings.
    (c) Select a second phrase and do another drawing.
    (d) In a group as a whole, discuss how you feel about discussing your feelings about yourself with others. Did the drawings express your true feelings?
2. Behavioral Objectives
    Participants will:
    (a) Show that they have become more aware of their self-concepts or body images by drawing themselves and interpreting that to one other person.
    (b) Show they have gained in ability to interpret verbally their drawings to at least two other people.

Session Ten

A. Content

1. Drawing positive and negative assets.
    (a) Draw three positive characteristics of self.
    (b) Draw one negative characteristic of self.
2. Attempt to evaluate the drawings realistically to the whole group in a discussion period. Evaluate each other's drawings.

B. Behavioral Objectives

Participants will:
1. Attempt to realize their self-worth by drawing symbols that represent positive things about themselves.
2. Help others to realize their personal, positive characteristics by discussing their drawings with them and the way each perceives the others in the group.

Program III: Group Activity Session Plans for the Perceptual-Motor Development of Kindergarten Children (Louise Streator)

All activities used in the following group activity sessions for kindergarten children deal with the development of perceptual-motor skills. The general objectives of the lessons are to develop specifically the skills of laterality, directionality, balance, and body image. All activities planned for the children are purported to contribute to the development of one or more of these skills. Sessions are planned for 20 minutes and involve minimal equipment.

Session One

A. Behavioral Objectives

Children will be able to:
1. Demonstrate the locomotor skills of running, walking, skipping, and galloping in different directions.
2. Distinguish their own self-space and move quickly to it on command.
3. Move in different directions in self-space.
4. Balance on three different body parts.
5. Touch five body parts correctly on command.

B. Procedures

The children enter a multipurpose room and sit in circle. Discuss the self-space (the space closely surrounding and containing them) concept, and instruct them to choose their own carpet square and sit on it. They then explore self-space by showing the instructor how tiny their space is, how tall, wide, low, fat, etc.

Discuss general space as being all other space in the room that is not their space. Play the *freeze game* where the children move in general space until the instructor calls, "Freeze!" at which point they stop and hold their positions until told to move. Names of body parts can be called out for the children to touch. In this game include the locomotor skills of running, walking, skipping, and galloping in various directions.

When the children return to their carpet squares they explore different ways to move in their space or general space using the square. For example, they can move over it, with it, on it, above it, around it, and so on.

Ask them to balance on the carpet squares with at least three different body parts touching the square. A headstand would be an example of a three-part balance. The leader moves them from a one-part balance to five-part balances.

Play a *body-part name game* in which the students touch the body parts as called out by the leader. The leader should make sure both members of a pair of body parts are touched, for example, the ears.

Session Two

A. Behavioral Objectives

The children will be able to:
1. Review the freeze game and correctly identify the body parts called out, and add three new parts not used during the previous session.
2. Review the name game and identify seven body parts.
3. Review that self-space activities and be able to perform all of them correctly.
4. Review the balance activities and correctly balance on the three body parts in the three positions called by the leader.

5. Do locomotor skills in place.
6. Play "Duck, Duck, Goose" and demonstrate ability to follow the directions of the game.

B. Procedures

For warm-up activities play the freeze game using all locomotor skills going in different directions and speeds in general space. When frozen, the leader calls out several body parts to be touched, adding new ones to those given in the session before.

Instruct the children to find a self-space and review dimensions of it themselves. *Examples:* "Show me how small you can be in your space, etc." Then instruct them to do the various locomotor skills while staying inside their spaces. *Example:* "Hop on one foot while staying in your space."

Review the balance activities with the children being asked to take a balance position with a certain number of body parts touching the floor. This lesson includes an addition of three body parts while on the side or on the back, using the shoulders as one part. Introduce "Duck, Duck, Goose" and play until all have at least one turn being "it."

Session Three

A. Behavioral Objectives

The children will be able to:
1. Perform the freeze and name games correctly for all directions given.
2. Learn the listening game utilizing auditory memory skills and show that they have by responding correctly once to the clap sequence.
3. Imitate movement skills of the leader and get at least five arm and leg movements correct.
4. Show development of balance skills using a low balance beam by going across forward and sideways correctly.

B. Procedures

Warm-up by playing the freeze game, adding the new dimension of levels: high, medium, and low. The children explore how they could move at a low level (crawl, roll, etc.), medium (run, skip), and high (jump, hop).

Teach listening game. This involves the leader teaching the signals for movement and the proper response for them. Example, 1 clap = lie down on your back; 2 claps = jump up to your feet. When they can all quickly respond to this, the leader tries to confuse them by clapping two times when they are already standing, etc. Then a new response is taught, for example, 1 clap = lie down prone, 2 claps = sit up.

Divide the class into groups with each group having one balance beam. The children take turns crossing the beam in various ways: forward, backward, sideways, forward halfway, then turn and continue going backward, forward and then using a 1-foot balance, and finally exploring their own ways of going across safely.

Play the name game, this time have children touch the body parts with their eyes shut. If they have difficulty, the leader should permit them to open their eyes and find the part. Play the circle name game. This involves the children standing on a circle and putting a certain body part into or outside of the circle. *Examples.* "Put your right foot in, take it out; put both elbows inside, etc." (This is similar to Hokey Pokey with no music. Singing could be added to it.)

Play "Follow the Leader" around the room with the leader using various locomotor movements as well as arm movements with the children imitating. Having the leader start leading and then designate a child to take over.

C. Equipment

Balance beams, 4 inches high.

Session Four

A. Behavioral Objectives

The children will be able to:
1. Perform the gross motor skills correctly.
2. Review balance skills.
3. Develop three ways of moving a ball on two different levels.
4. Show at least three ways of throwing and catching a ball correctly using the wall as a partner.
5. Show they remember the auditory memory skills for the previous lesson by following all the clap commands correctly twice through.
6. Identify the body parts out loud while lying down with the eyes shut.

B. Procedures

Play the freeze game utilizing different verbal directions. The leader, for example, says, "Move any way you want in a sideways direction; now go to the other side in a different way." When "Freeze" is called out, a number is given by the leader and the children quickly balance with that many parts touching the floor.

Have each child get a yarn ball, find a self-space, and explore the many ways a ball can be moved on a low level. Guide them to use a medium level and finally a high level. Ask what they can do with the ball. Find a partner and explore what they could do with a partner and one or two balls.

Review the auditory memory skills from the previous lesson and add one new response to the claps.

While the children are lying down, instruct them to shut their eyes and touch the body parts names by the leader. Then standing, with eyes open, review all of the parts and respond to commands such as "point in front of you, behind you, above you, etc."

Play "Follow the Leader" as done in the previous lesson.

C. Equipment

One ball of yarn for each child.

Session Five

A. Behavioral Objectives

The child will be able to:
1. Remember to follow the command after first stopping still in the freeze game.
2. Explore more than three ways to move a hoop in two different levels.
3. Review body part locations by touching 10 parts with a hoop both by oneself and with a partner.
4. Correctly follow the auditory cues given in the listening game.
5. Review "Follow the Leader."

B. Procedures

As a warm-up, play the freeze game with variations as follows: when "freeze" is called the children are instructed to stop and then do something specific. Examples: "When I call "freeze" put your hands on your knees; turn around one time; sit down; etc.

Give each of the children a hoop and explore the different ways it can be moved on all three levels. Review the body parts by touching the part with the hoop on command. Sometimes put a body part inside the hoop or on top of it or under it. With a partner, touch different body parts on command.

After the hoops are put away, play the listening game, vary the clap clues, and "Follow the Leader," led by the various children.

C. Equipment

One small hoop for each child.

Session Six

A. Behavioral Objectives

The child will be able to:
1. Perform all skills covered on the balance beam.
2. Perform all skills done with the balls and show one new way to use them.
3. Perform all skills done with the hoops and show one new way to use them.
4. Perform all listening skills covered.
5. Perform all imitation skills covered.

B. Procedures

Play the freeze game using all the basic locomotor skills with a command to remember, as was done in the previous lesson.

Divide the class into three groups and assign each group to a station; rotate among the three stations. At one station they practice all the ways known of walking on the balance beam. At another station allow them to use the yarn ball in any way they choose, and the third station, they use the hoops in ways they have been taught and in new ways they invent. To conclude the lesson, play the listening game with the leader, then the children give the clapping cues and follow the leader.

Program IV: An Outdoor Classroom Environmental Educational Survival Unit for Fifth and Sixth Graders (Ellen Kaspar)

This unit covers five 50-minute sessions conducted in an outdoor environmental education classroom. Total group size accommodated is 25 children, although smaller groups are possible and recommended. For events such as field walks, the group should be subdivided into smaller units of 6 to 10 participants.

Session One
Survival Needs: Food and Clothing

A. Content

1. Water
   (a) More important than food.
   (b) Sources include dew, plants, moss, and melted snow.
   (c) Grapevines, if used, should be slashed on top and then on the bottom.
   (d) Can be found above the high-tide line behind sand dunes.
   (e) If unsure of purity, boil water before drinking.
2. Food—edible wild plants.
   (a) Few sources in the winter.
   (b) In spring, cat-o'-nine-tails, dutch potato, wild strawberries, sweet clover, dandelion leaves, goldenrod leaves, and dried blossoms for tea, pond lily roots, wild onion, etc., can be eaten.
   (c) Poisonous plants and berries include rhubarb leaves, yew berries, holly berries and milkweed.
3. Clothing for warmth and protection
   (a) Cover extremities in cold weather: head, hands, and feet.
   (b) Properly cover each extremity.
   (c) Use wool and cotton, when appropriate.
4. Frostbite
   (a) Signs include gray or yellow waxy spots on skin.
   (b) First aid for frostbite.

B. Behavioral Objectives

Each participant will be able to:
1. Name six edible plants indigenous to the area in which you are hiking and three sources of water in the same area.
2. Demonstrate knowledge of correct clothing to take on a trip by packing the correct things for an all-day hike.
3. Demonstrate correctly, with a partner, the procedures for giving first aid for frostbite.

Session Two
Firebuilding

A. Content

1. Safety--clear spot 10 feet away from trees or bushes.
2. Procedures for building the fire. Understanding of tinder, kindling, logs, where and how to get fire wood.
3. Feeding the fire and knowing the proper size for the use.
4. Extinguishing the fire.

B. Behavioral Objectives

Participants will demonstrate that they know how to build, feed, and extinguish a fire properly by performing these steps correctly without help.

Session Three
Map and Compass

A. Content

1. Topography maps of the area and how to read and use them--explain map symbols
2. Compass use.
   (a) Parts of the compass.
   (b) Orienting and reading the compass.
   (c) Following assigned bearings.
3. Pacing.
4. Following map and compass courses.

B. Behavioral Objectives

The participant will be able to:
1. Name the points of the compass; explain or define: magnetic and true north, longitude, latitude, compass bearing; and pace correctly by defining them orally when asked.

2. Find and follow a bearing to a location using a compass and return to the original location by following correctly a bearing of 140º to a tree and a backbearing of 320º (140º and 180º) to the starting spot.
3. Follow a triangular course correctly that is set as follows: 40 steps 40º, 40 steps 160º, 40 steps 280º.

Session Four
Shelter Building for Warmth and Protection

A. Content

1. Kinds of shelter and materials, including snow, cave, overhangings, large logs or limbs, fallen trees.
2. Characteristics to look for: good insulation, surface to sit on other than bare ground (e.g., pine needles, evergreen boughs, dry weeds, or grass).
3. How to construct a proper shelter from natural elements, moving as quickly as possible while conversing energy.

B. Behavioral Objectives

Each participant will be able to:
1. On a walk through the woods, name the type of shelter appropriate to use and find the proper insulation by correctly identifying three kinds of natural shelters and two natural insulators.
2. Demonstrate correctly the construction of *one* kind of shelter.

Session Five
Problem-Solving Task–Survival

A. Content

In groups of three the participants will be given directional bearings to follow with a compass to a spot at which they are to build a small fire and construct a shelter. They will then find water and one edible plant.

B. Behavioral Objective

Each group of three will demonstrate their knowledge of survival skills by carrying out correctly (as judged by the leader) the task assigned. Tasks to be correctly performed include:
1. Arriving at the spot designated.
2. Correct safety procedures around fire.
3. Correct size of fire and correct use of tinder, kindling, and logs to build the fire.
4. Shelter protection from the wind and proper ground insulation, speed, and efficiency of construction.

5. Collection of water.
6. Choice of a correct, nonpoisonous plant.

Program V: A Resident Environmental Education Program on Energy, Streams and Water and Night Creatures (Susan Johnson)

These three sessions are designed to present materials to 30 fifth graders in 90-minute periods for Energy and Streams and 30 minutes for the night hike.

Session One
Energy Audit Hunt

A. Goals

1. To develop an awareness of energy use within the built environment.
2. To develop the skills necessary for assessing energy use and for recommending more energy-efficient methods.

B. Objectives

After completing the energy audit, students will:
1. Be able to identify energy-dependent systems within the built environment.
2. Be able to locate extremes in heat-temperature variations within the built environment.
3. Have identified points of heat loss within the built environment.
4. Be able to describe at least two energy-saving techniques.
5. Have made recommendations for creating a more-efficient built environment.
6. Be able to identify the types of energy sources utilized in the built environment.

C. Concept

Humans regulate and alter their surroundings in order to create a more comfortable lifestyle. They use energy to do this.

D. Activity

Role-play as if group were in a super-jet that could get anywhere in the world in 30 seconds. Have the group act out their arrival in several places with extreme differences in temperature (Alaska, African deserts, rain forests, etc.).

Discuss why people are able to live in a wide variety of locations. Compare to most animals who are habitat-dependent; humans are able to regulate their shelters in many ways and can, therefore, survive in a wide variety of locations.

1. How do we keep the temperatures in our homes comfortable in winter? In summer? Heating and cooling houses and other buildings require energy.
2. What other comforts in our homes require energy? Point out that these forms of energy cost money yet they identified places where we let heat escape and cold air get in.
3. Any ideas for keeping the warm air in and cold air out?
4. Discuss ideas for cutting down on costly energy in other areas (for heating, lighting, in the kitchen, etc.). Encourage students to use information they gained in learning about natural and historical uses of energy.

Activity: Energy Hunt

Lead-Up
1. Have students divide in pairs and give each pair the map sheet, the key and thermometer sheet, colored dots, two thermometers and a pencil.
2. As a group make up key to represent energy uses in building. Have each pair duplicate key on their individual keys.
3. Before energy hunt, instruct each pair to choose the spot that they think is the coldest and warmest in the building. Have them leave a thermometer in each spot. Also instruct them to check the thermostat and record on their sheet before the end of the Energy Hunt.
4. Set the time allowed for pairs to complete their maps.

Follow-Up
Using the individual maps as guides, fill in the big map together to create an "energy picture" of the building.
1. What kinds of things do we use energy for in this building?
2. What different kinds of fuel do we use as energy?
   (a) To heat our rooms?
   (b) To heat our water?
   (c) To cook?
   (d) To light the building?

Follow-Up: (Optional)
1. Demonstrate energy-saving techniques (window shades or curtains, insulation, bottles filled with colored water in windows, pipe insulation, weather stripping, etc.).
2. Distribute Energy Audit pins.

Session Two
Stream Study (Water)

A. Goals

1. To develop an understanding of the role of water in humans' lives.
2. To develop an awareness of plants and animals found in local freshwater streams, their habitats and the nature of their ecosystems.
3. To develop an awareness of how certain aquatic plants and animals may indicate the health of freshwater streams.
4. To nurture the ability to record observations of the environment.

B. Objectives

By the end of the stream study each child will be able to:
1. List human activities in which clean water plays a major role.
2. Identify the roles of different plants and animals in the aquatic food web.
3. Describe the differences in animal shape, structure, and movement among animals found in different stream locations: shore, still, and flowing water.
4. Describe the effect of moving water upon a biotic stream factors
5. Identify one animal from each of three classes of the Beck's Biotic Index, and what each animal may indicate about water "cleanliness."
6. Identify two distinct types of freshwater plants: algae vs. vascular plants.

C. Materials Needed

Pond Guides, Biotic Index Sheets
Dip Nets, Strainers
Hand lens
White-bottomed collecting dishes (plastic)
Butcher paper with pencils, markers, crayons, etc.

Activity
A. Introduction

Before reaching the stream, discuss human activities that involve water. Have the children list activities that involve water: drinking, bathing, cooking, recreational uses, construction, industry, waste removal, farming, etc. Where does water come from, where does it go, what may happen to it during use?

B. Before reaching the stream, establish the ground rules for the stream exploration:

1. Work in groups of two, have them choose or count off by two's, describe the reasons for the buddy system, especially safety.
2. Divide the groups of two into shore explorers, still-water explorers and flowing water group that will focus on when exploring.

3. Describe techniques of stream exploration; i.e., moving rocks while holding net downstream, need for quiet, etc.
4. Ask for suggestions as to how life can be effectively investigated without causing it harm; i.e., temporary restraint of organisms, then their release.
5. Point out that groups are to collect for a while and then come together to compare and discuss their findings.
6. At the stream, pass out collecting observing materials. When approaching the stream, listen to the sound of running water. Does a brook really babble? What sounds do you hear? What do you smell? Where does the stream come from? Where is it going?

C. Group Action
Allow the group about fifteen minutes for the stream exploration.

D. Group Discussion

1. Bring the group back together and gather around collected organisms in a circle. Discuss the stream following the questioning strategies below. Examine collected animals, plants, allowing each group to share their discoveries.Discuss differences, similarities, habitats, foods, plants and animals require.
   (a) Describe the banks of the stream. What may have caused their shape?
   (b) Examine the stream. Look for different sized rocks (their shape and texture), bubbles, currents, etc.
   (c) Is the water hot, warm, cold? Is it the same in all places?
   (d) How fast is the water flowing? How could we find out? Does it flow at the same speed in all places?
   (e) What kind of living things are found living in the stream? Define "organism" and "habitat."
2. Compare organisms based upon where they were found. Why do you think this animal picked this particular area in which to live? Are there differences, imilarities, in body size, shape, appendages, etc.? What importance do these adaptations (define) play in the animals' survival? Discuss what animals might eat; where they might live. Were there organisms seen but which the group could not catch? Why not?

Organism:	Any living thing, plant or animal.
Habitat:	The place where an organism normally lives where you would ordinarily go to find it.
Adaptation:	Changes in an organism's morphology, physiology or behavior, over time, that is in response to environmenta inputs.

3. Introduce the idea of water pollution and effects on aquatic organisms. Discuss the Biotic Index and compare index animals to what was discovered in thetors of relative pollution; different aquatic organisms have different tolerances to pollution/lack of oxygen).

4. Compare aquatic plant types; specifically, algae vs. vascular plants. What are the gross differences between the two? Describe some of the differences you see and try to explain them. Discuss possible plant responses to pollution.

5. Discuss differences between plant and animal responses to pollution. Do some of the plants and animals here depend on each other? In what ways? Describe several examples of interdependence you see, and try to explain them.

6. What happens to animals and plants that die in the water? Discuss recycling in water.

7. How do you think the plants and animals affect the water? In what ways?

8. How does your visit affect the water and the plant and animal life at the stream?

9. How are humans using this place? Think of as many ways as you can. Do you think human activities affect the water here? How? Discuss this question in relation to the initial discussion of human water needs; i.e., tie back to human systems and make the connection that humans are part/ components of the ecosystem.

10. Return all the organisms to where they were found.

E. Follow-Up/Optional Activity

Using butcher paper, have the group record their observations (collected and seen organisms) of the stream. Divide the butcher paper into the three areas of exploration: shore, still, flowing, and have children from each area draw/record their findings. Provide pictures, field guides if desirable.

Session Three
Night Hike (Creatures)

A. Goals

Introduction. The word at night is unique in many ways. A night hike will allow the students to experience this uniqueness. One problem that may be encountered is fear or uneasiness in children about being outdoors at night. One aspect of a child's fear is lack of knowledge and misconceptions about sounds they hear and what animal life they may come across. By helping the students correctly identify the various sounds they'll hear at night, some of these fears can be alleviated. Dispensing fears is a prerequisite before a student can appreciate the outdoors after dark.

B. Objectives

1. When attempting to identify observations/sounds, students will avoid the use of words or names connotating danger or fear and will primarily utilize the concepts discussed in the pre-show.

2. To have the group identify at least two (2) animal sounds without seeing what made the sound.
3. To have the group list the sounds they heard and observations they made on the bulletin board when they return to the lodge.

C. Concepts

1. Fear of darkness is often caused by misconceptions or lack of knowledge. Fears can thus be lessened by transmitting knowledge and by a positive night experience in the outdoors.
2. Sensory awareness is often heightened at night for most of the senses.
3. Silent cooperation is necessary in order to hear and see night activity.
4. Night time experiences are very much different than those during the day.
5. Nature is alive in the darkness.

D. Process

Introduction. Family groups will meet together outside after the pre-show, then embark on the hike via their designated trail.

1. A night hike is a quiet hike–stress this.
2. Encourage students to listen for sounds as given in the pre-show.
3. Students should walk in a single file–hand-on-shoulder or hand-in-hand if desired.
4. Be wary of uneasy or frightened children; keep them in front of you.
5. There should be perfect silence while walking. If a stop is made, gather all students tightly together and discuss the occurrence.
6. The counselor-teacher is the only one with a flashlight (red cellophane covered). If bright enough outside, don't use flashlight at all.

E. Activity

Remember that the two main groups are to help lessen the students' night fears and to provide a simple night experience in the outdoors.

1. Once along the trail, stop and sit down as a group in a circle. Have everyone keep completely silent for 5-10 minutes as they listen to the night. Encourage students to listen for the things given in the pre-show. After this, discuss the things everyone heard, saw and smelled.
2. At another area, separate each student by at least fifteen (15) feet and have them sit silently by themselves for 5-10 minutes. If any student is uncomfortable with this, sit near him/her. After this, return as a group to share feelings and observations. This part of the activity is an important one.

F. Evaluation

    1. Were there any references to negative concepts such as ghosts, being eaten or monsters that would indicate a continued fear of the outdoors at night?

    2. Was the group able to identify at least two (2) animal sounds of the night, especially those as given in the pre-show?

G. Follow-Up

    1. Discuss some of the interesting things that happened on the hike the next day and later in the week.

    2. Take another night hike (or dawn hike) some other time during the year with the class.

    3. Spend an entire night camping in the outdoors.

ACTIVITY ANALYSIS AND EVALUATION

Now that the means of establishing a variety of goals and objectives has been explored and formalized, the next step is to explore the ways in which the programmer can look at the cafeteria offering of activities and choose those things that can best meet the objectives stated. If the objective is written well, clearly there will be only one way to meet it, but in order to identify that choice, the expected outcomes (needs satisfied and goals met by any given activity) must be specified. The process of scrutinizing activities in this way involves activity analysis (Avedon, 1974; Wessel, Peterson, and Knowles, 1974) and cluster analysis (Burton, 1971). In the first category, each activity is broken down into its component parts so that the planner can better understand its qualities and contributions, and can assign to it those needs, goals, and objectives met by participating in it. In cluster analysis, an identification of recreation types is made, in which activities yielding similar benefits or that appear to belong together are, in fact, clustered. This clustering procedure and the rationale on which it is based is that of factor analysis. Incidentally, this cluster can also be done on people around activity preferences, as well as grouping the activities themselves. This capability allows flexible, alternative programming to meet the same needs with different facilities available.

Activity Analysis

The task of analyzing activities has been approached in many different ways and from many different perspectives, ranging historically from Hemphill's (1949) classification of 15 group dimensions such as size, homogeneity, etc.; to Gump, Sutton-Smith, and Redl's (1954) seven activity-setting dimensions of prescriptiveness, prop availability, physical locomotion, movement of body parts, competency required, effect of institutionalized control functions, and interactiveness, which are rated on a seven-point scale from very low to very high. These authors further described and expanded this idea in later writings on the dimensions of games, which they believed should be considered before determining what games are suitable to meet the needs of specific groups of children (Avedon and Sutton-Smith, 1971, p. 408). In addition to those most listed, the following dimensions are described:

1. Body contact—is it direct or with a prop, and is it aggressive (football) or noncompetitive (joining hands in a circle game)?
2. Element of chance.
3. Kind and intensity of competition.
4. Space required.
5. Time required.
6. Kinds and use of props.
7. Role taking functions.
8. Rules and their complexity.
9. Levels of participation–waiting, passive, active.
10. Leeway for emergent leadership.
11. Respite possibilities.
12. Suspense ingredient.
13. Switches between opposite roles.
14. Pleasure—pain content of winning or losing.
15. Spread of winning element—how many possible "winners"?
16. Penetration into the game of rewards and penalties.
17. Sanctions of bluffing or of misleading acts.
18. Nature of game obstacles.
19. Trust dependence.
20. Permanence of alliances.
21. Mirroring of real life themes.
22. Personalization of props—"my men" (checkers).
23. Amount of ritual.
24. "Genderizing" the game.
25. Humor elements.
26. Outcome clarity.
27. Challenges—the actor and the counteractor.

An inference from this analysis is that in programming for children, one might first determine the needs of a specific group and then assess which dimensions of their needs must be satisfied by the activities chosen for them and then match those qualities to the game or activity. For example, one might look for a short, noncompetitive game requiring a special space that encourages trust among competitors and allows for emergent leadership. This is obviously an excellent working approach in a therapeutic setting; whether or not it is as feasible in the community setting with larger groups is of concern to practitioners. Utilizing such analysis provides a way of assuring congruence between goals for the individual, knowledge about the needs of individuals, and activity settings and content.

Various approaches have been used for activity analysis. Avedon (1974) proposed classification by social pattern. The use of behavioral domains, cognitive, affective, and psychomotor (as described earlier), to classify the nature of activities is utilized frequently. Peterson and Gunn (1984) advocate this and provide a rating form. The authors also discuss activity modification. Activity analysis has, by some, been confined to a kinesiological analysis in the psychomotor domain, which is a more narrow interpretation than the one that we recommend. Further definition of these types of analysis is indicated.

Perhaps the most well-known model is that of Avedon (1971, 1974) and the various offshoots and applications of it by others. One such adaptation was that presented by Wessel, Peterson, and Knowles (1974) and expanded in Peterson and Gunn. The latter authors proposed a definition of activity analysis as "a process which involves the systematic application of selected sets of constructs and variables to break down and examine a given activity to determine the behavioral requirements inherent for successful participation" (1984, p.182).

This definition implies comprehension of expected outcomes, understanding the activity in terms of leadership and participation parameters, identification of the complexity of the activity's components, guidance as to adaptation of the activity for special populations, and information on its appropriateness in light of behavioral objectives. Many of the models presented in the literature, ostensibly for use in activity analysis, are in fact narrowly limited in potential application to physical activities only, which would considerably limit the capability of a recreation programmer. The basic tenets of Avedon's (1971) proposals, however, are applicable over a wider range of types of activities and can, as illustrated later in this chapter, be applied to music, drama, ceramics, and the like. In making application of this system, the programmer is required to make decisions regarding the behavioral domains touched on by the activity, the interaction patterns required of the participants, the leadership, equipment, and facility needs, the length of the activity, and participant characteristics. A worksheet used in this analysis is presented in Appendix B. First, the person making the analysis must be able to classify the activity into cognitive, affective, and psychomotor domains (discussed earlier) and furthermore, be able to decide which of these domains is primary, or the initial focus of that activity, which is secondary, and which is tertiary. To cite an example, if one were analyzing a basketball game, the primary focus would be psychomotor, at a high skill level (passing, dribbling, shooting the ball). The secondary domain would be cognitive, at a fairly high level (rules, plays, strategy), and the tertiary domain would be affective, at an average level of skill (sportsmanship).

The interaction patterns used in this analysis model for classifying relationships within and between participants and their environments are those classified according to Avedon:

1. Intra-individual—within a person and involving no outside person or object. *Example* : yoga.
2. Extra-individual—directed to an outside object and not involving another person *Example*: making a shell pin.
3. Aggregate—a number of persons each concentrating on an object, with no interaction among themselves. *Example:* an orchestra tuning up.
4. Inter-individual—dyad on a one-to-one basis and competitive in nature. *Example*: a log-rolling contest.
5. Unilateral—competition involving three or more persons, one of whom is "it." *Example*: keep away.
6. Multilateral—competition involving three or more persons, but no one is "it." *Example:* spelling bee.
7. Intra-group—cooperation between two or more persons with the same goal. *Example*: choral society.
8. Intergroup—competition between two or more intragroups. *Example*: debating team (1974, pages 162-172).

A low-skilled group in a given area may not be capable of participating at all the levels possible for the activity, and many special population groups cannot reach intergroup performance, but nevertheless the potential goal remains for each. In relation to the basketball game analysis mentioned above, interaction patterns to be checked are extra-individual (dribbling), aggregate (whole team practicing shooting), inter-individual (guarding the person with the ball), intragroup (the team effort to win), and intergroup (the game itself). In terms of the other items on the worksheet, the game requires facilities, equipment, and leadership, has a set time duration, and is for junior high and up. Similar analysis for an improvisation task in creative dramatics (Figure 3.1) and for throwing a pot in ceramics (Figure 3.2) follow that for basketball.

If this type of analysis is combined with behavioral objectives for the participants in a given program, a leader has the means to answer any accountability questions asked, which is part of the reason for utilizing such a system, and once the initial groundwork of analysis has been laid, it is a simple matter to face ten junior-high age youngsters in the Y on a given afternoon and choose things that would be applicable and satisfying to their needs, or to take a group of educable mentally retarded (EMR) children at day camp and know how to choose activities for them to meet criteria set.

Activity Analysis Worksheet #1

Activity:		*Improvisation*		

Behavorial Domains:

1. (Primary) *Affective*

Skill level:				X
	Low			High

Nature of skill: *Role playing, expressing and interpreting feelings*

2. (Secondary) *Cognitive*

Skill level:		X		
	Low			High

Nature of skill: *Processing the role for characteristics of movement*

3. (Tertiary) *Psychomotor*

Skill level:		X		
	Low			High

Nature of Skill: *The movement itself*

Interaction patterns:

X	X	X				X	X
Intra-individual	Extra-individual	Aggre-gate	Inter-individual	Uni-lateral	Multi-lateral	Intra-group	Inter-group

Leadership:

X		
Minimum		Maximum

Equipment:

X		
None		Required

Duration:

	X	
Set time	Natural end	Continuous

Facilities:

X		
None		Required

Participants:

	Small group	
Fixed number of multiples		Any number

Age: Any

Comments:

Figure 3.1 Worksheet

Activity Analysis Worksheet # 2

Activity:		*Throwing a pot (ceramics)*	

Behavorial Domains: 1. (Primary) *Psychomotor*

Skill level:		X
Low		High

Nature of skill: *Working the pot with the hands, wheel with foot*

2. (Secondary) *Cognitive*

Skill level:	X	
Low		High

Nature of skill: *Planning pot design, processing steps in the procedure*

3. (Tertiary) *Affective*

Skill level:	X	
Low		High

Nature of Skill: *Expression of creative self in throwing pot*

Interaction patterns:

	X	X					
Intra-individual	Extra-individual	Aggre-gate	Inter-individual	Uni-lateral	Multi-lateral	Intra-group	Inter-group

Leadership:	X	
	Minimum	Maximum

Equipment:		X
	None	Required

Duration:		X	
	Set time	Natural end	Continuous

Facilities:		X
	None	Required

Participants:	Alone	
	Fixed number of multiples	Any number

Age:	Any

Comments:

Figure 3.2 Worksheet

In this system, as soon as one can assess the needs and capabilities of a group, then one can match those with appropriate activities. For this reason, activity analysis is a particularly useful tool for the recreation leader of all types of groups because it allows accurate matching of ability with activity. An expansion of the analysis of activities for recreation therapy was presented by Gunn and Peterson (University of Illinois) at a workshop; for more detail, see the PRPS Therapeutic Recreation Workshop Report (Gutjahr, 1976).

Cluster Analysis

As has been indicated, cluster analysis is a means of grouping together similar activities or the people with these activity interests by means of a factor analysis technique formulated after the historical early work of McQuitty (1954). In this process each activity becomes a variable and the correlation between participation in two variables is computed. Variables are then grouped according to similarity of correlation so that activities having a relatively high correlation among themselves and a relatively low correlation with activities outside that group are clustered together, and the participants in them tend to confine themselves to that set of activities. An example of this in a team game series would be first to take the highest coefficient between two sports, say, between soccer and cricket. Following that, examine the other activities in which participation in them is correlated with either soccer or cricket to see which ones, if any have their highest correlations with either soccer or cricket and then look further to see what the highest coefficients are of other sports with those tertiary elements. In Burton's (1971) study, golf, fishing, and table tennis were correlated first with soccer or cricket, and tennis was correlated with table tennis in the third order of correlation. Burton carried out such an analysis using 71, 59, and 40 activities, respectively. The first analysis of Burton yielded 14 cluster groups which are presented in Table 3.1. Activities analysis was focused on the degree of skill required for the activities, level of activity, nature of the group needed, amount of risk or danger, and special facilities needed.

TABLE 3.1 Burton's Fourteen Cluster Groups

Group 1	**Group 5**	**Group 9**
Rugby	Hobbies/Do-it-yourself	Sailing
Athletics	Outdoor bowls	Rowing
Basketball	Motor racing	Motorboat cruising
Badminton	Motorcycling/Racing	Messing about in boats
Fitness exercises	Scrambles	Evening classes
Cycling	Rally	
Amateur dramatics/Music	Flying	**Group 10**
	Gliding	Visit to a cinema
Group 2	Sky diving	Visit to a theatre concert
Archery	Squash	Visit to a library
Go-cart racing		
Winter sports	**Group 6**	**Group 11**
Fencing	Bingo	Hockey
Surfing	Dancing	Netball
Water skiing	Picnicking/Driving	Gymnastics
Aqualung diving	in the countryside	
Canoeing	Gardening	**Group 12**
Hunting	Dining out	Mountaineering
	Visit to a pub or club	Potholing
Group 3		
Hill walking	**Group 7**	**Group 13**
Rambling	Visit to a community	Painting/Drawing/
Camping/Youth hostelling	or church center	Sketching
Caravanning	"Old tyme" dancing	Going to a party
Walking/Visit to museum	Photography	Boxing
art gallery		Wrestling
	Group 8	Judo/Karate
	Youth clubs	Other activities
Group 4	Horse riding	
Soccer	Ice skating	**Group 14**
Cricket	Bird watching	Tenpin bowling
Tennis	Roller skating	Swimming
Golf		Table tennis
Fishing		

This analysis permits means of judging substitutions of activities across groups of similar activities, if this appears possible, or if restrictions in facilities and equipment dictate the need to do so.

This same cluster analysis for 40 activities is presented in Table 3.2. These analyses indicate that people can be grouped into recreation types on the basis of activity choice.

TABLE 3.2 Burton's Eight Cluster Groups

Group A
Soccer
Cricket
Tennis
Golf
Table tennis
Fishing
Hobbies/Do-it-yourself
Other activities

Group B
Rugby
Netball
Athletics
Basketball
Badminton
Fitness exercises
Cycling
Amateur dramatics/Music

Group C
Outdoor bowls
Tenpin bowling
Swimming

Group D
Ice skating
Roller skating
Horse riding
Youth club

Group E
Rowing
Motorboat cruising
Messing about in boats

Group F
Hill walking
Rambling
Camping/Youth hostelling/
Caravanning
Walking

Group G
Picnicking
Driving in the countryside
Gardening
Dining out
Visit to a pub or club
Visit to a community or church center
Bingo

Group H
Visit to a cinema
Visit to a theatre or concert
Dancing

Evaluation

The final step in the program activity model is one in which the programmer finds out how well the goals of the program have been met in both a qualitative and quantitative sense. In this step, the experience is evaluated. Based on the outcomes of this evaluation, either revisions are suggested or the program continues as is. If the decision demands revision, then each step along the way must be reconsidered and adjusted; that is, the needs, objectives, and program analysis are all reassessed. This process is continuous, since accountability demands evaluation and the demand for accountability is always present. Refer to Chapters 7 and 8 for an in-depth discussion of measurement of program effectiveness and steps to take in implementing the evaluation process.

SUMMARY

Program planning starts with need assessment and moves quickly to establish goals and objectives. The first type of objectives to be set are performance or behavioral objectives, which are statements of the intended result of the participation for the clientele served. Objectives are considered in terms of whether or not the content of the program is related to thinking, feeling, or action. These areas are called domains by Bloom and are classified as cognitive, affective, and psychomotor. All objectives can be categorized into one of these domains and ordered from simple to complex.

The programmer's next step is to pick activities that will meet those objectives through activity analysis, or the identification of expected outcomes of the activity. There are many approaches to activity analysis in use, but all of them involve consideration of group interaction, level of skill needed, amount of time needed for completion, the complexity of the task, environment in which the activity takes place, and the motor requirements of the task.

Following the program experience, the final step in the activity model is one in which the programmer finds out how well the goals and objectives have been met. That is, the program is evaluated and, based on the outcome of this evaluation, either revisions are suggested or the program is continued as it is.

BIBLIOGRAPHY

Armstrong, R. J., et al. (1970). *Developing and writing behavioral objectives.* Tucson, AZ: Educational Innovators Press.

Avedon, E. M. (1971). The structural elements of games. In E. M. Avedon and B. Sutton-Smith, *The study of games.* New York, NY: John Wiley & Sons.

Avedon, E. M. (1974). *Therapeutic recreation service.* Englewood Cliffs, NJ: Prentice-Hall.

Avedon, E. M. and Sutton-Smith, B. (1971). *The study of games.* New York, NY: John Wiley & Sons.

Bloom, B. S. (Ed.). (1956). *Taxonomy of educational objectives, Handbook I: Cognitive domain.* New York, NY: David McKay Company.

Burton, T. L. (1971). Identification of recreation types through cluster analysis, *Society and Leisure,* 1: 47-65.

Caporale, D. (1974). *The effects of participation in a physical activity program upon the social interaction patterns of mentally ill adults.* Master's thesis, The Pennsylvania State University, University Park, PA.

Chapin, F. S. (1974). *Human activity patterns in the city.* New York, NY: John Wiley & Sons.

Compton, D. M. and Price, D. (1975). Individualizing your treatment program: A case study using LMIT, *Therapeutic Recreation Journal,* 9: 4: 127-139.

Esbensen, T. (N.D.). *Writing instructional objectives.* Mimeographed paper.

Gronlund, N. E. (1970). *Stating behavioral objectives for classroom instruction.* New York, NY: Macmillan Co.

Gump, P., Sutton-Smith, B., and Redl, F. (1953-1954). *The influence of camp activities upon camper behavior.* National Institute of Mental Health, M-550 Grant, Educational Research Project. Detroit, MI: College of Education, Wayne University. Mimeographed.

Gutjahr, M. A. (Ed.). (1976). *Selected workshop proceedings, 8th Annual Therapeutic Recreation Institute.* University Park, PA: Pennsylvania Recreation and Park Society.

Hayes, G. (1971). Activity analysis: Finger painting for the mentally retarded, *Therapeutic Recreation Journal, 5:* 3: 133-138, Third Quarter.

Hemphill, J. K. (1949). *Situational factors in leadership.* (Bureau of Educational Research, Monograph No. 32). Columbus, OH: Ohio State University.

Johnson, S. L. (1982). *The effect of three training methods on the teaching preparation of counselor-teachers in a resident environmental education program.* Master's thesis, The Pennsylvania State University, University Park, PA.

Kaspar, R. R. (1974). *Achievement of fifth and sixth grade students in environmental education using the indoor and outdoor classroom.* Master's thesis, The Pennsylvania State University, University Park, PA.

Knight, D. C. (1975). *The effect of participation in art activities on the self-concept of institutionalized alcoholics.* Master's thesis, The Pennsylvania State University, University Park, PA.

Krathwohl, D. R., Bloom, B. S., and Masia, B. B. (1964). *Taxonomy of educational objectives, Handbook II: Affective domain.* New York, NY: David McKay Company.

Kraus, R. (1977). *Recreation today.* New York, NY: Appleton-Century-Crofts.

Mager, R. F. (1975). *Preparing instructional objectives* (2nd ed.). Belmont, CA: Fearon Publishers.

Maslow, A. H. (1972). *The farther reaches of the mind.* New York, NY: Viking Press.

McQuitty, L. L. (1971, Autumn). Comparative study of some selected methods of pattern analysis. *Educational and Psychological Measurement, 31:* 607-626.

McQuitty, L. L. (1954). Pattern analysis–A statistical method for the study of types. In Chalmers, et al., *Labor Management Relations in Illini City.* Urbana, IL: University of Illinois Press.

Morris, L. L. and Fitz-Gibbon, C. T. (1978). *How to deal with goals and objectives.* Newbury, CA: Sage Publications.

Nafziger, D. H. and Helms, S. T. (1974, June). Cluster analysis of interest inventory scales as tests of Holland's occupational classification. *Journal of Applied Psychology, 59:* 344-353.

Neulinger, J. (1974). *The psychology of leisure.* Springfield, IL: Charles C. Thomas.

Peterson, C. A. and Gunn, S. L. (1984). *Therapeutic recreation program design* (2nd ed.). Englewood Cliffs, NJ: Prentice-Hall.

Plowman, P. D. (1971). *Behavioral objectives*. Chicago, IL: Science Research Associates, Inc.

Streator, C. L. (1976). *The effect of a supplementary program on the development of perceptual-motor skills in children*. Master's thesis, The Pennsylvania State University, University Park, PA.

The Urban Institute and International City Management Association. (February 1974). *Measuring the effectiveness of basic municipal services:* Washington, DC: The Urban Institute and International City Management Association.

U. S. Department of the Interior, Bureau of Outdoor Recreation. (1973). *How effective are your community recreation services?* Washington, DC: U. S. Government Printing Office.

Weiss, C. H. (1972). *Evaluation research: Methods of assessing program effectiveness*. Englewood Cliffs, NJ: Prentice-Hall.

Wessel, J. A., Peterson, C. A. and Knowles, C. J. (1974, September 24-27). *Activity analysis and prescriptive programming: State of the art purpose, procedures, applications*. Paper presented at the NRPA research needs conference. Columbia, MO.

Wolfensberger, W. and Glenn, L. (1975). *Pass 3: A method for the quantitative evaluation of human services*. Toronto, ON: National Institute of Mental Retardation.

CHAPTER FOUR

PROGRAM CONSIDERATIONS AND FORMAT STRUCTURE

As the program staff begins to chart the task of designing the program activities for their constituency, there are a number of considerations that must be given attention. These are mostly theoretical and philosophical. Take a moment to think about some of these considerations and what this means to the programmer. In previous chapters you have read about the process of programming; how to work your way through selecting approaches to programming, categorizing the program areas, looking at life stages in an attempt to understand the shift in needs as an individual progresses through life, the breadth of leisure service agencies, and some ideas about how the program should be guided through policy decisions, and how to shape program goals and objectives. Now we ask you to think again, and in a different way, about the participant.

PROGRAM CONSIDERATIONS

Consider Participant Readiness

All people are not at the same level of readiness to participate at a required level of expectation in a single activity. There are a number of factors operating in this concept. First, it is important to note that with any given activity all individuals will spread themselves along a continuum of "eager interest in participation" to "flight from the thought of having to participate." Readiness to participate is activity specific. Someone eager to sing in a youth choir may flee from being in the community center thespian group. It is useful to see the readiness concept as a three step process. Beginning with no interest or an almost total unwillingness to even show up; to the next step which is one of observing and measuring one's self into the activity against those who are already participating; to finally taking the major step of joining into the activity itself. Each person must come to the final step through whatever process is necessary.

Wise programmers facilitate opportunities for people to move from one stage of readiness to another. It rests with the individual participant to determine how quickly that journey can be accomplished.

A second aspect of participant readiness is a consideration of whose responsibility it is to motivate the client. Again, agencies vary regarding this matter. Some programmers are evaluated by measuring how many people are involved in the total program. Others are measured by how a client's progress toward goal has been accomplished. In any situation, it is useful to understand that the more attention one gives to being sensitive to the variety of readiness levels, the more people are going to feel good about joining into the activity.

Clearly skill level is a key factor. Few people are anxious to join an activity where the skill exhibited by the majority of the participants if far above their own to the point where they may look foolish in their participation.

Attention to the consideration of participant readiness requires that provision of many levels of ability in the program offerings be planned. In this planning strategy, care must also be taken in recognizing the insecurities of the hesitant participant. To give an obvious example, if a person has finished the formal education phase of life and has not yet had the opportunity to learn a skill, being placed in an environment with young children is not going to be seen as a way to solve the problem. Lessons for adults, teaching senior adults how to use computers, learn to swim programs for those afraid of the water, etc. need to be given special attention to the readiness of the learner.

For those programmers who work with individuals with handicapping conditions, participant readiness takes on a little different meaning. For some individuals, the spirit of readiness is there and willing, yet the ability of the individual may require caution until certain stages have been accomplished. The intent here is not, in any way, to limit a person; but rather, to assure a safe and confident move into the full participation role. Sensitivity is required here such that the inherent paternalism is diminished and the individual involved retains her or his own self-confidence. Learning through the school of hard knocks may be fine for some people, but programmers working with special individuals need to diminish the number of hurtful experiences in a life that is in your professional hands.

Consider Specialization

Bryan (1979) developed an idea of participant readiness as it applies to levels of specialization within an activity. He characterizes participants in relation to their behavior as they progress through the learning stages up to highly specialized ability. Such items as equipment, adherence to rules, dress, devotion to excellence and selectivity of others in the same activity become graded points on a specialization scale. A few examples might be useful in exploring this point.

Take the activity of tennis as an example. The beginning tennis player knows that the game is played on a fenced-in court with a net and some lines as boundaries. A racquet and balls–it is not until later that the player understands that balls for tennis are usually three of the same kind–are about the only equipment one needs while dress is related to weather. And some type of sneaker would probably be best for footware.

As the beginning player matures, equipment and dress improve dramatically. The first evidences of specialization surround the equipment. Racquet quality becomes extremely important; new balls or the life of used balls gets shorter and shorter. If choice is possible, the selection of tennis surface on which to play becomes a critical factor in the game.

The game itself takes on an emerging pattern. From the novice who simply plays at tennis until one or both players tire, those who move up the specialization scale play a prescribed number of games or sets. The nature of the time playing tennis is clearly defined from a warm-up period into the actual competitive play. When the sets are completed, play is finished.

Specialization is not confined to sport exclusively. For instance, musicians progress through these same levels as skill and interest increase. Beginning singers are grateful to have the music or "the tune" played for them while the learning pattern is frequently a rote process or listening to someone else sing the tune. As the musician matures and is able to read music, match vocal or instrumental sound with the sound in the ear (generally referred to as "being in tune"), the interests begin to change. Now the musician is ready to play or sing for higher purposes. Small ensemble work, solo activity, and practice become the focus of the activity. Having your own copy of the music, working to perform correctly and well are but two aspects of the upward ladder levels in this activity specialization.

Making music becomes serious business to the highly specialized participant. Acoustics of the space in which the music is "made" become critical to the activity. In contemporary terms we could think of the loudness of sound as being related to the level of specialization. When was the last time you heard a performance and there was no microphone and an absence of stacked speakers. Technology use is embedded into the musician's specialization ladder.

Think about examples that you have noticed in the past or can now be more keenly analytical about when you put participation in a context of a specialization continuum. Consider your own participation patterns. People continue to do things when there is success in the doing. Or to put this idea into a programmer's terms, the more participants succeed in doing an activity, the more likely they are to return to the activity and desire to keep on succeeding and getting better. Therefore, the more the programmer understands about specialization the more likely it is that the program design and planning will focus on accommodating a variety of levels through which individuals can more toward continuing challenges and higher levels of specialization.

Consider Urging Programmers to Work Themselves Out of a Job

This idea has not been buried inside this chapter to hide some bad news. This concept must be given careful thought such that a programmer can continue to do the job that one is expected to do. A professional conference held a session for program managers entitled "So many hats, so little time." The program staff can only carry so many specific programs in its portfolio. What happens when the portfolio is full? Does the programmer stop programming? Of course not! What must be considered is to design strategies that let those with vested interests "run" the activities and let the program staff focus on program development.

The principle here is to be an initiator and an enabler serving the program interests of your constituency. Use the professional skills you have as a programmer to get special programs started correctly. This means solid organization within the philosphical context of your agency. If you have worked well in the program development stage, you will have some key participants who form the core of the program's interest group. These may be participants themselves, parents of children who participate, or perhaps other people who simply are devoted to a particular activity and have found a home interacting with others who enjoy the same activity.

Once the program professional staff members have done all of the organizational work and the program continues to attract interested participants; then it is time for the staff to consider turning over the management of program details to responsible key participants. Of course there are many matters that require sound consideration. Remember that the idea is to continue the program as it was generally designed (changes will always be necessary), and to have the recreation agency continue its sponsorship and legal authority for it. This means that care must be taken in assigning responsiblity to those not on the payroll for oversight duties.

This strategy can have its down side. In today's litigious society, some people are reluctant to accept any volunteer role in which someone may get hurt or some accident has the potential of happening. However, there are still people in society who are willing and very capable of handling program supervision once a pattern has been established.

Contact is still retained with these people by the program staff. They are not cut adrift, but the volunteers now are responsible for doing the job of the program staff; i.e., unlocking the facility (this means giving them a key or access code), seeing that the area or facility is ready for activity, checking in the participants and maintaining a decent atmosphere for the activity. After closing up for the day or period, they should be asked to record the regular activity report noting any accidents, damage as well as attendance, game score tallies or needed equipment requests.

When the program staff have identified people who can handle these duties and are willing to do so, imagine how much time can be gained by the staff to expand further activity that has been requested. Now the professional staff can be more cost effective to the agency by doing what professional staff should do. The programmer who insists on holding onto all programs is limited in the amount of program service that a single individual can do.

Wise programmers see this consideration as a cost effective *staff multiplier*. Work at starting and stabilizing a program, then work yourself out of that program and go onto the next opportunity.

Consider the Affiliation Opportunities With Other Leisure Special Interest Groups

This concept may well be a partner to the previous notion of working yourself out of a job. But in this case, the program staff are urged to consider assessing all of the special groups in the service area of the agency, and make some determination about whether the interests of both groups–the recreation agency and the special leisure interest group–would be better served by a partnership of some sort. Your authors have used the word affiliation to articulate this partnership.

The intention of this affiliation status is to assist special interest groups in providing them with a link to a professional office. This could mean an affiliation that could span help with publicity of interest group events only to the offer of office space, phones, printing, maintainance of membership lists, etc.

One warning point is offered at this time. The recreation agency must be loyal to its policy and philosophy of service to its constituency. For instance, if the recreation agency is a public department then it must not and cannot affiliate with a special interest leisure group that has an exclusive membership policy. On the other hand, if the recreation agency is a for profit enterprise then it must be made clear at the beginning of the relationship that there will be times when the recreation agency will expect services in kind or perhaps rentals of some sort to help defray the costs. Why should either party be interested?

Let us first consider the positive aspects from the point of view of the recreation agency:

1. The agency can be viewed positively by the special interest group members and be made aware of the broad range of programs within the agency.
2. The agency now has individual people who have special talents that may be called upon when an appropriate occasion occurs.
3. The agency is viewed by the total area as a place where support for all leisure activity interests is a possible home.
4. The agency gets credit for "sponsoring" a wide variety of activities.
5. The agency has a more complete sense of the leisure interests in the service area.
6. There is sure to be spillover from one special interest group to another when they all are using the same homebase for their organization.

Just as there are benefits to the agency as a result of affiliation there is a down side as well:

1. There will be an increase of activity in the agency office; phone answering, people traffic, additional requests for help, and the usual amount of interruptions as a factor of more people accessing the office.
2. There will be certain costs associated with assisting these groups.

3. Given an inch, some people will take a yard. There are certain to be times when the affiliate groups (or individuals within the group) will assume that staff in the recreation office are there to serve their exclusive wants. This is usually directed at the clerical staff members. Special interest members must be oriented to what rights they have to use staff for their specific organization.
4. Communication is sure to be troublesome and steps must be taken to diminish these potential problems.

As far as the special interest groups are concerned, there are many advantages to affiliating with the recreation enterprise:

1. If the agency has some indoor facilities that can be modified for office and storage space (storage space in a computer file system as well), this would be a tremendous help to organizations whose membership and particularly elected officers tends to change regularly over the years. Having a home base for files, and some small equipment storage would establish a permanent place for the office activity of an organization.
2. The use of conference rooms and space for meetings would be a useful benefit.
3. If enough affiliate groups were linked with the recreation agency, it would be useful for a "leisure activities calendar" to be coordinated and printed for free distribution throughout the service area.
4. Affiliated groups could learn organizational techniques from each other since they would all be working in the same space or be close together in the agency.
5. Having a phone number that would stay constant over the years would help communication enormously.
6. Having a sophisticated system for handling membership lists would help every treasurer and secretary responsible for contacting members.
7. If the recreation agency has access to space in the schools with a priority higher than a special interest group, the group would benefit by having the recreation agency do the scheduling of their activities.
8. When a special interest group runs into problems they can easily seek assistance from the professional staff of the recreation agency without feeling that they are competitors.
9. If the recreation agency is willing, the special interest groups may be able to have the agency handle the collection of funds; either by being the mailing address for the organizations or by being a place where ticket sales are handled Money taken in is all covered by receipts and deposited into each groups fund.

Affiliation has its disadvantages as well:

1. Those who affiliate may find that they inherit the reputation of the recreation agency.
2. People may be unwilling to be a part of the recreation agency and enjoy the pecial and exclusive nature of the interest club.

3. Some members may see that by affiliating, the club is losing a lot of freedom and special identity.
4. If the agency costs get too high, surely special interest groups will be asked to contribute to their space by way of some rental scheme.
5. The recreation agency may want to control the groups more than they are willing to be controlled.

FORMAT STRUCTURE

It is a common notion that a sound recreation program is designed to meet the needs and desires of all potential participants. Activity for everyone who wishes to participate is a goal for professional programmers. Although there has been passing concern given to those who do not participate in the agencies' programs, usually staff are so involved serving those who have an interest, that this concern for non-participation receives low priority.

In discerning what elements are necessary and what ingredients are required to facilitate a sound program for all, the use of a model that assists the programmer in seeing where gaps might exist in the program plan is suggested. This model is based on a behavioral design in which people are seen as participants who can be grouped together in certain situations, with some refinement regarding how broadly based these groups can be. People engage in behavior patterns that reflect satisfaction of internal drives (see Chapters One and Two). In the broadest sense, a single recreation activity illustrates that participants vary in what expectations they have about that activity. For example, if when reviewing a music program in a recreation agency, the specific activities found were (1) the fifth- and sixth-grade singers, (2) guitar lessons, and (3) a drum and bugle corps, it would be difficult to make any substantial statement about whether or not these activities were serving the music needs and desires of the potential constituency of this particular agency.

When examining the functions of the recreation programmer, it is reasonable to assume that within this responsibility rests the authority to see that programming principles are translated into actual recreation activities. In Chapters One and Two, a brief overview of program areas and life stages was given. One method of reviewing program variety and balance would be to place each of these classification systems on a two-dimensional grid. The agency's program activities that satisfy each dimension can then be inserted in the matrix (see Figure 4.1).

This two-dimensional field has limitations. The matrix may not be an accurate description of the agency's program. One important element in the review of a full variety program is the format structure through which an activity is presented.

Figure 4.1 Two-dimensional Grid

Program Areas	Preschool	Early childhood	Late elementary	Youth	Etc.
		Life Stages			
Art	Finger painting				
Dance		Square dancing	Ballet lessons		
Sports		Leadup games	Soccer Biddy basketball Newcomb	Softball Flag football Volleyball	
Environmental Etc.			Junior Museum		

A comfortable way to design the overall program is to establish broad age groups toward which all programs will be directed. The material in Chapter Two addressed these issues of age clustering or attempting to categorize age into useful cohort groupings. Once these clusters are established, plans to provide a variety of program offerings to each age group makes managing the programming task more efficient.

Programming in this fashion permits the program manager to test for balance and some aspects of variety, as well as a double check on whether the programs are age-appropriate and meeting the desires of certain age groups. Listing programs in this fashion in promotional materials assists the potential customer in finding program offerings appropriate for their age group. If the program grid could be established as represented in Figure 4.1 the program staff would have an easy reference for a quick idea of the extent of program offerings for the constituency.

The major drawback to this two-dimensional grid system of portraying the program is the critical element missing in regard to variety. There needs to be a third element in the formula; thus, requiring the grid to become three dimensional. We need to look at the form that each activity takes. For example, take the sport line under program area in Figure 4.1.—What do we know about soccer? Is it a league activity? Is it a series of clinics for the volunteer coaches? Is a visit planned to some semi-professional soccer team in the city? Just knowing sport and soccer is not enough.

In this chapter we concentrate on exploring formats and how each can be a unique tool for use in designing a meaningful and total program. Five program formats will be considered with variations on each one. As noted in Figure 4.2, these five formats are labeled (1) self-improvement, (2) competition, (3) social, (4) participant spectator and (5) self-directed. In each format a different environment exists for the activity experience available to the participant. The well-rounded program must provide this type of variety for the participants. It is possible for an agency to use one or two formats while others are ignored, but a good program administrator will not allow this situation to exist, no matter how limited the program budget.

The authors are using the term program format structure then to express the idea of "what form the leisure experience takes." In the conceptual model presented in Figure 4.2, the five different forms of experiencing leisure are present. The following sections of this chapter address and explain the nature of the ideas in this model and an attempt is made to identify characteristics of people who prefer each format for their leisure experience.

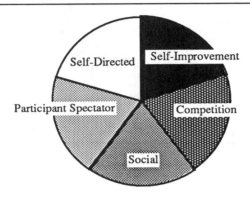

Figure 4.2 Five-Format Structure Model

Format: Self-Improvement

The self-improvement format includes those program activities often referred to as classes, clinics, workshops, field trips, and other similar offerings. The purpose of these programs is skill learning, skill development, education or skill refinement. Generally there is a high level of administrative organization effort in providing these programs. The program model provides an educational environment that includes (1) specialized leadership skills in the activity itself, (2) a limited number of participants, (3) a series of activity meeting times and dates, and (4) provision of space and perhaps special equipment. It is not unusual for activities offered within this structure format to carry a special fee or charge to the participant, especially when participation or enrollment in the activity is limited.

This format pattern is popular in recreation agencies. It carries a high level of leader control and clear reservation of program activity space for things scheduled for a given period of time. It assures the participant that all of the details have been taken care of, and that all the participant needs to do is to come and learn. For this service, as well as the convenience of arrangements, recreation agencies have found it propitious to place a reasonable fee on these programs. In light of today's scarcity of

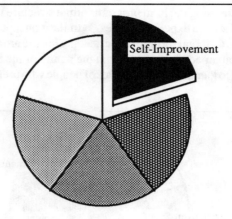

Figure 4.3 Self-Improvement Format

indoor and outdoor recreation facilities, the opportunity to use any facility comes as a rich privilege. Hence, being a member of an activity group that has priority use of a specific facility is another benefit of participating within this type of format.

The program administrator finds this format a particularly useful one. It has flexibility in that the periods for classes and the like generally last from four to ten weeks. Therefore, a facility can be engaged for set periods of time that are short enough to permit the offering of many sequences of these structure formats throughout a year. Most recreation agencies utilize three or four seasons for these activities in a single year. The four-sequence pattern follows the yearly seasons, while the three-sequence pattern generally provides for an October to December, February to May, and a summertime frame for programming.

This format allows the programmer to be responsive to potential participants interests. Classes or workshops can be offered in a wide variety of activities. Those classes that do not fill or clear the registration minimum can be cancelled prior to any expensive investment on the part of the recreation agency. On the other hand, those activities for which participants are turned away as a result of full enrollment can serve as a good barometer to what program needs exist within an agency and suggest that more classes of that activity be offered in the future.

Most recreation agencies operate some program activities on a fee basis. This educational structure format is a popular one for employing the fee element. When the participant receives specialized services, it is a common practice to charge a fee for that service. Generally the fee structure in recreation agencies is designed on a break-even philosophy. Although there has been much discussion among recreation programmers as to what break-even means, it is suggested here that it means program costs are covered. A more detailed discussion of this issue is presented in Chapter Five under budgeting techniques for program structure formats.

A common fee philosophy subscribed to in the last few decades has been to have activities free for children whenever possible. Adults were expected to cover these special costs in their own programs. It was difficult to carry this value through into the 1980s. Support for recreation programming has always been a hard item to get as a top priority in the budget. As a result most programming for children was on a mass participation budget or was not provided. Thus the small clinic, class, or workshop has not been an easy format to include as far as young people were concerned. The last decade has seen growth in fee programming for children. An unfortunate consequence of this practice is that those unable to afford the program receive little attention, or there are programs that are so out of touch with current interests that the agencies would be better off not to offer any program at all.

Swimming lessons, master dance classes, batting clinics, and outdoor cookery workshops all have common elements. The participants attend because they want to learn. The leadership provided by the agency sponsoring these activities must be highly skilled in terms of knowledge of the activity and be effective in the ability to facilitate skills learning. Recreation agencies have learned to tap specialists outside of the onboard staff for these assignments. It is unreasonable to assume that the professional recreation program administrator is going to be able to handle leadership for all classes, clinics, etc. that his or her own agency sponsors. In considering the four activities mentioned above, why not employ the high school swim coach, a studio dance instructor, a semiprofessional or professional baseball player, and a scout leader in the area to assist with these activities? It should be noted here that the program administrator may well wish to instruct in some of these activities but should not be expected to be a highly skilled specialist in all facets of all activities under the recreation program umbrella.

An important current trend, which may have implications for programmers in the near future, is the temporary society phenomena with the short-term residence patterns of many Americans. This life-style affects the length of the scheduling period. Perhaps the five-week workshop in carpentry, which met commonly in the past for five successive Tuesday nights from 7:00 to 10:00 PM, will be more successful in the future when it is scheduled Friday night and all day Saturday and Sunday in a weekend woodworker's workshops. The most recent experience of programmers has been that ten weeks is too long to sustain interest. This trend is definitely to a shorter more intensive learning experience.

Format: Competition

As the name implies, this structure format includes those organizational patterns that are addressed to facilitating tournaments, contests, and league activities. The purpose of using this format is to provide the participant with a competitive experience at any level that he or she feels is desirable. One tends to hear about highly competitive programs as opposed to recreation contests, that is, less competitive. Since this dichotomy is a difficult one for us to support, it will not be discussed in this book.

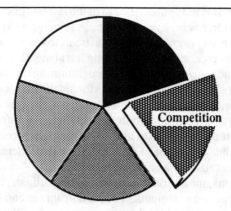

Figure 4.4 Competition Format

Various levels within the competitive experience can be clearly seen, but to designate these on a continuum of highly competitive to recreative is not appropriate for our purposes; more important is the organizational structure required for each level of competitive experiences. Competition is a complex concept. To assist the reader's understanding of competition, we give special attention to this concept.

This program model provides the participant with (1) a similar skill group(s) against which to compete, and (2) a proper environment that permits a fair contest, space, and perhaps limited equipment. When this format is discussed a wide variety of experiences are included. High- or low-level competition is not important to the concept; only the structure is of interest here.

In many agencies, this format is the bread-and-butter style of the department. Sports have traditionally dominated agency programs, and it is not difficult to move directly into a competitive format with this sports interest. Competition has been championed as the American way of life, and therefore strong support has been given to recreation programmers who want the green light to focus on this format. In most recreation agencies it is disappointing to note that competition is aligned only with the sports activities when the performing and visual arts, as well as camping and nature programs, have similar needs and do lend themselves to appropriate competitive activity.

The competitive format demands strong organizational skills in the program administrator. A high level of structure is required to present a quality, competitive experience. From the Class A softball league for adult women to the playground frisbee contest, someone must go through the steps of signing up players, setting up the league or the matches, seeing that the games are played by prearranged rules, and finally tabulating scores and determining the winners. Someone must be assigned the responsibility for managing this process, so that attention to and control of the competitive details are well covered. It can be described as labor intensive.

Variety in competitive experiences is one of the important tools in a recreation programmer's kit. Long-term round robins to single-day contests are only a part of the wide selection of experiences available to the programmer for use in planning a diversity of competitive activities. These programming techniques will be discussed in Chapter Five of this text. The programmer must approach competition from the viewpoint that the participation is likely to prefer more than one type of competitive experience. A program that utilizes only one style is far too limited.

In some competitive experiences, the model includes a long time frame. Most popular is the league experience in which a round robin tournament is planned. To complete one or two rounds of the league, it is not unusual for the time frame to be 10 to 12 weeks. Games or matches can be planned in terms of one game per week. This long-term approach assists the programmer in knowing what facilities are needed and have to be reserved. Round robin scheduling can provide for efficient use of specific playing facilities and related areas. It also provides a guarantee to the participant that facilities will be available for this special time period. Constituents learn that each Wednesday evening, the gymnasium has been reserved for corecreational volleyball from 8:00 to 11:00 PM. The casual user learns to avoid these times for drop-in activity, and knows that the gym must be vacated by 7:55 PM.

Another familiar system that facilitates a competitive experience is the highly concentrated time frame of a weekend or a three- to six-day period. It is not unusual for the competitor to play two, three, or four contests in a single day. There are obvious differences among games, related to the nature of the games themselves, that affect how many matches a person can play. Two games of field hockey represent a physical maximum, while many games of chess, bocci, or shuffleboard can be handled easily by a participant. The quick elimination type of tournament often is the technique used for structuring the competition. As long as one is winning, that winner remains in the tournament. Other types of tournaments that establish a winner by a highest or lowest score do not have an elimination feature. They focus on every player or team experiencing in turn a similar set of circumstances. These would range from fastest times, such as in a cross-country ski race; judges scoring, as in a one-act play festival; to total points accumulated, as in a scavenger hunt; to lowest score in the medal play public links golf tournament.

There are many variations in the types of tournaments that can be programmed. The available time of the participants and availability of facilities are two important aspects to consider when arranging the competitive experience.

The financing pattern used in this program format style is again one that links directly back to department philosophy. Popular patterns include fees attached to leagues where high costs accompany the activity experience, such as ice hockey teams in league play where officials are secured, ice rental is necessary, and costly awards are a part of the program plan. For other competitive activities, the events include the provision of some equipment and an entry fee that is charged to cover that equipment cost and perhaps the prizes. This is a popular style used in racquet sports in which it is necessary for all competitors to play with the same kinds of birdies or balls. Thus, to standardize the play as much as possible, the tennis tournament committee provides the balls and the cost of these is, in reality, covered by the entry fee of each competitor. For some contests there is no cost other than the organizational and administrative staff work involved. Some agencies agree to absorb these kinds of costs and provide the competitive experience at the lowest possible cost–free, if possible–to the competitor.

Of all the endeavors attempted by a program administrator, there is no other area in one's job for which there is a higher probability of outside, ready assistance. In almost every area in which the programmer would be interested in facilitating competitive experiences, there is usually someone in the community willing to help or lend expertise. Specific sports tournaments, music contests, art shows, and athletic contests all have a clientele of both participants and active affiliates who are more than willing to pitch in and lend a hand. The opportunity to involve many people in these concomitant activities in the organizational and managerial aspects of competition is also the job of the program administrator.

One of the unique aspects of competition that is common to many activities, particularly in sports, is the booster club or group of support family and friends. This type of club has been particularly popular in sports for which many people are needed to administer the competitive activity itself. For example, a swimming meet must be staffed by timers, lane and turn judges, scorers, announcers, and a starter, to mention only a part of the staff needs. It is obvious that volunteers and many extra hands are needed. In order to keep the cost of providing a swim meet within reason, people other than the competitors themselves are needed. Parents and friends of the swimmers are often pressed into service. The fact that one is needed and that there are plenty of roles for people to fill draws a large crowd of support personnel for the swimming program. It has been an easy step to have these "friends" form booster clubs and begin a progression of bake sales and other money-raising activities to provide things for the team, such as turning boards, uniform warm-ups, lane floats, banners, etc. The wise program administrator solicits the aid of these booster clubs and endeavors to find a meaningful role for their energies. Often such clubs have become a trail to be endured, but there is always the possibility of turning these interests into a positive contribution to the program.

Every activity in which there is opportunity for a competitive experience has its eager and dedicated organizers and helpers. Every recreation agency programmer will meet these people very quickly, and it is the skillful professional who maximizes these talents to the benefit of the overall program.

Format: Social

Since humankind is a social animal, it is not unexpected that a popular style for experiencing leisure activity would be in some social context. Recreation managers will need to consider the enormous variety of opportunities to provide these social situations in which people seek participation. Generally this variety ranges among such activities as using some activities in every program activity, hobby clubs or any special interest club activity, child care services while the parent is participating in a separate activity, social special events such as parties and the rich variety of festivals and celebrations.

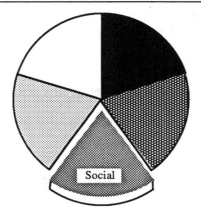

Figure 4.5 Social Format

Of particular importance and opportunity is the potential to facilitate a variety of special interest clubs. These surely will range from hobbyists, visual and performing arts groups, booster clubs, etc. to less formal social groups that may have a variety of purposes; for example, a tennis club that mostly meets for the purpose of playing some social tennis, yet may hold auctions, promote used equipment sales, have annual dances and picnic times together. In some instances, the total purpose of an activity group is devoted to the enhancement of developing social skills among those people who have difficulty relating easily with others.

The level of organization within social clubs can vary dramatically. Some clubs will have a formal structure—one that has by-laws, elects officers, and supports a membership/fee schedule, etc. This format provides for self-direction for the members within an organizational structure defined by the clubs' bylaws or constitution. Many different programs are possible. Members assume a variety of roles to sustain and enjoy the purposes of the organization. These purposes in recreational clubs vary, but generally they endeavor to provide an opportunity for anyone to enjoy, learn, share, and promote the activity focus of the club.

The organizational patterns of the club format structure usually include minimal directions from the recreation agency's program administrator once the club has been established. In the creation of a club, an interest group will need assistance in formalizing itself through the development of written agreements, in selecting leadership, and in establishing a financial base relationship both internally and with the recreation agency. Usually, all of these items are defined in the club's bylaws, which mandate officers, duties of officers, and dues structures. The various activities programmed by the club are then the responsibility of the club officers and members.

The recreation sponsoring agency has a unique opportunity in working with these clubs. For a minimal amount of supervisory work, a substantial amount of programming can be offered to others through the efforts of volunteers who themselves share an interest in the activity. The agency program administrator must be prepared in the early stages of a club's development to devote a good bit of organizational time to the core interest group of participants. Setting ground rules, establishing requirements that an affiliate club must meet to be a part of the recreation agency, and determining budget request procedures and a fiscal policy are but a few of the matters to be determined.

As a general rule, a recreation agency that serves the general public has very specific criteria for clubs to become affiliates:

1. Membership Must be Open to All Citizens. This requirement is an obvious one for a public agency but is not meant to preclude elimination from a club that establishes its group by audition or tryout. Those clubs that can only support their activity by a certain skill level or by limited parts must have this ability to limit members.

2. There Must be Some Club Guidelines and Rules. Since the purpose for a recreation agency sponsoring or having an affiliation with a special interest group is a reliance on self-direction by the membership, some document must guide this process. A constitution is typically the model used for this matter. The recreation agency must have some person or small group with whom it can communicate, thereby creating the need for a leadership structure of club officers.

3. A Financial Base Must be Supported by the Membership. For specialized programming there will undoubtedly be the need for special funding resources. Often it is difficult for a recreation agency to fund totally the specialized interest groups. It becomes necessary for club members to invest in the activity to support these special programs that are designated for their own select club membership. The recreation agency may well be able to provide some resources to the club, but after initial "seed money" support, the agency should be providing only services such as publicity, secretarial help for special projects, and bookkeeping if this is consistent with the agency's budget procedure. The program administrator will naturally keep in contact with the club by occasionally attending a club meeting or function, or meeting regularly with the club officers. The amount of the club dues must be carefully set, particularly if the club affiliates with a public recreation agency. The amount of these dues should be established at a reasonable level such that the club does not become exclusive and available only to the privileged. Scholarships or a certain percent of free memberships might be considered as options for clubs in which dues, of necessity, would be high.

4. Programs Must Operate Within the Philosophy of the Sponsoring Recreation Agency. It is obvious that many clubs can and do exist outside any formal recreation agency sponsorship. However, we believe that recreation agencies should be alert to providing an umbrella for all recreation interest groups who may wish to affiliate. The advantages to the constituency of the agency are many; calendar coordinations, central and combined publicity, wider awareness from the public of what recreational activities are available, and assistance from recreation professionals prepared to give reliable consultation. The interest group itself has much to gain through this affiliation and very little to lose. The club retains almost total autonomy while the recreational professional staff are free to devote time to other interests that may grow and develop in the future.

The public recreation program staff is in a unique situation to create an opportunity for leisure-oriented groups with an open membership focus to join with the public agency. Sailing clubs, musical groups, hobbyists, and theatrical and art alliances could well affiliate with the public recreation department.

Affiliation status would require the group to meet the four requirements for a social club, while the recreation department would take a passive role that would include making space allocations and assisting with promotion activities.

In most of our cities and smaller towns the specialized sport clubs and art groups form themselves independently from organized recreation units and, as a consequence, recreation departments frequently offer the bulk of their programs for children and do very little for adults. If efforts were made by the recreation agency to invite and bring these specialized clubs under a central umbrella *without the club losing its autonomy,* a broader variety of leisure experiences could be promoted for the community-at-large. Cooperation is the key. The clubs will need to retain their independence, budget control, pattern of operation, and general identity, while the recreation department will need assurances that the clubs will operate in patterns consistent with department philosophy. The club can help broaden the department's program, while the department can help the club with facility uses, program scheduling, promotion and general operational assistance.

The affiliation of special interest clubs with a recreation agency has the additional element of orientation of the club members to the department philosophy. Let us use the example of the model airplane club that wishes to hold a Delta Dart flying contest for children in its community. If the only facility large enough to hold this activity is the gym in the YM/WCA, this would appear to be a natural affiliation situation for the model airplane club and the family Y. With some initial orientation and organizational endeavors, the Y programmer and the Delta Dart Contest committee could establish the kind of arrangement that would serve (1) the interests of potential airplane builders and flyers among the children, (2) the program and exposure needs of the model airplane club and, (3) the YM/YWCA in assisting with a special event in which its members may have missed an opportunity to participate.

The cost of the Delta Contest would be minimal–perhaps only for awards, since manpower for both leaders and gofers would be provided by club members. The YM/WCA, by providing the facility and thus incurring some costs, may well realize food sales, future memberships, and exposure in this event, promotes participation in some future events that generate funds for operations. The contest could easily become an annual event both in the schedule of the Y's facilities and under the program schedule of the model airplane club. With minimal time expenditure on the program administrator's part, a good program that serves a specific interest group is able to be offered with a skill level and interest excitement (demonstration flying, exhibit models, etc.) that few recreation programmers have in their own personal skill bank.

Format: Participant Spectator

During the 1950s with the popularization of television, concern was voiced from many corners of our society that spectator-itis was becoming a serious matter. There is no doubt that by 1990 we had a fuller understanding of how much TV watching was going on per day when estimates of daily hourly television ranges between six and seven hours per day per person. Rather than despair over these data or argue about the believability of them, it is clear that there are many needs of people being met through this medium.

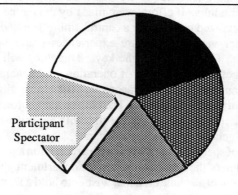

Figure 4.6 Participant Spectator Format

It seems that the key for all programmers to understand is that TV is a real competitor thus requiring our program opportunities to become a more attractive choice for people's time. In addition, it is critical that programmers understand that people need to be spectators. We like to watch other people and other things. Who would seriously argue with anyone wishing to attend a concert, a ballgame of one of your children, having patients bussed to a parade or fireworks show, etc., etc.

Perhaps the more appropriate point to be stressed should be made in terms of excesses. Can one imagine a parade that is unwatched, a football game or an outdoor band concert with no one in the stands, or the Special Olympics with no encouragers and friends looking on? Of course not. The world of performers needs the world of spectators. Just as an excess of spectating undoubtedly is harmful, so might one suggest that to perform always and never applaud the performance of others carries similar drawbacks.

The audience, the watcher, and the casual onlooker must always be considered in the special activities. There are many reasons for devoting a substantial amount of time to planning for these persons: (1) the program initially should be conceptualized as one including the spectator-participant; (2) for some people, this may be the only way in which they are able to participate; (3) by presenting this program in an area where you are not able to keep the spectator away, you may be legally responsible for them; (4) it is a good way to enhance support for future programs to help people become acquainted with your agency; and (5) the performing participant may have a richer experience when a crowd is present.

Let us explore each of these ideas further:

1. Include Space for Spectators. Programmers must give attention to the friends of the participant. Today's society tends to provide inadequate time for all we want to do. Couples, singles and families are having to maximize their time and coordinate their schedules. This creates patterns where, in order to meet everyone's agenda (many times this means who gets use of the car), people are doubling up and sharing experiences. For instance, the church youth group meets at 6:30 PM while mom goes straight from work to her aerobics group. This means that dad gets supper, takes the appropriate children to the church group and picks up mom so she can drop him off at his meeting, get the car home so the other children can use it for perhaps a school activity.

Hopefully not every day is so scheduled. But the example is not farfetched. The recreation staff needs to insist that there is a welcome mat out for those who have come to pick up someone, or there is a place for those who wish to observe the activity itself. Parents are usually anxious to review the experiences of their children, newcomers sometimes need an opportunity to see what goes on in a program before they enroll, while still others just like to watch in an interesting environment while getting ready to do something else.

During the planning phase of any new facility, program staff must insist that space be considered for the spectator. This sensitivity may mean the designation of cars to be parked, a small unit of bleachers to be installed, a particular area on the pool deck out of the way of staff or officials, etc. Whatever the activity, help the spectators understand that they are welcome and where is the best place for them to be.

2. Spectating the Only Way to Participate. Within the wide variety of leisure activities, people come to each one with different interests and abilities. If someone has limited interest in an activity the chances of that person wishing to be an active participant are slim. On the other hand they might at some point be interested in observing others engaged in the activity.

The more intriguing situation is the one where someone's interest is high, yet the ability level is below that which permits extended participation. It is to this potential client that the opportunity to be a spectator is going to be enthusiastically pursued. Watching the performance of others is this person's need. Programmers must be sensitive to the variety of opportunites this creates. The visual and performing arts, regardless of level of excellence, sport in all its forms, special events that provide a variety of spectating opportunities, and being a support person for any significant others in one's life.

3. Legal Responsibility for Spectators. Just as the programmer must assure the active participant that the conditions surrounding the activity are safe, so must the spectator participant have the same assurances. At times this will require special safety fencing plans while at other times the design of the activity can have designated space for spectators.

The use of rope, special yellow tape—similar to that used by police–or lines drawn on the surface should be considered. The important aspect to consider is the nature of the potential spectator. Is it young children who need careful attention? Is it a person who will be so curious that a firm barrier will be needed? Is it parents who need to understand that some distance would be appreciated by their children? Whatever the audience, serious consideration must be given to the appropriate area designation for all spectators.

With the current styles of selling tickets to events, there have been some tragic accidents among the spectators at some events. Give consideration to non-designated seating in ticket sales for large arenas. When seating is open, the crowd begins to form early so that *good seats* can be obtained. In the rush immediately after the doors are opened it is not hard to imagine the consequences of such a ticket selling strategy.

The solution of deciding to open the doors at an earlier time will not be satisfactory. Think about this decision. Now we still have lots of people coming early to get the best seats; but instead of solving the problem and potential hazzard, we have an additional problem of the long wait until the scheduled event. And generally people have planned ahead by bringing something to eat and drink, or you have decided to open up your refreshment areas for these sale opportunities. A restless crowd can find many negative ways to pass the time.

Open seating is fine for small numbers, but beware of using this strategy for large crowds. Also, never violate any occupancy code limits.

4. Enhance Support for Future Programs. In most corners of our society a significant communication network is mouth-to-mouth advertising. We discussed earlier in this chapter the process of how someone prepares to enter into an activity. The provision of spectator space helps strangers to an activity become familiar with it and whoever else is engaging in such activities.

Additionally, the provision of space for spectators signals an open philosophy about the program and invites everyone to browse and look at what goes on in the activities themselves. In some ways, having a philosophy about openness to others keeps the leadership and maintainance staff on their toes. This can create a positive viewpoint about the entire agency.

5. Audience May Provide Better Experience for Performers. In some instances the audience is critical for the activity. In other instances the audience may not be a positive aspect to the program. It is in the hands of the program staff to plan for and invite audience participation and spectators when and where it is appropriate. If parents are having a negative effect on the child's participation, strategies need to be designed regarding parent spectating rules. If rowdy spectators are ruining the activity for the active participants, some actions must be taken to retain the integrity of the program itself.

Format: Self-Directed

This program format structure seems to be the one type that is most difficult to define and manage. It is either overused or not used enough. Finding a middle ground is difficult because it is hard to set policy that has a chance of successful implementation. For all facilities under the jurisdiction of a recreation agency, some time blocks must be available for the drop-in or casual participant. To assign a certain percentage of time for this free play to take place has not been a common practice among recreation agencies. An open-use policy usually exists when nothing else has been scheduled for the field or in the multipurpose room, and when custodial or professional staff are supervising the building. Little effort has been made to keep facilities open for extended periods, even for 24 hours, if a scheduled program is not planned. Generally, recreational facilities are in short supply, and the scheduling of space, particularly indoor winter space, has become almost totally blocked into the scheduled, structured program. Little space or time is left for the programmer participant whose activity is self-initiated.

The key concept for the recreation programmer to remember is that this format needs as much careful consideration as the other four. Just as there are those individuals who require high structure to enhance their participatory experience, so are there many who are fully capable of planning, organizing, and participating in recreational activity without any assistance other than the use of a specific facility. All our efforts in education for leisure have been wasted if no provision is made for the independent recreator to use facilities. The program administrator must observe

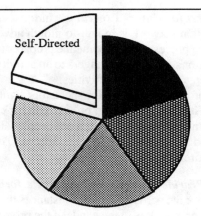

Figure 4.7 Self-Directed Format

facility use and ask: (1) "Is the facility free during hours when people in my agency will voluntarily use it for self-directed activity?" (2) "Are the only free, unscheduled hours at times when no one is free to use the facility?" (3) "What would the cost be of keeping facilities open later in the evening or opening earlier in the morning?" (4) "What steps need to be taken to encourage participants to do more self-directed activity?"

This structure pattern is common in the revenue-producing facilities such as swimming pools, ice arenas, golf courses, ski slopes, and bowling lanes. Recreation agencies use the facilities for classes and tournaments as well as making special arrangements for clubs to reserve specific hours; yet care must be given to providing open time for the drop-in participant to make use of space, and those times must be as widely publicized as the hours of special reserved use. Dark room hours, craft shop open times, open gym hours, nonleague open bowling times, and so forth, should be given.

With increases in the use of facilities, it becomes tempting to regulate use and schedule activity for the facility. As use on our flat water areas increases, the diverse users' interests often conflict. The sailors and the waterskiers find difficulty coexisting at the same hours of the day on the same body of water. It is not unusual to have one group or the other making requests to the park superintendent to "reserve" the lake on Sunday afternoons for the weekly sailing races or the weekly slalom competitions. The fishermen probably would be happy if neither group used the lake while the swimmers feel penned into their small area defined by buoy floats, wishing they could swim out into the middle of the area. Canoeists and skin divers are well aware that their lives are on the line with the hotdog, motor boat, or Sunday afternoon drivers on the lake and, as a result, the quality of the recreation activity experience on a weekend for any of the participants on the lake may diminish. Lake zoning becomes a necessary solution in many situations.

Providing special-use times for individual activity interests during the week has been only somewhat successful. Thus, the programmer who is committed to open-facility use often gets caught in the typical situation of trying to facilitate varied recreational interests that conflict with one another.

With careful and limited control of the facility, some scheduling can be done without destroying the open use of the area. Knowing the time of day when the winds are usually best might better serve the sailor. Since the skiers need calm water for best conditions, early or late in the day would be better for their participation time. Sound and strong leadership for programming the facility can assist the participants to understand the rationale behind this structure. Nevertheless, there must remain some hours in the day for the lake to be used in whatever way one wishes.

Another example that is currently cause for concern is the use of tennis courts. The dramatic increase in the use of courts and interest in learning the game have far outreached the number of facilities available to serve these interests. This is evident in the growth of indoor tennis arenas and the willingness of participants to pay up to $40 an hour for the privilege of using a court. Public courts have been receiving high play and long waiting lines. Even the extended time available with the installation of lights has not been able to satisfy the need for this activity. The recreation programmer is faced with the squeeze of open use versus highly structured use. If the courts are tied up with lessons and clinics 15 hours a week, is there ample time for free play? If four weekends during the summer months require the courts for tournament play, has this encroached too heavily into the free play zone? These and many other questions need to be faced squarely by the programmer. Pressures will be exerted from all quarters. In the long run the programmer must understand that there is no right or wrong answer as to what is the correct way to schedule the facility. Flexibility needs to be paramount, acknowledging that any excess of one use pattern over the other will probably put the programmer in a difficult position.

Indoor space for activity tends to be at a premium during the cold temperature months. There is no recreation agency that has too many indoor pools, gymnasiums, shops, crafts rooms, or the like. As a result, the use of such existing facilities is heavy. Many agencies are being pressed into permitting only those activities that serve large numbers to be included in the program, while the small interest groups are edged out of being able to offer their preferred activity. For instance, if a highly skilled ice figure skater is attempting to practice the free-exercise routine, the entire ice rink is needed for an hour or two. Can the programmer justify this kind of use when four hockey teams could be using the ice or general skating for 150 people could be taking place? The age-old problem of mass versus individual use rests squarely on the shoulders of the program administrator. Compromising, sharing the popular and unpopular times, and giving and taking, all need to be woven into the program fabric. If there were some magic answer to this dilemma, it would be presented here. There is no such easy resolution. We have attempted to clarify the importance of involving your clientele in the planning stages so that they can understand better why decisions are made.

As we become a more leisure-intelligent society that knows how discretionary time can be utilized and possesses the skills to engage in recreational activity, the more responsibility there will be that is placed on all recreation agencies to provide facilities for self-directed use. Either the recreation serving agencies will do this providing or someone else will. At this point, the choice is ours. Open meetings, called by the programming staff, with invitations to all potential users, would help people understand the problem and allow them to share in achieving the best possible solution.

PARTICIPANT CHARACTERISTICS AND FORMAT

Now that we have looked at the makeup and structure of these formats, the next question for the programmer to consider is what kind of clientele are attracted to each format? That is, what special characteristics, if any, must a person possess to be able to participate in activities under each category, what needs are met by each category, which ones appeal to the various life cycle groups, and are some formats more adaptable for those who are disabled? Let us briefly look at each format in turn from this point of view and with these questions in mind.

Self-Improvement

People sign up for lessons in order to learn the skill that is being taught and, because this is the case, they have expectations that it will have the flavor of an educational event with further expectation of achieving some performance goal in that skill. Although the initial establishment of what lessons are to be offered is in response to the expressed needs of the clientele and, in this aspect they would have some desire to give input, they are generally satisfied with a leader-centered approach. This fact may be even *more* true at the senior citizen level than at younger age levels. Lessons are, of course, appropriate at any age, provided that the learner meets the basic criteria needed to attempt the skill at the level it is offered. The mix of the group may vary. In most instances, it does not matter if the sexes are mixed, but the programmer must consider the interest appeal to males and females of things offered, as well as whether they appeal to family groups and/or its individual members. Often the key criteria for assignment to a given group is whether or not participants are beginners or intermediates, and not whether they are girl, boy, 15 years of age, or 40 years of age. Interest and appeal of the topic usually determine sorting, but the programmer should be sensitive to how they group lessons. The 60 year-old grandmother usually does not want to take novice swimming lessons with her neighbor's four year-old child!

Competition

The salient characteristic of the tournament participant is interest in competition, in contrast to the club member, who often participates as much for the sake of playing the game as for anything else. The tournament is played to be won. The rewards are extrinsic as well as intrinsic. The tournament offers a chance to perform in those areas where one has already acquired skill. There is some chance to demonstrate talents in front of an audience as well as to know within oneself the performance was well done. The tournament participant has many traits in common with the members of the performance group; having an audience is frequently important. The tournaments run by a town recreation department give the adults in the community a chance to keep in touch with a skill they mastered and used frequently as a high school or college student. Tournaments provide an arena in which these things may still be done. Tournaments are probably the *least* effective on the preschool and early elementary school level. Neither the temperament nor the skill development level of the child makes it appropriate here, and it is not a good time to "select" performers so that only the winners are getting extended participation time. At that age level the focus should not be on tournaments, least of all on elimination tournaments. The person who enters a tournament is probably not interested in extensive participant leadership. He or she is interested in having the tournament planned, organized, and run with little help from him or her. These persons want to devote most available time to being a participant in the tournament and are happy to have the event structured for them. Special tournaments may have to be run for the disabled, although there are many skill events that need no adaptation, either in equipment or approach. This format sometimes demands sex groupings as well as life cycle groupings. Athletic tournaments require classification by physiological and anatomical growth as well.

A popular dividing mechanism is to use age-group categories. In an all-comers road race, all runners will feel the competition is more fair if many age categories are used to divide awards and recognition. Adults tend to be comfortable with decade age divisions.

Special attention should be given to skill groupings. The one act play festival should not require that the junior high school players compete in the same category as the city theatre group. An optional "open" category is always possible.

Social

There is hardly any person who rejects the social context of activity, yet the thrust of this format and its attendant participant is a profile of a person who needs people to make the activity itself rewarding. The activity is frequently the means for getting together with others.

Naturally, many leisure activities require the presence of many people. The programmer must remember that the richness of recreation activities is their ability to meet a variety of needs. So for those who need to be with others can find a wealth of opportunity through any recreation program regardless of the sponsorship—church, resort, YM/W, club or community center.

In special interest clubs there exists a wide variety of roles within the club especially if a formal structure exists. Leadership in the officer's chairs, committee work, and other jobs inside the club or group provide chances for members to interact with others, test their own abilities, meet new members and generally widen the social sphere of one's life.

Participant Spectator

At the beginning of this chapter the idea of participant readiness was discussed. The typical participant spectator in leisure activities varies in relation to the activity itself. For those wishing to learn about specific activities, the place to begin is to go and observe. For those whose active participating days are over, enjoyment is still possible by taking a supportive role as the spectator.

In many activities there exists a support role with enormous opportunity for a "different" type of participation. Sport activities need people to coach, keep score, officiate and judge, people to manage equipment, arrange travel schedules or coordinate special tournament arrangements. For those no longer able to play the game, this concomitant role can be a satisfying experience.

The performing arts are similar to sport in this context. The need for people to do the back stage tasks provides opportunity for many who are no longer able or willing to be out front with the performance group. Those people most prized for their back stage contribution are those who do not seek the spotlight, are willing to let others be the noticeable ones, and those who find reward for thier quiet gifts of other talents. It is the wise programmer who is able to define this role and urge the right people to take responsibility in this support tasks.

Self-Directed

In consonance with the format of an open facility, the participant attracted to it is looking for an unstructured, unplanned, usually unsupervised recreation experience. It is a format that may not be possible to use with a very young group, because they may not be mature enough to handle it, and it may not appeal to the very old, because they tend to want more structure. Within these parameters, it appeals to a wide range of ages, and mainly to those who already have skills in the program elements offered. This participant is independent and can rely on his or her own resources. An open facility user usually knows what he or she wants, comes to get it, and leaves satisfied. The person may be highly self-actualized, but may or may not have strong sense of belonging, since one can use things in the facility that require a group, or choose activities that one can do in a dyad or even alone. The disabled person may actually have a better experience in this type of format than under some of the others, because of the opportunity to do what you want to plan for yourself.

SUMMARY

The successful programmer never loses sight of the participant's characteristics and needs. Some particular considerations staff must address as they begin to design the program are:

1. Participant readiness for the activity–skill level for example–and readiness to move from one level to another.
2. Specialization–becoming better and taking on the approach of the expert as opposed to a novice.
3. Participant ability to take over the management of program details, thus freeing up program staff.
4. Opportunities of participants from different agencies to affiliate with a central leisure service enterprise in sponsorship of events. Programmers must be aware of both the advantages and disadvantages of these affiliation opportunities.

One of the ways of reviewing program variety and balance would be to place each format style on one of the dimensions of a cubic matrix–with the other two axes being life stages and functional program areas.

Program format refers to the basic purpose for which a program is designed. Five program formats were proposed and labeled the Five Format Structure Model. Each format is a unique tool for use in designing a meaningful and total program. The five formats are:

1. Self-improvement
2. Competition
3. Social
4. Participant spectator
5. Self-directed

These five formats offer the programmer unlimited ways to think about structuring a single activity to serve a variety of participant needs. As can be understood, the amount of organizational structure required of the program staff varies dramatically among the five formats. It is incumbent upon the staff to understand the relationship between the requirements for staff organizational time and effort and the potential for designing a variety of program forms that permit leadership to emerge from the uses themselves.

Different formats generally attract people with similar characteristics. The person who signs up for lessons in a class usually chooses to learn a skill that is being taught and therefore expects to receive instruction and help in achieving some performance goal. Those who seek tournament experiences are characterized by their interest in competition, in winning the game, and in having a chance to perform in an

areas of a specific skill. The social interaction interests of people are central to our culture. People who participate for the social aspects of the experience are frequently affiliated with club-type activities. The variety of social roles available in these clubs permits a wide range of social needs to be fulfilled. As a society, we have many opportunities to become spectators and find this type of leisure activity extremely rewarding. Supporting family members, participating in the only way we can to experience certain events (particularly when our own personal skill level is too low to support being an active participant), finding needed anonymity in a large crowd watching something exciting and the sheer enjoyment of watching others perform all become the basis for this format style. There are those who seek an unstructured, unplanned and usually unsupervised recreation experience, which appeals to a wide range of ages of participants who already possess some skills to perform the activity. These people are generally independent and willing to rely on their own resources.

BIBLIOGRAPHY

AAHPER. (1975). *Leisure today: Selected readings*. Washington, DC: AAHPER.

AAHPERD. Neal, L., Editor. (1983). *Leisure, no enemy but ignorance*. Reston, VA: AAHPERD.

AAHPER. (1968). *Programming for the mentally retarded*. Washington, DC: AAHPER.

Bryan, H. (1979). *Conflict in the Great Outdoors: Toward Understanding and Managing for Diverse Sportsmen Preferences*. Sociological Studies No. 4. Birmingham, AL: The Birmingham Publishing Company.

Carlson, R. E., Deppe, T. R. and MacLean, J. R. (1979). *Recreation and leisure: The changing scene* (3rd edition). Belmont, CA: Wadsworth.

Colgate, J. A. (1978). *Administration of intramural and recreational activities: Everyone can participate*. New York, NY: John Wiley & Sons.

Hall, J. T. (1966). *School recreation: Its organization, supervision and administration*. Dubuque, IA: William C. Brown, Company, Publicationss.

Harris, L. and Assoc., Inc. (January 1976). *The myth and reality of aging in America*. Washington, DC: National Council on Aging.

Kando, T.M. (1980). *Leisure and Popular culture in transition, 2nd Ed.*. St. Louis, MO: Mosbey.

Kaplan, M. (1979) *Leisure, lifestyle and lifespan.* Philadelphia, PA: Saunders.

Kleindienst, V. K. and Weston, A. (1978). *The recreational sports program: Schools...colleges...communities.* Englewood Cliffs, NJ: Prentice Hall.

Kraus, R. (1978). *Recreation and leisure in modern society* (2nd edition). Santa Monica, CA: Goodyear Publishing Company, Inc.

Manjone, J. A. and Bowen, R. T. (1978). *Co-rec intramural sports handbook.* West Point, NY: Leisure Press.

McDaniels, C. (1982). *Leisure: Integrating a neglected component in life planning.* ERIC Clearinghouse on Adult, Career, and Vocational Education. National Center for Research in Vocational Education, No. 245.

Napier, R. W. and Gershenfeld, M. K. (1973). *Groups: Theory and experience.* Boston, MA: Houghton Mifflin.

Rojek, C. (1989). *Leisure for leisure.* Basingstoke, Hampshire,New York, NY: Macmillan Press.

Seabrook, J. (1988). *The leisure society.* New York, NY: Basil Blackwell.

Sessoms, H. D., Meyer, H. D. and Brightbill, C. K. (1975). *Leisure services* (5th edition). Englewood Cliffs, NJ, Prentice-Hall.

Stebbins, R.A. (1979). *Amateurs.* Newbury Park, CA: Sage Publications.

CHAPTER FIVE

TECHNIQUES FOR THE ORGANIZATION AND ADMINISTRATION OF RECREATION PROGRAM PLANNING

As the recreation program administrator functions in the role of planner, he or she finds that many additional skills are necessary in this phase of the job. The time of fathering activity-interest data is complete, and the participant input phase may have reached a point where no further advice from participants is possible until the professional programmer acts. The point in the planning process is reached when all the technical matters must be brought into focus and coordinated in such a way that the goals and purposes of the program have the best chance of being met.

There are a series of elements that must be coordinated for any program to have the opportunity of becoming a success. They are (1) selection of appropriate leadership, (2) program cost analysis, (3) scheduling a timetable, (4) facility availability, (5) promoting the program and inviting the participant, and (6) special program tools.

In this chapter each of these elements as they pertain to programs in general are discussed. There is no mystery to doing any of the above tasks, yet the successful programmer recognizes the importance of every minute detail in making decisions regarding each task. Being able to make sound choices in these areas of the programmer's job assures good results and avoids weak organizational work. A recreation agency should have formal procedures that consider each of these elements, which in turn guide the programmer in performing these tasks.

Before embarking on any of these tasks, the programmer must have clearly in mind the time frame available for the planning process. The usual Program Evaluation Review Technique (PERT) chart should be drawn for this type of task, just as PERT is used in any planning process. In utilizing the PERT systems, the planner proceeds to:

1. Bring together the people who will implement the plan and list all of the possible activities that might be included in the program or projects.
2. Plot the activities on a PERT chart based on the proposed sequence of activities and simultaneously start work on some of the activities.
3. Finalize the PERT chart and return to the key people indicated in number one for review and final approval.

4. Assemble the key personnel to determine the amount of time each activity will take in terms of weeks. Four times are determined. Three of these times are pessimistic time (PT) or the time it would take if everything went wrong; optimist time (OT) or the time it would take if everything went absolute right; and most likely time (MLT) or the best estimate of time. If these three are taken into account, then realistic time (RT) can be calculated and included on the PERT chart between activities. The formula is:

$$\frac{PT + 4(MLT) + OT}{6} = RT$$

5. Following this procedure, a critical path is indicated by a solid line on the PERT chart. This path is based on the longest sequence of activities that, when totaled, will give the total time it will take to complete a project.

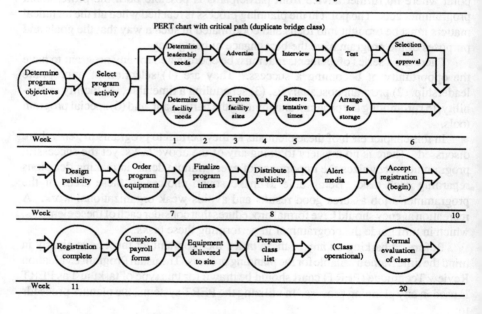

Figure 5.1 Sample Programs Evaluation Review Technique Chart and Steps in Development

Recreation activity programming is no different, as far as the process is concerned, from any other planning type function. Once this time calendar has been set, then the programmer can move into a smooth coordination of these elements.

LEADERSHIP

In literature dealing with the concepts of leadership, this element is often referred to as the most important factor for program success. The programmer needs to take some important steps to assure the participant that quality leaders are secured.

The process of leadership selection must be seriously approached. The first step is to identify what functions will be asked of the leader and at what skill level these tasks need to be performed. The alert program administrator has such task defined to the point that all leadership functions are written and collected into a personnel manual. These descriptions of leadership function go well beyond the generalized detail of a job description commonly used in advertising an open staff position. Although the job announcement type of description is beginning, the job function description is presented in much finer detail.

Once the functions required to perform a job are identified, then a parallel document must be written to describe the skills necessary to perform these functions. These descriptions need not be esoteric and theoretical, but instead should contain tight, specific words and active verbs that clearly describe and point directly to the assignment.

The next step is to secure the person or persons who possess the blend of talents needed to function well in his or her assigned tasks. In some instances a single leader must possess all of the talents that are sought, while at other times a team or group of leaders who complement one another might be the best choice. Other manuals and books have dealt with how one interviews and selects the best candidate, but this is not the purpose here. What is crucial to program effectiveness is the idea of a leader being able to function successfully at the level desired.

Throughout any diversified recreation program, all levels of leadership are needed. From the generalist park leader to the highly skilled lapidary specialist, all programs must be carefully reviewed for levels of leadership talent presently on-board. If quality of leadership has been sacrificed, then be prepared for fall off in program interest, unless the program is so popular it would succeed despite leadership quality. There are, in fact, some programs that *do* succeed in spite of weak leadership, which is dependent, ultimately, on what is meant by "success" in any given agency.

Every recreation programmer must be aware of both the internal and external leadership resources. A skill inventory of the agency's internal personnel would be a helpful early step in assessing leadership talents. This inventory might include, for instance, what staff members have audiovisual skills, social recreation skills, special hobbies, or special teaching skills in any of the program areas. Being prepared to maximize the talents of the staff, the wise programmer should plan for and find an opportunity to utilize these talents. When programs require talents beyond those of the on-board staff, careful review and selection must be made of potential supplementary sources. Every programmer should have, as a principal resource, a card file that has been carefully collected. Not only names and skill areas of those who have worked for the agency are listed, but also this file should contain names of those in the area who might have possible talent. Magicians, performers of one type or another, artists, hobbyists teachers in the skill areas, professional athletes, or amateur stars are among those whose names should be on file with the agency.

If no one person is able to meet the requirements for holding the leadership post, the program administrator must make one of two choices: (1) The program should be cancelled, or (2) special training should be provided to potential leaders in order to bring their skills into balance with program needs. Because of the usual pressures to proceed with specific programs, agencies have often been willing to accept lower levels of skill in leadership than they would like. Here is one of the most crucial centers of program quality control. Accepting less than the best at this stage puts the program on an unsound foundation; cancelling the program or training your own leaders appear to be the only options. Would anyone be foolish enough to open the neighborhood pool without qualified pool guards? Of course not. Then why would anyone even entertain the thought that unqualified leaders could make do in other program situations? Not all programs carry the life and death aura of the swimming situation, but the social, psychological, and environemntal life and death aspects should also influence decisions accordingly.

If training opportunities do not exist within the agency, then it is the responsibility of the recreation programmer to facilitate the potential leader's attendance at work-shops, clinics, etc., as they are offered in the area. Colleges and universities, professional organizations, and private firms, among others, are organizations from whom potential assistance might be asked. Camp counselor workshops, playground leader institutes, coaches' clinics, craft leader workshops, naturalist training programs for nature counselors and day camp leaders, and scout leader workshops are typical of the types of training experience that are available through various resource agencies. The alert program administrator should see that the recreation department is placed on the mailing lists of these agencies who run leadership training sessions.

After the identification processes of functions and qualifications is complete, and the leader is chosen on the basis of having met these specifications, the leader is contacted and hiring arrangements are made. The leader should be given some written assurances of what the job is to be. If the agency has a general type of contract that can be used, this would be preferable. Most recreation agencies rely heavily on part-time leaders to carry a heavy percent of the program leadership. Therefore, a contract form should be available that could be adapted easily to any activity.

Regardless of the leadership assignment held by a person with the agency, some written agreement should exist between the employer and the employee. The volunteer leaders should also have some document that designates their affiliation with an agency program. Thus, for paid or volunteer leadership, the commitment of the agency is binding and demonstrates good faith. Leaders then feel that serious attention, in addition to the paycheck, is being given to the importance of their participation on staff with the agency's program.

Volunteer Recruitment, Training, Assignment and Evaluation

Volunteers are people who give service of their own free will with no obligation to act. They come from diverse backgrounds, have varied skills and operate from different motivations. The demographics of the typical volunteer are changing, moving from the 30-44 year old, middle-class white woman (Cull and Hardy, 1974) to males and females of increasing age diversity who come more and more from grass roots environments. Motivation to volunteer is changing with this evolving new profile, and differences can be seen between demographic groups. Changing, also, is the need in the agencies for volunteers to assure maintenance of a broad breadth of program offerings. It is frequently crucial to the life of the organization that it keep a vital volunteer core in operation. This is no less true for recreation agencies than it is for other human service delivery systems.

Although volunteers may be classified in many ways, it is useful to make the distinction between *administrative* volunteers–those who serve on a committee or a board and participate in policy making; and *operational* volunteers–those who actually lead groups or program activity, help in the office, and help with fund raising (Naylor, 1967; Edington, Compton and Hanson, 1980). Recruitment of these two types may require quite different approaches to people who come from diverse backgrounds.

Established agencies are usually pretty well committed to having or not having volunteers as part of their service delivery system. New agencies must assess their goals and their budgets and decide whether they need to organize a volunteer group. Vital to the successful operation of a volunteer program is the commitment of the total organization, from the administration through all levels of supervisory and office staff to the maintenance personnel, including the agency's clients, to the acceptance of the volunteers (Cull and Hardy, 1974). There must be full cooperation among all of these groups with the volunteers or it will not work.

Once an agency has decided to recruit volunteers to help it meet its goals, the steps in establishing the volunteer program should include a plan for recruitment, orientation, placement, training, and evaluation.

Recruitment What should be considered when recruiting volunteers? Important to the programmer is having an understanding of the motivation of the volunteer. There is a thread that runs throughout the literature on volunteerism that says that it is vital to the success of the program to keep volunteers motivated and to challenge them with meaningful assignments.

Henderson (1980) suggested that intrinsic factors act as motivators. Volunteers may be achievement-motivated and excel in meeting standards. They may be affiliation-motivated, where social interaction and personal relationships are the key motivators, or they may be power-motivated and seek to encourage achievement in others. Henderson suggests that leadership and power are related and that the power seekers want to be dominant and to give advice. Motivation may be state related and shift with the situation and any leisure programmer needs to recognize that fact when dealing with volunteers.

Some people are motivated to volunteer by career interests. That is, they need certain experiences in order to sell themselves as knowledgeable and with given expertise, and to do so they must have worked in some given field and experienced the task and responsibilities involved. They may also do something for someone or some organization in the hope of receiving support from that source in return.

Volunteers are also motivated by a need to feel good about themselves, and further by achievement of their goals. When those goals are congruent with the agency's, that is a bonus. Motivation to start may be different from motivation to continue. It is up to the programmer to assess the motivation of the individual and capitalize on it. In any case it must be rewarding and fun, or it will not be repeated. Remember that it is possible that the volunteers' provision of service to others is leisure program for them (Henderson, 1980; Morando, 1986; Hayes and McDaniels, 1980). Vital to the successful operation of a volunteer program is the commitment of the total organization, from the administrator through all levels of supervisory and office staff to the maintenance personnel, including the agency's clients, and the acceptance of the volunteers (Cull and Hardy, 1974). There must be full cooperation among all of these professional groups with the volunteers or it will not work. Finally, do not assume that motivation is something once-and-done. The successful leader renews motivation frequently.

Following an exploration of motivation and the reasons people volunteer to give service, the programmer's next task is to operationalize this motivation and go out to recruit volunteers.

It has been shown that a one-on-one approach to recruitment is perhaps the best if it is possible to reach the potential group members in this way (Naylor, 1967). It is, of course, possible and often the only thing feasible to organize group recruitment sessions. When this approach is used, the basic discussion regarding the agency, its function, and its operation may be conducted in the large group and then individual interviews are held with interested persons. This type of recruitment plan is usually operationalized at the recruits' home area rather than at the agency (e.g., at a sorority house or a senior center). Members of the recruitment committee usually lead this session. Do not, however, overlook the potential influence a current volunteer can have on potential recruits, and put some present volunteers on the visiting team. If the agency is big enough, it may be a good idea to establish a recruitment committee. Be sure to include members of the community outside of the agency and to include within the agency personnel from various employment groups. Those involved in public relations may make a valuable contribution. It is also important to give careful thought and consideration to choosing the director of volunteers because the person in this position can make or break the whole effort. The director should have the major responsibility for drawing up the organization and recruitment plan.

It is suggested that the recruitment committee give careful thought and attention to publicizing the agency and its services so that the community members will be well educated about what the agency does. In fact, one of the first things to be done by the recruitment committee is to prepare a release to the media about the agency and its programs and to announce the upcoming volunteer program drive. If this step is followed by an open house of some sort, it helps to solidify the perception of the agency in the minds of those who might volunteer and lead them to a commitment to serve.

Placement Having recruited volunteers, the next step for the agency is to place them in a productive slot for them that matches their talents and makes both volunteers and agencies happy. It is important to recognize that volunteers have certain kinds of expectations, many of which relate to their motivation for volunteering and, in retirees, to their former work values and rewards. In placing the person, these expectations should be considered, so that the assigned task can serve to meet them (Saxon and Sawyer, 1984). In order to place people properly, information is needed about the skills possessed by the volunteer as well as some basic demographics. A form used to collect these data should include training history and work history, special certifications (e.g., Red Cross CPR training) and other volunteer experiences. For a copy of a sample form, see Appendix D for a sample form to use with volunteer staff.

After recruitment and prior to formal placement, there may be a period during which the volunteer is oriented to the agency and becomes familiar with the jobs to be done. This orientation should be completed in a fairly short time. Following that, the administrator and the volunteer meet to finalize the assignment with a clear understanding of the responsibility and authority that go with it. The administrator should know what to delegate and do it. To delegate and then fail to give flexibility to the volunteers to do what is asked of them often ends with the volunteer leaving the agency.

Orientation What should the content of the orientation sessions be? The general concensus is that it should contain: (1) some background and history of the agency, (2) a discussion of goals and mission, (3) a chance to meet the paid staff and veteran volunteers, (4) familiarization with the facilities and usage of them by the volunteers, (5) distribution of a pre-prepared handbook of policies and procedures, rules and regulations and a chance to discuss them, (6) a discussion of how volunteers relate to more experienced volunteers, staff and administration, and (7) distribution of the volunteers' job descriptions and a chance to address questions about expectations and agency operations.

Training Orientation is followed by actual training (or it can be considered part of the training session). The training program is planned by the administrator and the director of volunteers and uses the experienced volunteers as trainers. Training sessions can be in a workshop format in a single day, or spread out over a week in short sessions. The focus of the training is on developing, reviewing, or polishing the skills needed to do the job and to give an opportunity to talk with more experienced people who are doing the same or similar jobs. The trainees should be given a chance to observe the activities of which they will soon be a part. The changing demographics of the volunteers, with a higher percent of them technically rather than professionally educated dictates a different approach to skill training and the content of the training module. Training should be a continuous process and becomes an in-service training as the volunteer gains experience. Training may involve such things as newsletters, video tapes, movies, seminars, exhibits, etc. Training modules should contain process as well as content, but not too much of one and too little of the other. They should contain behavioral goals and not just skills to be learned. They should tell the volunteers what they are expected to know and how they are to demonstrate that they know. Finally, they should contain frequent supervisory input as to how things are going, with some formal summative evaluation.

Evaluation Evaluation of volunteer performance takes a page out of evaluation of staff performance. The process and how to go about it are the same; only the goals may be different. Goals form an important base in evaluation, since they are what evaluators use about which to assess performance. First they ask the question, "What are my goals?" and then "Have I met them?" The answers to these questions can come in the form of self-evaluation as well as supervisor evaluation. In addition, the organization should be having outside evaluation periodically, and the board of the agency should conduct its own internal evaluation.

Finally, it is wise to consider how volunteer service can be recognized by the agency. There is, certainly, great intrinsic reward in volunteering, but occasionally a pat on the back is in order. Many organizations have a volunteer of the year recognition banquet which they share as a community event. Whatever the culminating event, an occasional "well done" day-to-day is never remiss.

Application: Recruitment of Volunteers for Specific Situations

Let us take a look at the application of this theory in situational specific instances related to recruitment of volunteers. How could an agency go about recruiting a group of volunteers for specific events over a long-term basis and how could they recruit individuals for similar situations?

A. Volunteers to assist with the Halloween Parade: Group—One Shot
   1. Possible Motivation of Potential Volunteers
      a. To help and/or to work with children.
      b. To gain experience in leading large group activities.
      c. To experiment with or practice some "learned" skills.
      d. To participate in community action.
      e. To earn credits, badges or the like or to fulfill an assignment.
      f. To satisfy requirements for a class or club project.

2. Sources of Volunteers
   a. The local community college.
   b. The scout troops.
   c. The church youth groups.
3. Approach
   a. The first things in the Fall when those groups start up, find out who is in charge of each. Make contact with them to see if they are working on projects which would be fulfilled by organizing an event such as the Halloween Parade. This step may narrow down your choices. For example, the Scouts may need a Spring project, so they are not available for this one; the churches are involved in an ecumenical Fall Festival celebrating the harvest, so they are out; and you are left with the community college. A look into the situation shows that they offer a leadership class in the Fall (or their major's club is committed to community projects and does not yet have one for the Fall).
   b. Arrange for a time to come to meet the group either during class time or club meeting time. (You want to have a chance to make your pitch to the total group to maximize potential for attracting their interest.) Include such factors as:
      (1) Time and place of event.
      (2) Size or characteristics of the participants in the Parade.
      (3) Anticipated time commitment of the volunteers.
      (4) Types of tasks which will need to be done.
   c. Have a prepared sign-up sheet with you to pass around at the close of your presentation.
   d. Set a time and place for the organizational meeting of the volunteers to plan the event.
   e. Follow-up with a reminder card about the meeting, if there is time to do this. If there is not enough time, call to remind them of their volunteering to participate.

B. Volunteer to Run the Sidewalk Art Sale for the Summer Arts Festival: Individual—One Shot
   1. Motivation
      a Career interest—need to learn about running a large community event involving many people from a diverse constituency.
      b. Chance to use skills you have, but are not used in the job.
      c. Chance to be with the artists you would like to be, but do not have the talent to be.
      d. Political—good to do something for the town.
      e. Pride in town event and wish to contribute to its success.
      f. Need for a challenge (have done many of the smaller jobs for several years and feel ready for more responsibility).

2. Sources of Volunteers
   a. Adults in the community.
   b. Former workers for the Festival.
   c. Volunteers for other large projects in the community.
   d. Service clubs.
   e. Scouts.
   f. Church groups.
3. Approach
   a. Decide on the person you want to do this job and ask the President of the organization to approach him or her one-to-one and ask him or her to do it. Use the motivation factor you think fits the individual.
   b. Be prepared to "sell" the idea and let the person know why you think he or she is the best choice.

C. Volunteers to Run the Recreation Department's Age Group Hockey League's Season: Group–Long Term
   1. Motivation
      a. To do something for their children.
      b. Desire to keep in touch with sports.
      c. An opportunity to establish a social group linked through their children.
      d. A need to "change the pace" of life and be in charge of something.
      e. "Feel good" about themselves.
      f. A chance to use their organizational skills.
   2. Sources of Volunteers
      a. Parents of the children.
      b. Former coaches in the community.
      c. Former hockey players in the community.
      d. Teachers in the community.
   3. Approaches
      a. Call a meeting of all parents of children in the age groups to be served. Send flyers home through the schools to contact them and announce the meeting.
      b. Advertise in the local paper the need for coaches, drivers, a director.
      c. Get the Little League or Y swim team volunteer lists and mail announcements to them.
      d. If new activity, organize a meeting of the Parent Teacher Association and ask for an agenda item of support to start the league. If yes, start organizing the group into drivers, arrangements, treasurer, etc.

D. Volunteer to be a Docent at the Audubon Nature Center Year Round: Individual–Long Term

1. Possible Motivation
   a. Use skills learned but not yet applied.
   b. Use skills that represent pre-retirement job.
   c. Do something meaningful in leisure.
   d. Making volunteering recreation.
   e. Feeling good about themselves by helping others.
   f. Have sense of high success at task with low risk of failure.
2. Sources
   a. Retirement homes.
   b. Senior centers.
   c. Retirees' clubs (especially if there is a local university or community college).
   d. Women's groups at church or in town.
3. Approach
   a. Contact the recreation director at the centers to see if you can attend meeting. Similar contact with the president of the condominium association or women's club.
   b. Send material ahead regarding the nature center. Prepare a poster requesting volunteers and advertising that someone will come to the monthly condominium association meeting (or weekly center meeting or lunch on a given day) and talk about the program.
   c. In presentation cover:
      (1) Skills needed for the task–a job description.
      (2) Provisions of transportation. How meals will be handled?
      (3) Hours volunteers needed. Frequency per week/month.
      (4) Preparation time.
      (5) How long a commitment you are requesting.
      (6) How they should contact you if they wish to volunteer (directly through the recreation person, the center head or group president).
      (7) How you will let them know if they are accepted and what their assignments are.

PROGRAM BUDGETING

Within the overall budget of an agency is a portion devoted to the operational support of the recreation activity program. These funds are generally referred to as operational. In this book only the cost analysis aspects for this specific part of the budget are considered and the reader is referred to other sources on capital budgeting and sources of budget funds for more in-depth information regarding total department budgeting.

There are many ways to prepare a budget, and most agencies have a fairly clear process designed to guide budget planning. The programmer must fit the activity plan into these established systems. Designated categories, numbering systems, match-offs between projected expenses and anticipated revenues, all of these are elements of concern. The most practical way to approach the budgeting task is to cost out each individual program that the agency sponsors or plans to sponsor. This task demands attention to both direct and indirect costs, which will be determined by agency and programming budget philosophy.

Generally there are two budget philosophies that have impact on the program budget process. These philosophies are related to the handling of indirect costs. If the program administrator endeavors to get a clear picture of what each activity has for expenses and possible income, decisions must be made regarding indirect costs.

Direct and Indirect Cost Analysis

Direct costs refer to those expenses that are exclusively and totally related to a single program line item. This would include such expense items as equipment, leadership, publicity flyers, etc. The term *indirect cost* refers to budget expenses of a related and peripheral nature that have been incurred in presenting the program, yet may appear as hidden or uncounted costs. This category would include portions of program administrators' salaries, program wide promotion for which a single program has received publicity, and building rental costs such as heat, light, and custodian services. For departments that wish to display a realistic picture of program costs, the pattern used today calculates all program costs by way of the indirect method. The following budget samples reflect both of these philosophies.

Both systems reflect a break-even program, assuming that maximum registration for the class is met. The wise programmer will hedge by two to four spots in the class to assure that expenses are met when less than maximum enrollment is reached. A cautious rule-of-thumb is to analyze a program on the assumption that 80 percent of the anticipated registrants will enroll. This system has its advantages.

Table 5.1
Direct Cost Sample Budget

Class: Belly dancing	
Expenses:	
Instructor (10 wk—2hr/wk at $30.00/wk)	$300.00
Revenue:	
Class registrants (30 at $10.00/person)	$300.00

1. If a total of 30 do not sign up for the belly dancing class (let us suppose that 25 do), the class can still be offered at no loss. With our 80 percent rule, we would project 24 participants at $20 each. Therefore, our expenses are covered. See Budget Sample 2, Table 5.2.

2. Participants beyond the 24 figure puts a little extra revenue into other programs. This enables the programmer to continue another program that might have fallen short by only one or two registrants.

3. It is disappointing to potential participants to have programs cancelled. By building in a financial cushion, fewer cancellations will be necessary.

Table 5.2
Indirect Cost Sample Budget

Class:	Belly dancing	
	Expenses:	
	Instructor (10 wk—2hr/wk at $30.00/wk)	$300.00
	Equipment rental (record player, etc.)	$ 50.00
	Promotion percentage (TV ads, flyers, radio)	$ 25.00
	Program administrator's time (1/2 of 1%—$15,000)	$ 75.00
	Facility use percentage (heat, light)	$ 30.00
		$480.00
	Revenue:	
	Class registrants (30 at $16.00/person)	$480.00
	80% (24 at $20.00/person)	

The disadvantages to the 80 percent rule are that it drives the price higher for each person, and it is no guarantee that the class will meet minimum acceptable enrollment.

With the indirect cost buried elsewhere in the budget, the programmer can show fewer expenses and thus provide a lower class fee to the participant. Some agencies prefer to lump all indirect costs together and show these costs as total program costs. More and more agencies, however, are moving to a system that reflects the real cost of each individual program. In days of tight money and closer accountability, it is a more precise method to spread administrative costs into each function of the recreation department, and the program area must accept its fair share of these costs.

Therefore, the process of creating a budget is to look at each separate program and assign the appropriate expenses to it. Two forms are available for review in Appendix C (see Samples one and two) that would be helpful guides in giving direction to this process. Let us look at sample programs for a few of the format styles.

A. Program: Modern Dance Master Class

Sample Budget for Self-Improvement Format

Brief Description. A visiting dance company is to perform in the area and the recreation agency has contracted with a member of the troupe to present a master class that exemplifies the dance company's methods and style. Saturday, March 19, 10:00 AM to 12:00 noon; Senior high school gymnasium; class fee $4.00 for dancers; $2.00 for spectators.

As can be seen in Budget Sample Table 5.3 the program projects participant interest and utilizes the grant technique to assist in generating funds for an arts program of benefit to all. Without the funds from the endowment, entry fees would be higher or cutbacks would have to be made in crucial areas. It is always tempting to look at publicity costs as being an area where cuts should be made. This could well be the worst possible choice for expense reduction.

Table 5.3
Modern Dance Master Class Sample Budget: Self-Improvement Format

Expenses
Personnel
Instructor (from the troupe)	$300.00	
Accompanist (from the troupe)	$150.00	
Entry fee collector (ticket sale and entry control)	$ 25.00	
Locker room and towel attendant (4 hours at $3.80/hour)	$ 15.20	
		$490.20

Administrative Costs
Publicity—radio spots (ten 15-sec promos)	$ 45.00	
Flyers—500 at $50.00 and distribution	$ 75.00	
Newspaper ad—4 column inches, 3 ads/week	$ 75.00	
		$195.00

Prorated
Building costs for heat, light, water, and maintenance	$ 50.00	
Staff planning time	$ 75.00	
Phones, office supplies, etc.	$ 12.00	
		$137.00

Miscellaneous
Luncheon for dance professional and selected staff and guests	$ 90.00	
	$ 90.00	
		$912.20

Anticipated Revenue
Entry fee (150 participants at $4.50; 50 spectators at $2.00)	$775.00	
Prorated portion of National Endowment for the Arts Grant or Foundation Grant	$150.00	
		$925.00

Balance: $ 12.80

In reviewing the above cost items, the luncheon might be an easy item to eliminate. The programmer needs to weigh the consequences of this move. Good will and future support from the dance community might be worth four times the $90 expense item for this program. This budget sample is close to a bare bones cost-out for a program of this type.

B.   Program: Synchronized Swim Team

Sample Budget for Competition Format

Brief Description.   Twenty-three members of the Dolphin Club swim competitively in six dual or triangular meets during the January through March season as designated by the AAU organization. The club has always qualified to swim in the state meet, but has never sent any swimmers on to the regionals. This year three meets are at the home pool and three are away. The state meets are held in the capital city.

In Budget Sample Table 5.4, the agency has made a full commitment to this competitive program. There are many ways to bring revenue into the program. Swimmers could be asked to pick up travel and swim suit costs as well as membership fee in the area of $75 per participant. Merchants, service clubs, or others could be asked for support dollars. To recover the total amount of costs listed in the above program in this way would be difficult, so agency subsidy is nessarary. The decision to underwrite these costs within the operating budget falls squarely on the governing board of the agency.

C.   Program: Philatelic Society Annual Show and Sale

Sample Budget for Social Format

Brief Description.   The club meets every second Monday, for two to three hours, to trade stamps, build collections, and share stories and good fellowship. This event is their annual get-together with people in the region. A competition on displays is held and awards given. The club has been affiliated with the county park and recreation department for 37 years (see Budget Sample Table 5.5).

It is important to note that the leadership expenses are absent, yet leadership is certainly evident. The club member set up the area in which the activity will take place, sell tickets and refreshments, contact exhibitors and judges, buy trophies and organize the competition. Thus, with minimal expense, this type of event can be used as a money-raiser for a club and be a focal point of a club's yearly program. The county has benefitted by facilitating this group's project and perhaps given citizens a new hobby interest.

Table 5.4
Synchronized Swim Team Sample Budget: Competition Format

Expenses

Personnel

Coach for the team (contract is for total amount and portions are paid every two weeks)	$ 600.00	
Life guards (one on duty during practice hour for 5 hours/week for 12 weeks at $4.00/hour)	$ 240.00	
Locker and towel room attendant (prorated share: 25%, 60 hours at $3.80/hour)	$ 57.00	(of the $228.)
Judges (3 per meet at $50.00, 3 meets)	$ 450.00	
	$1,347.00	

Administrative costs—program operation

Travel (parents reimbursed if 4 or 5 swimmers are transported. Five cars at $.24/mile; average trip, 180 miles; 900 x .24 x 3 trips)		$ 648.00
Insurance—prorated share, $3.00/swimmer	$ 69.00	
Records and audio cassette tapes	$ 65.00	
Swim suits and costumes (makeup, etc.)	$ 250.00	
Spotlights, basic set, and lights equipment	$ 250.00	
Team expense account for AAU state championship (3 days, 10 swimmers; $22.00/day/swimmer, van rental and mileage $40.00/day, $.38/mile)	$1,027.00	
	$2,309.00	

Administrative costs—facility operation (prorated)

Heat and light, both for water and building	$ 150.00	
Chemicals (disinfectants, pH testing, etc.)	$ 65.00	
Safety equipment	$ 100.00	
Loudspeaker system	$ 125.00	
Laundry services	$ 70.00	
	$ 510.00	

Expense Total		$4,166.00

Anticipated Revenue

Fund raising activities held by Dolphin Booster Club	$1,350.00	
Total Income		$1,350.00
Balance: ($2,816.00)		

Table 5.5
Stamp Show and Sale Sample Budget: Social Format

Expenses

Awards (trophies, first, second, and third in 3 classes of competition at $5.00)	$150.00	
Publicity (flyers, posters, banners in school building)	$ 80.00	
County building rental and utilities (heat, light, custodian, etc.; prorated)	$150.00	
		$380.00

Revenue

Flat exhibitor fee of $125.00 for commercial collectors	$240.00	
10% of individual private collector sales	$ 80.00	
Snack bar sales (baked goods from members)	$110.00	
Entry fee ($1.00 per person)	$120.00	
Raffle tickets ($1.00 each)	$200.00	
		$750.00

Balance: $370.00

D. Program: Public Golf Course

Sample Budget for Self-Directed Format

Brief Description: The county golf course is open for play from sunrise to sunset. Walk-on players are welcome at all times except the following; Monday, Tuesday, Wednesday, and Thursday from 5:30 PM to sunset and on Tuesday mornings. Sample Budget Table 5.6, shows one month of operation.

Not included in this budget are the possible commercial items that help generate dollars toward a golf course operation, including golf shop, snack bar, and cart rentals, which could be factored in to reduce the deficit.

Table.5.6
Monthly Golf Operation Sample Budget: Self-Directed Format

Expenses (1/12 of actual expense is listed)
Personnel—starters and player control;
   three people full-time; two
   people part-time $12,000.00
Mowing, fertilizer, planning, landscaping,
   nursery management, watering, and
   all other maintenance aspects
   including wage payroll costs $ 9,200.00
                                                           $21,200.00

Revenue (3/4 of income goes to this budget)
Greens fee weekday and weekend rates
   for adults and children:
   Adults: $10.00 daily; $15.00 weekend
   Children: $4.00 daily; $6.00 weekend
To meet expenses, the golf course manager
   might hope to attract:
   Weekdays: Adults: 1400 $12,000.00
               Children: 150 $ 600.00
   Weekends: Adults   1000 $15,000.00
               Children   50 $ 300.00
                                                           $27,900.00
Balance: $6,700.00

Performance Approach to Budgeting

The above examples represent a small part of any budget process. These items were presented only to demonstrate the first steps the programmer will work with in calculating and juggling the hard dollar amounts. However, once these amounts have been determined in rough form, the program administrator will want to look at the efficiency and potential effectiveness of these dollars vis-á-vis programs. Most budget or accounting systems refer to this as a formulation of performance criteria process, or the performance approach to budgeting.

In the performance approach to budgeting, it is generally assumed that inputs and outputs will be given major emphasis. Expenditure data are utilized as they relate to anticipated program services for the dollars being sought. In this discovery process, one expects administrative efficiency to sharpen as well as budgets to reflect a clear interpretation of program goals and objectives. The programmer is interested in using a solid analytical process to measure the effectiveness of the programs that are being designed. In order to be able to know this, a budget process must be followed. The following is recommended:

1. Begin with well-defined objectives for the overall program. Work toward developing performance objectives for each individual program. If this step is neglected, the final measurement of effectiveness is impossible, regardless of the sophisticated method of counting participants or noting the strong feeling-sof success experienced by leaders.

2. If there has not been an element of measurement included in the statement of objectives, it should be established as the next step. Measures of performance can be one of three types—program size, efficiency, and effectiveness. (Chapter Seven of this book includes possible means by which program benefits of these three types can be measured.)

   (a) Program size is the traditional way of measuring performance. This measures the number of people attending an activity as a pure, quantitative process.

   (b) Efficiency is a ratio computation. The cost of a program per number of people served represents this technique.

   (c) Effectiveness is the qualification measure that is directed toward participant satisfaction.

3. If the decision is made to proceed, all agency budget forms should be completed, both by activity and summary. For samples of these pages, see Appendix C.

4. Most budget forms call for a short justification description for each activity. This justification should be given careful consideration so that facts and pertinent data are presented for the board to understand program goals and objectives.

5. It is an unusual situation when the administrator is not asked to present budget expenditures for the past one or two years. These should be readily available, and the program administrator must be prepared to justify any changes that are being recommended.

The final phase in the budget process is to control budget expenses such that there are no overages that are avoidable. Staying within the limits of the budget allotment is sound budget management of any agency program administrator.

SCHEDULING

It is necessary for the programmer to know well the calendar pattern of the constituency whom the agency serves. Are the participants into a traditional school pattern of September to May or into June? Is summer the time when people leave the area, or is there a large influx of different clientele into this same area? Are evenings a time when participation is popular? Work, school, meal times, and curfews are among the patterns that must be known. This step requires the programmer to know the people and their free time habits well.

Scheduling should be thought of in at least three different patterns. The first involves the seasons or the natural block periods in the year. It may be most convenient to program by calendar seasons, while in parts of the country where there is little seasonal change, it may be inappropriate. Consider the various holidays and the impact they may have on program continuity throughout the various seasons.

Familiar patterns in block period scheduling are seen by many departments or agencies as three or four, eight to ten week sessions. These blocks generally follow the calendar seasons of Fall, Winter-Spring, and Summer. This scheduling pattern serves to facilitate most easily those programs in the educational format structure. Classes and other programs that meet regularly can be scheduled during a single season. Publicity including pamphlets, flyers, newspapers, and tabloids can be coordinated to focus on every program that is being offered during a specific season. If a registration process is necessary, then one promotional effort can serve many programs rather than costly individualization.

The second familiar scheduling pattern is based on a monthly or weekly focus. Facility centered programs (i.e., buildings or park areas such as ski areas or lakes) will want to coordinate activities for participants who regularly visit these special areas. Monthly themes, special events, as well as weekly ongoing programs will keep the drop-in users informed. The casual skier may be interested to know of the upcoming NASTAR race; the new girl in town may be delighted to know of the gymnastics club that meets at the Girls' Club every Tuesday after school; the retiree at the YMCA may appreciate knowing that the Fitness for Fifties and Over swim is every Tuesday and Thursday at 10:00 AM for one hour. The skillful programmer keeps a good mix of special activities sprinkled throughout the months so that potential and past participants always have an opportunity to anticipate some future activity.

The third pattern for consideration in scheduling, and perhaps the most crucial, is the daily time frame for activity. This function demands that programmers understand completely the life style patterns of the people with whom they work. What are the discretionary time blocks in the weekday life styles? Are weekend days planned with time-use patterns similar to those of the weekdays? It is important that this information be known.

Usual patterns of daily scheduling will focus on five general time periods:

1. Morning Session. This time slot is a possible activity period for senior adults, preschool children, swing-shift workers, house-persons, and others. The time of activity rarely begins before 9:00 AM and is usually completed prior to noontime, although some meal may be a part of the program activity.

2. Early Afternoon Sessions. This period of time may well attract the same clientele as those listed above. The camp will incorporate a rest hour here, or the institution may choose this time period for special medication or treatments, such that immediately after the noon hour activity generally is at a lower level. After this normally slower period, it can be expected that activity periods will be popular.

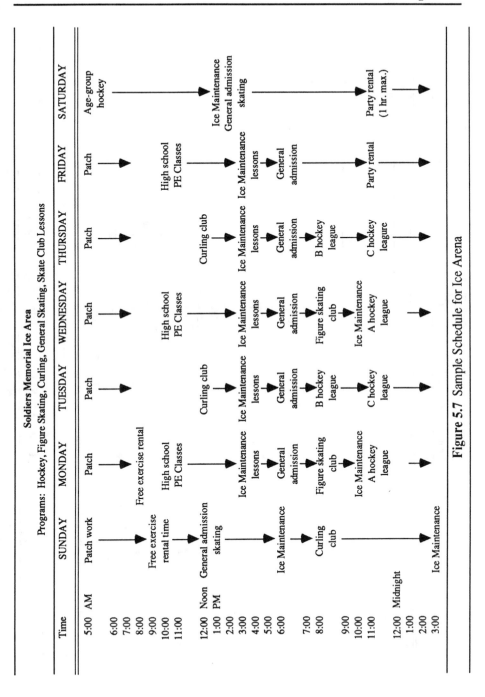

Figure 5.7 Sample Schedule for Ice Arena

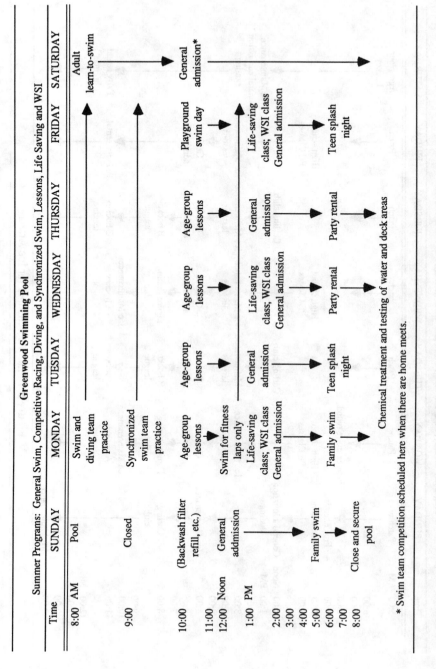

Figure 5.8 Sample Schedule for Swimming Pool

Multiple use
Gymnasium/Auditorum

Teen Center Gymnasium/Auditorium (Full Scale Programs for February)

	SUNDAY	MONDAY	TUESDAY	WEDNESDAY	THURSDAY	FRIDAY	SATURDAY
			1	2	3	4	5
Morning			Head start	Head start	B slimnastics T.O.P.S.		Badminton league
Afternoon			Baton lessons	Crafts for senior adults Baton and precision marching classes	Sport clinic— foul shooting	New games contest	hobby show
Evening			Senior basketball leagues boys and girls	Junior volleyball coed	Senior coed volleyball	Open mike cafe and dance	
	6	7	8	9	10	11	12
Morning		Head start	Head start	Head start	D slimnastics T.O.P.S.		Badminton league
Afternoon	Open activity	A slimnastics T.O.P.S. Skateboard club	Baton lessons	Crafts for senior adults Baton and precision marching classes	Sport clinic— jump rope for fitness	Service project: flea market sale	Decoration and preparation for Valentine dance and party
Evening		Junior basketball leagues, boys and girls	Senior basketball leagues boys and girls	Junior volleyball	Senior volleyball	Open mike cafe and dance	
	13	14	15	16	17	18	19
Morning		Head start	Head start	Head start Crafts for senior adults	B slimnastics T.O.P.S.		
Afternoon	Open activity	C slimnastics T.O.P.S.	Baton lessons	Baton and precision marching classes	Sport clinic— boxing	Performance: Bye, Bye, Birdie	
Evening		Junior basketball leagues	Senior basketball leagues	Rehearsal	Rehearsal		Performance: Bye, Bye, Birdie
	20	21	22	23	24	25	26
Morning		Head start	Head start	Head start Crafts for senior adults	D slimnastics T.O.P.S.		Badminton league
Afternoon	Open activity	A slimnastics Skateboard club	Baton lessons	Baton and precision marching classes	Sport clinic— indoor skateboard tricks	New games contest	Table tennis
Evening		Junior basketball leagues	Senior basketball leagues	Junior volleyball coed	Senior volleyball	Cartoon night— movies and snacks	Citywide tournament in badminton
	27	28	29				
Morning		Head start	Head start				
Afternoon	Open activity	C slimnastics	Pom-pom routines				
Evening		Junior basketball leagues	Senior basketball leagues				

Figure 5.9 Sample for Monthly Schedule for Gymnasium/Auditorium

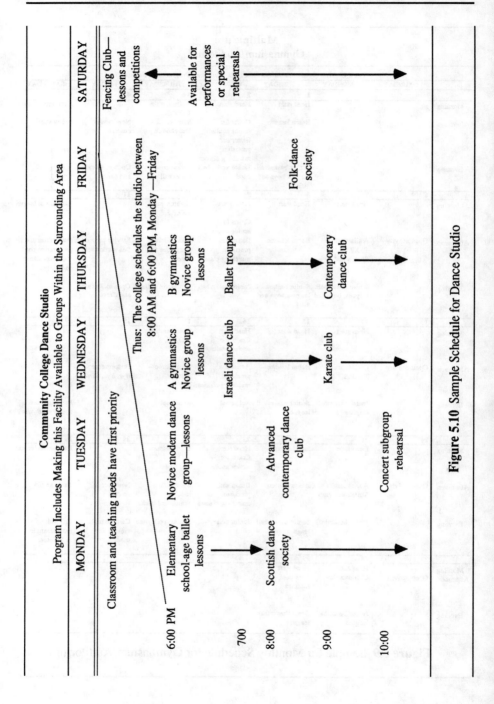

Figure 5.10 Sample Schedule for Dance Studio

Environmental Conservancy Nature Center—July
Program is Educational

	Week 1	Week 2	Week 3	Week 4	Week 5
Sunday	July bird count—mini-interpretive walks (led by staff)	Miniature walk—ducks—raise your own	Historical interpretation—miniature walks	Area geology—tree indentification walks	Mushroom study—miniature walks
Monday ↓ Friday	Displays and exhibits open to the public from 9:00 AM to 8:30 PM Regular daily programs: (a) 7:00 AM—Bird walks (c) 2:30 PM—Wild flowers walks (b) 10:30 AM—2-mile (d) 7:00 PM—Animals—Demonstrations touch and feel interpretive walk—general				
Friday	*Workshops: (a) Pond life (b) Bird banding (c) Edible plants	Workshops: (a) Nests and habitats (b) Ant farms (c) How to find water	Workshops: (a) Shooting wildlife with a camera (b) Wild flowers (c) Prey and predator	Workshops: (a) Photo blinds (b) Rock collections (c) Leaves for decoration	Workshops: (a) Orienteering (b) Life cycle (c) Butterflies—watch don't touch
Saturday	Evening star watch Movie feature	Movie feature—Camera club slide show	Movie feature "Best animal slide show and tell"	Movie feature	Survival talk

* All workshops will last for two hours and are offered twice, morning and afternoon. Registrations required

Figure 5.11 Sample Schedule for Nature Center

Neighborhood Park

Regular Summer Playground, Typical Day of the Weekly Plan

	Early Elementary	Late Elementary	Junior High	Senior High	Adult
10:00 AM	Play equipment	Softball practice	Basketball game	Free activity	
11:00	Crafts-masks in papier mâché	Tetherball, box hockey tourneys	Craft-puppet stage construction	Baseball/softball interplayground contest	
*					
1:00 PM	Tetherball, box hockey tourneys	Craft project-puppet heads	Music session-try out an instrument	Free activity	
2:00	Spray pool	Spray pool	Baseball/softball pickup game	Script writing for puppet show	
3:00	Free activity	Volleyball	Spray pool	Spray pool	
4:00	Drama-improvisations	Free activity	Chess tournament of the week	Foul shooting contest	
6:30	Low-organized games	Scavenger hunt	Basketball →	Basketball →	
7:30	Free activity	Field games-soccer/softball			Softball horseshoes

* Lunch, park closed

Figure 5.12 Sample Schedule for Neighborhood Park

3. Late Afternoon Session. This may be the busiest time during the school year in which children of school age will require programs and participate in recreational activities. During the summer months, however, this will not be a highly participatory time.

4. Early Evening Session. Aside from varying work shifts in the area, this remains a most popular time for recreational activity. There are many elements in a person's life that compete for this time of one's day. Television, part-time jobs, community service work, social clubs, family get-together time, school activities and studying, church work and fellowship groups, and socializing with peers; all tend to be competitors for activity during even discretionary hours.

5. Late Evening Session. Depending on the bedtime habits or possible curfew regulations in the area, this time block could extend well into the early morning hours. Although this tends to be an adult time period, there are many areas of the country in which younger children are out until well past midnight.

An important aspect that must be considered in this scheduling framework is the reservation of time to have major annual maintenance done. If a facility is used year-round, it is crucial in the use of such a facility that time be set aside from participation use for refurbishing. Hopefully, this type of work will not have to occur during high-use time in the area or facility. This type of scheduling is equally important to that of program use.

The following schedules are presented as samples of how a specific facility might well be programmed. We do not go into detail concerning each activity, its format, or sponsorship. The reader will be given only the activity name. The point to be made here is the scheduling possibilities, and not the generation of specific activity programs.

A. Indoor ice rink–County Recreation and Park Department (see page p. 143).
   Figure 5.7
B. Outdoor swimming pool–City Recreation Department (see page p. 144).
   Figure 5.8
C. Gymnasium in teen center (see page p. 145). Figure 5.9
D. Dance studio–Community College (see page p. 146). Figure 5.10
E. Nature center–environemntal conservancy (see page p. 147). Figure 5.11
F. Neighborhood park–Town Recreation and Park Department (see page
   p. 148). Figure 5.12
G. Camp Chickadee–Mental Retardation Association (see page p. 150). Figure
   5.13

Camp Chickadee Regular Resident Camp Day—Ongoing Program	
Thursday	
7:30 AM	Rising
8:00	Breakfast
8:45	Cleanup tent and tent area, chores
9:15	First activity block
	Activities available: archery, movement and dance, crafts, canoeing, or campsite building
10:30	All-camper swim
11:30	Preparation for lunch
12:00 Noon	Lunch
12:45 PM	Rest period
1:00	Second activity block
	Activities available: riflery, fishing, hiking, rowboating, sketching, or tumbling
3:00	All-camper swim
4:30	Closed waterfront, free activity for campers
5:45	Supper
6:30	Third activity block, canoeing, rowing, sing along
8:00	Tent get-togethers
8:30	Taps

Figure 5.13 Sample Schedule for Day Camp

FACILITIES

This section contains some suggestions about facility uses and how programmers might best advise the area or building designer so that the new facility will be programmatically well-planned as well as structurally sound.

Before any new project is begun or renovation work is attempted, it is paramount that the staff have a clear picture of what use the facility will serve. There are many excellent resources on how to design lands or buildings from a technical standpoint, but this is not our challenge here. The critical endeavor is centered on the facilitation of program activity that can best meet the needs of the agency's constituency. Of prime importance is not only program activity but also in what formats the activities will need to be offered.

If the pools is to serve class and general drop-in (open facility) types of swimming, there are variable water depths that will suffice. However, if diving, synchronized swimming, and racing activities and competitions are conducted, a deep pool is required. If the pool also serves as a center for social activities other than swimming, care and planning must be given to the amount of deck space, its surface, and other amenities. Club use and party rental groups could find this type of facility attractive.

Recreation agencies are faced with a number of programmatic considerations when planning areas and facilities:

1. What level of quality do we need and can we afford?
2. How many multiple uses should a single facility be asked to carry? How many is too many? If too few, will the facility lie idle?
3. Should facilities be clustered by like kind, or should they be decentralized into the various functional sections under the jurisdiction of a given agency?
4. Which facility development should be given priority?
5. As the population growth decreases and schools become vacant or up for public sale, should we renovate them and make do, or is it wiser to build our own new facilities?

The answers to these questions require individual department deliberation and resolution. There are no ready-packaged answers. Their resolution lies in department philosophy of service, citizen interest, and the economic abilities of the recreation agency. It is easy to take a philosophical position on the above questions in an environment totally unrelated to reality. Nevertheless, a close look at some of the guidelines may assist the programmer in resolving some of these dilemmas.

Some recreation agencies have cut corners by sacrificing quality in the development of areas and facilities. In some cases this has been done with little damage to the program, but high maintenance expenses have occurred as a result. Perhaps the most serious problem in the sacrifice of quality has been the overdevelopment of areas where the use impact has ruined the very substance of the amenity.

Multipurpose rooms were a fad in the building programs of the 1950s and 1960s. A single, large room was designed to serve as game room, auditorium, and cafeteria. It was generally unsatisfactory for the two former uses, but seemed to be a large enough place in which meals could be served. Magic squares were the outdoor multipurpose blocks. Areas paved with asphalt in a 120-foot square with a low curbing were designed. Holes for tennis and volleyball poles were set, while four to six basketball backboards were strategically placed around the edges. Therefore, court games of many kinds (often four square lines and hop scotch lines were painted on) were possible and the area could be flooded for winter skating. Few magic squares survived a two-year period. Seen as a boon to the user, they quickly became the center for fighting over which user group had priority. The age-old victors were the bigger kids.

Multiple use of our gymnasiums has been a temptation. So many lines have been painted on the floor, it has become impossible to know which line is for which game. Color coding has been of some help but, to the serious competitor, the confusion is real–to say nothing about what it does to the perceptually handicapped individual. Many floors carry basketball, volleyball, and badminton lines, and some modification of bases for whiffleball, kickball, or softball. Conflicts in use are sure to occur when we have jammed so many experiences into or on a single area.

Invention has answered necessity. New tape has been developed that can be placed on standard gym floor surfaces for establishing special court dimensions. It goes on easily and can be removed with no damage to the floor, Players report that it does not hinder the flow of the game. As basketball and volleyball vie for the same space, and basketball reigns supreme as far as permanent painted lines are concerned the volleyball program can still co-exist with basketball happily. The volleyball supervisor simply needs to plan for those extra 15 minutes of preparation. The new multiple-use concept seems to be occurring in the four- to six-wall cage games of squash, handball, racketball, and paddleball. The rules do differ slightly and lines are different. The baseboard requirement for squash can be portable, but the same use conflicts will still plague the drop-in user. Scheduling may have to be directed toward time block periods for the various games.

The third consideration to be examined relates most specifically to format programming. If the philosophy of the department is to being active in every neighborhood, then facilities should be decentralized so that easy access for open free-time use is facilitated. If the agency wishes to maintain an area such that it can facilitate large events in a specific activity, then thoughts will be given to clustering the facilities. If a department has determined that the interest in tennis such that 12 more courts are needed, it then becomes a matter of spreading them in three or four locations or placing all 12 courts in what will become the tennis center. Events such as tournaments, league play, lessons, and clubs would all have better use if these courts were centralized. The neighborhood casual user would probably prefer decentralization of these courts, since two or three of them probably would be "closer to home."

Back-to-back ball diamonds in one large area make the park a central focus for field games. Ball fields scattered throughout the district serve the scrub and pickup players. A crafts building that has rooms for many different crafts and arts activities becomes a solid focal point for classes, exhibits, and special events. One craft room in 8 or 10 centers throughout the city can bring crafts closer to home for many, but this arrangement lacks the depth and possible variety of a craft center. Perhaps a combination of both would be the ideal situation, yet, for most agencies, the matter becomes one of either clustering or decentralization.

All program activities have requirements for special area or facility amenities. In the chapter on program areas, we attempt to list special considerations that will enhance the activity experience itself. It is necessary to keep the program activities within the pocketbook of the constituency. Unless the citizens are willing to support a facility, it is unrealistic to plead for program activity. Ice rinks, swimming pools (year-round), and bike trails all are high-cost items. Can the people be happy playing street hockey or swimming only in summer? Can you ask for park roads to be closed to motorized traffic at certain times?

INVITING PARTICIPATION

Program staff must be prepared to see their job as requiring a solid background in promotion and marketing skills. Many good program plans have languished because there was little or no regard for how participants should be notified or invited to participate in the activities. Whether the programmer is working in the public or private sector, a sound marketing plan is as much a part of the programmer's job as the other elements in the organizational function.

In the earlier edition of this text this section was presented in a traditional fashion. Although these strategies for promotion are still valid, the plan for marketing has become much more sophisticated while the competition for participants and clients has become much more demanding for each competing agency. The following are good ideas and presented only as an introductory stimulus toward which you must expand. This expansion, or marketing plan, will follow this immediate section.

There are many traditional promotion techniques that are standards and still valuable:

1. Television spots/programs.
2. Radio ads/programs.
3. Newspaper ads, stories, special tabloid sections.
4. Posters and bulletin boards.
5. Flyers, handbills.
6. Banners.

These types of publicity or invitations reach only a certain percent of the potential clientele. Getting the attention of potential participants through media messages, when a recreation agency is competing with professional advertising agencies, can be a difficult assignment. The programmer has some choices in the performance of this job function. One might elect to employ a graphic arts specialist to prepare brochures, flyers, annual reports, and the like. A quality piece of promotional work from the recreation office reflects positively on the agency itself. Mimeographed work that has been hand stapled cannot possibly convey the same message as a printed piece of work that has contemporary sketches and a professionally designed layout. The determining factor in terms of what is done is the availability of funds. Within any agency, serious consideration must be given to budgeting appropriate amounts for public relations materials. Cost-cutting savings in this area may be a higher detriment to program success than cuts elsewhere.

Another choice for completing the publicity function is to purchase and have on file various available resources of sketches and drawings that can easily be traced onto the master copy for the various ongoing professional efforts. Lettering sets and style books, sketch files, letter sheets, and many other art supplies can be of assistance for the untrained but do-it-yourself staff. Careful records should be kept of the time this effort consumes. It may be discovered that the end product does not justify the cost of staff time.

A third obvious choice is to refrain from attempting fancy art work and simply provide facts, data, and short, written descriptions of activities. As far as costs are concerned, this will be by far the least expensive method. Whatever choice is made, the effect of the technique is what is important to the agency. The alert program administrator will evaluate regularly the impact of the various promotional materials being utilized.

Whatever style is chosen for publicity and promotion, the programmer should be aware of contemporary methods. What does an attractive looking newspaper advertisement look like? In order to promote a fall recreation and leisure educational package, what is the competition for potential participants? What is the best way to show off a new program or facility?

The area of promotion is one of the areas in which the recreation professional has been traditionally inexperienced. Many believed that, since recreation was so inherently good, people just naturally knew what services were provided by public and private agencies. However, the style of the forties, fifties, and sixties is not appropriate for our modern society. A fast moving, temporary society has no knowledge of patterns and tradition. When the average American family moves every five to six years, how can the clientele possibly know that registration for scout camp must be made by March 1st in order to receive special discounts? Without some promotional materials readily available, how does the new family know where the park facilities in the county or parish are located? So it is with all services to people. It is within this transient life-style that the programmer must consider new ways of presenting an invitation to leisure services.

In addition to the previous list of traditional publicity and promotion techniques, the following is presented to inspire all present and future programmers to create an exciting invitation to what they believe is a life-enriching experience. All of these may be commonly used techniques, but may still be helpful to the neophyte.

- Development of a quick set-up, knock-down display to be shown at shopping center malls, area banks, schools, and other public places.
- Use of small display racks and boxes into which promotional materials can be placed for free pickup near cash registers, sales counters, and in welfare and public service centers.
- Use of the postal service stamp cancelling machine for promotion of feature program events on every piece of mail. Agencies that have their own stamping postal machines may also be contacted for this type of promotion. Most large businesses will have these machines.
- Identification of an agency logo. This symbol could be represented on every piece of paper and promotional item that concerns the recreation services of the department. The logo should be a simple one and, as the constituency becomes more familiar with it, the quicker people will turn on, or off, to your message. Sell, promote, and invite by a single symbol.

- Installation of a recreation hot line. Citizens or members could call and find out pertinent program information. An adaptation of this might well be an invitation to call and leave an idea for a new program or a suggestion for program improvement.
- Would your local phone company give you the phone number 534-7873? If so, you could advertise for people to dial LEISURE. If the phone company refuses the special seven digit number, why not ask for the last four digits which might spell PLAY (7529) or PARK (7275). Here is an area that urges you to be clever and creative.
- Contact a local advertising agency. Work with this company on various promotional ideas, for example, buttons, bumper stickers, balloons, and key chains, for special seasons or events. Remember that your competition for the clientele's attention is powerful, professionally managed, and expensively designed. You must be more clever and more skillful with fewer financial resources.
- Perhaps the oldest and newest idea in promotional techniques is to help all recreation staff members endeavor to be sensitive to their own personal styles and work with all participants as they would like to be treated. The best promotion comes from the participant who has had a positive experience and urges others to seek the same.

Focus on Marketing Techniques

A wise saying in the business world is useful for programmers regardless of whether the agency is for profit or public. Think about minimizing your risk and maximizing your opportunities. This is good common sense. Throughout this book you have been urged to be in touch with client needs and desires, select programming approaches which have the potential to generate high client interest and participation, and to program activity with a variety of formats such that the most people within your constituency can be served in a cost effective way.

Now we must make a commitment to these perspectives and concepts by using some techniques that represent a professional approach to inviting the participant to become involved in one of our activities. Many commercial recreation enterprises require a business plan, certainly a must when a business is being started. Other recreation agencies are more interested in positioning themselves more competitively by doing a more serious job analyzing the market for their particular services and getting a larger market share in this environment. It is not the intent of this text to discuss the entire business plan, but it is useful to put forward some ideas and strategies for how to handle some thoughts about marketing the program and its individual activities.

Marketing Plan

Market plans are nothing new to the programmer. The plans suggest a logical order of events and techniques which assist in the decision making process. Much of the information needed for the marketing plan will already have been collected in the program planning process stages described in earlier chapters in this book.

There are four major steps and units within a marketing plan: a) consumer focused research which covers needs and interests and general program feasibility, b) segmentation techniques for disaggregating the potential consumer, c) attention to the life cycle potential of an activity, and d) an assessment of some supply and demand factors.

Consumer Research

Before any new programs are designed it makes sense to do some feasibility work on the potential each program has for success. Too many programmers design wonderful sounding programs in the relaxed atmosphere of the office only to find no takers when the program is offered. It may be incorrect to survey consumer interest in a simplistic fashion. Every step of the research phase must be sophisticated which means that good, solid research and evaluation techniques must be employed.

Perhaps the most important questions to be asked surround consumer behavior as it relates to interest. Then the next order of research is to ascertain whether program X is feasible for the home agency to manage, or whether the competitors are already into a major market share with which our agency cannot and should not compete.

Procedures for Segmenting the Market

If the recreation agency has been in existence for any time, the staff should be well-schooled on demographics of the potential clientele. Most larger recreation agencies have this type of information available such that the process may be one of reviewing and reassessing. Words that are typically used in this step are: demographics, geographics, psychographics and sociographics. These terms refer to data that may well be well-known to all program staff. Such data as age, gender, income, family size, etc. are common information. Most recreation departments are organized into zones or districts or specially defined neighborhoods that can be termed geographic units. And population density and travel time to activity are key pieces of information to understand.

Care must be taken when assessing the social and psychological climate of the potential participant. Life style, social class, needs, emotional stability all are matters of interest when considering the market plan, but seek help from other professionals when tackling these areas.

Market Life Cycle

Every program has a life of its own. Some activities are like fads and are over within a single season; while other activities seem to be staples of the department over the years and continue to attract participants. The program staff must be aware, and plan for the projected life of every new program. Then assessing how much investment into the activity in terms of personnel, facility development, and start-up costs is made more realistic.

There is no magic to the life cycle for a program. Staff introduce a new program, it may grow or have a growth period, it levels off (a popular term is maturity), and then decline may well be expected. Being able to know when maturity has occurred is essential and requires attention to certain evaluation strategies.

Assessing Market Demand
The familiar terms of supply and demand are useful in this final step of the marketing plan. There are four areas for consideration in this construct. Think of this problem as represented on an X and Y axis. Let the X axis represent Demand and it should range from low to high. Let the Y axis be Supply and it ranges as well from low to high.

There are four general areas or quadrants to consider: 1) high demand and high supply, 2) high demand and low supply, 3) low demand and high supply, and 4) low demand and low supply. All of the previous data collected for the market plan will help you assess both supply and demand. You will need to understand where the place of your agency will be, or should be in locating the appropriate quadrant for a specific program.

SPECIAL TOOLS AND TECHNIQUES

No book on programming would be complete without reference to some of the special tools available that give flair and extra interest potential to the many program areas. It is said that people are competitive and therefore thrive on any available, competitive activity. It has also been said the there is more to life than winning or losing, and it is the opportunity to play that has the greatest meaning.

Here we examine some recommended program enhancing techniques. However, the detail of how to do each in its specific way is left to other excellent manuals and texts (see end-of-chapter bibliography).

Grouping People for Activity

There are many activities that are age-group specific or for which a limited age span is recommended. On the other hand, there are activities in which a broad spectrum of ages makes a happy arrangement and, on occasion, is required. The same is true for sex specific and sex nonspecific activity planning. Consider the question of why people should be grouped at all. Is it for the safety, enjoyment potential, or probable interest the grouping is done?

People are grouped by age because of (1) assumed skill level and maturity or (2) peer group needs to be with others of the same age. Earlier we discussed the various cycles of life through which an individual passes. These groups are identifiable, since there are things common to one another in that cycle. Lives are lived with others of similar age and experience. If discretionary time is a normal part of an individual's life, then age-group preferences exist for recreational activity participation as well as for other facets of one's life.

In addition to participant preference for limited grouping, there is also the element of safety in some activities, particularly sports or strength activities that dictate special groupings. A general rule of thumb for children's groupings is not to mix more than two ages, possibly three, in a single activity. First and second graders, third and fourth, and the fifth and sixth graders make fair dividing lines most of the time. Perhaps grades one to three and four to six are acceptable. Separating boys and girls in the elementary years has been thought to be good for the safety of the girls. On the contrary, there is little to support separating girls and boys in the same activity until puberty. In recent research, arguments that cite unique cases or lean on emotional issues have little support.

It may make little sense to group by specific age. This can be seen clearly in many of the performing arts program areas and in our outdoor naturalist programs. For example, theatrical productions often require a wide age range, a county orchestra may enjoy talents from many age levels, and family camping programs will feature all family members participating equally. It has been convenient in programming to focus on participant expectations. If the purpose of the group is to make good music, then it seems that any musician who can make that happen should be welcome in the group.

It is equally important to ascertain which programs require various groupings and which programs do not. So much of one's life is spent in peer groups that open, mixed group activities should be encouraged. In some sports, rules might be modified to make a corecreational experience in high demand. This has been done with volleyball and softball. Racquet sports provide for good combinations of age-groups and partners, yet some activities will still be more successful as single sex or single life cycle programs.

Types of Tournaments

There are some useful tools in the form of various tournaments available to the programmer to use when different patterns and styles of competition are desired. These tournaments fall into four main categories: (1) elimination, (2) round robin, (3) challenge, and (4) scoring events.

Elimination. This type of tournament requires that the participant be ready to play and that the opponent be determined by the tournament staff, while the winner moves ahead and the loser is either dropped or slips into a consolation structure. It is used when:

1. A champion must be determined in the quickest way and shortest time possible.
2. There is limited time for a tournament.

3. Players' ability is known, and the tournament can be designed such that the two best competitive entries have a fair chance of meeting in the final championship. If player abilities are not known, the draw is blind.
4. Many people wish to enter an event.

The two most popular tournament types here are the single- and double-elimination setups. Single elimination means that once a participant has lost a game or match, they are out of the competition. A double-elimination tournament permits one loss, but a second loss eliminates the participant.

Organizational Techniques For Program Planning

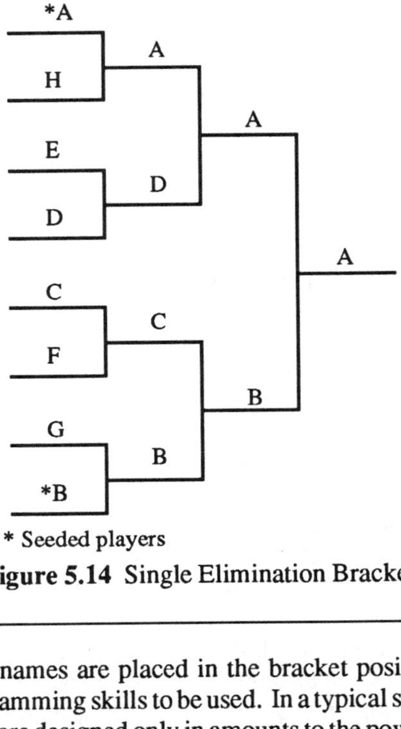

* Seeded players

Figure 5.14 Single Elimination Brackets

The draw, or how names are placed in the bracket positions for competition, provides for some programming skills to be used. In a typical single-elimination type of tournament, brackets are designed only in amounts to the power of ^{2}. Thus a bracket with eight entries can serve as an example, as in Figure 5.14.

This figure shows the easiest type of competition to set up. Letters represent the different participants; that is, A plays H and, as our example has reflected, A in defeating H moves to the next round while H has been eliminated.

This type of tournament permits known skill levels to be recognized. If one wants to have the best two players or teams face each other in the finals, then steps must be taken to see that these two known competitors are carefully placed in the brackets. This process is called "seeding" the players. The seeded players are the better players, perhaps last year's winner and runner-up, or even a ranked or undefeated player or team. There are usually two seeded competitors for each bracket of eight. In the above example, player A is the first seed and player B is the second seed. Every programmer or tournament director has a favorite way to set up these brackets with the seeded players. No one way is correct. It is simply a matter of preference. Secure your own favorite resource book that is acceptable to the agency. Use of the above example is perfectly appropriate for any elimination tournament.

In addition to seeding players into certain bracket slots, it is possible to place every competitor into a designated position. Letters A to H are listed in order from best performer to weakest performer. For instance, a bowling club may wish to have its monthly competition, and three lines are bowled to be used as a qualifying round to establish one's place in the tournament draw. The highest bowler is placed in the A position while the second highest bowler is put in the B position, and so forth down the line. If there are 32 bowlers, then brackets need to be drawn for 32 competitors.

It is also possible to draw the competitors' names out of a hat and place them at random in the brackets. This may be the only fair way to set the draw when no performance data are available on any of the competing teams. Thus the crucial step of getting the names into the brackets can be done by seeding, qualifying, or chance drawing.

If there are competitors in numbers that do not fit neatly into brackets set up in numbers to the power of ^{2}; that is, 2, 4, 8, 16, 32, etc., the next bracket number beyond the number of competitors must be used, and "byes" assigned to the empty slot opposing the status or seeded bracket positions. If six competitors enter a marble shooters tournament, the brackets must be drawn for eight players. One to six positions (A-F) are playing, while seven and eight (G and H) are byes. Thus the byes go to the better players. The philosophy here is that in order to dethrone the champion or the number-one seed, challengers must prove themselves in the process. The champion or number-one seed should have the easiest route to the finals.

Another useful tool in an elimination type of tournament is that by using either 8 or 16 unit draws, various skill levels can compete against one another. These brackets then represent "flights." As an example, the women's county golf tournament may require an 18-hole qualifying round. After all participants have turned in their scores, the draw committee takes the top eight participants (or the lowest eight scorers) and places them into the championship flight; the second group of eight players are put into the first flight, and so on until all golfers are in brackets with others of close skill. Thus, the golf tournament can accommodate as many golfers as the course can accommodate.

There are many advantages to the use of flights. It provides an opportunity for competitors at all skill levels. Naturally the greatest interest of most spectators will be in the championship flight, but there will be many winners and many runners-up. People enjoy competition when the match is close and competitors are well matched.

No one really enjoys a one-sided contest–either the players or the spectators. Greater spectator interest can be generated when some care has been given to the tournament structure and close competition is the end result.

One final tool that can assist the beginning competitor in tournament play in the elimination type of tournament is to arrange for consolation rounds. In some organizations the term "beaten fours" is used. Understanding that an elimination tournament has harsh consequences for the losers, it is possible to soften that loss with play-offs among those competitors who have lost in the first round of the tournament.

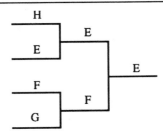

Figure 5.15 A First Round Consolation Draw

In the Figure 5.15 example, brackets would be drawn for those who lost in the quarterfinals, and they would play out their own consolation round.

It is possible to create consolations at any point in the tournament. When a person has entered a tournament, one can assume that most competitors are interested in playing as much as possible. The provision of consolation matches eases the consequence of losing and highlights the attention on playing for the sake of play.

Another useful and popular type of elimination tournament is the double elimination bracket arrangement. Again, every tournament director has a favorite way to draw these brackets. The following is presented as just one useful way.

Players are designed by letters A through P. The letters are marked in the brackets as if a qualifying score determined the skill level. A, B, C, and D were the top four scorers and could be called the seeded players, although in this draw, all players are placed by virtue of a score. A was the best qualifier; P was the poorest performer. Double elimination means that you remain in the draw or the competition until you lose two matches. Once a player loses, he or she is moved to the left side of the bracket and continues playing until the second loss indicated by superscript asterisk (*).

There is only one tricky spot for the tournament manager. To avoid playing the same opponent twice, it is necessary to switch players from the upper part of the bracket to the lower part, and vice versa. This is done after the second round results. The diagonal lines indicate where a loser from the right side of the draw goes after round two. On the left side of the bracket, round two eliminates the first four players, in this example, M, P, O, and N. (No surprises here; they were the four lowest scorers in the qualifying round.)

Organization Techniques for Program Planning

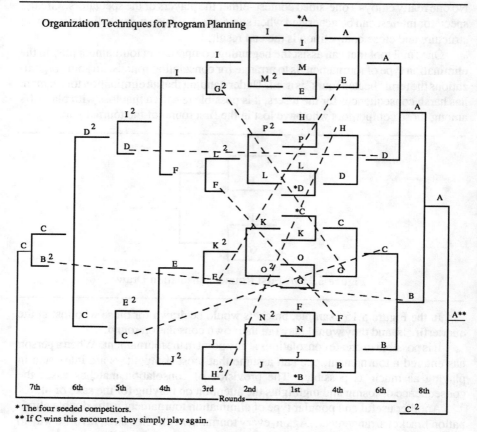

* The four seeded competitors.
** If C wins this encounter, they simply play again.

Figure 5.16 Double Elimination Tournament Brackets

As you will notice, there is more activity on the losers' side of the draw, the left side, than on the right. Keep the rounds in order, and you will have no difficulty. A word of advice. Be an assistant the first time you try this; it can be confusing.

Round Robin. This type of tournament provides an opportunity for every contestant to meet every other contestant on a one-to-one basis. Win/loss records are established as play progresses. The winner is that player or team with the best win/loss record. This type of tournament is used when:

1. It is desirable to have every player or team meet every other entry such that a true winner is determined.
2. Time is no particular problem, and it is possible to take weeks or months to complete the competition.

3. Games that often end in ties can be accommodated. A win, loss, and tie system can be handled easily.
4. Limited entries are anticipated.

A round robin type of tournament is an easy kind of competitive tool to manage. Used mostly with leagues in team sports, it provides each team—win, lose, or draw—to remain in the tournament and continue playing until the completion of the round robin. It is wise not to have too many teams in a single league. Six to eight teams is usually the maximum number included in this tournament style. The programmer may have 24 teams of six-man soccer, but these teams could be divided into three or four leagues. Perhaps the important factor in how many teams are to be included in the league is how much time and how often facilities are available for play.

Often the leagues that are established will schedule a meeting for once a week. If there are eight teams in the league, the minimum for one round would be seven weeks. If the leagues wished to play a double round robin, 14 weeks would be needed. Whether or not interest in the league can be maintained over this period of time must be given careful consideration.

The coordination of round robin play has a few special considerations that must be handled. There are many examples of how to set up a round robin tournament, and space will not be devoted to that purpose here. (See Bibliography for references on tournaments.) However the draw is done, it is often crucial for teams to know which one is the home team and which team is visiting. Many rules refer to home team/ visiting team rights and responsibilities. Teams should have an equal number of each assignment. Perhaps the league has drawn its own rules, requiring that the home team provide the officials, some equipment, or do some preparation or clean-up chores.

One of the convenient aspects of a round robin is that the entire schedule is determined prior to any play. This schedule can be submitted to a local officials' board. Arrangements for all games can be handled through the board; each player can have his or her own copy, and the press and other potential spectators can be alerted as to who plays where and when.

For a final note on the round robin tournament, it should be pointed out that if many leagues are established in the same activity, there will usually be interest in play-offs between the league champions. The usual way to conduct these play-offs is to utilize an elimination type of tournament.

Challenge. There are many different styles of challenge tournaments, but the overriding identification pattern here is that the scheduling of matches or games is in the hands of the competitors. This type of tournament is used when:

1. It is possible to leave the competitive arrangements to the discretion of the players.
2. Little structure is needed by the competitors from the agency programmer.
3. The rules of the particular activity do not need special officials and can be handled by the competitors.

4. Facilities are generally available in time periods when drop-in play is possible.
5. Small groups of competitors are interested in tournament play.
6. Time is not a problem in terms of a quick tournament completion.

A challenge tournament requires each play to understand the tournament rules. Whether the shape of the tournament is a ladder, crowns, or pyramid, the responsibility for moving in the structure rests with those in the challenge positions.

The program tournament director is responsible for announcing the rules by which the competition is governed. These rules usually include who may challenge whom, how frequently a person or team may be challenged within a given time span, what the consequences are when a challenge is refused, the day and time when tournament play finishes and a champion will be declared, how many contests constitute a "match," and when the challenger has successfully defeated the opponent, what change occurs in the draw. As can be seen, the more work that is done before the announcement of the tournament for names, the better are the chances for a smooth tournament.

Because of all the individual arrangements that must be made in this competitive process, it has been used successfully with individual and dual activities. Recreation centers, resorts, camps, and the like find that this informal structure has drawn many into the competitive ranks who otherwise might not compete. The draw or challenge board should be placed in a spot that receives a good bit of exposure. If the competitors do not know each other, it may be appropriate to have some identifying process built into the system, such as tent number, phone, room number, or some similar sign. If permanent staff are available to coordinate these arrangements, this would be an extra bonus. In a unique fashion this type of tournament almost runs itself.

Scoring Events. Because of the scoring method of many activities, winners are established by various point totals. Either as the result of judges' scores or earning points in a target concept game, winners are ranked without every meeting another competitor face-to-face. There is no particular limitation on activities that utilize this type of competition. One-act play contests, timed racing events, bowling, riflery, archery, golf tournaments, and puppet show selection for ribbons are among those kinds of activities for which this type of tournament is well suited. It is used when:

1. There is a large number of entries.
2. It would be impossible for each entry to play every other entry in a one-to-one situation.
3. A score of some kind is available that can permit the ranking of scores in a single array from high to low.
4. Those competing may not be able to be in the same location at the same time for the competitive experience.
5. Judges are the determining factor regarding scoring or placement.

The objective scoring events require special organization and usually a lot of manpower, particularly in timed events such as track, swimming, skiing, and sailing. Finish-line timers, race course clerks, and general flunkies are needed to perform tasks that enhance the competitive experience. For instance, a swimming meet requires two to three timers for each lane being used; a turning judge at each lane, scorers, starter, clerk, and announcer, to say nothing of the diving judges if this becomes a part of the meet. Without too much hesitation one can imagine the manpower needed to run track-and-field and swimming competitions.

In those activity areas in which judges score the performance and the winner is determined by various scoring systems, the competition may be quite different. The judged art show with ribbons awarded is a popular activity as are horse shows, ski jumping, talent shows, gymnastics, and musical instrument or vocal competitions. In the aforementioned activities and, of course, many more, the feature of one judge or many judges evaluating a competitor's performance through an intricate system of scoring criteria is evident. Many people believe that this is the most difficult kind of competition. The participant is at the interpretive mercy of an expert evaluator. Judges, like officials and others who enforce rules and regulations, are usually available to perform these tasks. If they are not available, the programmer may find serious program limitations.

Straight scoring events, in which the participant is totally responsible for determining one's own score, are among some of the most popular activities in our society today. Target games, where there is no mistaking point differences, should include all the totally objective activities such as golf. Usually these activities rely on the integrity of the competitor, but many still require a review of "close calls" by an activity arbitrator or rules committee. Pole vaulting, skeet shooting, discus, foul shooting contests, an archery double American, and a horseshoe ringers contest all have this in common. You can objectively measure performance. Either a ringer was thrown or it was not thrown. A basket was made or missed. The results are quantifiable, and winners are quickly determined.

A helpful technique for the programmer is handicapping different skill levels of the players. The concept of handicapping is to have all players compete from an event start. For instance, the handicap system in golf attempts to put all players equal to par. If golfer A consistently scored par on the courses he or she played, the handicap for this person would be zero. If golfer B consistently shot a score of 85 on par 72 golf courses, this player would carry a handicap of 11, which indicates that if we subtracted 11 shots from B's score, he or she would be a par golfer like golfer A. (See USGA handicapping guide.) Thus when A and B play together, A must give B those 11 strokes and theoretically they are equal players for their round of golf. Many activities have a system for helping players of unequal ability play evenly with some handicap adjustment. All in all, it makes for keener competition, and forces the better players to work harder. No match is a pushover for the better player or team, and the chances for the poor players are enhanced.

This section has been devoted to making some suggestions to the programmer about how a spark and new focus might be given to some standard programs. We would be remiss if we did not note that each activity has its own fanatics who know exactly how the competition should be run, as well as modifications and wrinkles that would make it more interesting to the participant. Be glad you have the fanatics; they will save you endless hours and silly errors. Know they love the activity and want others to love it as well.

SUMMARY

If any program is to be successful the following elements must be coordinated: (1) selection of appropriate leadership, (2) program cost analysis, (3) scheduling time-table, (4) facility availability, (5) promoting the program and inviting the participant, and (6) special program tools. A recommended first step in this planning process is the drawing of a PERT chart.

The steps in leadership selection are as follows:

1. Identify what functions will be asked of the leader and at what skill level these tasks will be performed.
2. Describe the skills necessary to perform these functions.
3. Secure the person or persons with the talents needed to function well in the assigned tasks. A skill inventory of the agency's personnel should be available. The administrator may have to go outside the internal on-board staff to get someone with a special skill, or train someone to do the job required.
4. Contact potential leader and complete hiring arrangements.

The overall budget of an agency will have a part devoted to operational support of the recreation activity program, and the programmer is especially concerned with the cost analysis aspects of this budget. The programmer should know the ways his or her agency plans a budget. The most practical way is to cost out each individual program that the agency sponsors or plans to sponsor. Both direct and indirect costs are considered. Indirect costs can be distributed throughout the program budget, or fees can be used to cover direct costs only, and the indirect costs can be picked up elsewhere in the budget.

Once budget amounts have been determined, the program administrator should look at the efficiency and potential effectiveness of the program in order to take a performance approach to budgeting.

It is necessary for the programmer to know the calendar pattern of the constituency the agency serves. Scheduling can be thought of in three patterns: (1) seasonal, lending itself well to the class, clinic, and workshop format; (2) monthly or weekly, needing schedule time for maintenance and repair–special activites fall under this pattern, and; (3) daily time frame for activity, in which the program falls into morning, early afternoon, late afternoon, early evening, and late evening sessions.

Programmatic considerations about planning areas and facilities should include:

1. What level of quality do we need and can we afford?
2. How many multiple uses should a single facility be asked to carry?
3. Should facilities be clustered by like kind or decentralized into the various functional sections under the jurisdiction of a given agency?
4. Which facility development should be given priority?
5. As the population growth decreases and schools become vacant or up for public sale, should we renovate or make do, or is it wiser to build our own new facilities?

The answers to these questions require individual department deliberation and resolution.

How are we going to invite the participant? There are many traditional promotion techniques such as TV spots, radio ads, flyers, posters, and banners. Whatever style is chosen, the programmers must be aware of contemporary methods of reaching the public and promoting their product: ways such as the quick setup and display at the shopping mall, asking the postal service to promote your event on the stamp cancelling machine, promoting the program on the agencies' vehicles, installing an agency hot line, or the like.

Programs can be enhanced by attention to ways in which people are grouped for activity and not just relying on grouping by same age-group or by sex. Tournaments styles can be used wisely to vary the format in which the activity is conducted and get away from offering only the familiar elimination tournament. Other styles are the round robin, the challenge tournament, scoring events where judges are used, contests where scores are totaled and ranked, and handicap scoring.

BIBLIOGRAPHY

AAHPERD. (1979). *Planning facilities for athletics, physical education and recreation.* Washington, DC: AAHPERD.

Allen, K. K. (Spring 1983). *The future of volunteerism: Impetus for a strong foundation.* Journal of Volunteer Administration, 1:32-38.

Bannon, J. J. (1976). *Leisure resources: Its comprehensive planning.* Englewood Cliffs, NJ: Prentice-Hall, Inc.

Baxter, McDonald and Co. (October, 1968). *Budgeting for development as state park sites.* Berkeley, CA: Baxter, McDonald and Co.

Berger, P. J. and Berger, M. L. (ND). *Group training techniques.* New York, NY: John Wiley & Sons.

Bureau of Outdoor Recreation. (August 1969). *Compare.* Washington, DC: Department of the Interior.

Cheek, N.H. (1976). *The social organization of leisure in human society.* New York, NY: Harper & Row.

City of Palo Alto. (July 1974). *Service management system handbook, City of Palo Alto, CA.* Springfield, VA: National Technical Information Service, Distributors.

Cull, J. G. and Hardy, R. E. (1974). *Volunteerism: An emerging profession.* Springfield: Charles C. Thomas.

Curtis, J.E. (1979). *Recreation.* St. Louis, MO: Mosbey.

Edington, C. R., Compton, J. L, and Hanson, C. J. (1980). *Recreation and leisure programming.* Philadelphia, PA: Saunders College.

Flanagan, J. (1981). *The successful volunteer organization.* Chicago, IL: Contemporary Books, Inc.

Gerson, R.E. (1989). *Marketing Health/Fitness Services.* Human Kinetics Publishers, Inc. Champaign, IL.

Hayes, G. and McDaniels, C. (September 1980). The leisure pursuit of volunteering, *Recreation and Parks, 15*: 54-57.

Henderson, K. A. (September 1980). Programming volunteerism for happier volunteers, *Recreation and Parks, 15*: 54-57.

Henderson, K. A. (1981). Motivations and Perceptions of volunteerism as a leisure activity, *Journal of Leisure Research, 13*: 3: 208-218.

Henderson, K. A. (Spring, 1983). The motivation of men and women in volunteering, *Journal of Volunteer Administration, 1*: 20-24.

Howard, D. and Crompton, J. (1980). *Financing, Managing, and Marketing Recreation and Park Resources.* Dubuque, IA: William. C. Brown Co. Publishers.

Kotler, P. (1980). *Marketing Management.* Northwestern University. Prentice-Hall Inc. Englewood Cliffs, NJ.

Mantilla, J.A. and James, J.C. (1977). Importance-performance analysis. *Journal of Marketing* pp.77.

Moore, R. L., LaFarge, V., and Martorelli, T. (1987). *Organizing Outdoor Volunteers*. Boston, MA: Appalachian Mountain Club.

Morando, V. L. (Summer 1986). Local service delivery: Volunteers and recreation councils. *Journal of Volunteer Administration, 4*: 16-24.

National Park Service. (1981). *Marketing Parks and Recreation*, New Directions in Leisure, Venture Publishing, State College, PA.

Navaratnum, K. K. (Fall 1986). Volunteers training volunteers: A model for human service organizations. *Journal of Volunteer Administration. 4*: 19-25.

Naylor, H. H. (1967). *Volunteers today–Finding, training, and working with them.* New York, NY: Association Press.

O'Connell, B. (1976). *Effective leadership in voluntary organizations.* Chicago, IL: Association Press.

Rokosz, F. (May/June 1990). The wave--a new tournament structure. *Journal of Physical Education, Recreation and Dance, 61*:92-93.

Saxon, J. P. and Sawyer, H. W. (Summer 1984). A systematic approach for volunteer assignment and retention. *Journal of Volunteer Administration, 2*: 39-45.

Tedrick, T. and Henderson, K. (1989). *Volunteers in Leisure.* Reston, VA: AAHPERD.

Wilson, M. (1981). *The effective management of volunteer programs.* Boulder, CO: Volunteer Management Associates.

CHAPTER SIX

RECREATION PROGRAM AREAS

A brief overview was presented in Chapter One of the various ways in which recreation activity might be classified into discrete units. In this chapter, the functional program area classification system will be explored and elaborations of each area will be presented. To the pragmatic programmer, these functional areas provide a simple method of coding activity into a system well understood by the person. This system is also a practical guide to the professional programmer who wishes to measure balance and variety within a total agency program.

It is not our intent to list all the possible programs that could be offered to the potential participant in each of the following program area sections, but instead to present ideas, techniques, and matters of common understanding and practice surrounding these program areas. There are many books, pamphlets, guides, and periodicals available that handle the specific activities, and these are listed in the bibliography at the end of this chapter. There is no intent to present rules of games, words and tunes, steps to dances, or tips on how to be better skilled in any activity.

It is assumed that the leader has the expertise necessary to lead the skill in question. Our purpose is to present to the program administrator all the tools necessary to help him or her be as effective and efficient as possible in providing program services.

The optimum concept of program variety is displayed in Figure 6.1. on the following page. Each dimension, represented by format, life stage, and the functional program areas, includes the total category for each area.

We propose that the programmer can make a final check on whether or not the program is servicing all life-cycles in terms of format and activities offered by presenting a three-dimensional diagram of each activity in the program, and what life-cycle stage and format it can service. One can tell at a glance if all clients are included adequately in the scope of the total program. One must look into the third dimension to see the actual intersection of all three factors in a single block, but diagramming all the third dimension blocks would be impossible here because it would be too complex to be effective as an illustration. The evaluation cube illustrates a diagrammatic presentation of this concept.

For most program administrators, the activity goal is to meet the leisure needs of a particular constituency. It is easy to believe that these needs are being served if no complaints are heard. The continuing dilemma in the programmer's job is not knowing whether the activity needs are being met. We suggest that the cube in

Figure 6.1 gives programmers a head start in identifying areas of potential neglect. By mentally pulling out a random subcube–for example, drama, later middle age, educational workshop–the program administrator can test whether a need existed and has been filled or not, or whether there is no need for such an activity as a result of empirical data.

As each functional program area is discussed, you will find only selected examples of program ideas. This chapter is not designed to amplify each category an every activity. The critical step for the reader is to see an example in one section and realize its usefulness in another and apply it there. This style of learning translates into excellence in performance as a programmer.

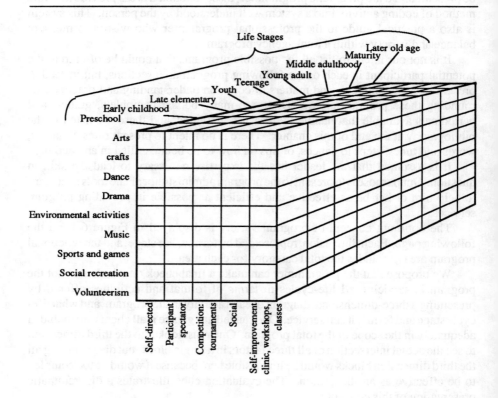

Figure 6.1 The Programmer's Evaluation Cube

ART

This program area encompasses all arts that serve solely the value of appreciation of the art form itself. Differentiation is made between the arts and the program area of crafts. *Crafts* are seen as those works that serve a functional purpose, while *art* encompasses those creations that are appreciated as objects d'art. We are all familiar with the popular term "arts and crafts," which usually connotes more craft activity than art for art's sake. This term will not be used in this coding system.

It is tempting to give an elitist flavor to art while suggesting that the craft area is rather plebian, thereby signifying lesser talent. Nothing could be further from the truth. The only reason for separating these two commonly joined areas is that the use to which art is put is quite different from the use of crafts objects.

With the advent of popular art festivals being held in many sections of the country, a distinction is being made between fine arts and crafts. Discussion could continue far into the evening regarding how the two differ. Rather than fall victim to this everlasting argument, we will leave the quarrels to others and take the authors' privilege of doing it our way. Thus, for the purpose of amplification, we will separate them in the way designated.

Although there are some who may disagree with the separation of these areas, it is of little consequence to the program planner outside of a theoretical mode. However, one of the continuing criticisms leveled at recreation agencies is relative to this point. The field is accused often of not providing an in-depth, intermediate or advanced skill level experience in programming. Art programs have invested heavily in activities and projects that can be easily handled and quickly completed. In service to those participants with needs for immediate gratification (and perhaps limited storage areas), arts and crafts programs have been designed to accommodate the 15 to 25 minute project, or other "quickie" programs. All too often, art programs have suffered in deference to a good craft program.

Scope of the Art Program Area

As we review the breadth of what is generally considered to be the visual art program area, the following categories appear to be the most discrete:

1. Graphics
2. Painting
3. Photography
4. Printing
5. Sketching
6. Sculpture/welding

Each of the above categories has subcategory variety. For instance, in the printing activities, included would be linoleum block printing, lithography, silk screening, stenciling, or the use of any carved object that utilizes any "inking" substance in order for a print to be made.

The painting group includes all of the traditional materials such as oil, watercolors, pastels, finger paint mixes, acrylics, and other new products appearing on the market. In the following section each category within the art program area is displayed. These lists are not meant to be all-inclusive, but instead a definition and refinement of the specific category.

A. Clustering of Grouping of Activities

1. Graphics
   - (a) Poster design, murals, cards, etc.
   - (b) Paper models
   - (c) Flags, banners
2. Painting
   - (a) Oil—on wood, canvas, other fabric
   - (b) Watercolor
   - (c) Gouache
   - (d) Acrylic
   - (e) Finger paint mixes
3. Photography
   - (a) Still, black and white, color
   - (b) Motion (8 mm, 16 mm, 35mm)
   - (d) Video tape
4. Printing
   - (a) Woodcarving blocks
   - (b) Linoleum blocks
   - (c) Silk screening
   - (d) Stencils
   - (e) Other miscellaneous materials
5. Sketching
   - (a) Pencil
   - (b) Etching on metals and scrimshaw
   - (c) Charcoal
   - (d) Pastel
6. Sculpture/welding
   - (a) Wood: walnut, oak, driftwood, etc
   - (b) Stone
   - (c) Clay
   - (d) Sand
   - (e) Metal
   - (f) Plastic
   - (g) Glass

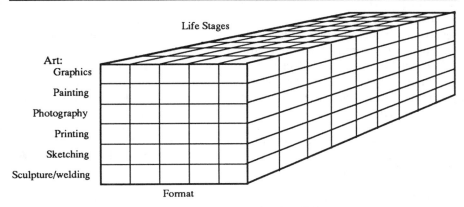

Figure 6.2 Art Evaluation Cube

B. Current Practices and Trends

Just as all art experiences renaissance, visual art has also become a part of this growth. Art has always been a high-cost program and, as people have extra discretionary income, there is growing interest in this area. Not only has the growth taken place in the number of participants who sketch or paint, but also growth among the art spectator participants and collectors whose interest has grown as well as the number of art museums in existence for many years.

Perhaps the significant trend to notice in art programs in recreation agencies has been the discovery that without top-rate, quality leaders in this area, the programs have had limited success. There is simply no substitute for the art leader who is secure in personal skills and confidence. In addition, there has been a high increase in certain types of art. Mural painting, either with or without a message statement, has been popular in some of our larger cities. Sculpture has been the popular activity in other areas–both metal and wood. Metal welding has been one of the newer entries in the summer art festivals in the past few years. Graphics work is perhaps the newest entry on the scene in recreation programming. The category is not new, but it is a new area to many agencies.

C. Patterns of Organization

Art activity is evident in every realm of American life. Ethnic art to pop art fills our everyday lives. Both professional and amateur artists abound in our society. Familiar patterns in our recreation agencies generally focus on the educational experience. Oil painting and watercolor classes tend to be the most popular. It is not unusual to find in any given area of the country many fine teachers for these activity classes. Art tends to be a "faddish" media. The past decade has seen op art, body painting, clown faces, painting on wood and antiquing, and painting and murals with a public statement. Art therapy has had some success as a healing tool. The recreation field has not been skillful in facilitating a broad range of programming in art. The costs associated with art activities are high. This could be reason enough for art activity receiving minimal attention in the overall program. There is a suspicion that art is not an area usually approached with confidence by recreation professionals and, as a result, is a difficult area in which to be enthusiastic and creative.

In the last ten years of tight dollars and limited budgets for recreation services, programmers have had to seek outside funding to enhance programs in art. Utilization of arts councils for advice and direction will also be a necessity.

D. Art Program Samples of Organization for Each Structure Format

For each of the different format structures an example is presented in this section. Art lends itself conveniently to each of these forms.

1. Self-Improvement Format—Silk Screening Set of Three Clinics. This program is designed to provide a learning opportunity for anyone who wishes to explore the silk screen process. An emphasis is placed on needed material, printing processes, and uses. It is expected that participants will have art work and designs in mind or ready to use at the beginning of the second clinic. The program administrator may find instructors from many different persons employed specifically for these clinics. A registration sign-up should be held for this series, which could be successfully planned for October or November, Saturday mornings from 9:00 a.m. to noon. The pattern for implementing this program might look like the following.

Instructor:	A former printer, a member of the retired person's club. He or she will handle all three clinics for $75.
Facility:	General craft room in the Y with work tables, hammers, screw drivers, etc.; running water and basin section of room able to be darkened.
Class size:	Twenty-five to thirty people—no age limitation.
Participant fees:	Twelve dollars ($12) per person.
Unit:	Three consecutive Saturday mornings.
Registration:	At the Y, one month prior to first clinic.
Publicity:	The fall activities brochure will carry the announcement of these clinics. A special silk screened poster will also be used to promote this activity.
Materials:	Wood for precut frames, as well as brackets, will be available for purchase. Other material will be provided free of charge. Participants will be responsible for photography costs.

2. Social Format–Oil Painting League of Artists. The league is the oldest art group in the county. They are quite active in promoting young peoples' art and have a major art competition every spring that features cash prizes and ribbons to the winners. The league meets in the county art center building and has use of the facility with minimal cost ($500/year) to the league. They have locker storage there for members. The county recreation department has a minor role with this group, which is little else than keeping in touch with their activities. A member of the league serves as a representative to the county program committee for the annual festival for the visual and performing arts, and contributes information for the recreation department's arts calendar. In return, the league members are called upon to judge art contests, give demonstrations, and occasionally provide exhibits for various department sponsored activities and projects.

Membership: Anyone may join who is over the age of 18 years.

Dues: Twenty-five dollars ($25) per year.

Meetings: Business meetings once a month. Regular meetings every Monday from 8:00 to 10:30 p.m. Club meets September through April. Program includes lessons, fall foliage trip, shows, special sessions by visiting local artists, and so on.

Officers: Elected annually as per the constitution and bylaws. Club president is official liaison person with the recreation department.

Club entry: Membership is open at all times for new member, yet fall is the time when publicity for new members is heaviest.

3. Competition Format–Black and White Photography Show. In this format, the programmer has a full role in either executing or facilitating the management and organization of this competition. Determining the rules of the contest with the coordinating committee, accepting entries, arranging for the contest location, judges, and awards are but a few of the programmer's tasks. Age groups should be established for this type of competition, and all work from a single grouping should probably be clustered in the same area of the contest display. It is important that the display be in an area in which the spectator-participant can easily gain access and security can be maintained.

Entry fee: None.

Entry requirement: All entries will be screened by jury. The top 50 entries will be exhibited.

Registration: All entries must be submitted two weeks prior to the show for initial jury screening.

Type of contest: Total award scores of five judges who rate each entry on a 0 to 100 mark; thus, this is a scoring type of tournament.

Location: One of the malls in the large shopping center.

Awards: Ribbons will be awarded to first, second, third, and honorable mention in each age group.

Publicity: Announcement of entry requirements and registration will be made in the papers, on radio, and through a display in major food stores of pictures of last year's winners. Pictures and names of all winners will appear in the newspaper media after the judging is completed.

4. Participant Spectator Format–Giant Sketch Board. This activity, and others like it, requires organizational skills of the program administrator. A midtown block of old buildings has been razed, and the construction company has surrounded this site with solid plywood fencing that has been whitewashed. The city recreation department has received permission to use the wall for a giant sketch board. Patches of varying size from two foot squares to ten by six foot rectangles are sectioned off and numbered. Artists from throughout the city apply for a patch and present their sketches. Rules must be drawn. If interest exceeds available patches, two different rounds could be planned.

Facility: Construction site walls.

Registration: For all ages with no charge. Two weeks prior to sketch day, application should be submitted for patch size.

Materials: Charcoal supplied by recreation department; all other material is the responsibility of the artist. All final sketches are sprayed with fixative.

Publicity: Local radio/TV station is cooperating with this program and is giving free promotion to it. Their on-site van broadcasts from the construction site location and interviews artists while they work.

Personnel: Recreation department staff member will be on site to assist all artists in finding their patches. Ladders and stools will be available while they last.

5. Self-Directed–Artist Areas in Parks. As a part of the design, special areas have been designated and designed for painters, photographers, or sketchers. These are special areas off the regular path where particularly pleasant vistas may exist. Vistas have been cut on the higher ledges, and low brush is kept trimmed so that lake views are possible. Low work tables are provided and secured, and sturdy benches placed in the areas. The park signing system identifies these locations and hopes that picnickers will avoid these places. Painters are welcome in any areas of the park, while these special spots are designated use areas. The artist is free then to use these areas whenever the park is open to the public.

If good planning design has preceded the cutting and development of these areas, sunrises and sunsets that may be of interest to photographers are possible; vistas with interesting forms are cut, as well as spots for close detail work. The park design team should have worked with some local artists in the design of these areas.

In terms of the program area of art, the program administrator needs to evaluate, among other aspects of the activity, whether or not program balance and variety exist within this area. Following the macromodel of the evaluation cube, art, as a single program area, might be placed under a similar test as displayed in the micromodel in Figure 6.2, p. 175.

CRAFTS

As you have noted, in the previous section we discussed the companion area usually associated with crafts, that of art. A firm distinction has been made between these two areas, assigning the form and aesthetic notion to art while assigning functionalism to the crafts area. In this section the wide variety that is present in the crafts area will be covered. Crafts hold a popular spot in most agency programs and usually stand in second place only to sports in almost every recreation program.

One of the reasons that a crafts program can find a comfortable home in many agency programs is because some craft projects can be simple to do, take very little time to complete, and are often inexpensive. With some minimal staff training, most leaders can carry through with a basic craft program idea. As long a someone else selects and plans the program, amateurs can be prepared to carry the program forward. This is often a satisfactory arrangement for young children's programs, but is not satisfactory once children become skilled craftspersons.

At the point where crafts become specialized into a single media, the costs take a quantum leap. In order to provide a well-rounded crafts program, the recreation agency must be prepared to provide high-cost equipment, such as looms, kilns, hand tools, and much more. An agency moves slowly into a full-range program, if at all. Equipment and quality leadership are costly. It is not surprising that crafts programs are mostly elementary in terms of target group sophistication, while homemaking and remodeling (do-it-yourself) types of activities are provided for adults. In this section, those craft activities for which some function is seen are discussed. For example, if a class is held for hooking rugs, it is assumed that the rug will be used as a rug and not as a wall hanging. Although the latter is certainly possible as an end result for the rug, the general purpose toward which the experience is focused is that of use and function.

A. Clustering or Grouping of the Activities

Perhaps the best way to observe the various categories within this area is to arrange a system by a combination of processes and materials. The following classification system is presented in this pattern.

1. Ceramics
2. Homemaking
3. Home repair
4. Jewelry
5. Leathercraft
6. Paper
7. Weaving
8. Woodworking

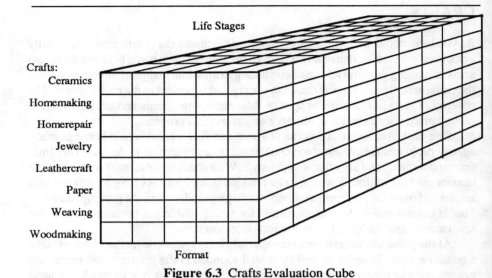

Figure 6.3 Crafts Evaluation Cube

There is a constant turnover concerning what is new and popular among the crafts. We have formerly seen macrame reach the pinnacle of popularity and, although it is still popular, there seems to be less interest in it. Indoor green plants then became the rage in homes and offices. Perhaps this was the result of the macrame and all of the pot slings that were made! At the time of this writing, cross-stitching and woodworking seem to be rising in popularity. Each of the above eight categories can be expanded by noting subgroups or activities within each of the major groups. Although these appear to overlap, they represent a general view of what is an extremely large area of programming:

1. Ceramics
   (a) Pottery
   (b) Mosaics
   (c) Plaster of Paris
2. Homemaking
   (a) Needlepoint, crewel
   (b) Sewing and millinary
   (c) Candlemaking
   (d) Quilting
   (e) Canning, cooking, baking
   (f) Gourmet cooking
3. Home design and repair
   (a) Furniture and carpentry
   (b) Electricity, heat, water, paint
   (d) Lawn and garden

4. Jewelry
   (a) Copper, silver, gold
   (b) Baubles, bangles, beads
   (c) Shells, stones, etc.
5. Leathercraft
6. Paper
   (a) Papier-mâché
   (b) Collage
   (c) Airplanes, kites, origami
7. Weaving
   (a) Card, loom
   (b) Macrame
   (c) Hooking, braiding, knitting
8. Woodworking

B. Current Practices and Trends

As we mentioned briefly, the crafts area is most susceptible to fads. One year it is beads; the next year macrame; another year paper dresses; who knows what will be next! The past years of this decade have seen the growth of the folk crafts. The *Foxfire* series brought forward some of the almost forgotten skills of those who used to be the craftspeople prior to mass production. If a single trend appears on the horizon, it is that of doing the craft project in the old way, perhaps with the old tools.

The do-it-yourself trend is still an important part of spending discretionary time, and one suspects that craft work will undoubtedly move in this same direction. The kit, the prepackaged job in which one is required only to follow directions (this is said with tongue-in-cheek) for quick completion, has left the participant with an end product but often still hungering for that creative experience. No longer is it pride in the fact of having done it oneself, but instead the feeling of designing and creating the job by oneself that brings true satisfaction.

A large percentage of people are quite content to do craft work that is prepackaged. Although there is a desire to diminish this emphasis, there must be an opportunity in the program for choices. If the program in crafts is weighted in either direction, this is probably a mistake.

The crafts area is a popular one. Interest abounds at all skill levels. What often begins as an avocation turns into a well-paying and enjoyable vocation. Few, however, reach the stage in their own abilities where they can continue to work in a craft area without assistance from a leader or someplace where special equipment is available.

C. Patterns of Organization

The most popular format used in crafts is the clinic or workshop. Adult classes are a popular program offering. Some agencies are unable to offer enough classes in ceramics and jewelry! The other organizational patterns of format share an equal position way down in second place. There is occasionally activity in competition; a club or two may form, but generally learning how to do a craft and perfect it is the main pattern for most agencies.

D. Sample Organization for Each Format

1. Self-Improvement Class–Advanced Pottery and Glazes. This activity would be open to those who have already proven that they can handle the basic pottery skills. The class will focus on mixed glazes and work toward unique glazing effects.

Instructor:	The person handling this class is a chemist for a local industrial plant whose hobby is ceramics. She has agreed to teach this class for $250.
Registration:	This class is one part of the Fall Leisure Series of the Township Park and Recreation program. Registration is limited to 15 people on a first come, first served basis. Registration will be held at the senior high school.
Fees:	Twenty-five dollars ($25) per person for township residents, $35 per person living outside the area. Any age welcome.
Class:	This activity class will meet in the high school art room every Wednesday for seven weeks. Participants will be responsible for their own materials, but firing can be in the kiln owned by the school district with no further charge to the class registrant.

2. Competition–Whittling Show. At the end of each camping period, each camper may enter his best piece for the show, but only one piece per camper may be entered.

Fees:	None.
Registration:	Informal. The craft pieces must be turned into the craft counselor the day before the judging, at the latest.
Awards:	Two judges review the whittling projects and award ribbons to the top six winners in each category, which include animals, chains, figures, and miscellaneous.

3. Social–The Jeweler's Guild. This activity is sponsored by the local YWCA and has emerged with an eye toward quality control. In order to obtain membership into the guild, one has to present jewelry to a jury of guild members, and then is either invited to join or present work for further review. The guild member is able to display the guild insignia on one's work and place pieces for sale in a guild display case in the local gift shop.

Personnel:	The club has strong leadership internally and has little need for the recreation staff of the YWCA to be very involved.
Fees:	Dues are $25 per year for each member.

| *Meetings:* | The guild meets the first and third Tuesday of every month in the Y craft room. Since members have their own equipment, they ask little of the Y except for the use of the room. |
| *Publicity:* | Mostly the guild becomes known through its sales areas and from calling cards distributed by the members. The YWCA always promotes the group in its seasonal brochures to the membership. |

4. Participant Spectator Activity–Sidewalk Craft Fair. A mall or a special section of sidewalk that can be closed off without curtailing business is secured for this type of event. Craftspersons are assigned a certain amount of footage on the sidewalk, and they are responsible for setting up their booth and operating their own sales. This kind of event takes an enormous amount of organizational and planning work yet, by the time the event is happening, the programmer ought to be free to enjoy the show. The main purpose of the fair is to provide the craftspeople with an opportunity to display and sell their work.

Fees:	Each booth entry space is set at $25. A participant can purchase no more than two spaces.
Location:	Once the stretch of sidewalk (or parking lot) is determined, matching the entries with their designated spots is done by drawing numbers out of a hat.
Publicity:	Vigorous promotion work has been done by the media and the Chamber of Commerce. Not only do the craftspeople enjoy sales but also additional business is brought into the fair area.
Registration:	Applications are made to the recreation department. A craftsperson must designate what will be featured in the booth and return the application by a date at least two months in advance of the fair dates with entry fee. Rules and regulations are then mailed to each entrant.

5. Self-Directed-Craft Room. Because of the equipment needs for most craft projects, it is not the usual pattern for the crafts area to have open facilities that one uses at anytime. Usually there is some kind of supervision. As people become trusted in the facility it is easier to permit a room to be used without staff being there. This is a slow process at times, but the crafts center staff quickly learn new faces, and these people in turn learn how the center operates. Staff need to make this learning process happen.

E. Special Facility Needs

Perhaps there is no area, other than sports, where special facilities are more often needed, and which in turn facilitate its experience, than the crafts areas. A building either totally devoted to craft activity or permanent rooms in existing center facilities is desirable.

The building or room(s) can be in less than spotless shape, and usually the craft area can be placed in an older facility and not be a harmful environment for the participant. An old store, remodeled building basement, or an abandoned garage can be adequately renovated to serve the craft activity program. The participant in a crafts activity is often more comfortable in a "used" environment rather than sterile, shiny accommodations. One should not interpret this environment as a messy one, but instead as a place where pounding, sanding, painting, and spilling would be acceptable activities.

Areas with tables, easels, storage closets, baskets or lockers, running hot and cold water, heating equipment, and basic supplies would be necessary to enhance a good crafts program. For those who are familiar with crafts programming, it is a well-established fact that storage room and space is crucial. Many crafts programs work heavily with scrap materials. Local industry is frequently seeking an inexpensive way to dispose of their scrapage. For example, a cork producing company or a tannery may sweep away end cuttings. The alert crafts director will make arrangements for pickup and storage of such material at the center, not only for these materials but also for anything else the programmer can scavenge.

In order to look critically at variety and balance in the crafts area, the programmer could place the crafts categories in the program spot on the evaluation cube displayed in Figure 6.3, p. 180.

DANCE

The program area in which dance movement activity is the focus is one of great variety and depth. Program planners will find a wealth of opportunity in it to provide a wide range of experiences to their clientele. From activity of a general, basic skill level engaged in largely for personal enjoyment, to refined, intricate, and specific activities demanding high skill-level expertise, to one presented in show form for the enjoyment of others as well, the dance area is rich in potential for meeting a variety of participant needs and interests. People dance in order to perform, to exercise, to meet others, and to learn new skills. It is a fertile ground for programming.

A. **Clustering or Grouping of Activities**
   1. Ballet
      (a) Classical
      (b) Modern
   2. Children's rhythms
   3. Contemporary or modern dance
   4. Country and round dance
   5. Folk dance
      (a) Ethnic dances: Israeli, Balkan, Irish, Scottish, etc.
      (b) Square dancing

6. Popular or current dance
7. Precision movement skills
8. Show dance or modern jazz
9. Social dance and chorus line
10. Tap dance
11. Concomitant activities
    (a) Choreographing
    (b) Costuming, makeup
    (c) Directing

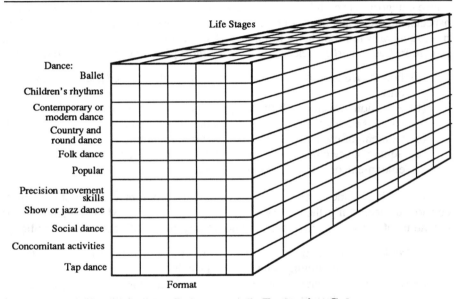

Figure 6.4 The Programmer's Evaluation Cube

B. Current Practice and Trends

The most popular activity design through which participants engage in dance activities within a recreation setting is in the self-improvement format. Ballet classes, modern dance workshops, square dance, or social dance lessons are all standard programs in many recreation agencies. As has been noted throughout this book, leadership is the critical ingredient in this process. The programmer who decides that just anyone can teach dance is doing a disservice to both the participants and the agency program. Attention to quality leadership is the key to good program interest in dance. It is the responsibility of the program administrator to secure top talent (professional or volunteer) to work in these programs.

C. Patterns of Organizations

Typical dance programs through the high school years are generally established on an age-group basis, and the type of organization may be classes, social dances, or shows. After the high school years there appears to be little reason to establish programs on any age-group criteria. Dance provides a life enriching factor where, in fact, there are many age groups within a single dance activity.

D. Sample Organization for Each Format

1. Social Format–Dance Group. Although the clinic and workshop format for dance is most popular, it is not unusual to find interest in clubs forcing around a specific dance category. The club itself may give some time and attention to educational aspects, but this is not the only option served by it. Some clubs organize in a way that dance generally is an end in itself. Other clubs meet to prepare for concerts, festivals, or demonstration performances. Perhaps the most popular dance club groups are:

(a) Folk dance groups. Both general in scope and for specific ethnic dances only.
(b) Precision movement skills groups. Main purpose is to perform in parades as marching units, give demonstrations, etc.
(c) Contemporary dance clubs. Usually program oriented.
(d) Square dance clubs. Weekly or monthly dances for member enjoyment, only occasional performances.

In offering a dance group within a program, the program administrator needs to consider the leadership, the facility, cost, age-groups to be served, accompaniment or not, hours of scheduling, final performance arrangements (if needed), and publicity.

Example:	Contemporary Dance Club–A club for serious dancers in the community who enjoy high culture.
Leadership:	Volunteer. The assistant dance instructor at the nearby university who wants experience in organizing and running a dance club and is interested in keeping her own skills sharpened. Accompanist is a local music major graduate living in the town and paid $10 an hour.
Facility:	A room at least 60 by 90 feet. For special facility considerations, see format 5, Specific Facility Needs, p. 189.
Membership:	Open to men and women of high school age and above.
Fee:	To cover the cost of the pianist and reproduction costs, $10 per person per year.
Hours:	Every Tuesday evening from 7:00 to 9:00 PM form October 1 to May 1 (with a break Christmas week). Extra times will be needed prior to scheduled performances and extra club activities.

Registration:	9:00 AM to 5:00 PM daily at the recreation center the last two weeks in September and at the first meeting of the club.
Publicity:	Posters will be placed in the shopping centers and flyers posted in drug stores; publishing of department's and other agencies' programs should appear in the local newspapers. Club members from the previous year who are still in the area are notified. Short demonstration performances are given on Saturdays in September at the shopping mall.

2. Self-Improvement–Folk Dance Classes. In this format, the emphasis is on learning skills; participants who were in the classes one year often join the folk dance club the next. The instructor is a member of the permanent recreation staff and draws on the club members to come as visitors to the class to teach a favorite dance or two. The focus is on folk dances in general, representing many countries. The format is strictly a learning one, and no performance is planned. In offering this program, the department considers the size of each class, when and where it can be offered, equipment needed, whether or not fees are to be charged, registration, and publicity.

Instructor:	Salaried, full-time recreation department employee.
Facility:	The recreation center gymnasium, 6:30 to 8:30 PM, Wednesday evenings in the fall. (Demand on the gym is lower in the fall and dance is not seasonal.)
Fee:	Five dollars ($5) per season.
Membership:	Limited to 100 people, preferably evenly divided between the sexes. Must be high school (10th grade) and above.
Registration:	From 6:00 to 8:30 PM the day of the first class.
Equipment:	Record player, sound system, and records (department budgets regularly for record replacement and augmenting the present collection).
Publicity:	Notices through the schools, as well as regular channels of the newspaper, and posters in the shopping centers are covered. Flyers are sent to the folk dance club members so that they can tell their friends who might want to learn to dance. The Welcome Wagon visitors promote these classes so that the information will reach the new couples in town.

3. Competition Format–Dance Contest. The primary purpose of this type of a contest is to produce better quality dancing. Judging and awards should be made with this in mind. The contest may be conducted in an informal manner, with plenty of time given between announcement of the event and the actual contest, or they may be even more formally conducted with tryouts required and contestants usually selected by a group of judges. The programmer must decide which of these formats to use, select judges, establish clear contest rules, decide whether to solicit cosponsorship from civic or business groups to finance the awards, whether to charge an entry fee, what age-groups to open it to, and what dance steps to include in the contest (the formal waltz, tango, etc.), as well as other things, considered for any program, such as publicity.

Leadership:	Assigned to an agency, full-time employee, salaried. Three judges: the part-time social dance teacher, the local Arthur Murray Studio instructor, and the high school physical education teacher.
Facility:	The recreation center gymnasium from 7:00 to 11:00 PM, Friday night, and Saturday afternoon from 1:00 to 4:00 PM, with awards given at 4:00 PM. Conducted in late March or after the basketball season is over.
Fee:	One dollar ($1) per entrant couple. Spectators are charged $.50 each.
Eligibility:	Open to anyone. Contestants must enter as couples.
Equipment:	Record player and sound system. Records available or contestants may bring their own. Tape cassette available as well.
Registration:	One hour prior to start of the contest in the lobby of the gymnasium; members of the folk dance club will collect entries and run the registration table.
Publicity:	This will be handled by the recreation department through its regular channels, and by the cosponsor through its publicity media.
Trophies:	There will be trophies for the first three places for each dance step judged.

4. Participant Spectator-Square Dance Roundup. In this event clubs from the state are invited to attend for an evening of square dancing and barbeque; demonstrations will be given, and new dances will be taught. A door prize will be awarded along with prizes for the best dressed set. The programmer will need to plan for a caller and a facility that will accommodate both the dances and the barbeque, decide on charges, hire cooks, get an organization to help, choose the demonstrators, buy prizes, choose judges to select the best dressed winner, print and sell tickets, and arrange for publicity.

Leadership:	The recreation department will provide a regular staff to act between the agency and the local folk and square dance club who are the organizers of the event. The club dance committee will decide on the demonstrations needed and invite groups performing at least three months ahead of the event. A caller will be hired from the state Honor Your Partner Caller's Association along with an orchestra (three-piece) for $225, total costs.
Barbeque:	A local caterer will be contracted to provide the barbeque. He/she supplies all food, serving tables, warming utensils, serving utensils, etc.

Facility:	Arrangement will be made with the local high school to use the gymnasium there, which is bigger than the recreation center's largest room and also has bleachers for spectators and resting dancers. The gym opens out into a grassy courtyard to accommodate the barbeque. Permission to use the cafeteria is assured in case of rain.
Participants:	Limited by ability to pay the fee and the requirement that people must come as a set.
Fee:	Six dollars ($6) per person (includes the barbeque).
Tickets:	Sold on order through the mail by clubs throughout the state; also from the home club and at the recreation center daily. No tickets will be sold at the door, since the meal must be guaranteed. Tickets are numbered to facilitate drawing for a door prize.
Publicity:	Publicized through the folk dance club and its branch organizations. Local publicity might invite spectators in order to enhance interest in the area in square dancing.

5. Specific Facility Needs. In planning for a dance facility, there is, of course, considerable variety depending on what type of dance is to be held. Things that are important for modern dance or ballet may not matter for folk or social dance. In any case, the following characteristics should be considered:

(a) Adequate floor space to accommodate locomotor movements of the group.
(b) For modern dance and ballet, mirrors, at least along one wall from one end to the other. Barres are helpful to the ballet dancers.
(c) Sound system capability.
(d) If performances are to be given, there should be:
   (1) Control over the lighting systems, so that they can be in full force or at a minimal level.
   (2) Control at entrances for ticket taking.
   (3) Accommodation of an audience.
   (4) A stage area set at one end that can be curtained off appropriately.
(e) A resilient floor, preferable for all dance, but a must for modern and ballet.

Since other program areas have been submitted to the evaluation cube test for balance and diversity, so too, can dance be placed on the same dimension (see Figure 6.4, p. 185).

DRAMA

Whether the name is theatre arts, drama, or stage and screen, the activity has a single flavor that is the exploration of portraying someone else, something else, becoming a pure fantasy world. This area is distinguished by its wide variety of activity experiences in a finely focused perspective. The central theme is performance on the part

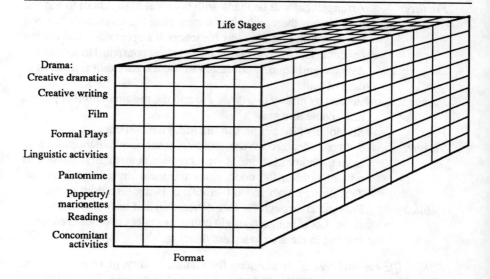

Figure 6.5 Drama Evaluation Cube

of one type of participant; assistance and support on the part of another type of participant; and appreciation on the part of a third type of participant, the spectator. Perhaps it is the wide variety of participatory roles that makes dramatics the popular activity it has been and continues to be today.

Scope of the Area

This area does not lend itself to clear categories, but an attempt will be made to display the area's breadth, knowing that some overlap will exist:

1. Creative dramatics
2. Creative writing
3. Film and video tape
4. Formal plays
5. Linguistic activities
6. Pantomime and clown activities
7. Puppetry/marionettes
8. Readings
9. Concomitant activities

As we take a closer look at the performing arts areas, we see the existence of all the mixes and support skills needed to back up the main theme of drama. These activities are called concomitant activities. These functions are simply a different way to participate in drama activity other than as the traditional, out-front actor. Drama activities must have a fair share of out-front and backstage participants. One role is no more important than the other; it is a matter of the roles being different.

Each of the above major categories has its own subcategories. The following list is not meant to be conclusive, but it may well be a start for any programmer to plan depth into the drama experience.

A. **Clustering or Grouping of Activities**
  1. Creative dramatics
     (a) Improvisation theatre
     (b) Creative play
  2. Creative writing
     (a) Poetry
     (b) Short story
     (c) Fiction, science fiction
     (d) Limerick writing
     (e) Script writing
  3. Films
     (a) 8 mm, 16 mm, 35 mm
     (b) Betamax or VCR tape
     (c) Review and critique
  4. Formal plays
     (a) One and three acts
     (b) Musicals
     (c) Children's theatre
     (d) Mobile street theatre
     (e) Theatre-in-the-round
     (f) Shadow plays
  5. Linguistic activities
     (a) Debate society
     (b) Toastmaster/toastmistress
     (c) Choral speaking
     (d) Story telling
     (e) Monologues
  6. Pantomime and clown activities
     (a) Face painting
     (b) Juggling
     (c) Magic tricks
  7. Puppetry/marionettes
     (a) Punch and Judy
     (b) Puppet therapy
  8. Readings
     (a) Book reviews

(b) Play reading groups
(c) Great books program
9. Concomitant activity
  (a) Costume design and completion
  (b) Makeup
  (c) Stagecrafts–lighting, set design, and construction
  (d) Direction
  (e) Production–props management

B. Current Practices and Trends

As discussed with the program area, art, there also seems to be a renewed interest in dramatics in general. Whether this means that many better works are available, or that there is an interest in rerunning so many of the great plays of past decades, is for the student to decide. When summer stock companies and arts festivals in general are announcing seasons that "bring back the great hits of the 1940s and 1950s," it is tempting to believe that audiences are more willing to see the more comfortable material of those years instead of the difficult contemporary works of today. Traditionally, the spectator public is well behind the artist in being ready to accept the new. The 1960s saw exciting growth in drama with a message, whether it was street theatre, puppetry, or debate topics. The 1970s saw a modifying trend to more relaxed themes and certainly more humor than was apparent in the 1960s; while the 1980s were characterized by more violence and more open displays of sexual activity. Television has had an enormous impact on the exposure of the public to making home videos, use of puppets, which has had a positive result in many recreation agency programs.

Drama traditionally has been one of the program areas in which the professional recreation programmer has not been highly skilled. The college graduate may have had one course in dramatics as an introduction to this entire field of activity. Any further exposure had to be on one's own. Unfortunately for most, there was little to nothing beyond the single class. As a result, attempts to work drama into the overall agency program were either totally voided or minimally tried. Large agencies were able to employ drama specialists but the small departments had to use the generalist in hopes that skills were available in this area. As a result, most recreation programs have not provided many activity experiences in this program area.

C. Patterns of Organization

Two patterns have emerged as the most popular form in which to serve the drama interests of the constituency. Classes or other educational experiences and drama clubs seem to be found most often in recreation agencies.

Classes have been most successful with children in the area of creative dramatics and puppetry. One trend is that classes are continuing well into the junior and senior high school years. Under strong leadership, this type of interest should not be unexpected. There has been difficulty in most school systems to include drama in any form other than in speech classes or the traditional thespian-type, extracurricular activities. As a result, drama activity has been exposed only to a small percent of our population, unless one is a spectator.

Club structure, perhaps because of the usual high school model, has been by far the most popular avenue for dramatic participation. Indigenous leadership has emerged, and drama groups have had various levels of continued success. It is to this type of group that an affiliation invitation by a recreation agency can be most helpful both for the drama club and the group's program offerings. Drama or theatre groups have generally been resourceful in finding and modifying facilities for their use. Old barns, abandoned schools or armories, or vacant stores have been popular in serving drama clubs. In affiliating the club with the recreation agency, there may not have to be this expense of modifying another facility, and the stage or gymnasium of a recreation center could be used for drama activity.

If a drama interest club is free of many facility problems, the usual pattern for the club is to branch out and work with junior groups, acting competitions, puppet interest groups, to mention a few of the typical patterns. If the recreation department encourages the drama groups to branch out with other interest groups, the benefits will be far reaching and beyond those possible if the group remains a separate entity.

D. Samples of Organization for Each Structure Format

The five examples mentioned in this section are only a taste of what might be possible for a recreation agency to organize in its drama activity program. A professional dramatics artist on staff would be limited only by his or her imagination and enthusiasm. The nonprofessional drama person should seek advice and counsel from available resources.

1. Self-Improvement Format–Film Making Class. This activity is designed to explore film making techniques and teach the participant to judge between a good film and poor film presentation. Sponsored by the Jewish Community Center (JCC).

Instructor:	The instructor has been secured from the local vocational-technical school and has agreed to teach a seven-week class for $300.
Participant fee:	Forty dollars ($40) per person (includes developing costs).
Class limit:	Twenty (20) people must sign up to hold class; no more than 25 may register.
Time and location:	Class will be held at the vocational-technical school Wednesday evening from 7:30 to 9:30 PM for seven Wednesdays in March and April.
Registration:	First come, first served. Fees are payable in advance. Applications are available at the JCC information desk and fees can be paid there in person or by mail. Open to members only.
Other costs:	Class members will be required to purchase their own film from the instructor but developing film and use of splicing tools and all other equipment will be provided free for all participants.

2. Social-Centre Circle Theatre. This is one special interest club operating under the overall program of the college student union. A theatre group has formed to become a totally student-run organization. There is a link with the college's drama department, yet this group is totally supported by the student union program as one of many such clubs. The Centre Circle Theatre presents four productions during the school year in the student union ballroom. All plays are performed in the round and require minimal scenery and lighting. Of necessity, these are low-budget productions, and it is not unusual to perform works written by the students themselves.

Leadership: Internal and among the members of the club. The union's program director works as official advisor to the group and assists with administrative matters of budget and policy.

Membership: Membership is open to any student who is matriculating at the college. Dues are $5 per year.

Program: The shows committee selects the plays to be given for the year and sets the calendar. Directors and producers are assigned (after reviewing applications) and the schedule for auditions is determined. No member may act in more than two plays and must work "backstage" in at least one.

Meetings: In September and October meetings are held every Tuesday evening. In the other months, business meetings are held once a month.

Productions: All monies for Centre Circle productions are deposited in the union program budget general fund. Since disbursements are made through the union's financial officer, all monies are handled centrally. Each club within the union's program division participates in the budget process of requesting budget funds and operating its own financial allotment.

3. Competition–Playground Puppet Show Contest. In addition to the continual competition among those who audition for acting parts, there are many other ways in which competition can enhance the dramatic experience. A good program in puppetry on the playgrounds could begin a wave of interest that might result in a citywide competition for the year's best winner, the Punch and Judy blue ribbon. The top puppet show could be given time on television; it could be taped and shown in schools, hospitals, and churches; the show could be a special feature at the country fair; or it could be used by the recreation agency for any number of special occasions.

Type of tournament: A scoring event as a result of points awarded by a panel of judges at various levels. Each playground would select its best show. Regions within the city or county would be designated. The top playground shows would travel to the regional location to be judged. Regional winners would move to the next step until the single winner is determined.

Fee: None.
Contest   All puppets and scenery must be handmade, and the script may be
requirements: original or adapted. All rules and regulations would be circulated
                    at the beginning of the summer to all playground leaders.
Personnel: Playground leaders are responsible for assisting with this program
                    as a part of their usual duties.
Materials: All materials should be free and a part of the regular crafts supplies
                    assigned to a park site.
Awards: Banners are given to the regional park winners and ribbons and
                    puppetry books to the winning show.
Registration: At the regional competitive level, it will be necessary to know how
                    many entries there are. This is the job of the playground supervi-
                    sor for the region, who will also have to schedule the times for
                    judging the puppet shows.

4. Participant Spectator–Mobile Theatre-of-the-Streets. In this program, the
play is taken into those neighborhoods that probably would have little opportunity to
see live theatre or meet and talk with actors. The mobile van driver reaches the target
neighborhood street and parks the van in a predetermined location. The street is
blocked off while chairs, benches, and sit-upons are placed about the area. The stage
is set for the early evening performance while the neighborhood children and adults
have an opportunity to talk with the theatre troupe as they make the preparations. The
final preparation step is to rope off the area for the night's performance.

Admission   Children free, adults $1.00 each.
fees:
Publicity: An active campaign must have been launched with posters on the
                    block the week prior to the show, flyers under doorways the day
                    before, reminder notes in the media about the troupe and their
                    total summer schedule.
Personnel: The theatre troupe is a totally self-contained unit. It exists either
                    under the umbrella of the recreation agency, or is a separate group
                    that has been put under contract for the summer by the agency.
                    The responsibility of the agency staff will vary depending upon
                    which of the above options has been utilized.
Locations: Determined by the agency. Three or four performances per week
                    each in a different neighborhood.

5. Self-Directed. Many parks have natural amphitheaters that could easily
facilitate the development of a simple stage and back screen. This stage area would
be available for groups needing a facility for an impromptu or practice session. Scout
troups, 4-H clubs, and many groups would like the use of such a stage area for special
meetings. A large, formal stage with auditorium seating is too intimidating for these

kinds of groups. Park designers are remiss if this easy development chance is missed. The stage can be used for church services and weddings, as well as all types of drama activity. It can become a focal point for impromptu dramatic activity. No registration would be required unless a reservation system was in operation. It would be available for use during the usual park hours. Depending on how much investment was put into the stage area (light panels and sound system), it would take very little supervision from park staff.

Dramatics should be exposed to the evaluation cube test as has been done with art and dance (see Figure 6.5, p. 190).

ENVIRONMENTAL ACTIVITIES

Environmental activity focuses on the environment in its totality: natural and manufactured, ecological, political, technological, solid, cultural, and aesthetic. It is an interdisciplinary concern and takes place in the camp, the school, the institution, and recreation agency programs, among others. The goals of such a program include both learning about the environment and learning to behave in the environment–to know how to utilize it and preserve it at the same time. The ways in which recreation touches these things are mainly through day and resident camping playground programs, nature center programs, and outdoor educational programs, with emphasis on the understanding of and developing an appreciation for the natural environment through the use of the out-of-doors as a living laboratory.

A. Scope of the Area
   1. Camping activities
      (a) School camping
      (b) Day camping
      (c) Resident or established camping
      (d) Trip camping
      (e) Family camping
      (f) Senior citizen camping (day or resident)
   2. Nature-oriented activities
      (a) Interpretive programs
         (1) Nature centers
         (2) Nature trails
         (3) Nature museums
      (b) Nature crafts
      (c) Nature games
      (d) Identification activities

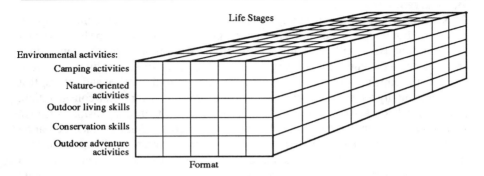

Figure 6.6 Environmental Activities Evaluation Cube

3. Outdoor living skills
    (a) Firebuilding
    (b) Use of tools
    (c) Knots and lashing
    (d) Cooking and meal planning
    (e) Shelters
    (f) Map and compass
4. Conservation skills
    (a) Soil and water conservation activities
    (b) Wildlife activities (animals, birds, insects)
    (c) Activities related to conservation of flowers, trees, mushrooms, and such
         plants that grow in the wild as well as in highly populated areas.
    (d) All of the above are related to conservation at the campsite
    (e) Conservation games
5. Outdoor adventure activities
    (a) Backpacking and camping
    (b) Cycling
    (c) Orienteering
    (d) Rock climbing
    (e) Rope courses, bunji diving
    (f) Skin diving, tubing, and rafting
    (g) Spelunking
    (h) Winter skills and activities

B. Current Practices and Trends

This is an area that has grown rapidly in the last ten years in terms of the emphasis given to it in both school and recreation agency programs. Although camps have emphasized outdoor living skills and nature crafts activities, it was only with the tremendous impetus given the importance of a need to attend to the environment by the environmentalist groups and the various government groups in the 1960s and 1970s, that environmentally selected activities moved to the forefront as a program consideration. Although schools and camps have often been endowed with the responsibility to take care of environmental education, it has only been recently that the other recreation agencies have recognized their responsibilities to offer programs in this area and have seen that they, in fact, do have the skills to do so. The trend in these programs has been to be less simplistic and to take on more complex issues in terms of the management of the environment, the place of human beings in this space capsule called Earth, to learn about the economic and technological aspects and impacts of the use of the environment, and to conserve the environment as we know it. Much more emphasis has been put on the biological characteristics of the environment and the environment as a resource base.

C. Patterns of Organization

Environmental knowledge, attitudes, and skills are most often conveyed in interpretive and nature centers (educational), clubs, classes, playground activities, special demonstrations and events, day camping, and through consultants to school and private groups. *All* age groups participate in environmental programs. Groups are more often age heterogeneous than homogeneous.

D. Samples of Organization for Each Format

1. Social Format–Cardinalville Audubon Society. This club was organized by the local community recreation agency, but is affiliated with the National Audubon Society. Club programs include annual bird counts, maintenance of photograph blinds, a weekly column for the local newspaper, and other activities. Considerations for the programmer in establishing this club in response to the expressed need of the residents include the facility in which to hold meetings, leadership, fees, publicity, and membership.

Facility:	A room in the recreation center basement that is used as a nature center with displays, a small library, comfortable chairs and tables. The club meets regularly on the third Monday of each month.
Leadership:	Provided by the club. The agency supplies the place to meet and use of its landscape equipment for bird club events, but the leadership is all volunteer.
Fee:	There are $8 membership dues, part of which goes to affiliation with National Audubon Society and part of which goes to purchase new library materials on birds, contribute to a display, or the like.

Membership: Potential members are eligible as specified by the club constitution and bylaws and may join at any meeting of the club.

Publicity: Publicity is done through the usual agency channels. Flyers are also sent to the Sierra Club and other environment-oriented groups in the area.

2. Participant Spectator/Format–Nature Crafts Show at Potter's Creek. Local craftspersons as well as members of the various agencies' nature programs are given a chance under this format to display completed products, as well as to demonstrate such skills as candlemaking, woodcarving, drying and preserving flowers, making jewelry from indigenous materials, basket making, and the like. Cider, fruit, and nuts and other natural foods will be available (donated) and sold to the show visitors.

Leadership and facility: General direction will be given by the interpretive naturalist at the Potter's Creek Nature Center, which was donated to the town in the form of a cabin on the edge of town near Potter's Creek and has been developed by the town recreation department into a nature center. One large, special event is scheduled at the center each season. This one takes place at the center in late fall on a Sunday afternoon. It is open to all ages.

Fee: There is a $.40 admission charge per person. Local craftspeople who display their wares for sale are expected to return to the agency ten percent of monies realized from sales.

Publicity: Notification of the event will be sent to local craftspersons, leaders of nature groups, shops in town catering to nature crafts, and the newspapers. Posters will also be placed in shopping malls, laundromats, or the like.

Registration: All persons wishing to display or demonstrate crafts must register with the naturalist two weeks before the event is to take place. Included in the information needed from registrants is the size of the space needed, and the title of the display. Displays will be set up on the morning of the day of the event by those who have displays, assisted by the naturalist and members of the nature crafts class at the agency. Docent leaders will be greeters and provide hospitality.

3. Competition Format–Fire Building Contest. This event comes at the end of the outdoor living skills course at the agency day camp. It involves selecting the proper tree to cut down; use of the proper tools to do so; felling, chopping, and splitting techniques; and firebuilding for boiling water. The contest is over when a kettle of water is brought to a boil. The group is divided into teams and the winning team has supper cooked for them by the others.

Facility:	The contest takes place in the outdoor living skills instruction area adjacent to the nature center at the edge of town.
Leadership:	This event is organized and run by the outdoor living skills instructor who is a summer employee of the recreation department and salaried.
Fee:	No charge, as this is part of the coursework.
Registration:	Scheduled as part of the program on the next to last day of it.
Publicity:	None needed.

4. Self-Improvement Format–Field Training Course for Teachers. This field training course is directed toward teaching interpretive skills to the teachers in the local school district so that they, in turn, may work with the children. The focus is on plant and animal interpretation. The course will meet in the spring on three consecutive Saturdays and has been authorized by the local college as a one-credit course applicable to teacher certification.

Facility:	The field training course will be held at the nearby state park.
Leadership:	The naturalist biologist at the college will conduct this class three Saturday mornings from 9:00 AM to 12:00 noon and will be paid out of fees contracted for by the college ($300).
Fees:	The participants will pay at the standard college rate of $65 per credit. A limit of 20 people has been set for the course.
Publicity:	The course will be publicized out of the college's continuing education department.

5. Self-Directed–Nature Crafts Center. Next door to the nature room in the basement of the recreation center is a crafts room. This room is open two evenings a week from 7:00 to 9:00 PM as a drop-in center for people to come to work at their leisure, with the center providing space, tools, equipment, and help if needed. Materials are generally supplied by the participant, although certain items are available at a minimal fee. Carving, weaving, basketry, and jewelry with nature materials are the main crafts available. This program opportunity is publicized through the regular department seasonal program literature. Special effort is made to get the information to the retirement homes and senior citizen housing units in the area.

E. Special Facility Needs

Although it is not a necessity, it is desirable to have some sort of a nature center and access to some natural wooded area. Centers essentially fall into three categories: (1) those in close proximity to the homes of the major participants, (2) those that are far enough away to make transportation a key organizational factor, and (3) the large city center (or section of a center) in which an outdoor area is an impossibility (Smith, Carlson, Donaldson, and Masters, 1972). There should be space for meetings, displays, and a work room, with adequate storage space. A library reading room would

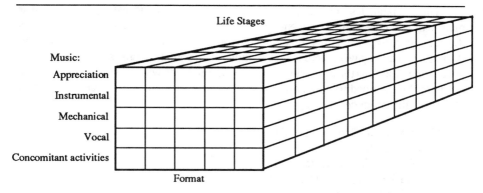

Figure 6.7 Music Evaluation Cube

be preferred, but that function can be handled in the display room. Places for practice in outdoor living skills are also desirable. Of course, any center located on several hundred acres of land would be a boon to the program.

Following the format of previous sections of this chapter, environmental activities should be placed in the program slot of the evaluation cube to test for variety and diversity (see Figure 6.6, p.197).

MUSIC

The program area of music has many similarities to other functional areas of the performing arts. The participant has many open avenues in which he or she can experience the area of music. In music there are three ways to participate: actively, in support, and in appreciation. For those who believe they lack musical talent, again, the latter two participatory roles are possible. Persons who perceive themselves as having musical ability have all three roles as possible activity outlets.

Many grand and elegant claims have been put forward about the universality of music, the healing power of music, and the value of music to increase production and ease tension, yet the scope of possible music experiences is quite simplistic.

Scope of the Area

Music can be approached from a couple of directions as far as classification is concerned. We have chosen a simple system to classify music experiences:
1. Appreciation
2. Instrumental
3. Mechanical
4. Vocal
5. Concomitant activities

These categories are broadly defined. Refinement is necessary to get a clear picture of what the scope really entails. Sounds can be produced in many ways. It is the intent here to present only those subcategories that can be easily communicated to the reader. The key word here is music, rather than sound. If this is seen as elitist, so be it. Sounds such as the train whistle, footsteps, bubbling water, or a typewriter being used are not intended to be within this classification system (i.e., mechanically and electronically produced sound).

A. Clustering or Grouping of Activities
1. Appreciation
   (a) Attending performances
   (b) Listening to reproduction
   (c) Studying music
   (d) Acting as patron or sponsor to activities
2. Instrumental
   (a) Orchestra
   (b) Band
   (c) Strings
   (d) Brass
   (e) Woodwinds
   (f) Percussion
   (g) Same or mixed instrument ensembles
3. Mechanical
4. Vocal
   (a) Choir, chorus
   (b) Soprano
   (c) Alto
   (d) Tenor
   (e) Bass
   (f) Same or mixed voice ensembles
5. Concomitant activities
   (a) Composing
   (b) Conducting or directing
   (c) Accompanying vocal areas
   (d) Acting as librarian
   (e) Acting as business manager

B. Current Practices and Trends
Some trends have been identified in the music area in the last decade or two. After the folk singing years of the 1960s, there appears to be high popularity for country music and a diminishing attention to jazz. Volume was important in the late 1960s but that seems to have softened. Perhaps the most recent trend is the move to more complex and sophisticated chord progressions and harmonies. To be an important musician in the popular mode, one needs to be a good musician. There is no more faking it simply with loud noise and a knowledge of five different chords.

Electronic and mood music appears to be in the wings fairly solidly, while gospel singing is front row center. Most music activity is still taking place in schools, churches, and private clubs and organizations. The men's and women's barbershop groups, church choirs, drum and bugle or fife and drum corps form the largest group of music activities available today. Choruses, community bands or orchestras, choral societies (or specific groups such as Bach or Haydn societies), and occasionally youth singing ensembles or gospel groups fill out the music activity found in most communities and cities in America. Colleges and universities are engaging in probably the most exciting music programming that is happening today.

On a positive note, it is encouraging to see growth in music performances of all kinds throughout America. A 1974 Ford Foundation report indicated that attendance was up, and members of performing groups were on the increase, while financial difficulties still remained as the number one problem. Yet as the government in the early 1980s reduced funding to all the arts, much greater effort was required from recreation programmers to seek new funding sources and continuing support for the arts.

The emergence of the small performing ensemble group has been an exciting new trend in the music area. This is probably a contemporary version of the popularity of string quartet works, woodwind ensembles, and barbershop quartets. We also see a high number of groups of five to twelve performers whether they be vocalists, instrumentalists, or a combination of both.

Concerts in the park, brown bag concerts, and other performance opportunities for amateur groups have given impetus to groups forming and competing for these treasured public appearances. Mobile stages have facilitated bringing music performances into areas where this type of activity never before took place. Seeing, hearing and being touched by the experience has given new options to those people who knew some kinds of music to be only a remote happening.

C. Patterns of Organization

For most recreation agencies the programming of music activity has not gone much further than contracting for a band to play at some special dance. Thus, the most popular format structure has been the special event or performance activity at which a big effort has been made for a short period of time, with little being done in this program area for many months.

Lessons and clinics have not been in popular use, but social activity has had small successes. The Y-teen chorus, the community band, or Legion Posts band have taken hold in a small percent of the recreation agencies. The unaffiliated singing groups are where most music experiences are made available. This fact should be a signal to agencies that might want to explore the possibility of bring one or two music groups in under the program umbrella. Gospel singers, barbershoppers and special instrumental groups all need rehearsal and performance space. Recreation agencies could be of assistance by permitting these groups the use of their auditoriums, multipurpose rooms, or basements.

D. Sample Organization for Each Format Structure

Each of the formats lend themselves easily to program administration within recreation agencies. Programmers can take heart that any effort toward facilitating a music experience is probably breaking new ground. The following are meant only to serve as examples:

1. Self-Improvement Brass Instrument Group Lessons. This series of lessons is available for four popular brass instruments, which are the trombone, tuba, French horn, and trumpet/cornet. Each instrument has a group lesson once a week for six weeks. Therefore, the brass series is a twenty-four-week season. Classes meet twice a week for one hour.

Instructor:	Band director at the junior high school is a trombone player and stays after school Monday and Thursday for group lessons. Her salary is $20/week or $120 for the trombone series.
Registration:	All children eight years and older who want to play trombone may apply. First ten registrants are accepted.
Fee:	Each participant pays $12 for the series of six lessons.
Location:	Since the instruments are available in the school, the class is held in the band room, and horns are made available to class registrants.
Publicity:	This aspect of the program is managed through flyers and announcements at the city schools. This type of class can be held for any of the instrumental or vocal subcategories. The simple offering of classes requires only the promotion and arrangement. The key, as it is with all of the visual and performing arts areas, is quality leadership.

2. Social Format–Camper Vesper Choir. Almost every camp will program some type of religious ceremony on a regular day in the camp schedule. It is usual to have some singing at this service, which becomes a perfect occasion for a special interest group to get together or be called together. The camper vesper choir or the counselor choir may well be the special performing group at the service If the camp season is longer than two weeks, this group might work on some fairly sophisticated choral programs. When such a group is formed and becomes active, it may be called on to sing for many other kinds of occasions, such as campfires, taps, serenades in the grove, etc.

Instructor:	Camp Treble Clef has many counselors who are interested in working with the vesper choir. The camp director has assigned his post to one of the counselors as a part of her regular camp duties. Depending on camper interest, auditions may or may not be held.

Registration: The tradition of the vesper choir has a long history in this camp and the campers are usually anxious to belong. Out of the 180 campers a limit of 15 has been set for the choir.

Rehearsal Meetings: Wednesday and Friday nights before supper (5:00-6:00 PM), the choir rehearses, with a warm-up time before services. Since all formal camp activity closes at 5:00 PM, the choir practices while others are getting ready for the evening meal.

Fee: None. Any sheet music needed is provided by the camp. The music selection is determined by the counselor in charge, and all work is performed either a cappella or with available instrument accompaniment.

3. Competition Format–March Composition Competition. The park district, through its concerts in the park program, wishes to have a march piece with which the band could open every program. A band patron has put up some prize money for the winner of the march composition competition in the style of John Philip Sousa. Rules for the composer will be determined by the contest committee and circulated to band members, newspapers, and the like. A jury must be determined to judge the compositions as played by either the composer or some other competent musician.

Registration: Participants register when they pick up the contest rules. A registration period is announced three months before the due date for entries. The contest is open to anyone who holds official residence in the park district.

Finances: Entries are free. Prize money is $500 to the winner and $250 to the runner-up.

Publicity: Newspapers, flyers, and posters in all music stores, and a radio station will feature the contest. Having a march written specifically for the summer concert series will be the main selling point.

Timing: The contest deadline of mid-April would permit the band to get the orchestration in hand and perform the march at the first concert, perhaps Memorial Day.

Jury: These people must be carefully chosen. They would be responsible for judging all entries in light of predetermined criteria that were clearly announced and given to each entry.

4. Participant Spectator–Benefit Concert by The Golden Oldies. In order to raise money for the new recreation center a singing group has been contracted for an outdoor concert at the band shell in Greenway Park. This project demands a great deal of organizational work from the professional programmer as well as assistance from many volunteers and helpers. In a project of this magnitude, it is wise to set a coordinating committee to control all aspects of the event. When 5000 spectators are expected to congregate in one place, all systems must be brought into a single focus for this event.

*Contact
with talent:*   Arrangements to contract the hottest contemporary singing group are made. The Golden Oldies were signed through their Chicago agent. Performance date, fee, and ticket prices are the main elements in the contract negotiations. The agent is from a eputable firm and had sample contracts for signature. A "rider" was added to that contract, asking the group to be in the band shell at least four hours prior to performance, so that lights and sound levels could be set.

Tickets: These are to be sold in three locations in the city and at the door if any are left. Prices were set at:

> $ 1.50 for children under 13
> $ 2.00 for teenagers
> $ 5.00 for those 20 or over

Talent cost: Because the show is a benefit to help pay for a recreation center building, the agent cut the group's usual fee in half. The contracted price is $4000, payable immediately after the show. Ticket prices must be kept as stated above.

Publicity: The agent supplies 300 posters and 5000 flyers, which would need to be filled in with dates, ticket prices, location, and time of the concert. Assorted glossy black and white photographs with accompanying news releases would also be provided. A budget of $600 is set for promotion.

Personnel: Union and safety regulations require a full complement of staff to assist with this concert: electricians, sound technicians, lighting experts and operators, piano tuner, stage manager and ushers, firefighters, security staff, first aid crews, ticket sellers and takers. If concession stands are available, they need to be operable with program salespersons, restroom attendants, etc., on hand. The Golden Oldies may wish to have an announcer, a curtain puller, and other personnel which will be stated in their contract. The programmer must be aware of local union requirements as well as requirements noted in the contract.

*Ticket and
program
printing:*   Ticket control is absolutely essential. For most shows of this type the ticket should be designed and printed so that it cannot be duplicated easily. Programs may or may not be needed. As a general predictor, it is safer to assume that you will sell 80 percent of the house rather than believe you will have a sell-out, SRO crowd. Estimates on income or profit are much more realistic if based on the 80 percent figure. There are many other considerations that need attention in this program plan, but the above discussion is a good head start.

5. Self-Directed–Piano in the Union Lounge. Every afternoon between 3:00 and 6:00 PM, students are able to use the piano for a total time limit of 30 minutes or longer if no one else is waiting to play. The lounge is not an area that can be completely closed off. Since day students use it as a study hall area, the piano may not be used during the earlier hours. It should be anticipated that the piano will get hard use, and all kinds of music will fill the lounge. Union building personnel could keep the lounge on their program of supervision to keep chopsticks and other old favorites of the non-piano player to a minimum. If the piano is there to play, however, then one must be prepared for the consequences.

Since music is alphabetically at the end of the performing arts cluster of functional program areas–that is, art, dance, drama, and music–perhaps this is the place to mention what has been missing in each of the categories of these single program areas. The missing feature is a mixture of these areas in all kinds of combinations. Dance is usually supported with music. Much of theatre is in the form of musicals. Music productions in the opera area require drama and dance to complete the production. Scenery, backdrops, and scrims necessitate good artistic creations. One may argue the point that the performing arts should never be separated. We contend that the arts can only be combined in a multimedia program when each is able to lend its uniqueness to the whole. We leave this discussion to the professional performing artists while we work at perfecting and enjoying the building blocks to that position.

The evaluation cube would reflect the above, with music in the program area slot (see Figure 6.7, p. 201).

SPORTS AND GAMES

Sports and recreational games may well be the single biggest area in recreation programs. Part of this may be due to the importance of sports and exercise in the lives of the American people with the tremendous impetus given in this direction by the commercial interests that sell sports equipment, and partially by the fact that physical education had an early influence in the development of recreation programming. Whatever the reason, there is hardly a household that does not have at least one bicycle, or a tennis racquet, or a basketball, or the like. Bowling has reached practically every economic level, and family picnics are focused around the interminable softball game. Most people fancy themselves as an expert in some game or another and know exactly how it should be programmed, taught, and officiated. All of these facts present a challenge to the programmer to present a sports program geared to fit the needs and expectations of a wide variety of participants, ranging from experts to beginners of all ages, both able bodied and disabled. Participation in sports and games is possible for everyone. The problem in this area is selecting from an extremely large offering the things most appropriate for any given clientele. The programmer is urged to utilize a need estimate of some sort to aid in this decision. To what sports are the environmental parameters of the area most conducive? What can the agency support financially? Within these two considerations, in what are the residents most interested? Let us take a look at the possibilities.

Scope of the Area

The following categories are meant to indicate the broad scope of the area, but no attempt is made to include every possible element under each category. Whole books have been written on such a topic. In selecting sports and games for inclusion in a program, the programmer should play close attention to the current trends in participant interest (discussed under each format):

A. **Clustering or Grouping of Activities**
    1. Field and team sports
        (a) Football, flag football, baseball, soccer, softball, field hockey, lacrosse.
        (b) Basketball, volleyball, ice hockey.
        (c) Lead-up games for all team sports for the early life-cycle groups or when the space is small, the group is large, and the full game cannot be played.
    2. Individual and dual sports
        (a) Racquet sports
            (1) Tennis, paddle tennis, three-wall racquet ball.
            (2) Badminton, racquetball, squash, table tennis.
        (b) Archery, bowling, cycling, fencing, golf, gymnastics, handball, ice skating, riding, roller skating, skiing, both downhill and cross country, weight lifting, and wrestling.
        (c) Aquatics
            (1) Swimming of all types, diving, surfing, water skiing, polo.
            (2) All kinds of boating.
        (d) Martial arts.
        (e) Track and field for all life-cycles and both sexes.
        (f) Environment-related activities–rock climbing, hiking, cave exploring, etc.
    3. Recreational games
        (a) Shuffleboard, deck tennis, croquet, box hockey, horseshoes, lawn bowling, bocci, tetherball, etc.
        (b) New games and less competitive games.
        (c) Games with little organization.
    4. Fitness activities
        (a) Running and jogging.
        (b) Weight training.

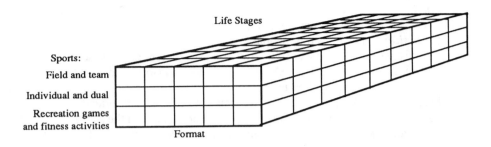

Figure 6.8 Sports and Games Evaluation Cube

B.   Current Practices and Trends

As mentioned earlier, the programmer must not only be aware of the tried and always popular sports that one can count on to be well attended by participants, but also must be alert for trends in the sports culture that indicate an upsurge in popularity of activities among the general public. There are some trends that are evident at present. These include the development of co-recreational activities encompassing competition between and among men and women, the increase in lifetime sports emphasis, and a rapid growth in fitness programs for all life-cycles after preschool and for both sexes. Community sports clubs and sports camps are increasing rapidly in number, water-based activities, which grew rapidly in the 1960s, are still in a growth cycle, and Special Olympics for the disabled are well-established.

C.   Patterns of Organization

In organizing groups for sports and games, there are several typical patterns from which to choose. They are largely related to the factors of group size, purpose of the event, and facilities and leadership available. Sports activities can easily fit into all formats discussed in other program activities. The tendency has been to view this program area as the "competition" area. The programmer must not be satisfied with only this type of format structure.

D.   Sample Organization for Each Format

1. Self-Improvement Format–Tennis Class. In this pattern, the programmer needs to assign the leadership to a qualified tennis instructor either from the permanent staff or as special part-time help, reserve the courts for class time and post it as such, decide if fees are to be charged, and, if so, how much, decide on size of the class for each skill level, decide on length of the unit, amount of time for each class, how registration is to be handled, and plan publicity. Sample decisions are presented as follows:

Instructor:	Summer sports instructor with $100/week salary.
Facility:	Six tennis courts reserved from 9:00 to 12:00 PM, Monday, Wednesday, and Friday.
Class size:	Twenty-four people.
Ability levels and ages:	From 9:00 to 10:00 AM, young beginners and intermediates; from 1:00 to 11:00 AM, older beginners and intermediates; from 11:00 AM to 12:00 noon, advanced.
Fee:	Seven dollars and fifty cents ($7.50), balls provided.
Unit:	Two weeks per participant; four sessions in the summer.
Registration:	At the center, a Saturday, one week before start of unit, 9:00 to 11:00 AM.
Publicity:	In all newspapers and on local radio and television stations, on posters in shopping malls, in flyers with the total summer program listed sent through the school to each family with children.

2. Social Format–Tennis Club. In this organizational pattern, tennis will be offered to those 16 years of age and up at a special fee. It will draw for membership from the older students in the tennis classes, as well as from the general community adult population. No instruction will be offered. The club needs to reserve the facility; it also needs someone available for maintenance purposes, to check member's cards, take court reservations, and handle emergencies; a member to work with the recreation agency on club hours; issue membership cards; set up tournaments and decide on a time limit on each court. This tennis club might be organized, then, as follows:

Facility:	Six tennis courts.
Personnel:	The same summer sports instructor who handles lessons serves as recreation agency liaison with the club.
Membership:	Self-limited to those who pay dues. Limited to those 16 years of age and up.
Fee:	Thirty dollars ($30.00) for eight weeks.
Hours:	Tuesday and Thursday, 9:00 AM to 12 noon (will probably draw housewives and retirees), Wednesday, 5:00 to 7:00 PM (will draw the working person), and Saturday and Sunday, 9:00 AM to 12:00 noon (for all members).
Registration:	Wednesday, 5:00 to 7:00 PM, the week preceding the program start, at the recreation center.
Publicity:	Local newspapers, radio and television, posters in shopping malls, flyers with the whole summer program sent home with the school children.

3. Competition Format–Tennis Tournament. The culminating events for the tennis season are the annual community tennis tournaments: singles, couples, and mixed doubles. The programmer must decide on the dates for the tournament, places the matches may be played, type of tournament (and draw it up), who is eligible, entry fees, awards, whether or not to have officials for the finals, registration, and publicity. The organization for a typical sequence of tournaments might be as follows:

Facilities:	Six community courts.
Dates of the tournaments:	Last three weekends in August; singles the first week, doubles, the second, and mixed doubles the third.
Type of tournament:	Double elimination.
Eligibility:	An open tournament to anyone in the area.
Fee:	A $7 entry fee for each tournament (balls provided).
Awards:	Serving dishes engraved on the bottom. Presented on the courts at the close of the finals match. Have photographer available.
Registration:	Anytime from 9:00 AM to 5:00 PM, Monday through Friday, and Saturday from 9:00 AM to 12:00 noon, at the center the week before the start of the specific tournament. (Leave two days to prepare the draw.) All participants report to the courts at 8:30 AM the Saturday of the tournament to receive court, time, and opponent assignment.
Publicity:	Through tennis classes, club, posters, newspapers, and radio.

4. Participant Spectator–Tennis Moviehouse. There are many possibilities for special events within a program that will serve to highlight the program, bring special attention to it, and bring in people who are not engaged in it at the time of the special happening, but who may be enticed into future participation. An example of this is the tennis demonstration. Such a demonstration might have been opened up to nonparticipants in the workshop, and families coming to pick up their child or husband or wife could come a little early to watch. In planning an event one must consider its feasibility, how much appeal it will have, whether it is too similar to something else done recently in the area, if the residents will pay for it and, if so, how much, how many people it will take to run, and if such people are available, whether the facility is available, and how it should be publicized. A second example of an event connected with tennis might be a night of tennis movies, oldies but goodies of former Forest Hills or Wimbledon matches, and a current film on improving your tennis with the pros. The organization for this would be as follows:

Event:	Tennis moviehouse with two hours of tennis with the masters. Oldies but goodies and a current film on improving your tennis.
Time and place:	Wednesday, 7:00 to 9:00 PM, the sixth week of the program in the recreation center gymnasium.
Fee:	One dollar ($1) per person, $.50 for children under 12.
Personnel:	The tennis instructor, a projectionist, and a ticket taker.
Publicity:	Newspaper, local radio station, announcements in tennis classes and the club, posters at the courts and in the shopping malls.

5. Self-Directed Format–Free Court Time. There must be time within the summer program for the courts to be open for general use by anyone desiring to play tennis. The programmer must decide whether or not the demand is great enough to limit time to play to an hour or embark on a reservation system. If so, such regulations must be posted at the courts and at least a spot check conducted by the tennis instructor to make sure it is being adhered to by everyone. Open hours for the program described here would be:

Time and place: Monday, Tuesday, Thursday, Friday–all afternoon and evening. Wednesday–12:00 to 5:00 PM and 7:00 to 9:00 PM. Saturday and Sunday afternoon and evenings.

E.   Special Facility Needs
An indication of the types of facility needs for sports and games has been illustrated in the samples just presented. Since each sport and game is almost unique in the facility required, refer for details to a general facility book or to the sports and rules guides listed in the bibliography, which include the specifications of playing areas for the sport being addressed.

Although the categories of this program area are few in number, as illustrated in Figure 6.8, p. 209, the concept of the evaluation cube could be expanded to include every subcategory for all life stages and formats. Space limitations prohibit the display of this feature.

SOCIAL RECREATION

This functional program area has tremendous variety in that much of the activity in it crosses over into some of the other program areas. The main purpose of social recreation is to provide activity that primarily facilitates the social interaction process. In one sense, this means providing an atmosphere in which people can get to know one another without having to go through awkward situations. The program planner for such gatherings is aware of how difficult it is to enter a new group in a new setting. Plans are made and social recreation programs are designed so that this step is an easy one.

One aspect of social recreation is the party plan and the large celebration. Both of these events require organizational expertise and a good bit of creativity. Whether the event is a county fair or a simple birthday party, the organizational process is similar. Every recreation agency will embark into this program area regularly. Many of the activities organized and sponsored by the recreation agency will be for the sole purpose of socializing. Teen centers, coffee houses, dances, such as square and social, and board games have socialization as the key element.

Hobbies constitute another area of interest under the umbrella of social recreation. Although an individual may work quite independently with a hobby interest, a recreation agency would be unique if it served various hobby enthusiasts. Grouping the hobbyists would be a possible program through the hobby night or in an after school hobby program. In the rehabilitation setting it is more popular to work on a one-to-one basis, and this is the kind of agency in which the fostering of a single person for a single program idea might be possible. In addition to the programs that are focused directly toward the social interaction purposes, the elements of this area are used while enhancing many other types of programs. Any leader should have an entire skill bank of abilities in the social recreation skills. These skills are also useful in emergency situations in which a leader or program director is often found. When filler activity is needed, the extemporaneous song leader or magic games director can make the time quickly with an enjoyable experience.

A. Clustering or Grouping of Activities

This is a particularly difficult area in which to establish discrete categories of activities. Some authors have attempted to separate the social recreation area from the hobbies and special events. These types of activities should be included here. The cluster will purposely have some overlap simply to assure that all categories are given some attention with words that are familiar to the field. These categories are:

1. Celebrations and festivals
2. Easy equipment games
3. Guessing and magic games
4. Hobbies
5. Mass participation games
6. Parties
7. Social interaction games
8. Table and electronic games

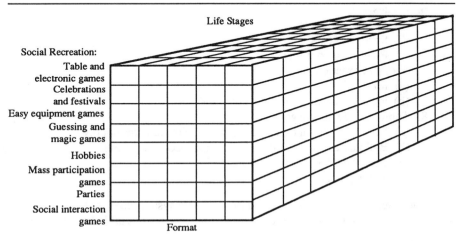

Figure 6.9 Social Recreation Evaluation Cube

Each of the above categories has many specific games that would be included within the grouping as well as subgroupings. The following list is not meant to be all-inclusive, but a few examples may serve to assure that we are both on the same track:

1. Celebrations and festivals
   (a) Pageants
   (b) Holiday celebration events
   (c) Parades
   (d) Fairs and circuses
2. Easy equipment games
   (a) Paper
   (b) Aluminum foil
   (c) String
   (d) Balls
3. Guessing and magic games
   (a) Riddles
   (b) Quizzes
   (c) Magic tricks and stunts
4. Hobbies
   (a) Creative
   (b) Collecting
   (c) Educational
5. Mass participation games
   (a) Leader/audience response stories
   (b) Group singing
   (c) Motion stories
6. Parties
   (a) Special holidays
   (b) Special events
   (c) Picnics and outings
7. Social interaction games
   (a) Mixers
   (b) Ice breakers and early arriver activities
8. Table and electronic games
   (a) Board games such as cards, puzzles, checkers, monopoly
   (b) Ball games such as billiards, bumper pool, Ping-Pong
   (c) Hand held battery-powered games
   (d) Video games

The categories may be too varied in size. The system does include very small activities to large projects, yet it appears that these activities all belong in the same home base.

B.   Current Practices and Trends

The emphasis in this area generally surrounds the parades and celebration types of activity. The smaller social interaction activity is left to the skill development of the individual leaders to use as they see fit. Some efforts are being made to provide an opportunity for all hobbyists to get together in a single place at the same time. This has been particularly popular in small areas where there are not many people who share similar hobby interests but are hobbyists.

Workshops abound in teaching registrants the social skills. Precamp training sessions, 4-H leadership development clinic weekends, and senior citizen program workshops all find a ready audience for these social skill training experiences. Church recreation programs are certainly near the top of any list identifying agencies that are active in this area. Also, those agencies that are building-centered have given attention to a social recreation room in which pool tables and Ping-Pong tables are located. Programming has not been heavy among all agencies in this functional program area.

C.   Patterns of Organization

The most common patterns in the area for participants have been in the special event or performance category. There is little that needs to be elaborated on in this context. The area of social recreation has always been a bit of a misfit, and it is obvious that there are many irregularities when it is put to the scrutiny demanded by this chapter design. Social recreation is that extra polish that is often added to another purposeful program. It is rarely the main course. Thus, to be involved in a singing or icebreaking activity is a special program and should be classified in that particular type of format structure.

D.   Sample Organization for Each Format

In the following section potential program development in this area is described. They are intended only as samples. Adaptations and revision will undoubtedly need to be made when these are applied to a specific agency program:

1. Self-Improvement Format–Winning Chess Workshop. A leader has been located in the area of the JCC who is a master chess player. He has agreed to explain and teach advanced chess to anyone who would like to attend this particular workshop. The chess club is most interested in sponsoring him for this event and has agreed to provide hosting and arrangements the day of the event.

Instructor:	For an honorarium of $50, our expert has agreed to provide an advanced workshop for all ages with up to 50 participants. The workshop will be held on a Sunday from 10:00 AM to 5:00 PM with a break for lunch.
Registration:	The first 50 people to register for this workshop will be accepted Registration will be handled at the center desk, and members as well as nonmembers are invited to attend.
Fees:	Members will be asked to contribute $1; the fee for nonmembers will be $2, payable at the time of registration.

Location: The workshop will be held in the center in the multipurpose room in the morning and in the lower gymnasium in the afternoon so that spectators might be accommodated to watch some of the play.

Publicity: A "challenge the master contest" will be held at one of the shopping malls. Members of the chess club will take turns running a booth that invites any challenger to sit down and have a game with a "master." This will be promotional for the workshop as will regular flyers in the center; there will be some newspaper coverage.

2. Competition Format–Hobby Day. This contest is open to all people. Two age categories are planned: Group A for people 18 and under and Group AA for people over 18 years of age. The young people will have an opportunity to display their hobbies and compete, within various prearranged area group sings, with those in like categories; this does not necessarily mean with others who have the same hobby, but instead a similar type of hobby. These categories will be announced prior to the acceptance of any entries or registrations. All hobbies will be given a set amount of space in which the hobby can be displayed.

Personnel: The regular full-time staff of the Boys' and Girls' Clubs will serve to coordinate the event. Volunteers from the Lions Club will also be available to lend a hand and carry various assignments. The Lions participate in this event as a part of their community service program.

Registration: Persons must indicate their intent to participate in the show at least ten days prior to the event. They may register at either the Boys' Club or the Girls' Club main office. Contest regulations and requirements will be available at that time.

Fee: No charge is made for the hobby show entries, but a $.50 donation is collected at the door on the day of the event from all visitors over the age of 12.

Location: This event will be held in the Girls' Club gymnasium. Each entrant has an eight- or six-foot regular banquet size table and one chair. No electricity will be available at these booths. Each hobbyist is presented with only the table and chair. It will be the results of their effort at displaying their hobby that will be an important feature in the judging.

Awards: Trophies will be awarded to the top three winners in each of the categories. Participant ribbons will be given to all entries.

Categories: Four categories will be set for three age groups. Categories will be animal-based material, vegetable-based material, mineral-based material, and a combination of any of the above. Age groups will be under 12, 13 to 15, and 16 to 18.

3. Social Format–Paper Folders Club. One of the oldest and most popular uses of paper is to fold it into various shapes that fly, that hold water, or that look like something real. This art was developed in Asia, and the Japanese have made an art form of it. The paper club meets once a week at the hospital, and its members share new ideas and techniques with one another.

Personnel:	The club has an internal structure and needs very little assistance from the recreation therapist other than to be on the fringes and assist when needed. The club folds paper and sells these objects in the hospital gift shop, so it is a serious get-together.
Materials:	Special paper is provided at minimal cost to the club members, $.25 per 100 sheets. The recreation staff believes, however, that to give the special paper to them would be a poor learning experience. Tweezers and pins and all other materials are provided from the crafts room supply closet.
Dues:	None.
Membership:	Membership in this club is very fluid. Participants come and go, but the purpose that binds the group together is to be doing an interesting task with other people and receiving the special reward of that finished product. The hospital staff makes special efforts to encourage membership for this group.

4. Participant Spectator Format–St. Patrick's Day Celebration. This activity would be no different from any other special program, except that it focuses on an ethnic group (although everyone seems to be a wee bit Irish on March 17th). The usual committee structure should be formed to manage each of the celebration functions. Whether in terms of a parade, block party, Irish dance exhibition, or a shillelagh throwing contest, each needs to be surrounded by strong organization and planning with a keen eye to publicity and arrangements. Although this date usually falls in the middle of Lent, there is always a good bit of natural celebrating that accompanies this day. Almost every community will have some Irish descendents, so that opportunity to have an early spring special event is a good time in the programming calendar.

Publicity:	An event of this magnitude will need the support of all the local media. Someone from the media should be on the coordinating committee. Developing a PERT chart should be an important task in identifying publicity deadlines.
Personnel:	If the local recreation and parks department is sponsoring this event, there will be a need for many helpers and volunteer workers. Organizations such as service clubs, church groups, and scouts should be willing to assist with these events. It is the job of the recreation programmer to coordinate all of these volunteer groups. The reader is encouraged to look back at some of the other organizational outlines for specifics so that this section does not become redundant.

5. *Self-Directed Format–Recreation Room Amenities.* The alert center programmer will see that the recreation room has available Ping-Pong ball rental machines so that players can purchase a ball and sign out the rackets. Some board games available for sign out or at least some card type tables with the black and red square patterns could be provided so that players might bring their own chess or checkers pieces. Also, playing cards as well as mimeographed paper and pencil games could be in a ready supply for use by the casual drop-in participant.

A sign out/sign in system may have to be developed for some of these materials, but this should be a standard procedure in any center building. If the center has been well designed, the supervision of this room from a central office should be easily managed.

E. Special Facility Needs
A large recreation room that can be used for parties but in which table and board games can also be set up represents the essential needs for this program area. Other needs may be specific to the event and dealt with in that context.

Social recreation can also be tested by the programmer, placing the categories on the program axis, as is done in Figure 6.9, p. 213.

VOLUNTEERING

Volunteering is thought of mainly as a service activity. The programmer needs to keep in mind that while it is, indeed, a service, it is also leisure programming for many volunteers across the life span.

The details of setting up a voluntary staff in any given agency are presented elsewhere in this text. Here we will deal with it as a leisure activity. It must be approached a bit differently from the other areas, since it does not have solely designated activity-related facilities, equipment, etc., but does fit under the format umbrella, see Figure 6.10.

A. Scope of the Area
Any agency or recreation organization can recruit volunteers, so the scope of volunteering encompasses the entire leisure delivery system. (Tedrick and Henderson, 1989. See Chapter Five for complete reference.) Samples of categories of activity in which you might find volunteers are:

1. Working with the disabled.
2. Serving as docents in museums or nature centers.
3. Serving on advisory groups, boards, and commissions.
4. Working with the court system.
5. Coaching.
6. Running social events.
7. Fund raising.

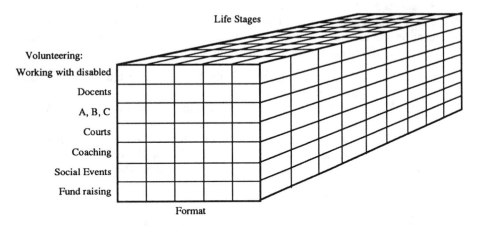

Figure 6.10 Volunteering Evaluation Cube

B.   Current Practices and Trends

Volunteering has regained stature and recognition in recent years, recovering from an era when volunteering was unpaid "woman's work" and expected of them especially of middle and upper class women. Women in the late 60s and 70s were examining carefully how what they did was valued, and volunteering though expected, had a second-rate aura about it and service of this kind was seen to be taken for granted. Women's response was to say, what I do is valuable enough to be paid to do it, and volunteering was not supported as much as it had been in previous years. This point of view has moderated and paralleling it, was the onset of financial crisis in public recreation. There are some events in communities which would not occur if volunteers were not available to run them. Currently volunteering has become a national goal.

C.   Patterns of Organization

Volunteer situations run the gamut from one-on-one situations such as a reader for a vision-impaired cliente to 2,000 volunteers running a week-long summer arts festival. The pattern includes highly sophisticated training and practicing before being assigned to an actual situation (taking American Red Cross Life Saving before volunteering as a life guard at the lake) to showing up on the day of the race, being instructed on how to read a stop watch and being shuttled off to person the one-mile station of the Run-for-the-Fall Colors 10K at the local park. All age groups of all sizes and shapes are volunteers.

D. Samples of Organization for Each Format

1. Social Format–Church Youth Club–Annual Picnic for Area Children at Risk. In this format the total membership of a youth club volunteer to take on the organization and running of a picnic for at-risk children living in group homes and various special living arrangements in the county.

Facility:	The picnic takes place at the largest city park with a playground and softball field.
Leadership:	The event is planned and run by the Club members. All leadership is volunteer, including the club advisors.
Fees:	No fees. Earlier in the year the Club had held a hoagie sale to earn the money to pay for the picnic food and event prizes.
Publicity:	Not needed. Groups will be invited individually.

2. Self-Directed Format–All Comers' Track Meet.

Facility:	Track and surrounding fields at the local high school.
Leadership:	The local track club provides the main leadership, but all individual event timers, starters, finish judges, field judges, are volunteers who show up at 9:00 AM on Saturday morning and are assigned on a first come, first assigned basis.
Fees:	None.
Publicity:	Article on the sports page in events for the week (for the day). The track club also puts out a flyer at the beginning of the Fall that lists events it will sponsor for the year. Both of these sources request volunteers to help run the meets.

3. Competition Format–Scouts' Annual Litter Clean Up Rally. The troop collecting the most litter from 9-5 on a Spring Saturday is the winner. Top prizes are awarded.

Facility:	Large field to use to congregate, put the collecting bins and act as headquarters for the rally. Collecting bags are needed. Scouts are asked to bring gloves.
Leadership:	The Scout leaders of all troops will act as the organizers with the Eagle Scouts in the squad leaders of individual working groups. Each year a different troop is designated as the lead troop to chair the event.
Fees:	None. Bag lunches are provided by the local Rotary Club.
Publicity:	None needed.

4. Participant Spectator Format–Judging the Summer Festival Sidewalk Art Sale.

Facility: Room in the Festival office complex for the judges to meet with their volunteer recorders and assistants before and after the judging of the booths.

Leadership: The volunteer in charge of the event contracts with three expert judges and lines up the three volunteers to help as recorders; one per judge.

BIBLIOGRAPHY

Crafts

Bohm, H. (1972). *Making Simple Constructions*. New York, NY: Watson-Guptill Publications.

Boyes, J. (1974). *Making Paper Costumes*. Boston, MA: Plays, Inc.

Britton, D. S. (1973). *The Complete Book of Bazaars*. New York, NY: Coward, McCann and Geoghegan, Inc.

Cumings, R. (1968). *101 Masks*. New York, NY: David McKay Co., Inc.

D'Amato, J. and D'Amato, A. (1972). *American Indian Craft Inspirations*. New York, NY: M. Evans and Co., Inc.

Fleming, G. (1969). *Scrap Craft for Youth Groups*. New York, NY: The John Day Co.

Gould, E. and Gould, L. (1974). *Crafts for the Elderly*. Springfield, IL: Charles C. Thomas.

Ickis, M. and Esh, R. S. (1974). *The Book of Arts and Crafts*. New York, NY: Dover Publications.

Johnston, R. W. (1970). *The Book of Country Crafts*. Cranbury, NJ: A. S. Barnes and Co.

Linsley, L. (1977). *Wildcrafts*. New York, NY: Doubleday.

Nueckel, S. (1973). *Selected Guide to Make It, Fix-It, Do-It-Yourself Books*. New York, NY: Fleet Press Corp.

Parker, X. L. (1974). *Designing for Crafts*. New York, NY: Charles Scribner's Sons.

Parker, X. L. (1972). *Working with Leather*. New York, NY: Charles Scribner's Sons.

Snook, B. (1967). *Making Clowns, Witches and Dragons*. Newton Centre, MA: Charles T. Branford Co.

Wiseman, A. (1967). *Making Things*. Boston, MA: Little, Brown.

Crafts Periodicals

Art Teacher. Reston, VA. (Published three times a year.)

Arts and Activities. Van Nostrand Reinhold, Skokie, IL. (Published monthly except July and August.)

Craft Horizons. American Crafts Council, New York, NY. (Published bimonthly.)

House and Garden. Nast Publications, Inc., New York, NY. (Published monthly.)

School Arts. Worcester, MA. (Published ten times a year.)

Dance

AAHPERD. (N.D.). *The art of disco dancing*. Reston, VA: AAHPERD.

AAHPERD. (1981). *The guide to dance production: "On with the show."* Reston, VA: AAHPERD.

Cheney, G. (1989). *Basic concepts in modern dance* (3rd ed.). Pennington, NJ: Princeton Book Co.

Emery, L. F. (1988). *Black dance* (2nd ed.). Princeton, NJ: Princeton Book Co.

Furst, C. and Rockefeller, M. (1981). *The effective dance program in physical education.*, West Nyack, NY: Parks Publishing.

Harris, J. A., Pittman, A., and Waller, M. S. (1988). *Dance a while* (6th ed.). New York, NY: Macmillan Publishing.

Heaton, A. (1976). *Fun dance rhythms*. Provo, UT: Brigham Young University Press.

Horst, L. (1973). *Modern dance forms*. Brooklyn, NY: Dance Horizons, Inc.

Joyce, M. (1973). *First steps in teaching creative dance*. Palo Alto, CA: National Press.

King, B. (1970). *Creative dance. . .Experience for learning*. New York, NY: Bruce King, 180 West 75th Street, 10025.

Morgenmoth, J. (1987). *Dance improvisations*. Pittsburgh, PA: University of Pittsburgh Press.

Murray, R. L. (1975). *Dance in elementary education* (3rd ed.). New York, NY: Harper & Row.

National Square Dance Directory. (1985). Winder, GA: Prameadero, Inc.

Nevell, R. (1977). *A time to dance.* New York, NY: St. Martins Press.

Dance Periodicals

American Journal of Dance Therapy. New York, NY: Human Sciences Press, Inc. (Published Spring/Summer.)

American Square Dance. Sandusky, OH. (Published monthly.)

Ballet Review. New York, NY. (Published bimonthly.)

Dance Magazine. New York, NY. (published monthly.)

Let's Dance–The magazine of international folk dancing. Folk Dance Federation of California, Inc., San Francisco, CA. (Published monthly, with the exception of two combined issues: May-June and July-August).

Drama

Barry, J. G. (1970). *Dramatic structure.* Berkeley, CA: University of California Press.

Chambers, D. W. (1970). *Storytelling and creative drama.* Dubuque, IA: William C. Brown Co., Publishing.

Fordyce, R. (1975). *Children's theatre and creative dramatics: An annotated bibliography of critical works.* Boston, MA: G. K. Hall and Co.

Gillies, E. (1972). *Creative dramatics for all children.* New York, NY: Citation Press.

Mahlmann, L. and Jones, D. C. (1974). *Puppet play for young players.* Boston, MA: Plays, Inc.

McIntyre, B. M. (1974). *Creative drama in the elementary school.* Itasca, IL: F. E. Peacock Publishing, Inc.

Styan, J. L. (1975). *Drama, stage and audience.* London, England: Cambridge University Press.

Ward, W. (1952). *Stories to dramatize.* Anchorage, KY: The Children's Theatre Press.

Wethered, A. (1973). *Movement and drama in therapy*. Boston, MA: Plays, Inc. (Printed in Great Britain: Macdonald and Evans, Ltd.).

Drama Periodicals

Television Quarterly. National Academy of Television Arts and Sciences, Beverly Hills, CA. (Published quarterly.)

Theatre Crafts. New York, NY. (Published six times a year.)

TQ Theatre Quarterly. London, WC2, England. (Published quarterly.)

Environmental

Darst, P. W. and Armstrong, G. P. (1980). *Outdoor adventure activities for school and recreation programs*. Minneapolis, MN: Burgess Publishing Co.

Donaldson, G. and Swan, M. (1979). *Administration of Eco-education–A handbook for administrators of environmental/conservation/outdoor education programs*. Reston, VA: AAHPERD.

Ford, P. (1985). *Leadership and administration of outdoor pursuits*. State College, PA: Venture Publishing.

Lewis, W. J. (1980). *Interpreting for park visitors*. Washington, DC: Eastern National Park and Monument Association.

Meier, J. F., Morash, T. W., and Welton, G. E. (1987). *High adventure outdoor pursuits: Organization and leadership* (2nd ed.). Columbus, OH: Publishing Horizons, Inc.

Mitchell, A. V., Robberson, J. D., and Obley, J. W. (1977). *Camp counseling* (5th ed.). Philadelphia, PA: W. B. Saunders Co.

Mitchell, G. (1981). *Fundamentals of day camping* (rev. ed.). Martinsville, IN: American Camping Association.

Musselman, V. W. (1980). *The day camp program book*. New York, NY: Association Press/Follett.

Rohnke, K. (1977). *Cows tails and cobras: A guide to ropes courses, initiative games and other adventure activities*. Hamilton, MA: Project Adventure Press.

Sharpe, G. W. (1982). *Interpreting the Environment* (rev. ed.). New York, NY: John Wiley & Sons.

Smith, J. W., Carlson, R. E., Donaldson, G. W., and Masters, H. B. (1972). *Outdoor Education*. Englewood Cliffs, NJ: Prentice-Hall.

van Matre, S. (1972). *Acclimatization: A sensory and conceptual approach to ecological involvement* (rev. ed.). Martinsville, IN: American Camping Association.

Fitness

AAHPERD. (1981). *Health related physical fitness test manual.* Reston, VA: AAHPERD.

AAHPERD. (1989). *Physical best, a national health and fitness program.* Washington, DC: AAHPERD.

Decker, J. I., Oncult, G., and Sammann, P. (1989). *Y's way to fitness walking.* Champaign, IL: Human Kinetics Publishing.

Espeseth, R., Jr. (1989). *The complete rowing machine workout* (VHS video). Champaign, IL: Sagamore Publishing.

Flynn, R. B. (Ed.). (1985). *Planning facilities for athletics, physical education and recreation.* Reston, VA: AAHPERD.

Franklin, B. A., Oldridge, N. B., Stoedefalke, K. G., and Loechel, W. I. (1990). *On he ball: Innovative activities for adult fitness and cardiac rehabilitation programs.* Carmel, IN: Benchmark Press.

Franks, B. D. and Howley, E. T. (1989). *Fitness leader's handbook.* Champaign, IL: Human Kinetics Books.

Golding, L. A., Myers, C. R., and Sinning, W. E. (1989). *Y's way to physical fitness.* Champaign, IL: Human Kinetics Books.

Hockey, R. (1989). *Physical fitness* (6th ed.). St. Louis, MO: Times/Mirror Mosbey College Publishing.

Hoeger, W. W. K. (1989). *Lifetime physical fitness and wellness.* Englewood, CO: Morton Publishing.

Kingsbury, B. D. (1988). *Full figure fitness.* Champaign, IL: Human Kinetics Books.

Mazzeo, K. S. and Kisselle, J. K. (1987). *Aerobic dance* (2nd ed.). Englewood, CO: Morton Publishing.

Mood, D. P., Musker, F. F., and Rink, J. E. (1987). *Sports and recreational activities* (9th ed.). St. Louis, MO: Times/Mirror Mosbey College Park.

National Fitness Coalition. (1988). *Fitness and disability resource handbook.* Alexandria, VA: NRPA.

Spitzer, T. A. and Hoeger, W. W. K. (1990). *Physical fitness: The water aerobic way.* Englewood, CO: Morton Publishing.

Winnick, J. P. and Short, F. X. (1985). *Physical fitness testing of the disabled.* Champaign, IL: Human Kinetics Publishing.

Music

Baird, F. J. (1963). *Music skills for recreation leaders.* Dubuque, IA: William C. Brown Co., Publishing.

Batcheller, J. and Monsour, S. (1972). *Music in recreation and leisure.* Dubuque, IA: William C. Brown Co., Publishing.

Cargher, J. (1970). *Music for pleasure.* Sydney, Australia: Ure Smith.

Gaston, E. T. (1968). *Music in therapy.* New York, NY: Macmillan Publishing Co., Inc.

Hopkins, J. (1969). *A book of American music celebrations, festival!* New York, NY: Macmillan Publishing Co., Inc.

Howe, H. S., Jr. (1975). *Electronic music synthesis.* New York, NY: W. W. Horton and Co., Inc.

Roberts, J. S. (1972). *Black music of two worlds.* New York, NY: Praeger.

Music Periodicals

American record guide. Melville, New York, NY. (Published monthly.)

The American music teacher. Cincinnati, OH. (Published six times a year.)

Billboard. New York, NY. (Published weekly.)

Downbeat. Chicago, IL. (Published biweekly.)

Guitar player. Saratoga, CA: GP1 Publications. (Published monthly.)

Jazz journal international. London, England. (Published monthly.)

Music and musicians. London, SW1, England: Hanson Books. (Published monthly.)

Music educators journal. Reston, VA. (Published monthly except June, July and August.)

Music journal. New York, NY: Sar-Les Music. (Published ten times a year.)

The school musician director and teacher. Joliet, IL: Ammark Publishing Co., Inc. (Published monthly except July and August.)

Sports and Games

Adams, R. C., Daniel, A. N., and Rollman, L. (1975). *Games, sports and exercises for the physically handicapped* (2nd ed.). Philadelphia, PA: Lea and Febiger.

Armbruster, D. A., Musker, F. F., and Mood, D. (1979). *Sports and recreational activities* (7th ed.). St. Louis, MO: Mosby.

AAHPERD. (1980). *Rules for coeducational activities and sports* (rev. ed.). Reston, VA: AAHPERD.

Bellisimo, L. (1975). *The bowler's manual* (3rd ed.). Englewood Cliffs, NJ: Prentice-Hall.

Bergstrom, C. and Bergstrom, J. (1988). *All the best contests for kids.* Alexandria, VA: NRPA.

Bloss, M. W. and Brown, V. A. (1975). *Badminton* (3rd ed.). Dubuque, IA: William C. Brown Co.

Bowers, C. O., et al. (1972). *Judging and coaching women's gymnastics.* Palo Alto, CA: National Press Books.

Byl, John. (1990). *Organizing successful tournaments.* Champaign, IL: Leisure Press.

Cooper, P. (1973). *Feminine gymnastics* (2nd ed.). Minneapolis, MN: Burgess Publishing Co.

Egbert, B. J. (1985). *A handbook of physical conditioning for pregnant women.* Columbus, OH: Publishing Horizons.

Ferretti, F. (1975). *The great American book of sidewalk stoop, dirt, curb, and alley games.* New York, NY: Workman Publishing Co.

Fluegelman, A. (Ed.). (1981). *More new games.* New York, NY: Doubleday.

Fluegelman, A. (Ed.). (1977). *New games.* New York, NY: Doubleday.

Gill, J. G. (1977). *Games, games, games.* Columbus, OH: Publishing Horizons.

Johnson, C. and Johnstone, A. C. (1975). *Golf: A positive approach.* Reading, MA: Addison-Wesley Publishing Co., Inc.

Kenfield, J. F., Jr. (1973). *Teaching and coaching tennis.* Dubuque, IA: William C. Brown, Co.

Matthews, D. O. (ed.). (1987). *Managing collegiate sport clubs.* Champaign, IL: Leisure Press.

Midtlying, J. (1974). *Swimming.* Philadelphia, PA: W. B. Saunders Co.

Mueller, P. and Reznik, J. W. (1979). *Intramural-recreational sports: Programming and administration* (5th ed.). New York, NY: John Wiley & Sons.

National Archery Association. (1974). *Instructor's handbook.* Lancaster, PA: National Archery Association.

Orlick, T. (1978). *The cooperative sports and games book.* New York, PA: Pantheon Books.

Pacivek, M. J. and Jones, J. (1989). *Sports and recreation for the disabled: A resource manual.* Carmel, IN: Benchmark Press.

Powell, J. T. (1971). *Track and field fundamentals for teacher and coach* (3rd ed.). Champaign, IL: Stipes Publishing Co.

Stillwell, J. L. (1987). *Making and using creative play equipment.* Champaign, IL: Human Kinetics Books.

Stumbo, N. J. and Thompson, S. R. (1989). *Leisure education: A manual of activities and resources.* State College, PA: Venture Publishing.

Turner, M. A. (1975). *League constitution and bylaws for girls' interscholastic program* (Suggested guide). Washington, DC: AAHPERD.

Vogelsinger, H. (1973). *The challenge of soccer.* Boston, MA: Allyn and Bacon.

Wakefield, F., Harkins, D., and Cooper, J. M. (1977). *Track and field fundamentals for girls and women* (4th ed.). St. Louis, MO: Mosby.

Werner, P. H. and Simmons, R. A. (1990). *Homemade play equipment for children.* Washington, DC: AAHPERD.

Rules

Aerial Tennis. Sells Aerial Tennis Co., Box 42, Kansas City, KS 66103.

Archery (field). National Field Archery Assn., Route 2, Box 514, Redlands, CA 92373.

v*Archery (target).* National Archery Assn., 1750 East Boulder Street, Colorado Springs, CO 80909.

Badminton. U. S. Badminton Association, 501 West 6th Street, Papillion, NE 68046.

Baseball (nonprofessional) Guide. National Baseball Congress, 338 South Sycamore, Box 1420, Wichita, KS 672201.

Baseball (American Legion). American Legion, Box 1055, Indianapolis, IN 46206.

Baseball (Babe Ruth League). Babe Ruth League, Inc., P. O. Box 500, 1770 Brunswick Avenue, Trenton, NJ 08638.

Baseball (Little League). Little League Baseball, Inc., P. O. Box 3485, Williamsport, PA 17701.

Baseball (Little League Umpire's Handbook). Little League Baseball, Inc., P. O. Box 3485, Williamsport, PA 17701.

Baseball (Bronco-Pony-Colt). Boys Baseball Inc., P. O. Box 225, Washington, PA 15301.

Baseball Scorer's Handbook (Does not include actual rules). American Amateur Baseball Congress, 215 East Green Street, Marshall, MI 49068.

Baseball League Organization. American Amateur Baseball Congress, P. O. Box 5332, Akron, OH 44313.

Basketball. Amateur Basketball Association, 1750 East Boulder Street, Colorado Springs, CO 80909.

Bicycling. Bicycle Institute of America, 122 East 42nd Street, New York, NY 10017.

Billiard (rules and records). Billiard Congress of America, 717 North Michigan Avenue, Chicago, IL 60611.

Boccia. General Sportcraft Company, Ltd., 140 Woodblue Street, Bergenfield, New Jersey/Lignum-Vitae Products Corp., 96 Boyd Avenue, Jersey City, NJ 07303.

Bowling (lawn). American Lawn Bowling Assoc., 445 Surfview Drive, Pacific Palisades, CA 90272.

Bowling (ten pin). American Bowling Congress, 5301 South 76th Street, Greendale, WI 53129.

Croquet. U. S. Croquet Assoc., 500 Avenue of Champions, Palm Beach Gardens, FL 33418.

Curling. U. S. Curling Assoc., 100 Center Point Drive, Box 971, Stevens Point, WI 54481.

Cycling. U. S. Cycling Fed., Inc., 17509 Boulder Street, Colorado Springs, CO 80909.

Darts. American Darts Organization, 13841 Eastbrook Avenue, Bellflower, CA 90706.

Deck Tennis. General Sportcraft Co., Ltd., 140 Woodbine Street, Bergenfield, NJ 07621.

Fencing. U. S. Fencing Assoc., 1750 East Boulder Street, Colorado Springs, CO 80909.

Football (six man). (See high school listing.)

Golf. U. S. Golf Assn., Golf House, Fair Hills, NJ 07931.

Gymnastics. U. S. Gymnastics Federation. P. O. Box 4699, Tucson, AZ 85717.

Handball. U. S. Handball Association, 903 North Beaton Avenue, Tucson, AZ 85711.

Horseshoes. National Horseshoe Pitchers Assoc., Box 278, Munroe Falls, OH 44262.

Ice Skating. Amateur Skating Union., Edward J. Schmitzer, 4135 North Troy Street, Chicago, IL 60618.

Indoor Hockey. Cosom Corp., 6030 Wayzata Boulevard, Minneapolis, MN 55416.

Marbles Shooting. National Marbles Tournament, Cleveland Press Building, Cleveland, OH 44101.

Paddle Tennis. U. S. Paddle Tennis Assoc., 186 Seeley Street, Brooklyn, NY 11218.

Paddleball. National Paddleball Assoc., P. O. Box 712, Flint, MI 48501

Quoits. General Sportcraft Co., Ltd., 33 New Bridge Road, Bergenfield, NJ 07621.

Racquetball. International Racquetball Assoc., 4101 Demster Street, Skokie, IL 670076. American Amateur Racquetball Assoc., 815 North Weber, Suite 203, Colorado Springs, CO 80903.

Scoopball (Rules for 26 different games). Cosom Industries, 6030 Wayzata Boulevard, Minneapolis, MN 55416.

Shuffleboard (deck). National Shuffleboard Assoc., Trailor Estates, Box 63343, 2010 Iowa Avenue, Bradenton, FL 33507.

Skating (speed). Amateur Skating Union of the United States, 1033 Shady Lane, Glen Ellyn, IL 60137.

Skiing (downhill slalom, giant slalom, jumping and cross-country, FIS and USSA rules). U. S. Ski Assn., 1750 Boulder Street, Colorado Springs, CO 80909.

Soccer. U. S. Soccer Federation, 1750 Boulder Street, Colorado Springs, CO 80909.

Softball (16"). Edw. Weinstein, Chairman Rules Committee, Umpires Protective Assn. of Chicago, Apartment 710, 3550 Lake Shore Drive, Chicago, IL 60607.

Squash Racquets. U. S. Squash Racquets Assn., 211 Ford Road, Bala-Cynwyd, PA 19004.

Table Tennis. U. S. Table Tennis Assoc., 1750 East Boulder Street, Colorado Springs, CO 80909.

Tennis Umpire's Manual (includes rules). United States Tennis Assn., 51 East 42nd Street, New York, NY 10017.

Tether Ball (inflated ball). W. J. Voit Rubber Corporation, 3801 South Harbor Boulevard, Santa Ana, CA 92704.

Touch Football. The Athletic Institute, Merchandise Mart, Chicago, IL 1 60654.

Volleyball (includes rules). U. S. Volleyball Assn., 1750 East Boulder Street, Colorado Springs, CO 80909.

National Collegiate Athletic Association, P. O. Box 1906, Shawnee Mission, KS 66201.

Basebal	*Ice Hockey*	*Swimming*
Basketball	*Lacrosse*	*Track and Field*
Fencing	*Skiing*	*Water Polo*
Football	*Soccer*	*Wrestling*
Gymnastics		

National Federation of State High School Athletic Associations, P. O. Box 20626, Kansas City, MO 61195.

Basketball Rules	*Football Rules*
Basketball Casebook	*Football Casebook*
Basketball Player Handbook	*Football Player Handbook*
Basketball Official's Manual	*Football Official's Manual*
Baseball Rules	*Football—Touch Football*
Baseball Casebook	*Six-Man Football and Soccer*
Baseball Umpire's Manual	*Track and Field (Rules and Records)*

Amateur Athletic Union of the United States, 3400 West 86th Street, Indianapolis, IN 46268.

Basketball	*Swimming, Water Polo, and Diving*
Boxing	*Swimming (Synchronized)*
Gymnastics	*Track and Field*
Handbook	*Weightlifting*
Judo	*Wrestling*

AAHPERD, NGWS Guides, Official Rules. AAHPERD, 1900 Association Drive, Reston, VA 22091.

Field Hockey	*Softball*
Gymnastics	*Tennis*
Soccer	*Volleyball*

National Association for Disabled Athletes, 17 Lindley Avenue, Tenafly, NJ 07670.

National Handicapped Sports and Recreation Association, P. O. Box 33141, Farragut Station, Washington, DC 20033.

Tips and Techniques for Teachers and Coaches. AAHPERD, 1900 Association Drive, Reston, VA 20091.

Even Years:	*Soccer*			
Odd Years:	*Aquatics*	*Basketball*	*Volleyball*	*Track and Field*

NAIA (National Association of Intercollegiate Athletics), 1205 Baltimore, In the Dixon Inn, Kansas City, MO 64105.

White, J. R. (ed.). (1990). *Sports rules encyclopedia* (2nd ed.). Champaign, IL: Leisure Press. (An excellent comprehensive source of rules.)

Social Recreation

Ahl, D. H. (1979). *More basic computer games.* Morristown: Creative Computing Press.

Kraus, R. C. (1979). *Social recreation: A group dynamics approach.* St. Louis, MO: Mosby.

Milberg, A. (1976). *Street games.* New York, NY: McGraw-Hill Co.

Scarne, J. (1973). *Encyclopedia of games.* New York, NY: Harper & Row.

Schwartz, A. (1972). *Hobbies.* New York, NY: Simon & Schuster.

Smaridge, N. (1976). *Choosing your retirement hobby.* New York, NY: Dodd, Mead.

CHAPTER SEVEN

EVALUATING PROGRAM EFFECTIVENESS

Evaluation is the key to successful program planning, since inherent in it are suggestions for increasing effectiveness. It is a process whereby, through systematically judging, assessing, and appraising the workings of a program, one gains information that indicates to programmers whether or not they are getting results or getting where they want to go–in sum, whether or not the program has value. In order to accomplish these things, the programmer needs to:

1. Be cognizant of and knowledgeable about the terminology used in evaluation.
2. Know the place of evaluation in recreation and its relationship to the planning process, particularly to program objectives.
3. Know the areas that need to be evaluated in terms of the total program.
4. Be able to select the proper approach to the evaluation that is to be made and put into effect.
5. Be able to analyze and interpret the results.

In this chapter the following topics are presented: (1) definitions of evaluation, measurement, testing, and research, (2) models for evaluation, (3) areas to evaluate, (4) competencies needed to evaluate, (5) approaches to evaluation, (6) tools of measurement, (7) development of measuring instruments, and (8) evaluation of specific areas related to programs.

EVALUATION, MEASUREMENT, RESEARCH

Evaluation

Evaluation is defined in varying ways in the literature, with perhaps as many subtly differing nuances as there are authors writing about it. However, all of the definitions seem to possess two common points: ascertainment of value and assessment of whether or not program objectives have been met. Program evaluation has been more formally defined by Rutman and Mowbray (1983) "...as the use of scientific methods to measure the implementation and outcomes of programs, for decision-making purposes" (p. 12). All definitions carry with them implications for the necessity of collecting qualitative and quantitative data in either a subjective or an objective manner and comparing these results in some way to some preset standard or goal. All of these elements are essential to evaluation and they imply, further, that evaluation is a process that employs measurement. What about measurement; what is it?

Measurement

This term has implicit in it the characteristic of determination of the quantity of a thing, the answer to the question, "How much?" or "What is the degree to which a person or a program possesses that quality?" It further implies the use of tools to measure the quality selected. Again, in a formal sense, measurement may be defined as ". . . a technique of evaluation which makes use of procedures which are generally precise and objective, which will generally result in quantitative data, and which characteristically can express its results in numerical form. It may be applied to qualitative procedures, however, when its techniques are objectified" (Barrow and McGee, 1979, page 7). One of the tools of measurement is a test, which might be defined in terms of a presentation of a task or series of tasks, so designed as to provide the evaluator with a systematic recording of behavior representative of certain traits possessed by the person tested.

If one uses tests to measure traits in order to evaluate behavior, is one engaged in research? Not necessarily, although evaluative research is of vital importance to the continued growth of recreation as a profession. What, then, is research?

Research

Research implies hypothesis testing, the systematic delving into a subject to discover facts, to create and test theories, and to revise application of those theories. Suchman (1967) suggests that one should distinguish between evaluation as the process of judging the worthwhileness of an activity and "evaluative research as the specific use of the scientific method for the purpose of making an evaluation" (page 31). The scientific method is the key to the difference, with its inherent criteria of forming an hypothesis and testing it scientifically as one pursues an inquiry into truth. All programmers may not be conducting research (although it is certainly encouraged), but all programmers *must* conduct program evaluation.

The Process of Evaluation

One can hardly exist without evaluating. Evaluative adjectives are in constant use in ordinary conversation. Things are cited as good, bad, wise, useless, with heavy reference to the affective domain in which one assigns value to things and people. Any social group carries the potential for probing evaluation, and that potential should be harnessed and brought to bear in solving the problems of the system and helping to increase its effectiveness. The process itself may be looked at in terms of Baumgartner and Jackson's (1975) three broad steps:

1. Collecting suitable data (measurement).
2. Judging the value of these data according to some standard.
3. Making decisions based on these data and the alternative courses of action available (1975, page 3).

In this process, one is concerned with *formative evaluation,* those things, evaluated during the formative stages of a program, that give immediate feedback, and the results of which lead to ongoing revision; and *summative evaluation,* which takes place at the conclusion of a program and contributes to comprehensive decision making about the disposition of the program. It is important to note that both of these forms are necessary for good evaluation to exist.

This process may also be looked at in terms of five steps, based on the early work of Danford and Shirley (1970), for the programmer to include in a total evaluation plan.

1. Prepare clear goal statements.
2. Interpret these goals in terms of the behavior of the people served—that is what behavior indicates progress toward achieving the goals?
3. Provide the kinds of recreation experiences you believe lead toward achieving these goals. For example, if you want to promote social interaction, the activity must include an opportunity for people to be together.
4. Observe and assess behavior of the participants in terms of the behaviors to be displayed that indicate goal achievement.
5. Analyze the results of the observation and assessment in terms of causes of success or failure and change the program as indicated by these results.

MODELS FOR EVALUATION

This discussion of process leads to the consideration of models for evaluation that have proliferated in the literature and form a useful schematic base for the understanding of how evaluation fits into the total program planning process.

The systems planning model is one that is used more and more frequently and addresses program design in total, including implementation and evaluation (see Figure 7.1). Such a model provides for accountability from the planner at each stage of the design by means of its evaluation component. Each step in the plan is evaluated, including the overall evaluation, and the results are communicated through the feedback loops, leading to revision at any stage of the plan. A typical systems model includes inputs (resources needed to establish and process the program), processing (the program process or planning and delivery of the program), and outputs (the program outcomes in terms of objectives) with feedback on the outcomes. Such a model for comprehensive planning was presented by Bannon (1976) and illustrates where evaluation is in the total picture (See Figure 7.1)

Evaluation then is actually the end product of a process that starts with planning, the setting of goals and objectives, the establishment of needs, a statement of the kinds of needs met, and the actual assessment of these needs. One must know what is planned for in order to evaluate wisely. To complete the model, feedback from the evaluation is used in further analysis and planning.

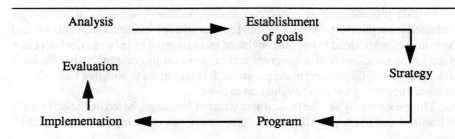

Figure 7.1 Comprehensive Planning Model (Courtesy of Bannon, 1976, p. 3)

Models of the evaluation segment of this planning model have been presented by many authors in slightly different ways (see Figure 7.2). Suchman's (1967) model does allow the evaluator to enter it at different points and carry on the evaluation from there. For instance, the organization administrator and staff may want to set the values and establish the objectives or goals and allow the evaluator to establish criteria by which to measure the accomplishment of goals. If the evaluator is the administrator, of course he or she will carry through all of the steps in the model.

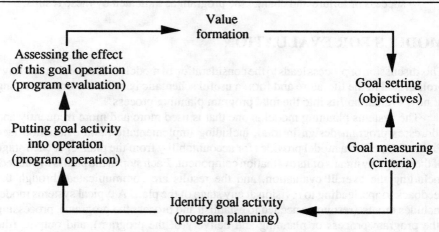

Figure 7.2 Evaluation Process (Courtesy of Suchman, 1967, p. 34)

In this process the objectives are set by the programmer, the program is planned, conducted, and evaluated, and modification, if needed, is made to the objectives or the program itself and then reevaluated. One can do this to miniunits of a program (formative) or maxiunits (summative). As always, the link between program performance and the objectives set for that program is maintained and evaluated. (See Bannon (1976, page 281) for a more extensive evaluation model.)

Another model for evaluation with good potential for use in recreation programs is the Discrepancy Evaluation Model (DEM) (Yavorsky, 1976). Evaluation in this model is considered to be the comparison between what is performance (P) to what should be standard (S), and if a difference is found between the two, it is called discrepancy (D). Discrepancies may be positive when the performance exceeds standards, or negative when the performance does not measure up to the standard. If the latter happens, the evaluator may have to (1) redesign an unrealistic standard, (2) suggest that management exert greater control over the performance, or (3) terminate the program. The model is illustrated in Figure 7.3.

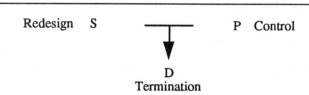

Figure 7.3 Discrepancy Evaluation Model (Courtesy of Yavorsky, 1976, p. 3)

Areas to be Evaluated

Having chosen a model for application of the evaluation process, what needs to be evaluated and how is that to be done? Let us look first at the areas of evaluation and more specifically, later, at how each area is to be evaluated. There are essentially four aspects of the programming process that are necessary to its success, which include the administration under whose auspices it is conducted, the specific face-to-face leadership who actually bring the program to the people, the program itself, and the facility in which it is conducted. All of these areas must be fully effective if the total program is to be successful. More specifically, each area involves assessment of the facets of each as listed:

1. Administration. Is the agency organized so that it can meet the demands or needs of the residents? Are executive officers competent in the areas of (1) planning, (2) organizing, (3) staffing (including the training functions), (4) directing the work of the personnel under them, and (5) exerting control over their domains. All of these areas include the financing that goes with them (Bannon, 1976).

2. Leadership or Personnel. What are their qualifications for the job they are doing, what is their performance in that job, and how effective are they in their jobs? This is obviously a key area, since poor leadership can rapidly destroy even the most well-conceived program.

3. Program. How is this related to participant needs? What are the philosophy, goals, and objectives? How do the program content, scheduling supervision, and records kept hold up? What is the relationship between goals and program-participant behaviors and outcomes, and what is the appropriateness of the activity for the community and the client group involved? This area is the crux of the evaluation process.

4. Areas and Facilities. These include the physical planning process with all of its ramifications, the management of areas and facilities, and the meeting of standards set for various types of facilities in terms of design, construction, and maintenance, as well as program and client appropriateness (e.g., a swing set in the yard of an adult MR facility is *not* client appropriate).

Competencies Needed to Evaluate

The evaluation process itself is initiated and participated in by many people, from the face-to-face leader to the supervisor to the board of the recreation department, the hospital or the camp, and the outside consultants called in by the administration. This is not to mention the day-to-day evaluation given by the participants themselves in their action of either continually supporting the program or in not supporting by failing to come a second time.

If the kind of formal evaluation referred to here is to be conducted successfully, it must be done by qualified personnel. This means qualified at the specific level of evaluation one is talking about. If it is self-evaluation, any given leaders should be able to make some significant self-assessments; if it is a systemwide evaluation, a team of outside consultants may be desired. At any rate, the evaluator should possess the following competencies, that is:

1. Be familiar with the field of recreation and leisure services.
2. Have knowledge of the availability of measuring instruments, on what they are based, the techniques necessary to use them, and how to administer them.
3. Know how to evaluate and select tests for specific purposes.
4. Be able to analyze results of the tests and interpret them to all concerned, relating results to the goals set by the program.
5. Be able to construct measurement instruments when none are available for the specific circumstances.
6. Have knowledge of elementary statistics (Barrow and McGee, 1979).

APPROACHES TO EVALUATION

The process of evaluation involves (1) setting goals for evaluation and (2) choosing an approach through which to meet these goals. In simplistic terms, the job might be seen as one of saying, "Yes, the objectives were met" or "No, they were not," claiming that if the behavioral objectives referred to earlier are well written, then the means for assessing whether or not the goal has been reached is already made clear and subjectivity is kept at a minimum. That statement is true as far as it goes. It is a good method of checking whether or not each participant reached a certain level of behavior—for example, chopped down the tree, ran the mile in seven minutes, completed a puppet that worked. But is the success of the program necessarily the sum of the individual accomplishments of each participant? Since it is important to remember that objectives are based on needs, this approach is also satisfying the criteria of measuring whether needs are met. This type of procedure is called *evaluating by objectives* and is one viable approach to the process.

Evaluation by Objectives

This may be the most important evaluation that is done because evaluation is mandated by the demand for accountability for the program. Why should it be supported in preference to spending the same money on health or welfare, or the like? Recreation departments compete for public funds and are constantly called upon to justify their existence. If one evaluates a program in terms of its objectives, then one will find that this process encompasses evaluation of facilities, leadership, participant benefits, and administration. Good evaluation leads to a revision of objectives, better policy decisions, and a better, stronger operational base for the program. Carrying out an evaluation also serves to bring the administration into all phases of the service-delivery system so that they observe, firsthand, what is going on—an outcome applauded by all programmers.

Referring to the steps in the evaluation process and the discussion of formative and summative evaluation, we find that in evaluating by objectives we start at the planning stage of the model and, using the formative approach, evaluate the objectives themselves as to their intrinsic worth as objectives before we try to evaluate whether or not they are met in a behavioral sense. This means that a preliminary step in evaluation by objectives is to evaluate the objectives and then proceed to evaluate the program by its objectives.

In evaluating by objectives we generally consider two types: (1) the broad objectives for the program itself, and (2) the specific behavioral objectives for the participants. (See Chapter Three for a complete presentation of writing of objectives.) The program objectives are established cooperatively by the professional deliverer of the service and the lay consumer of the service. (This process is outlined thoroughly in Bannon's mode; see Figure 7.1.) There is a link from these program objectives to the participant goals, since the broad goals are largely interpreted through the behavior of the participant. These latter goals are, of course, more specific than the former.

The evaluation process, then, starts with the formulation of broad goals. These goals for recreation are well known and appear in many texts. Some examples are:

1. To improve the quality of life–the joy of living.
2. To provide lifetime enjoyment.
3. To contribute to democratic citizenship–the welfare of all citizens.
4. To contribute to the search for excellence.
5. To provide a program for everyone.
6. To promote moral and ethical values–a code of living.
7. To contribute to good mental health.
8. To help satisfy basic, human needs.

Given these broad goals, the evaluator is faced with the problem of how to determine whether they are met. The programmer cannot simply answer, "Yes, the quality of life is improved for each participant in my program." He or she has to show specifically how the quality of life was improved. Therefore, one sets less broad objectives for each phase of the program, and these *must* be measurable. For example, the last broad goal cited above involves satisfying basic human needs. If we assume that a basic human need is for activity and its concomitants–strength, endurance, and fitness–then we can focus our objectives on something that is both programmable and measurable. We can include in our offerings a fitness and games program for youth, apply the AAHPERD Fitness Standards to a participant's performance in the activities of that program, and measure quite clearly whether each child has met the objectives dealing with increasing strength, endurance, and fitness in achieving broad goals under basic human needs. This kind of procedure must be followed for each broad goal agreed on.

Another example of moving from broad goals to specific participant objectives that are measurable was cited by Danford and Shirley (1970). Suppose that a broad program goal was to strengthen the quality of cooperation in children and youth. The specific behavioral objectives that would show participant attainment of this goal might be stated for a crafts program as is done below. In each lesson, each child will:

1. Share equipment with others.
2. Help clean up after crafts club.
3. Assist others less capable than oneself.
4. Contribute to the common pool of scrap materials.

If one did not expect perfect performance from everyone in the first lesson, one might make this more specific by stating exactly what percent of the time these behaviors should be shown. (See Chapter Two for specific examples of participant objectives for various programs.) If the objective calls for the participants to perform certain skills a given number of times, and all of them consistently meet this objective

50 percent of the time, that says a great deal about how successful leaders are in achieving these goals. If the town has invested a lot of money into its tennis program and if at the end of a season only 25 percent of the 10 to 12 year-old group can rally the ball and serve into the correct court, then the administration has a right to question the quality of instruction, just as they have a right to insist that the program leaders set reasonable objectives and report the facts regarding whether or not they are met.

Having formulated the objectives to meet the broad goals of the program, the next step is to weigh the different objectives in terms of their relative importance, so that counting something double and other things not at all is avoided. In this process one deals with varying degrees of tangibility that must be accounted for, for example, to measure whether or not a goal of having 80 percent of the tent sites in a given park occupied during the week is a more tangible task than measuring whether or not camper attitudes toward the park rangers is positive 80 percent of the time. Both types should be evaluated, with the tangible being given a little more weight, on the theory that in the *long run,* attitudes will correlate with the more tangible performance indicators (Rossi and Freeman, 1989).

Control Groups Before and After Evaluation

We may be interested in evaluative research on whether a program is accomplishing given objectives better than other programs, or we may want to know not only whether participants could achieve specific performance objectives but also what difference our program made to that person–that is, what was he or she able to do after the program that they could not do before they participated in it? To do this, we cannot simply measure where the participants are performing at the point of the evaluation, but we must go further than that. Two approaches could be used: (1) Establish a control group that is not involved in the program, but in all other aspects is exactly like the program group. We then measure each group on the trait(s) we are interested in and compare the resulting scores of the two groups to see if our participants have more of the quality we are measuring than the control group does; (2) we use the program group as its own control and measure the trait(s) before the program and again after they have experienced it. In many programs, one may not have a choice of which of these to use, or whether to use a combined approach, because no control group is available. However, when comparisons are only made within the group, if a difference is found, the evaluator does not know for certain whether or not the program experience made that difference without a control group against whom to compare changes.

Evaluation by Standards

A second approach to evaluation is that of *evaluation by standards.* Such standards can be either norm referenced or criterion referenced.

Norm Referenced

In this method the assumption is that program outcomes can be judged as effective if they are compared to a norm of success established for a group of similar programs. This technique allows the programmer to compare the present group's performance with that of previous groups for the same program, or with that of a neighboring town or agency. A greater element of objectivity may be evident than is found in using behavioral objectives, provided that the item is quantifiable and can be converted to a numerical score for comparison. There are numerous examples of these available in the literature. One example is the AAHPERD Fitness Test National Norms (1976). This normative approach is characterized by the use of some scale by trained examiners for rating or assessing the element to be judged. These raters give the element a score that can be converted into percentiles, T-scores, stanines, or the like. Norm-referenced performance, for example, may be reported as: 64 modified sit-ups in 60 seconds for a 15-year-old-girl equals a 99th percentile for the girl's placement.

The normative group must have similar characteristics to the population the programmer is currently rating. In utilizing this approach, the programmer must be wary of making the assumption that, if the participant is high on some quantity of standard behavior, then the program is necessarily good. That is the hope, but this is only true if the norms were established with great care to make certain that an excellent score was equated with ideal performance. Norms or standards often deal with quantity and exclude the consideration of quality. Other examples of quantity assessment are to count participant hours in activities, count activities available, chart how many leader hours go into a specific task, tally what activities are most popular, how many dollars are spent per capita, the number of classes, meetings, and games held, the number of acres per 1,000 population or even square footage used, or the number of campground visitations per month in the state parks.

Criterion Referenced

Criterion referenced refers to a system whereby one assesses the degree to which a person has attained some set standard or level of performance set by the evaluator and related to the group. For example, a girl of 15 must perform 37 modified sit-ups in 60 seconds in order to be eligible to join the tumbling club. Another example of a criterion-referenced system of evaluation is the ACA Camp Standards (1980). Using standards against which to compare programs is probably the most common approach to evaluation of any service delivery system in the public domain, recreation included. This approach allows a program to be evaluated in terms of standard criteria that represent some desirable level of performance, such as so many campers per counselor, so many beds per ward, or so many sit-ups per person. All of these things can be quantified in some way. A standard is defined as "a degree or level of requirement, excellence, or attainment" (Anderson et al. (1975), page 386).

How do standards come into being, and who says that these specific things are the standards of performance for all groups? Who enforces standards? Usually standards are developed in response to a felt need from those responsible for the operation of any given agency or service group. There is some effort made to establish uniformity in meeting objectives, to maintain a given level of performance, to assure a certain quality of program for the participants, to assess effectiveness of methods of doing things across a system, to be able to have confidence that all members of an organization meet some minimum level of criteria, to present evidence of accountability or to receive accreditation from some national group such as the American Camping Association or National Recreation and Parks Association. The expression of these needs leads to the establishment of some authoritative group within the organization who is charged with the task of developing standards for that organization in the general areas of (1) philosophy and goals, (2) administration, (3) programming, (4) personnel, (5) areas, facilities and equipment, and (6) evaluation. Following this step, criteria for measuring each of these standards are developed. Usually several working subgroups within the organization will meet then to discuss the criteria, rework them, and bring them back to the parent group. Discussions and workshops take place until consensus is reached that these standards and their supporting criteria represent as much as possible what the members of the organization believe it stands for and can achieve. Paralleling this procedure, a scoring system for use in assessing standards is also developed. That system is then checked for reliability (test-retest), validity (often construct is accepted), and objectivity (interrater correlations). These terms are discussed in greater detail later in this chapter. Examples of such standards are the Standards of the American Camping Association, Evaluation and Self-Study of Public Recreation and Park Agencies, and Program Analysis of Service Systems (PASS).

When utilizing the standards approach to evaluation, there are certain considerations one should be cognizant of in applying the findings. The measurement tool used is usually a checklist with interview schedules employed in a supporting role. This type of tool has the advantage of being fairly easy to construct and may be utilized validly by personnel without extensive training, but it is also sometimes too global in nature, yielding data that are too general to be useful, and it is difficult to weight the important things more heavily than other items, thereby giving the impression that all things are relatively of the same concern (Bannon, 1976). Another point here is that although there are inherent, viable differences within different systems or communities and their programs, given standards do not allow for "equally good, but different." There is some danger in believing that standards are absolute and in pursuing them as though they are ends in themselves. Standards tend to take on the perspective of things that can be counted (e.g., beds, pushups, and staff) and ignore the impact of the program on people.

When choosing standards for use with a given program, several points should be noted:

1. Does the system cover all the areas adequately that need to be evaluated?
2. Are there basic criteria listed for each standard? Are they clear and scorable?
3. If you use the system, what will you know when you finish it? Does that meet the objectives you set for evaluation?
4. Is the scoring system clear?
5. Are there implications within the scoring system for remediation?

Evaluation by Effects on the Participants

A third means of assessing a program is by *evaluation of effects on participants*. As a result of being in the program are they stronger, happier, more skillful, or more integrated in the group? What are the gains in the affective domain? Here the programmer is looking at the qualitative outcomes of the program and assessing whether or not the program made a difference to participants. Were they changed in any way by participation? At this stage one begins to move into evaluative research.

Examples of this type of evaluation would involve measurement of such things as (1) the difference in attitudes toward the environment before and after participation in a nature center program, (2) the change in body image of mentally retarded adolescents after undergoing a fitness program, or (3) the effects on asocial behavior exhibited by predelinquent boys enrolled in a recreation program. Assessment of all of these things is in the scope of the recreation programmer's day-to-day operation but, too often, is considered the sole concern of the researcher, and not that of the practitioner. Yet, the practitioner has the real and continuous contact with the clients and has the unique opportunity to effect lasting change. Such change must be planned to be effective, and no one is in a better position to do it than the programmer, nor in a better position to make it meaningful. Let us look at this more closely.

Objectives, once set, are translated into some experience that will help the participant to achieve that objective. Since some experiences may serve to meet a given objective, but rarely does any one experience serve to meet *all* objectives, the professional chooses those activities that he or she believes will best meet the objectives stated. We then look at what happens to the individuals who are engaged in that experience and evaluate the effects on them. These effects can be categorized into four groups:

1. Psychomotor
   (a) Developmental–body image, skill.
   (b) Physiological–strength, endurance, fitness, relief from stress.
   (c) Rehabilitative–remediation, therapeutic, prescription.
2. Psychological
   (a) Behavioral aspects–self-concept, attitudes, personality, human need satisfaction.

(b) Self-actualization–value enhancement through play.

(c) Play therapy.

3. Sociological

(a) Enhancement of group or community.

(b) Collective behavior–small and large group, leisure norms, belongingness, social behavior, integration.

(c) Increase social organization (reduce disorganization, i.e., delinquency).

4. Educational

The question then arises as to how to measure these outcomes. One approach is to design your own instruments. The mechanics of doing this are presented in the following section. The second option is to choose a test developed and standardized for each category listed. A disadvantage to this choice is that each test is developed for some given population, and if the characteristics of the present population to be measured are not the same as the normative population, then the test should be revalidated. If, however, the populations are similar, and if the objectives of the test are satisfactory for your purposes, much work and time are saved by using such instruments. A complete bibliography of measuring tools related to assessing effects on the participants is in Appendix E.

TOOLS OF MEASUREMENT

It has been established in this discussion that in order to evaluate, one must first measure certain specified qualities or traits possessed by the focus of the evaluation. This measurement requires the use of data gathering tools or instruments appropriate to the approach to be used and the population evaluated. Typical of the instruments used in recreation are questionnaires, attitude scales, rating scales, observations, checklists, and sociograms. The development, meaning, and interpretation of these and other tools are presented here, along with general characteristics of measuring instruments used in program evaluation. These instruments include:

1. Anecdotal records
2. Observational methods
3. Questionnaires
4. Inventories
5. Interviews
6. Checklists
7. Rating scales
8. Standardized tests
9. Personal diary reports
10. Case studies
11. Cumulative records
12. Sociometric methods

13. Self-appraisals
14. Reaction sheets
15. Various types of hardware instrumentation
16. Videotape and motion picture films

Characteristics of Measurement Instruments

There are certain definable qualities or characteristics of an instrument that are essential, and without them one can put little faith in the data resulting from the use of that instrument. These characteristics are reliability, validity, and objectivity.

Reliability

Reliability implies consistency or dependability. A test is said to be reliable if similar results occur when the test is repeated under like conditions. When a test is reliable, a person taking it twice (whose ability in the trait being tested has not changed) will receive a similar score. Extraneous factors can influence this and introduce variability into the measurement. For example, the person being tested can feel tired or sick on one of the days tested, motivation could change, or test effect could be operating (learning from taking the test). Reliability is expressed on a scale from 0 to + or -1.00, with 1.00 expressing a perfect, positive correlation between the scores of two performances. There are several ways of generating these scores. These methods are called test-retest, split halves (odd-even), and parallel forms.

1. Test-retest. This method requires that the measure be given at one time and repeated at another time fairly close to the first, so that forgetting, practicing, and learning will not be factors influencing the results. It is sometimes called the stability-reliability method (Baumgartner and Jackson, 1975) because it assumes that the conditions under considerations are stable from day to day. This type of reliability should yield a correlation of .80 to .95 if the test is to be considered reliable, especially if a skill performance is being measured. This method is time consuming.

2. Split Halves. Often it is impossible to retest a subject on a given trait, and yet one would like an estimate of reliability. If a test has a given number of trials or statements, it is possible to give the test only once and to correlate scores on the odd-numbered trials (1, 3, 5, 7, 9) with the even-numbered trials (2, 4, 6, 8, 10) or the first half of the test against the second half. Statistically, it is then possible to predict what the correlation would be for the whole test. One method for computing correlations is presented in Chapter Eight.

3. Parallel Forms. In this method, two supposedly identical forms of a measuring instrument are given and, if performance on one correlates highly with performance on the other, the test is said to be reliable. This method is used mostly with paper and pencil tests in which those taking the test are given Form A at one session and Form B at another.

Validity

A measuring instrument is said to be valid if it measures what it is supposed to measure. In order for a test to be valid it must be reliable, although the reverse is not true, since a test could measure the wrong thing with great consistency! For example, counting the people who pass through the gate is a valid measure of how many visitors there are to a park, but not of how many people used the fireplaces; or scores on the Attitude Toward Disabled People Scale is a valid measure of what people say their attitude is, but it is not a valid measure of how they would vote on raising taxes to provide the money to make town buildings accessible to the handicapped. Validity can be divided into four types : (1) content, (2) construct, (3) concurrent, and (4) predictive (Baumgartner and Jackson, 1975).

1. Content Validity. An instrument is said to have content validity if it measures the factors about which conclusions are to be made. Does it do what it says it does? Does the attitude toward the handicapped test have questions in it pertaining to the handicapped, or does the program evaluation instrument contain items related to the objectives of the program? The judgment of this quality is obviously subjective, and no statistical assessment can be made of it.

2. Construct Validity. The traits that form the basis of a total test are called constructs, and it is assumed that these constructs are legitimate parts of the whole. For example, if passing, blocking, and tackling are constructs of the game of football and a combination of these would be a legitimate test of football playing ability, then the test has construct validity and the best players will receive the best scores on the test.

3. Concurrent Validity. Testing for concurrent validity requires the correlation of the test results with some known criterion measure of the same trait. An example of this type of validity would be correlating the scores on a test of attitudes toward littering with actual littering behavior, or correlating the scores on a newly constructed test of self-concept with scores of the same children on the Piers-Harris Children's Self-Concept Scale. Expert or judges' ratings are often used as criterion measures.

4. Predictive validity. This validity represents the ability to test for performance on one trait in order to predict performance on another trait. For example, if the Tennessee Self-Concept Test has predictive validity, then those who score high on the positive scales will demonstrate favorable attitudes toward themselves. Undergraduates who score above the mean on the entrance predictor scores will graduate from college.

Objectivity

Objectivity is often referred to as rater reliability, or it represents a quality of agreement among users of the instrument. It implies that two people looking at the same performance will judge it the same way. If it is objective, there is lack of personal influence from the rater on the score or rating given.

Attributes of a Good Measuring Instrument

1. The first attribute and the most important one is that the test should possess reliability, validity, and objectivity. If these qualities are missing, then there is almost no need to judge it further; it is not adequate.
2. The tool should measure the important factors. What these factors are should be determined by the objectives of the program or its subparts.
3. It should be appropriate to the participants evaluated in terms of things such as age, sex, and special factors (e.g., reading level). For example, the Tennessee Self-Concept Scale requires a sixth-grade reading level and is therefore inappropriate for young children.
4. It should discriminate between those people, programs, or facilities that possess the trait being measured and those who do not have it, and be sensitive enough to identify a real difference if one exits.
5. It should be given in a reasonable length of time. For example, a questionnaire that takes one and one-half hours to administer would not be the tool of choice at the formative evaluation stage of a new crafts program.
6. A good test should be easy to prepare and administer. The less complex the better, providing it still does what it is purported to do.
7. Availability of norms and standards should be considered as they serve to strengthen interpretation of test results.
8. There should be clear, concise directions.
9. The scores should be readily interpretable.
10. The attribute that is measured should be clearly delineated so that it is clear specifically what was lacking in performance and what type of modification is needed. For example, if a campsite in a state park were rated on a score of 1 to 10, and it received a 4, what does the park superintendent know in terms of modifying the sites in order to receive a 10? He has no idea on the basis of score only. The person receiving the evaluation should gain some suggestion of what to change. Feedback should be provided by the instrument.
11. Tested scoring directions should be provided.
12. It should measure unique data that have not already been gained in some other way.

DEVELOPMENT OF MEASURING INSTRUMENTS

Questionnaires

A questionnaire is a device used to gain information by having a respondent fill in answers, or give the answers in an interview with the evaluator. This is the basic data collection instrument used in conducting surveys and is of common usage in the recreation and parks field.

Questionnaires are used to make descriptive assertions about population, for example, the percent of the community likely to support a new swimming pool, the geographical origin of campers at a state park, or the age, sex, and disability of the handicapped citizens patronizing the town recreation programs. It is used to explain something about a population, that is, to try to link an answer to a given variable; for example, if users of the tennis courts at 10:00 AM on a Tuesday are typically female, age 25 to 35, and the users at 4:30 PM on Wednesday are male, age 30 to 50, can any explanation be drawn for the pattern of usage? What questions might be asked to strengthen the implication already evident in these data? A third purpose of a questionnaire might be to explore how a given segment of a population feels about an issue before delving into it too deeply. For instance, one might conduct a survey on a limited basis in a community to explore attitudes toward building a swimming pool before working toward a referendum among the voters on the issue.

Data collected through the use of questionnaires to survey an issue can be gathered by means of a *cross-sectional technique* (data collected at one point in time from a sample selected to represent a larger population in existence at the same time). A typical question is, "If the election were held today, how would you vote?" This is the most common design. Data may also be collected by means of a *longitudinal technique* in which data are collected from a given population at different points in time. Based on these data, the evaluator is able to report change.

Backstrom and Hursh (1963) suggested some steps to take in the development and administration of a questionnaire that are pertinent here:

1. Hypothesizing–deciding what you want to study.
2. Designing and planning the procedures to be used and the personnel needed.
3. Financing–arranging support for the survey.
4. Sampling–choosing the people to be questioned.
5. Drafting and constructing the questionnaire.
6. Pretesting it at a preliminary stage to see if it is collecting desired data.
7. Training those who will administer the instrument.
8. Administering the questionnaire.
9. Verifying the data collected.
10. Processing and analyzing the data.
11. Reporting and interpreting the results (1963, page 19).

Structuring the Questions. In this section a presentation is made of (1) types of format, (2) kinds of questions, (3) formulating the questions, and (4) sequencing the questions.

A. Types of Format

1. *Fixed alternative items.* This type of item offers the respondent a choice among two or more alternative answers. This is also called a closed format. Examples are:
   - (a) Yes-No, True/False.
   - (b) Multiple choice.
   - (c) Rank order.
   - (d) Checklist.
   - (e) Scale.

   Advantages: This provides greater uniformity and thus higher reliability. It is easily coded for analysis and it forces answers into the categories desired.

   Disadvantages: This type of question may encourage superficiality, since it may never get any deeper than the choices offered. It may often irritate the respondent who does not want to choose any of the responses offered. It can also cover ignorance of the subject or fail to reveal answers that are given because they are believed to be socially desirable.

2. *Open ended items.* An open ended item supplies a frame of reference for the respondent, but puts minimum restraint on the answer. It can be a completely free response or a request to list.

   Advantages. This type of question offers flexibility and a possibility to get an in-depth response. There may be a chance for better estimates of true beliefs, to detect lack of knowledge and open up estimates of true beliefs to detect lack of knowledge and open up the possibilities of getting information not previously considered.

   Disadvantages: There is a real possibility that the answer will be so broad or multifaceted, that it will be too hard to link to specific objectives and to analyze and interpret. Open ended items are unwieldly and take a relatively large amount of space. There is also a possibility that the respondent to a written questionnaire will simply skip the open ended type items.

3. *Scale items.* This is a special type of closed format in which a set of verbal items is stated and the respondent expresses degrees of agreement or disagreement with it. This is a familiar format used with attitude questions.

B. Kinds of Questions

1. *Fact questions.* These questions are often used in gathering demographic data on age, sex, income, group affiliations, and so on.

2. *Opinion or attitude questions.* This type of question is often in the affective domain and deals with feelings, beliefs, and ideals.
3. *Information questions.* These questions are included to get data on how much respondents know, how they know, or what they know.
4. *Self-perception questions.* Here the evaluator deals with questioning the respondent regarding his or her behavior in relation to others. For example, one cmight ask, "Are you a leader or a follower?"

C. Formulating the Questions

In choosing and phrasing the questions, it is advisable to follow some specifics do's and don'ts. Some suggestions are given below.

1. Be concise, precise, and avoid subtleties. Avoid ambiguity such as misperception and loading ("Do you think we should waste any more of the town's money on a ballfield in that low class area?").
2. Ask only one thing per question. Avoid double-barreled statements such as, "Do you think Mr. Playback should direct the theater group this summer, or should we get a better person?"
3. Keep the questions short. The respondent should not lose track of what you are asking.
4. Be sure the respondent has the knowledge and competence necessary to answer the question. Do not ask the citizen how much of the budget should be allotted to each activity. Most of the time citizens do not know the true costs involved, and the answer cannot be meaningful.

D. Sequencing the Questions

Typically, a questionnaire is in four parts. (1) The introduction, which identifies the sponsor, the topic, and the interviewer if that is how the data are to be gathered; it is designed to create a good impression of the evaluator and win the confidence of the respondent. (2) The warm-up, or a series of questions that may have no great meaning but lead to respondent rapport and proceed easily into the main purpose of the questionnaire. (3) The main body of the questionnaire. (4) Demographic characteristics.

The questionnaire should demonstrate smooth transitions from one part to another with the simple things leading to the complex. However, complex items should not be left past the point of informant fatigue, estimated to occur at about 15 to 20 minutes into the questionnaire.

E. Designing the Questionnaire

1. General format
   (a) Spread out and uncluttered.
   (b) A new line used for new questions.
   (c) Enough space allotted for open-ended questions.
   (d) As short as feasible. As a general estimate, up to 10 well-spaced pages will take 30 minutes.

(e) Items in a consistent format and question style.

(f) Items sequenced logically.

2. Specific suggestions

   (a) Precode if it is to be computer analyzed.

   (b) Use good stock paper, and color code the different parts of the questionnaire.

   (c) Give specific directions such as: "Circle one," "Check one," "Put an X in the box."

   (d) Decide on boxes, brackets, lines, and be consistent.

   (e) Have a set format for contingency questions, for example, "Have you every belonged to the Recreation and Parks Society?"

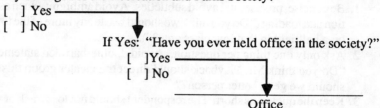

[ ] Yes

[ ] No

If Yes: "Have you ever held office in the society?"

[ ] Yes

[ ] No

Office

   (f) Include clear, concise instructions.

   (g) End the questionnaire with a "Thank you."

For more details regarding the administration of an interview questionnaire, see Dillman (1978) and the Survey Research Center's *Interviewers' Manual* (1976). Examples of questionnaires used in evaluation are given in Appendix E.

Observations

An observation is a planned, systematic procedure designed to note and record specific, selected occurrences. The tools used to do this are checklists, anecdotal records, rating scales, or the like. The choice really depends upon the type of answer or data needed. Unlike the questionnaire, which requires cooperation of the subject, the observation can even be done with the subject unaware of it (provided that the code of confidentiality is not violated). This flexibility allows the evaluator to look at behavior that is neither staged for the observer nor stilted because the observer is known to be there. Participant observation is also used, which means that the observer is part of the group, has a vested interest in it, and may gain greater access to information. A disadvantage to the latter approach is that, when a person becomes a part of the group, he or she then has a position in it, with a potential leadership role, which changes the group, in a sense, so that it is not the same group as it may have been if the evaluator were not there. Another consideration is that the evaluator may lose objectivity. In relation to this final point, in all observations, the observers must be objective and trained both in assessing the behavior they are observing and recording it appropriately.

It is essential, if the results are to be valid, that the behavior to be observed is clearly and specifically defined. For example, if leader behavior is being observed, it is not enough, say, to look for democratic behavior. One must answer, "What characterizes democratic behavior?" It must be clear what actions will be recorded and classified as democratic. In doing this, the evaluator should assign behaviors to mutually exclusive categories that are divided into clearly identifiable units.

Observer's inference is practically always present, but it should be kept in control. The greater the inference factor anticipated in any given observation, the more trained the observers should be.

Observation systems may either be developed for the specific situation for which they are to be used, or an already devised system such as a modified Bales Interaction Analysis may be used.

Observations are set on a time sampling or an event sampling basis. The former is a recording of behavioral units at given points in time, for example, ten minutes of a program every other night for six weeks, with a specific plan made for which ten minutes will be sampled each time. In event sampling, an observation is made of a complete behavioral event, for example, the interaction between two players in a game of checkers. An advantage to event sampling is that there is an integrated unit of behavior from start to finish. It also can provide information as to how events follow to their conclusion. An advantage to time sampling is that the evaluator gets random samples of behavior if they occur frequently. But if the behaviors are infrequent, they may be missed altogether in this approach, and the reported data may not have a great deal of continuity to them. Because observations are done on behavior, there may not be any better way to get information about how program objectives are being met. There should obviously be a direct relationship between the behavior specified in the objectives and the behavior rated in the evaluation process (Cartwright and Cartwright, 1974).

There are three primary ways to collect observation data:

A. Checklists.
A checklist is a list of actions that the observer may see occurring and on which he or she tallies occurrences. For example, a checklist item may look like this.

Check all that apply.

The leader of this activity is:

___ Well organized.
___ Well prepared.
___ Knowledgeable about the activity.
___ Motivating.
___ Dull.
___ Uninformed.
___ Not effective.
___ Disorganized.

A checklist is used when the behaviors that will be exhibited are known in advance, and there is no need to indicate frequency or quantity or to give any explanation about the presence or absence of a behavior. One can almost take the behaviors specified in any given objective and put them in checklist form. Be sure to group together those items most likely to occur in the same sequence of behaviors.

An advantage to the use of a checklist is that a lot of information can be recorded in a relatively short period of time.

B.   Anecdotal Records.

An anecdotal record is a narrative account of an incident and is often used in case studies and not often used in evaluating day-to-day operations. The record usually contains a statement of the situation being observed, what subjects said or did, and how they reacted to their role in it. For example:

> Child X was playing on the floor with a toy truck. Child Y came up to child X and took the truck from child X. Child X sat there and did not do or say anything.

One event is not usually sufficient, but a series of related events must be recorded.

C.   Rating Scales.

A rating scale is a measuring device that requires the rater or observer to assign the rated factor to categories on a continuum that usually have numerical values assigned to them so that the data may be quantified. The common types of scale are (1) category, (2) numerical, and (3) graphic (Kerlinger, 1973).

1. Category. This type utilizes verbal categorization of strength or frequency of the behavior, for example:
   (a) Strongly agree, agree, neutral, disagree, strongly disagree.
   (b) Excellent, good, fair, poor, very poor.
   (c) Always, sometimes, never.
2. Numerical. The categories above can be assigned numerical values so that data can be treated statistically. For example, excellent = 5, good = 4, fair = 3, poor = 2, and very poor = 1.
3. Graphic. In this type, the categories are distributed along a line graph, and specific points on the scale may be identified. In other words, one takes, for example, three categories of never, usually, and always and puts them on a line as follows:

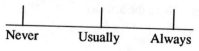

Never   Usually   Always

The rater is instructed to check the spot on the line that applies to the behavior rated. This has the effect of expanding the scale because, if a check is placed between never and usually, one could assign that a verbal category of sometimes, and if it is placed between usually and always, the verbal category would become often:

| Never | Sometimes | Usually | Often | Always |

This type of scale can be vertical or horizontal, which suggests to the raters that there are equal intervals, and it fixes a continuum in their minds that word categories alone do not do. The Likert technique used in preparing scales is presented later in this chapter.

A caution is indicated regarding rating scales; because they are so easy to use, they are often used indiscriminately without proper training, and then the results are interpreted by equally untrained people. Rating scales are also prone to observer bias, since there is a tendency for the fact of rating one characteristic to influence the succeeding rating of other characteristics. There are several possible error sources that an observer utilizing these technique should be cautious about (Sax, 1974). Three of these are:

1. Error of severity–utilizing only the low side of the scale.
2. Error of leniency–utilizing only the high side of the scale.
3. Error of central tendency–utilizing only the middle of the scale.

Rating scales are often used by participants to evaluate a program they have attended. Some examples of scales are presented in Appendix E.

Attitude Scales

An attitude is a learned predisposition to think, feel, perceive, and behave toward an object, person, or situation (Kerlinger, 1973). Attitudes are generally evaluated by means of measurement by a paper and pencil test of some sort. There are three major types of attitude scales generally in use. These are (1) the summated rating scale (Likert), (2) equal appearing intervals (Thurstone), and (3) the cumulative scale (Guttman). Only the Likert technique will be detailed since it is the most widely used.

Summated Rating Scale (Likert)
The Likert rating is a scaling technique in which a large number of items have the characteristic that the more favorable an attitude, the higher the score on the item. Responses to an item are frequently given on a five-point scale of strongly agree (SA) as equal to 5, agree (A) as a 4, undecided (U) equal to 3, disagree (d) scoring a 2, and strongly disagree (SD) equal to 1. Scoring is reversed for negatively worded items. Some specific elements are present in this method of scaling (Kerlinger, 1973).

1. The universe of items is conceived to be a set of items of equal attitude value, that is, one item carries the same value as any other item.
2. An intensity of feeling or expression of attitude is possible through the strongly agree/to strongly disagree format.
3. It is possible to assign numerical value to categories (as indicated above) and utilize these values in statistical analysis such as rank order subjects, figuring averages, etc.
4. Respondents can be placed on a favorable-unfavorable continuum, although the middle category on a five-point scale is difficult to interpret.
5. Standard scores may be computed from the raw attitude scores, allowing comparisons between groups and easy interpretation to the lay person.
6. Likert scales are typically reliable.

Steps in Developing a Likert Scale
Although there are many scales on the market designed to measure attitudes toward a wide variety of attitude objects, it is often desirable to design your own scale, which will be specific to your given program situation. Suggestions for a procedure to be followed in developing a Likert scale are presented here:

1. Review any available literature, talk to experts, ask open-ended questions regarding the attitude object (e.g., littering), and based on these contacts, compose an item pool representing the salient factors in proportion to their importance to the factor studied.
2. Form these items into statements that are phrased in the same format and are grammatically correct. Avoid long, complex sentences. Prepare more items than are desired in the final scale.
3. Choose a three-, five-, or seven-item format.
4. Give the items to a group that is similar to your target group.
5. Compute a total score.
6. Correlate the score of each item with this total score and keep those items with the highest correlations, or keep those items with correlations significantly greater than zero. Look at the items thus omitted to see if, with some rewording, they could be revised and kept. Check to make sure that the remaining items still represent the salient items in proportion to their importance to the factors as they were originally represented. If there are subscales, compute reliability of the subscales, as well as that of the total scale. If a statistical analysis is beyond the scope of your present skills, look at the total score and the item to see if each agree in the direction supported. For example, if the total score expresses a positive attitude, does the single item also?
7. Resubmit the scale for analysis. The items that now receive the highest correlations are retained for the final scale. The final scale should have about 30 items on it.

An example of a Likert item is the statement, "Recreation programs should be provided by a public agency."

SA   A   U   D   SD   (Circle one.)

Other Attitude Measurements
There are some additional, more specialized techniques by which attitudes are measured, which are not really scale construction methods in the strict sense of the term. Two of these utilized most frequently by evaluators in recreation are the semantic differential technique developed originally by Osgood, Suci and Tannenbaum (1957), and the Q-sort technique developed by Stephenson (1953). These techniques may also be used in need assessment.

Semantic Differential. Osgood's technique is designed to measure the meaning of an object to a person. The technique consists of establishing a number of what could be termed, scales, each of which consists of a bipolar adjective pair (good-bad), to which a respondent is requested to respond regarding any given concept. The person is asked to rate this concept on a seven-point scale between the two adjectives that represent how he or she feels. Adjectives used are usually (1) *evaluative* in nature, such as good-bad, (2) show strength or *potency* of an idea, such as strong-weak, or (3) show motion or *action* such as fast-slow (Kerlinger, 1973). As an example, we could take the concept of recreation and ask people to respond on a semantic differential, ranking each pair along the specified continuum and it would look like this:

E	1.	Pleasant	: : : : : : :	Unpleasant
A	2.	Angular	: : : : : : :	Rounded
A	3.	Passive	: : : : : : :	Active
E	4.	Ugly	: : : : : : :	Beautiful
P	5.	Delicate	: : : : : : :	Rugged
A	6.	Fast	: : : : : : :	Slow
E	7.	Good	: : : : : : :	Bad
P	8.	Weak	: : : : : : :	Strong
A	9.	Dull	: : : : : : :	Sharp
P	10.	Deep	: : : : : : :	Shallow
P	11.	Heavy	: : : : : : :	Light
E	12.	Dark	: : : : : : :	Bright

E = evaluative;   P = potency;   A = action

Numbers are assigned to the spaces between the dots with 7 in the space nearest the positive adjective and 1 at the other end. (Note that some scales are reversed in position, such as weak-strong, so that the respondent does not simply check all the same position without assimilating the meaning of the adjectives.)

Case Study Approach

An approach that is being used with increasing frequency in evaluation and research in the behavioral and sociological domain in the case study. In this method, detailed information about an individual, an institution, or a situation is gathered, as the evaluator records specific behaviors, often of a highly individualized nature. The case study can lead to the formulation of theories about things that can be submitted to more rigorous testing, which would not be possible otherwise. It is a good way of identifying what is actually happening, provided well-trained, highly objective observers are used. It has been classified as being a method of looking at social reality. Although the focus on this discussion to date appears to be on the individual as an object or a case study, it is also used to study communities, organizations, and institutions.

Data for the case study are collected by means of anecdotal records, observation, and rating forms, mentioned earlier in this chapter, as well as direct interviewing and testing of the individuals on the variables of concern. It really accommodates broad input of information. The point is to gather all the relevant information available to explain a given condition as it exists at the time it is being studied. For example, a case study approach could be used:

1. To investigate a particularly successful program if one were interested in identifying all those things that went into making it successful, so that they could be studied and adapted for use in similar programs that were less successful.
2. When there is a particular problem in a program or area, the cause of which is elusive.

The case study often brings to light the specific area of difficulty, and then the avenue to solution becomes clearer. General steps in the case study approach are:

1. Identify the focus of the investigation. Is it the behavior of an individual, a study of a community, or is it a program with a larger structure?
2. Identify the nature of what needs to be studied in regard to this focus. Is it in the affective, the cognitive, or the psychomotor domain? For example, evaluation of the leader may be in the affective domain, the participant in the psychomotor, and the agency in the cognitive.
3. Select the measurement tools to collect the appropriate data. The tools used are such things as questionnaires, rating scales, anecdotal records, logs, diaries, attitude scales, life history or biographical forms, and various sociometric instruments.
4. Collect the data in a planned, systematic way. (See specifics under the individual methods described earlier.). Optimize the available evaluators to get the most usable data in a reasonable time frame.
5. Collate and present the data in a logical way.

6. Interpret data in a way appropriate both to the situation studied and the audience to whom the report is directed.
7. On the basis of the findings, prepare solutions to problems and make general recommendations.

Guidelines for effective recording of case study data are:

1. Records should be accurate, objective, complete, concise, and clear.
2. Be brief enough for clarity and complete enough for objectivity.
3. Utilize chronological and topical presentation of the data (sometimes in combination) so that it can be easily followed.
4. Present the background against which any behavioral incident occurred.

The case study really represents a specialized approach that deserves mention. It is called the qualitative approach to evaluation research.

Qualitative Evaluation

An alternative approach to data collection that should be mentioned is through qualitative measurement. "Qualitative data consist of *detailed descriptions of* situations, events, people, interactions, and observed behaviors; *direct quotations* from people about their experiences, attitudes, beliefs, and thoughts; and excerpts or entire passages from documents, correspondence, records, and case histories" (Patton, 1980, p. 22). Contrary to quantitative data, qualitative interview data are collected in narrative form from people who respond in their own words, rather than reacting to preset statements.

Further the evaluator tries to record the subject's words the way they were given, and not to translate them or assign them numerical values. The researcher who uses qualitative approaches is mainly searching for the meaning of leisure behavior for the participant. Two main approaches to collection of qualitative data, then, are qualitative interviewing (Howe, 1988) and observation of behavior. The data collection techniques commonly used are ". . .simple observation, participant observation, unstructured nonstandardized interviews, key informant interviews, open ended questionnaires, the review of documents or other artifacts and physical traces and/or some combination of these techniques. . ." (Howe, 1985, p. 218).

Once the data are collected, the most challenging task is the analysis of them. This analysis must be unambigious and rigorous. It must have the same credibility and interpretability as quantitative data have. The programmer must be meticulous in assigning meaning to the behavior and exceptionally careful to present conclusions clearly and consistently. Potential bias must be anticipated and accounted. It is suggested that triangulation be used in any study in which the researcher uses a qualitative approach so that more than one perspective is covered.

Whether to use and when to use the qualitative or the quantitative approach to data collection is often a difficult question to answer. Probably a combination of the two is best. They are not mutually exclusive.

EVALUATION OF SPECIFIC AREAS RELATED TO PROGRAM

It is important at this point to look at the use and application of these tools in the actual evaluation of those areas impinging on total program effectiveness. The key areas are leadership (personnel), administration, facilities, and the program itself.

Leadership

"The leader is the most important single factor influencing the success or failure of any recreation department" (Danford and Shirley, 1970, page 373). At least once a year, regardless of what type of agency is being considered, there should be some kind of evaluation of the performance of all personnel. This process should involve self-evaluation of the leader, participant evaluation, and supervisor evaluation. After all of these evaluations are solicited and compiled, there should be feedback of the results to that leader. Such an evaluation serves as a basis for rehiring, promotion, salary increase, and most important of all, improvement of performance. Criteria for good leadership were covered in Chapter Five. Some steps in leadership evaluation are:

1. A *must* starting point is with the job analysis and job specifications of what the person was hired to do.
2. Tools and methods of approach are selected that will assist the evaluator in gathering data relative to the accomplishments of the tasks specified. Standards of acceptable performance are set.
3. During the process of job performance, the leader is observed by the supervisor. Be sure to evaluate a representative sample of performance.
4. The supervisor rates the performance.
5. The leader rates his or her own performance.
6. The participant rates the performance.
7. A record is kept regarding whether or not tasks assigned are completed.
8. The supervisor collates the information.
9. The supervisor and the leader sit down together, go over the evaluations, review strengths and weaknesses, and formulate recommendations for the leader's future behavior based on the findings.

Lopez (1968) suggests that when choosing an evaluation instrument for leadership, one should consider three key points:

1. Is it really measuring the trait it purports to measure?
2. Is this trait significant for effective job performance?
3. Is the evaluation predictive of future performance?

Also, is the measure consistent over time? It is suggested here that the instrument be checked for validity and reliability.

In this evaluation one is obviously looking at: (1) The general and specific traits of a person, measured by rating scales, adjective checklists, personality tests of various traits, and leadership inventories, indicating style preference among other things. (2) Comparison with other employees in comparable jobs, utilizing such things as a paired comparison sort in which each leader is paired with every other leader and one is chosen as the better of the two and assigned as 1; after everyone being evaluated is paired with every other person evaluated, the scores are added and the group is ranked on the basis of the totals. (3) Actual rating of the job performance as carried out by the leader. This could be based on a checklist of performance as presented by Lopez (1968) or the leader self-evaluation form suggested by Danford and Shirley (1970, page 375).

In relation to job performance, the evaluator must consider the importance of the ramifications of the situation in which the leader is performing. So much of leader and participant behavior is situation specific, that it is not enough to know the traits possessed by the person, but one must know the conditions, both physical and social, in which those traits are manifested in behavior. One can possess the competencies to perform in a certain way, but the environment may prohibit effective interaction with others and thus block the achievement of positive outcomes. In addition, one simply behaves differently from one situation to another. Current research design for studies of attitudes, personality, and interactions includes consideration of the situation in which the measures are to be made. Any evaluation of performance should be made in the same way.

Examples of evaluation instruments and source references for this area are presented in Appendix E.

Administration

The administrator is the person responsible for the operation of the department and may be known by a variety of titles, such as superintendent, director, or commissioner of recreation; but whatever the title, he or she must be a managerial specialist. Such a specialist should have three main qualifications: (1) to know the technicalities of the field of recreation, (2) to be able to work through and with people, and (3) to get subordinates to work together (Jucius and Schlender, 1965). The functions of an administrator include planning, organizing, directing, and controlling the work of others (Jucius and Schlender, 1965; Bannon, 1976). *It is within this framework of reference that evaluation of administrator effectiveness should be carried out.* Effectiveness may be defined as "...the extent to which a manager achieves the output requirements of his position" (Reddin, 1971, page 3). Reddin further suggested that a manager show effectiveness and be appraised in terms of that effectiveness in the following areas: (1) working with subordinates, (2) working as a member of a system, (3) innovation on the job, (4) completion of projects associated with the job, (5) meeting the objectives of the position, and (6) working with other department administrators if they exist in the system.

For each of these areas, objectives should be developed that have as a key characteristic–*measurability*. If this is true, the evaluator is in the role of measuring by objectives, which is the preferred approach. Thus, if the goal of administrators is to increase the effectiveness of their subordinates, an objective might be to have subordinates set aims for their performance for the subsequent year and, together with the administrator, agree on each objective, how it is to be met, and how its achievement is to be measured. Administrators then set out the activities through which they can meet this objective such as "Hold monthly meetings with subordinates regarding their objectives," "Be available for 30-minute meetings within three days of request for one from a subordinate," or the like. It is easy enough, then, to measure whether or not these objectives have been met by an administrator. It is important to recognize that managers should be evaluated both in terms of how well they met their own objectives as well as how the objectives of subordinates are met. Whether or not the latter are met probably is related in some way to how well they were managed.

Administrators should be evaluated by the following groups or people:
1. The lay board if they are the top executive in the system.
2. By their immediate superior if (1) is not the case.
3. By their subordinates.
4. By others in a working relationship to the administrator.

The results of the evaluation should yield information regarding strengths and weaknesses of performance and recommendations for improvement of performance.

How can these data be gathered? There are various sources of information and methods of accessing it. Suggested approaches are: (1) personal observation of performance by the superior, (2) group appraisal by several raters who first rate independently and then meet to present a composite rating (may be external), (3) interview with staff, (4) self-evaluation, (5) evidence from performance records of the organization, and (6) administration of various tests and scales.

What tools can be used to collect such data? The techniques of development of observation forms and rating scales were discussed earlier, and quite often a form designed for use with a given, specific organization is really the most valid; the items on it should be based on the objectives specified for performance in the areas observed. The items in the job analysis are often an excellent source of items for such a form. All of the systems utilize some sort of a rating scale, but all are not equally well designed to feed back information useful to the administrator in terms of strengths, weaknesses, and remediation if the ranking were low. Qualitative assessment is often weak in this type of rating. All of these do lend themselves to utilization in group appraisal with room for meeting to reach consensus. PASS (Wolfensberger and Glenn, 1975) is the best noted for this purpose. Checklists, attitude scales, and leadership style inventories may be used in self-appraisal as well as utilizing the same scale to rate oneself as the supervisor or lay board is using. These two ratings should be reviewed in conference. One can also list one's own strengths and weaknesses and check them out against those listed by other evaluators. One could use the semantic differential in this process or a form of an adjective checklist (see Appendix E for sources of such checklists). Departmental records are an obvious source of information because they give concrete information as to what the departmental objectives are to see whether or not goals are being reached. This process can be applied at any given point in time to see what is happening at that point, and can also be used to give a clear picture of what is happening over time. Many of the standardized tests are used more in the hiring of an individual in order to assess style, philosophy, traits, and skills and are not as useful in the later job performance evaluation, unless one of these is a particular problem area and it is necessary to have present data to support the recommendations of an evaluator in a current situation. In any case, the evaluation must illustrate specifics if it is to be useful; for example, if a rating scale includes the item, "The department has a written policy of nondiscrimination," and one is to rate that on a 1 to 4 scale, a rating of 2 does not tell you much about how the administrator implements this policy, nor is it particularly helpful to say that an administrator earns a 3 or "holds formal consultation meetings with staff." What staff, how long, how often, and regarding what issues? If the evaluation is to be meaningful, it must provide opportunity for feedback and recommendation.

Areas and Facilities

It has been suggested that what needs to be evaluated in terms of areas and facilities are their (1) adequacy, (2) safety, (3) availability, (4) attractiveness, (5) appropriateness, (6) multiple use, and (7) accessibility (Shivers, 1967). In any case, one of the important factors is whether the areas and facilities complement and facilitate the program, and whether both of these reflect the interests and needs of the community. In this regard, for example, an institution proudly displayed a weight training room, complete with expensive bicycle ergometers and rowing machines, all in mint condition, with the room never used! Some fitness enthusiast with a hand in the budget decision had ordered the equipment and had the room set up with no regard for the fact that weight training was neither in the planned program of the institution, nor was the weight training room one of the places available to the residents in their nonprogrammed hours. Since that particular facility was not reflective of the program it was to serve, although it could be rated highly for most of the characteristics listed above, it was entirely inappropriate for the situation as it stood.

This type of incident is multiplied many times over, where beautiful buildings are built with little or no consultation with the programmers and turn out to be low functioning in a program sense. Therefore, a key step in evaluation of facilities is to measure whether or not they meet the program needs and whether or not they are adequate to allow program objectives to be met. One of the sources for evaluation of areas and facilities in relation to the program among other categories are the various standards referred to on page 243 (ACA, Berryman, NRPA, PASS), and these reflect the common usage of checklists and rating scales as the main data collection instruments in this area. On the whole, it is suggested that each programmer-evaluator devise her or his own questions in this regard in order to reflect the objectives of individual programs.

The data collected as a result of application of the measuring tools described in this chapter will be of greater value to the evaluator if these data are analyzed in some formal manner and conclusions are reached based on a statistical treatment of scores, ratings, checklist tallies, and so forth. Data of this type are often presented in terms of frequencies and percentages, standard scores such as percentiles, means or averages, relationships or correlations between one factor and another, and by some method of testing associations between scores for one group and the scores of another such as the chi square technique. How to perform some of these statistical manipulations is covered in Chapter Eight. The skilled evaluator is expected to know how to utilize such basic statistical techniques.

SUMMARY

A good programmer must be able to evaluate. In order to do so, the programmer needs to:

1. Be cognizant of and knowledgeable about the terminology used in evaluation.
2. Know the place of evaluation in recreation and its relationship to the planning process.
3. Know the areas that need to be evaluated in terms of the total program.
4. Be able to select the proper approach to the evaluation that is to be made and put it into effect.
5. Be able to analyze and interpret the results.

Evaluation really tells the programmer how well objectives have been met or what the discrepancy is between what was supposed to happen and what actually took place. Evaluation takes place essentially at two key times: (1) when the program is developing, called formative evaluation, and (2) at the conclusion of the program, called summative evaluation. Both of these forms are necessary for good evaluation to exist.

There are many models for evaluation that basically set the stage for establishment of goals or objectives, the conduct of the program, assessment of the outcomes of the program, and revision of the program on the basis of the evaluation results.

Although the program is evaluated as to how it works as a total entity, specific evaluation should be made of the administration, leadership or personnel, the program itself, and areas and facilities.

Evaluation is approached through objectives, standards, and effects on the participant. In the first of these, the evaluator must consider the broad objectives of the program itself as well as the specific behavioral objectives for the participant. There is a link from these program objectives to the participant's goals, since the broad goals are largely interpreted through the behavior of the participant. In order to assess whether or not goals or objectives have been met, they must be set so that they are measurable, and one must know the relative importance of each objective to the total operation in order to determine how to weight it in the total program evaluation. Utilizing standards is perhaps the most common approach to evaluation of any service delivery system in the public domain. This approach allows a program to be evaluated in terms of standard criteria that represent some desirable level of performance, such as so many campers per counselor, so many beds per ward, or so many sit-ups per person. Examples of standards are those of the American Camping Association, the National Recreation and Parks Association's *Self-Study of Public Recreation and Park Agencies,* and Berryman's Standards and Criteria Checklist. Evaluation of effects of program on the participant can be categorized in four areas: (1) psychomotor, (2) psychological, (3) sociological, and (4) educational. Information is gathered by means of attitude scales, questionnaires, observations, and sociograms.

Instruments used to evaluate should be established as reliable (consistent) by means of test-retest, split-halves, or parallel form methods of comparison. A second characteristic of a good test is that it possess validity–it measures what it is supposed to measure–as exemplified by (1) content validity–it measures the factors about which conclusions are to be made, (2) construct validity–the constructs or traits measured in the test are legitimate parts of the whole, (3) concurrent validity–correlation of the test results with some known criterion measure of the same trait, and (4) predictive validity–the ability to perform one thing will predict performance on another.

Questionnaires are one type of data gathering instrument used extensively in recreation and are used to make descriptive assertions about a population, explain something about a population, or explore how a given segment of the population feels about an issue before delving into it too deeply. Data are usually gathered by means of a cross-sectional technique (in point of time) or a longitudinal technique (several points in time).

An *observation* is a planned, systematic procedure designed to note and record specific, selected occurrences through data collected by means of checklists, anecdotal records, rating scales, or the like. The choice of instrument depends on the type of answer or data needed. Observations are done on the basis of time sampling (behavior units at given points in time) or event sampling (observation of a complete behavioral event).

There are three major types of attitude scales in use: (1) summated rating scale (Likert), (2) equal appearing intervals (Thurstone), and (3) cumulative (Guttman). Other suggested ways of measuring attitudes are by means of a semantic differential (Osgood, Suci and Tannenbaum), and the case study approach.

Evaluation of leadership starts with the job analysis of what the person was hired to do; standards of expected performance are set and measured by the supervisor, the participant, and the leader; a record of successfully completed tasks is kept; and the supervisor and leader sit down together to discuss the results and plan for future performance.

Administrators are evaluated on how well they perform the functions of their job, which are to plan, organize, direct, and control the work of others. Administrators are evaluated by (1) the lay board if they are the top executives in the system, (2) by their immediate superior if (1) is not the case, (3) by their subordinates, and (4) by others in a working relationship to the administrator.

Areas and facilities are evaluated in terms of their (1) adequacy, (2) safety, (3) availability, (4) attractiveness, (5) appropriateness, (6) multiple use, and (7) accessibility. It is important in this evaluation that the areas and facilities complement and facilitate a program that reflects the interests and needs of the community.

Data collected as a result of the measuring tools described in this chapter will be of most value to the evaluator if they are analyzed in some formal manner and conclusions reached based on their statistical analysis. The reader is referred to the bibliography of this chapter for sources of methods to use in statistical analysis.

BIBLIOGRAPHY

AAHPERD. (N.D.). Health related physical fitness test manual. Washington, DC: AAHPERD.

AAHPERD. (1976). *AAHPER youth fitness test manual* (revised edition). Washington, DC: AAHPER.

American Camping Association. (1980). *Camp standards with interpretations for the accreditation of organized camps*. Martinsville, IN: American Camping Association.

Anderson, S. B., Ball, S., Murphy, R. T., and Associates. (1975). *Encyclopedia of educational evaluation*. San Francisco, CA: Jossey-Bass, Inc., Publishing.

Backstrom, C. H. and Hursh, G. D. (1963). *Survey research*. Evanston, IL: Northwestern University Press.

Bales, R. F. (1951). *Interaction process analysis: A method for the study of small groups*. Cambridge, MA: Addison-Wesley.

Bannon, J. J. (1976). *Leisure resources: Its comprehensive planning*. Englewood Cliffs, NJ: Prentice-Hall.

Barrow, H. M. and McGee, R. (1979). *A practical approach to measurement in physical education* (3rd edition). Philadelphia, PA: Lea & Febiger.

Baumgartner, T. A. and Jackson, A. S. (1975). *Measurement for evaluation in physical education*. Boston, MA: Houghton Mifflin Co.

Baumgartner, T. A. and Jackson, A. S. (1987). *Measurement for evaluation in physical education and exercise science*. Dubuque, IA: William C. Brown.

Bloom, B. S., Hastings, J. T., and Madaus, G. F. (1971). *Handbook on formative and summative evaluation of student learning*. New York, NY: McGraw-Hill Book Co.

Bultena, G. L. and Klessig, L. L. (Autumn, 1969). Satisfaction in camping: A conceptualization and guide to social research. *Journal of Leisure Research*, I:4:348-354.

Cartwright, C.A. and Cartwright, G.P. (1974). *Developing Observation Skills*. New York, NY: McGraw-Hill Book Co.

Danford, H. G. and Shirley, M. (1970). *Creative leadership in recreation*. Boston, MA: Allyn and Bacon, 1970.

Dillman, D. A. (1978). *Mail and telephone surveys*. New York, NY: John Wiley & Sons.

Farrell, P. (1972). The meaning of recreation experience in music as it is defined by urban adults who determined typal singer profiles through Q-technique. Doctoral dissertation, The Pennsylvania State University, University Park, PA.

Farrell, P. and Lundegren, H. M. (1978). *The process of recreation programming: Theory and technique*. New York, NY: John Wiley & Sons.

Fisher, J. N. (1977). *The effects of participation in a creative dramatics program on the self-concept of mentally retarded children in a six-week day camp*. Master's thesis, The Pennsylvania State University, University Park, PA.

Fowler, F. J., Jr. (1984). *Survey research methods*. Newbury Park, CA: Sage Publications.

Howe, C. Z. (1985). Possibilities for using a qualitative research approach in the sociological study of leisure. *Journal of Leisure Research, 17*: 3, 212-224.

Howe, C. Z. (1988). Using qualitative structural interviews in leisure research: Illustration from one case study. *Journal of Leisure Research, 20*: 4, 305-324.

Jucius, M. J. and Schlender, V. E. (1965). *Elements of managerial action.* Homewood, IL: Richard D. Irwin, Inc.

Kerlinger, F. N. (1973). *Foundations of behavioral research.* New York, NY: Holt, Rinehart and Winston.

Lavrakas, P. J. (1987). *Telephone survey methods.* Newbury Park, CA: Sage Publications. Personnel Association.

Lopez, F. M. (1968). *Evaluating employee performance.* Chicago, IL: Public Personnel Association

McIver, J. P. and Carmines, E. G. (1981). *Unidimensional scaling.* Newbury Park, CA: Sage Publications.

Mercer, D. (1973). The concept of recreational need. *Journal of Leisure Research, 5*: 1:37-50.

Osgood, C. E., Suci, G. J. and Tannenbaum, P. H. (1957). *The measurement of meaning.* Urbana, IL: University of Illinois Press.

Patton, M.Q. (1980). *Qualitative evaluation methods.* Newbury Park, CA: Sage Publications.

Reddin, W. J. (1971). *Effective management by objectives.* New York, NY: McGraw-Hill Book Co.

Robinson, J. P. (Winter 1969). Social change as measured by time budgets. *Journal of Leisure Research, I*: 1:75-77.

Rossi, P. H. and Freeman, H. E. (1989). *Evaluation* (4th edition). Newbury Park, CA: Sage Publications.

Rutman, L. and Mowbray, G. (1983). *Understanding program evaluation.* Newbury Park, CA: Sage Publications.

Sax, G. (1974). *Principles of educational measurement and evaluation.* Belmont, CA: Wadsworth.

Shaw, M. E. and Wright, J. M. (1967). *Scales for the measurement of attitudes.* New York, NY: McGraw-Hill Book Co.

Shivers, J. S. (1967). *Principles and practices of recreational service.* New York, NY: The Macmillan Co.

Sideralis, C. D. (1976). Factors influencing effectiveness in municipal recreation epartments. *Journal of Leisure Research, 8*: 4:289-291.

Staley, E. J. (Winter 1969). Determining neighborhood recreation priorities: An instrument. *Journal of Leisure Research, I*: 1:69-74.

Stephenson, W. S. (1953). *The study of behavior.* Chicago, IL: The University of Chicago Press.

Suchman, E. A. (1967). *Evaluative research.* New York, NY: Russell Sage Foundation.

Survey Research Center. (1976). *Interviewers' manual* (revised edition). Ann Arbor, MI: The University of Michigan.

Theobald, W. F. (1979). *Evaluation of recreation and park programs.* New York: NY: John Wiley & Sons.

Vartiainen, W. (1975). *The determination of leisure education objectives for selected disability groups.* Department of Leisure Services and Studies, Florida State University, Tallahassee, FL.

Vershaw, C. L. (1974). *A study of leisure time interests of teens.* Department of Recreation and Leisure Studies, California State University, Long Beach, CA.

Wolfensberger, W. and Glenn, L. (1975). *Pass 3: A method for the quantitative evaluation of human services.* Toronto, ON: National Institute of Mental Retardation.

Yavorsky, D. K. (1976). *Discrepancy evaluation: A practitioner's guide.* Charlottesville, VA: Evaluation Research Center, The University of Virginia.

CHAPTER EIGHT

TREATMENT OF DATA

Once the data are collected, it is incumbent upon the program evaluator to do something meaningful with them, keeping in mind that the purpose of the analysis is to contribute to answering the evaluation questions and to indicate whether objectives have been met. It is important for the evaluator to see that the proper analysis is made. He or she does not have to conduct this analysis but does have to understand what is being calculated and what it means. Keeping in mind that the evaluator's job is to match the data collected with the statistical technique to use in its analysis, we should ask the questions, "What kinds of analytical techniques are available and what is the purpose of each?" "Under what circumstances would I use each technique?" and "How do I interpret the answers?"

In this chapter we will attempt to answer these questions by (1) presenting a brief introduction to and an overview of terminology used in statistics and approaches used in solving problems and answering questions, and (2) going through the steps used in calculating selected statistics.

OVERVIEW OF APPROACHES TO STATISTICAL ANALYSIS

The choice of approach to the statement of statistical data has its origin in the objectives set, both for the program and for the evaluation, because it is these things that determine whether you are looking for a description, a comparison, a relationship, a difference, or for something else. For example, if evaluators are seeking to find out the characteristics of participants in a program, they would include in the measurement instruments questions regarding demographics, and, using descriptive statistics, would count how many people in the sample are in each category (frequency analysis). If they wanted to know the average age of the group, and how the ages were distributed around the average, they would apply a measure of central tendency (average or mean) or a measure of variability (spread of scores, standard deviation). Finally, if they wanted to know if participation is related to age, they would apply a measure of relationship (correlation).

On the other hand, evaluators may want to know whether groups differ from each other in attitudes toward leisure or toward the services provided by the agency, or may want to know if the program made a difference. If so, the approach might be to compare the means of two groups (t-test) or the means of more than two groups (analysis of variance). These are called parametric tests. If the data do not meet some basic requirements for the use of parametric tests, then nonparametric tests could be used. For example, if you wanted to know the association between frequency of participation of senior citizens and distance from the senior center, you might used a technique called chi square.

In order to understand an expanded discussion of these techniques, it is important that definitions of terminology be addressed so that a common basis is established regarding what the terms used mean.

TERMINOLOGY AND BASIC STATISTICAL CONCEPTS

Measures of Central Tendency

A measure of central tendency is an average value, and there are three measures typically used.

(1) The mean (symbolized as $\bar{x}$) or the arithmetic average, is calculated by dividing the sum of all scores by the number of scores such that:

Figure 8.1 Formula for Calculation of Mean

$$\bar{x} = \frac{\Sigma X}{N}$$

This is probably the most widely used measure of central tendency (see Figure 8.2).

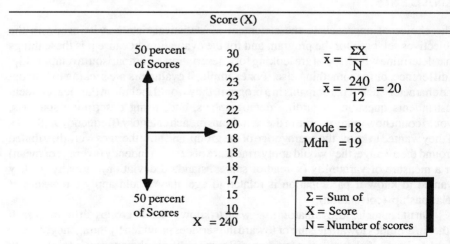

Score (X)		
50 percent of Scores	30	$\bar{x} = \dfrac{\Sigma X}{N}$
	26	
	23	$\bar{x} = \dfrac{240}{12} = 20$
	23	
	22	
	20	Mode = 18
	18	Mdn = 19
	18	
	18	
	17	
50 percent of Scores	15	Σ = Sum of
	10	X = Score
X = 240		N = Number of scores

Figure 8.2 Measures of Central Tendency

(2) The mode is the most frequent or commonly appearing score in the distribution of scores. The mode is also shown in Figure 8.2 for the distribution presented there and is determined by inspection.

(3) The median or 50th percentile (mdn or P_{50}) is that score in a distribution of scores above and below which one half of the frequencies fall. It can be found by arranging the scores in order of size and counting up or down to the midpoint of the scores. If the number of scores is even, the median is halfway between the two middle scores. When the number is odd, the median is the middle score. This is shown in Figure 8.2.

Frequency Distribution

A frequency distribution represents a list of scores from high to low, tallying how many cases occurred at each score (indicated by the symbol f). For example, using the scores from Figure 8.3, the cumulative frequency (cf) indicates how many scores in the distribution lie below the upper limit of that interval. To get cf, start with the lowest score and add the frequencies for each succeeding score. The highest cf value should equal the total N of the scores.

X	Tally	f	cf
30	1	1	12
29			—
28			—
27			—
25			11
24			—
23	11	2	10
22	1	1	8
21			—
20	1	1	7
19			—
18	111	3	6
17	1	1	3
16			—
15	1	1	2
14			—
13			—
12			—
11			—
10	1	1	1

Figure 8.3 Frequency Distribution

Measures of Variability

A measure of variability shows the spread of the scores around the mean (or around the measure of central tendency). There are three measures commonly used: (1) the standard deviation, (2) the range, and (3) the quartile deviation. The first two of these will be described.

The standard deviation (**SD, S**) is the average of the degree to which scores deviate from the mean. The sum of the deviations equals zero. Three **SD** above and below (+ or -) the mean include 99.7 percent of the scores, between +1 and -1 **SD** represent 68 percent of the scores and between +2 and -2 **SD** account for 95 percent of the cases. This concept is best understood in relation to another type of distribution called the normal curve. This is a symmetric curve that has been mathematically defined; it is often referred to as a bell-shaped curve (Figure 8.4).

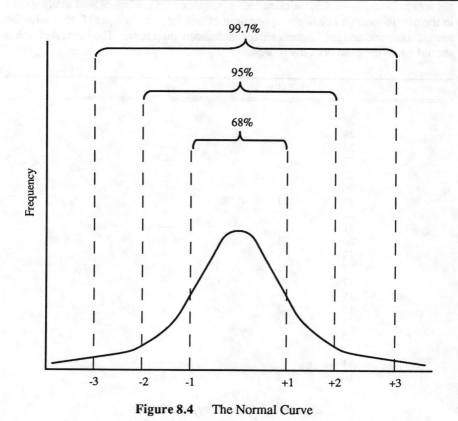

Figure 8.4   The Normal Curve

The normal curve depicts a massing of scores or data at the center with gradually diminishing numbers or percentage of scores toward both extremes; the mean, median, and mode coincide (Barrow and McGee, 1983). The normal curve, for example, is used to show the distribution of attributes thought to be evenly distributed throughout the population, such as IQ scores. A concept associated with the normal curve is that of skewness; if the tail is to the right, it is positively skewed. These concepts are illustrated in Figure 8.5.

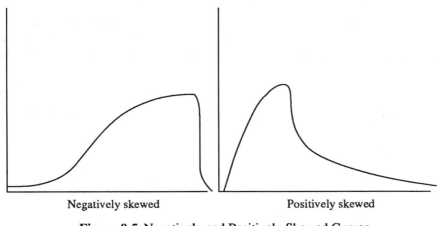

Negatively skewed   Positively skewed

Figure 8.5 Negatively and Positively Skewed Curves

One of the reasons the evaluator looks at a standard-deviation value is to gain some idea of how scores are dispersed around the mean. The closer they cluster around the mean, the smaller the standard deviation and the more it can be concluded that everyone is performing at approximately the same level. On the other hand, if one score is three standard deviations from the mean, it might be considered so unusual an occurrence that it is not used in decisions about the group for which the scores are being analyzed. Uses for **SD** are presented later in this chapter.

One formula used to compute **SD** is:

$$SD = \sqrt{\frac{\Sigma x^2}{N}}$$

Figure 8.6 Formula for Mean Deviation Method for Computing
Standard Deviation

The steps in computing **SD** by this method are as follows:

1. Compute the mean of the distribution.
2. Subtract the mean from each score (X) to get the deviation from the mean (symbolized by x).
3. Square the deviations to get x^2.
4. Add the x^2 column to get sum of x^2 represented as Σx^2.
5. Divide Σx^2 by N. This gives you the variance; since SD is really the square root of the variance, take the square root of this figure.

This method of computing SD is sometimes call the mean deviation method and demonstrates what is happening conceptually. You can see that it is dealing with the sum of the deviations around the mean. Calculations are shown in Figure 8.7 in that case.

Score (X)	Deviation (x)	Deviation Squared (x^2)
30	+10	100
26	+6	36
23	+3	9
23	+3	9
22	+2	4
20	0	0
18	-2	4
18	-2	4
18	-2	4
17	-3	9
15	-5	25
10	-10	100
$\Sigma X = 240$		$\Sigma x^2 = 304$

$$SD = \sqrt{\frac{\Sigma x^2}{N}}$$

$$SD = \sqrt{\frac{304}{12}}$$

$\bar{x} = 20$
$N = 12$

$$SD = \sqrt{25.33}$$

$$SD = 5.03$$

Figure 8.7 Computation for Standard Deviation Using Mean Deviation Method

If you have large values and a large number of cases, use the raw score method, using a calculator or a computer. A formula used is:

$$SD = \sqrt{\frac{\Sigma x^2}{N} - \frac{(\Sigma X)^2}{N^2}}$$

Figure 8.8 Raw Score Formula for Standard Deviation

The data in our earlier example would look as shown in Table 8.1 using this method. The raw-score method is as follows:

Table 8.1 Raw Score Method for Calculating Standard Deviation

Score X	x^2
30	900
26	676
23	529
23	529
22	484
20	400
18	324
18	324
18	324
17	289
15	225
10	100
$\Sigma X = 240$	$\Sigma x^2 = 5104$

$$SD = \sqrt{\frac{\Sigma x^2}{N} - \frac{(\Sigma X)^2}{N^2}}$$

$$SD = \sqrt{\frac{5104}{12} - \frac{(240)^2}{12^2}}$$

$$SD = \sqrt{\frac{5104}{12} - \frac{(57600)}{144}}$$

$$SD = \sqrt{425.33 - 400}$$

$$SD = \sqrt{25.33}$$

$$SD = 5.03$$

The range, a second measure of variability, is the difference between the highest and the lowest score. In our example, that is 30 minus 10, or 20. This gives us some idea of the spread of scores, but it does not give much information. However, it is valuable because the mean and some other measures are not too meaningful if you do not know the range. Suppose the possible range is 1-40 and your group scores 10-30, but a second group scores 18-22; the mean is the same, but the distribution is quite different.

Kinds of Data

It becomes important in deciding what statistical technique to use to know what classification the data fall into, because the choice of one is dependent on the other. The terms we are most concerned with here are discrete and continuous data and data that are said to be parametric or nonparametric.

Continuous
These data are on a continuum, can be expressed in fractions and have the possibility of taking on an unlimited number of intermediate values, such as weight, time, or speed. Values are approximate rather than truly exact because of this. It is important here that the unit of measurement be the same throughout the scale.

Discrete
These data are finite and noncontinuous and are often whole numbers. That is, a scale could have partial units on it, which are not whole numbers, but the value is either that number or it is not; it cannot be in between. An example is the number of bicycles owned by a family, or the number of boys and the number of girls in a house. Here we are really counting things; the number of visitors to a park or the number of people at an exhibit. Discrete measurements are exact, not approximate.

Parametric
Parametric data are those that are assumed to be normally distributed. Some parametric tests of significance are t-tests, the analysis of variance (ANOVA) and correlations (PPMCR).

Nonparametric
Nonparametric data are those about which no assumptions can be made regarding their distribution. Some frequently used nonparametric tests of significance are the Mann-Whitney U test and the Wilcoxon signed-ranks test.

Ways Data Are Scaled

It is also important to the choice of statistical technique to know how data are scaled, that is whether data are nominal, ordinal, interval or ratio.

Nominal
These data may be placed in discrete categories only, and are used to name things. Frequency counts or tabulations of occurrences are used with nominal data. Examples are sex, voice classification, and team affiliation. This is the simplest scale used. Chi-square is used to analyze nominal data.

Ordinal

This is the next level of scale to nominal and includes data that can be ordered in some way from least to most or smallest to biggest, but do not have any given unit of measurement between them. The things being measured stand in some relationship to each other. As with nominal data, you cannot add, subtract, multiply, or divide, but you can rank them and apply techniques that utilize ranking, such as the rank-order correlation, to study relationships, for example, between two groups in terms of their order of finish in a race.

Interval

These scales are based upon numbers, are truly quantitative, and allow arithmetic operations. Equal differences between points on any part of the scale are truly equal; that is, the difference between 8 and 10 degrees is the same as the difference between 28 and 30 degrees. The interval scale has an arbitrary, not true, zero point. That is, although a 0 might be scored on a pop quiz in a water safety instructor course, it does not mean that the examinee knew nothing about water safety, but only that he or she could not answer any questions on that quiz.

Ratio

The ratio scale is much the same as the interval scale, but it has a true zero. If you measure something with a ruler divided into inches, the difference between 8 and 10 inches is the same as between 28 and 30 inches, and we also know that 0 inches is truly no inches. We can also talk about scales in relation to the ratio of one number to another, such as 4 inches is twice as long as 2 inches or 4 is to 2 as 2 is to 1.

Standard Scores

To be able to compare people with others on a known scale, it is beneficial to convert raw scores to some known, standard scale. This also allows comparisons of performance of skills measured in different units, such as inches and seconds. One cannot compare 3 inches to 3 seconds, but one can compare performance by percentile rank in each case, and it sets some standard so that we can qualify the performance, putting it in perspective. One way of doing this is to convert to percentile rank, that point below which some given percentage of the scores fall. For example, if the percentile rank is 90, this means that this score is better than those of 90 percent of the people taking the test. Another standard score commonly used is the z-score.

Percentile Rank

Percentile rank is that point below which some given percentage of the scores fall. For example, if the percentile rank is 90, it means that this score is better than those of 90 percent of the people taking the test.

z-Score

A z-score is a standard score that indicates how many standard deviations above or below the mean a given score is. As stated earlier, they are often used to convert results from several tests having different scoring units so that the scores can be treated in the same way. For example, we cannot average scores in inches with one in seconds, but we can convert each to z-scores and average those. The formula for z is:

$$z = \frac{x - \bar{x}}{s}$$

Figure 8.9 Formula for Calculation of z-Score

How do you use this value? If, for some given score (let us say 30), z were equal to 0.55, then this value can be converted to the percentage of area under the normal curve that is between the mean and that point by using Table F.1 in Appendix F entering the left-hand column at 0.5 and then moving over to the 0.05 (This takes care of both numbers of the 0.55). The value there is 20.88. This means that 20.88 percent of the scores lie between 30 (in this example) and the mean of the distribution from which the score of 30 was taken.

SAMPLING

Before we get into specific statistical tests, we address the question of drawing the sample who will eventually produce the data to be analyzed. "Survey sampling is the process of selecting certain members of a group in such a way that they will represent the total group about which we wish to make generalized statements" (Survey Research Center, 1976, p. 35). The total group is called the population.

Sampling becomes necessary when the total population is not available to the evaluator, or when it would be too expensive or too time-consuming to question the entire group. For example, if the programmer wants to know how satisfied the participants in the two tennis tournaments were with the organization of them, there is no need to draw a sample; the total population is available. On the other hand, if the director of the Metropolitan Opera wants to know if those who attend the opera performances during a season are happy with the programming, it may be more feasible to sample a representative segment of all those who attended the opera because the task of trying to sample everyone who attended might be overwhelming and the result biased. In choosing the sample, whatever the system used, a sufficient number must be chosen to represent the group adequately and each person in the population should have an equal chance of being chosen.

The most familiar term in sampling theory is random sampling and the simplest way to do this may be to put the names of each member of the group to be sampled on a piece of paper, put the papers in a hat, mix them up, and draw them out one at a time without replacement until you have the number of subjects you had set as sufficient. This technique would probably be adequate for program evaluation in small communities, agencies or commercial enterprises when you want, for example, a sample of 25 from a population of 100. (You could also use a table of random numbers.) However, it would be difficult to imagine, for example, putting the names of everyone in the City of Philadelphia on separate pieces of paper in a hat to draw a sample of 10,000 households representing different economic levels, ages, sex, and so on. You could employ a computer to do this, but there are more efficient ways to get to the same end and produce an acceptable sample, particularly if you want subjects in subgroups. Therefore, the evaluator should consider an approach to sampling other than drawing names out of a hat. Some of these ways are: systematic sampling, stratified random sampling, simple random-cluster sampling, paired-selections cluster sampling, and Multiple-matrix sampling. Terms and labels for sampling methods may differ and this list is by no means inclusive of all possible methods. In the types of evaluation studies conducted in most agencies, the simple random sample (discussed already), the systematic sample, the stratified sample and something call a convenience sample may be all that is needed, so we will primarily address these approaches.

In simple random sampling we have indicated that the evaluator selects a sample or subject (n) of the total population (N) and that this choice is made at random. In stratified random sampling you divide the population N into subgroups (also called strata) and then you choose subjects from each subgroup by means of random or systematic sampling to get the sample n. You do this when you want to be sure you have a representation from some given subgroup and you do not want to leave that representation to chance. For example, you might want both males and females in your sample, or adolescents and young adults, or people whose incomes are in different categories. If so, you split the group up into these desired categories–e.g., males and females–and then use one of the methods described earlier (table of random numbers, drawing from a hat) to get a simple random sample from each strata.

Although stratified random sampling requires more effort and a larger initial sample so that the subset of each category will be big enough to satisfy sample-size criteria, it is more precise than simple random sampling.

To take this in another direction, you can also do simple random-cluster sampling, in which you really choose a group (cluster) rather than an individual, and then, having chosen the cluster, conduct simple random sampling of that cluster. For example, if you want a national sample of 1,000 leisure studies educators from colleges and universities across the country, the first thing you have to do is identify the colleges and universities and draw a sample of them (a school represents a cluster); then you are ready to draw the sample of the educators. Another approach would be to draw the schools first and then sample every leisure studies educator in each school. A further example of this would be if you had 30 softball teams and you wanted to try out how well a given uniform held up. By means of simple random-cluster sampling, you could draw, say, five teams, and everyone on the chosen teams would wear the outfit.

In systematic sampling a person is chosen for sampling from a list at planned intervals, such as choosing every tenth name. The assignment may start by picking the first name at random, and then choosing every tenth name from that point. In using this method, one should be sure that the list is set up on a random basis so that some systematic error is not introduced because of the arrangement of the list.

Using a convenience sample means that you use individuals who are convenient for you without regard for randomness. For example, in a shopping mall you might take up a position by the sporting goods store and stop the first person who appears to meet the criteria for which you are looking (e.g., male older than 20 years), and when you finish with one subject, you look for the next. This is an imprecise method and the findings based on it are not generalizable to the larger population. It is not known whether such a sample is even representative of the total population.

Sampling can be quite complex, but it is unlikely that in evaluating the delivery of service of a private, community, or state agency or institution, one will be called upon to use the more complex methods. They are in the domain of evaluation research.

TREATMENT OF DATA

Conducting an evaluation of an agency and its programs yields a large amount of data needing analysis and interpretation. Therefore, one of the responsibilities of the evaluator is to decide at the planning stage of the evaluation not only what data are needed to answer the evaluation questions, but also how they will be treated to provide these answers. In other words, collecting data is not enough–proper analysis is an integral part of a good evaluation plan. This type of planning will also ensure that only meaningful data are collected, because its use will be projected and there will not be a temptation to gather information with little intent to use it to answer your specific questions. A good evaluator resists asking something that "might be interesting to know" without any idea of what it relates to in the primary planning model.

In this section we present some options regarding what to do with data of certain types. We have just finished defining these various types and suggesting that they should be treated differently. For example, parametric and nonparametric data cannot be treated statistically in the same way because there are certain basic assumptions underlying the use of certain statistics that one or the other of these types of data violates. Some of this theory goes beyond that needed by a basic evaluator. Although the details need not be expanded upon, the fact that they exist must be recognized and considered in decision making.

It is assumed that the reader has access to a calculator, or possibly a microcomputer, and so we will not deal with how to group data in order to reduce the task of computation. However, if information on how to group data is needed, consult one of the following references found in the bibliography of this chapter: Barrow and McGee (1983), Gronlund (1981), Runyon and Haber (1980) or Morehouse and Stull (1975).

Since this is not a statistics text, only the broad concepts and some basic selected approaches are presented here. For greater insight into the intricacies of data analysis, the reader is referred to any of the statistical texts appearing in the bibliography at the end of the chapter.

Parametric Statistics

When the data that you have meet the criteria of a normal distribution (described earlier in this chapter), the tests used to determine significance of difference or relationships are called parametric tests. The tests in this category presented here are the independent t-test, the dependent t-test, and the Pearson product-moment correlation technique.

Independent t-test

The t-test is used to test the differences between two means. If two samples are drawn at random from two different populations, the samples are said to be independent. For example, you would use this test if you wanted to demonstrate whether a group of leaders participating in an in-service program performed better on some selected measure of leader performance than a group that did not have the program.

The formulas used to solve for t are:

$$\boxed{\text{Independent}}$$

$$t = \frac{\bar{x}_1 - \bar{x}_2}{s_{\bar{x}_1 - \bar{x}_2}}$$

$$s_{\bar{x}_1 - \bar{x}_2} = \sqrt{\left(\frac{\left[\Sigma x_1^2 - \frac{(\Sigma X_1)^2}{n_1}\right] + \left[\Sigma x_2^2 - \frac{(\Sigma X_2)^2}{n_2}\right]}{(n_1 + n_2) - 2}\right) \cdot \left(\frac{1}{n_1} + \frac{1}{n_2}\right)}$$

Figure 8.10 Formula for Calculation of Independent t

1. This means that we have to start our computations by finding x^2 for variables X_1 and X_2, and finding the means for both groups. Let us use an example based on the data presented in Table 8.2.

2. Solve for $s = \frac{\bar{x}_1 - \bar{x}_2}{s_{\bar{x}_1 - \bar{x}_2}}$. The degrees of freedom for two means are $(n_1 + n_2)$ -2, or in our example $(10 + 10)$ -2, or 18.

Table 8.2 Data for t-Test

Experimental		Control	
X_1	x_1^2	X_2	x_2^2
7	49	8	64
20	400	11	121
24	576	22	484
10	100	20	400
11	121	6	36
18	324	14	196
17	289	11	121
15	225	9	81
5	25	5	25
14	196	5	25
$\Sigma X_1 = 141$	$\Sigma x_1^2 = 2305$	$\Sigma X_2 = 111$	$\Sigma x_2^2 = 1553$
	$\overline{x}_1 = 14.1$		$\overline{x}_2 = 11.1$
	$n_1 = 10$		$n_2 = 10$

3. Solve for t.
4. Look up in the **t** table (Table F.2 in Appendix F) to check for significance.

The degrees of freedom for two means equal $(n_1 + n_2)$ -2, or $(10 + 10)$ -2, or 18 in this sample. The **t** value needed for 18 df at the 0.05 level of significance is 2.101. Since 1.13 does not exceed that value we can conclude that there is no significant difference between the means.

Dependent t-test
When the same group is tested again, or when two groups are matched on some variable so that in each case you could say that the groups are matched, the test used is called a dependent t-test. There are two ways this t can be calculated. In one method, a correlation is computed between the scores for the two test administrations, and that correlation is entered into the formula for **t**. In the other method a correlation is not used and the standard error of the difference is calculated directly. This method is called the direct-difference method and is the one shown in this section.
    The formula is:

$$\boxed{\text{dependent}} \quad t = \frac{\overline{D}}{s_{\overline{D}}}$$

Figure 8.11 Formula for Dependent t (Direct Difference Method)

where $\overline{D}$ = the mean of the difference between the two distributions.

$s_{\overline{D}}$ = standard error of the mean difference

$$s_{\overline{D}} = \sqrt{\frac{\Sigma d^2}{n(n-1)}}$$

$$\Sigma d^2 = \Sigma D^2 - \frac{(\Sigma D)^2}{n}$$

n = number of pairs of scores.

Figure 8.12

The steps in calculation are as follows:

1. List the pairs of scores and obtain the difference between each. Enter the value in the **D** column and compute the algebraic sum of the column. In the sample **D** = 87   (see Table 8.3, p. 287).
2. Square the difference scores and enter the values in the **D²** column; then sum the column. In the example, **D²** = 755.
3. Compute **d²**, using the preceding formula, so that:

$$\Sigma d^2 = \Sigma D^2 - \frac{(\Sigma D)^2}{n}$$

$$\Sigma d^2 = 755 - \frac{(87)^2}{21}$$

$$\Sigma d^2 = 755 - \frac{7569}{21}$$

$$\Sigma d^2 = 755 - 360.42$$

$$\Sigma d^2 = 394.58$$

Figure 8.13

4. Solve for $s_{\bar{D}}$ by dividing the value you derived in Step 3 by n $(n-1)$ and taking the square root of that value, thus:

$$s_{\bar{D}} = \sqrt{\frac{\Sigma d^2}{n(n-1)}}$$

$$s_{\bar{D}} = \sqrt{\frac{394.58}{21(20)}}$$

$$s_{\bar{D}} = \sqrt{\frac{394.58}{420}}$$

$$s_{\bar{D}} = \sqrt{0.93947}$$

$$s_{\bar{D}} = 0.969$$

Figure 8.14

5. Solve the $\bar{D}$ by dividing the sum of Column D by n: Where n = number of subjects
6. Now you have all the data needed to solve for t, so:

$$t = \frac{\bar{D}}{s_{\bar{D}}}$$

$$t = \frac{4.43}{0.969}$$

$$t = 4.57$$

Figure 8.15

7. To see if this value is significant, look it up in Table F.2 in Appendix F. The degrees of freedom for the dependent t-test are $n-1$, or in this case, 20. A t of 1.725 for 20 df at the 0.05 significance level is needed to indicate a statistical difference. Since the computed t of 4.57 is greater than this value, we can say that in our example it indicates a significant increase in situps performed by the group after participation in an aerobic dance program.

If there are more than two groups to be compared, some form of an analysis of variance (ANOVA) should be used. Since this computation is beyond the scope of this book, the procedure is not presented here, but the reader should be aware of it since it is a frequently employed technique. There are a number of computer programs available for computing ANOVA.

Table 8.3 Table of Values for Computation of a Dependent t-Test

Subject	Pre	Post	Difference	D^2
1	12	26	14	196
2	0	4	4	16
3	9	19	10	100
4	18	20	2	4
5	20	28	8	64
6	9	10	1	1
7	2	1	-1	1
8	10	10	0	0
9	12	15	3	9
10	0	4	4	16
11	10	14	4	16
12	23	21	-2	4
13	11	17	6	36
14	17	23	6	36
15	10	15	5	25
16	19	16	-3	9
17	18	19	1	1
18	16	18	2	4
19	23	35	12	144
20	10	13	3	9
21	13	21	8	64
(n = 21)			$\Sigma D = 87$	$\Sigma D^2 = 755$
			(ΣD is +93 −6)	

Pearson product-moment correlation technique

Tests of relationships between variables are used frequently in recreation evaluation research, and form the basis of more complex computations than are presented in this text, such as multiple correlation and regression. The basic parametric test for a linear (straight line) relationship between two normally distributed intervally scaled variables is the Pearson product-moment correlation technique (PPMCR). The meaning of a correlation was discussed earlier in the text under reliability and validity. The reader is reminded that the correlation falls between -1 and +1 and indicates whether there is any relationship between how one person scores on one variable and on another, or on two performances of the same test. If the correlation is high and positive, subjects will have scored in a similar position on each variable. That is, those who are high on one will be high on the other, and those who are low will remain low.

We will use an example here in involving a therapeutic recreation leader who was trying to find out whether a special camping program would have any effect on the emotional control of disturbed adolescents. She also hoped to increase their ability to delay gratification. Before administering the program, it was decided to see if any relationship existed between the two variables. That is, do those with poor emotional control have trouble delaying gratification? If so, the question might become, if I can increase emotional control, will the ability to delay gratification also increase? If the variables are not related, then participating in a program geared to emotional control cannot be expected to affect ability to delay gratification.

The formula for PPMCR is:

$$r = \frac{n\Sigma XY - (\Sigma X)(\Sigma Y)}{\sqrt{\left[n\Sigma X^2 - (\Sigma X)^2\right]\left[n\Sigma Y^2 - (\Sigma Y)^2\right]}}$$

Figure 8.16

where   r = correlation coefficient
         n = number of subjects
         X = one variable
         Y = the other variable
         XY = the product of the paired scores

$$r = \frac{n\Sigma xy - (\Sigma x)(\Sigma y)}{\sqrt{\left[n\Sigma X^2 - (\Sigma X)^2\right]\left[n\Sigma Y^2 - (\Sigma Y)^2\right]}}$$

$$r = \frac{10(2501) - (130)(180)}{\sqrt{\left[10(1842) - (130)^2\right]\left[10(3678)^2\right]}}$$

$$r = \frac{25,010 - 23,400}{\sqrt{\left[18,420 - 16,9000\right]\left[36,780 - 32,400\right]}}$$

$$r = \frac{1610}{\sqrt{\left[(1520)(4380)\right]}}$$

$$r = \frac{1610}{\sqrt{6,657,600}}$$

$$r = 0.624$$

Figure 8.17

The steps in solving for **r** are as follows:

1. List the scores for the two variables in columns X and Y. Sum each column.
2. Multiply each pair (X AND Y) and enter in column XY. Sum this column.
3. Square each X and enter in a column x^2. Sum this column.
4. Square each Y and enter in a column y^2. Sum this column.
   All of these values are shown in Table 8.4, p. 289.
5. At this point you have all the data needed to solve for r. Complete the formula as follows:

6. The final step is to look up the critical table values for **r** found in Table F.3 of Appendix F.

Table 8.4

Values for Computation of Pearson Product-Moment
Correlation Between Emotional Control and Inability to Delay

Ss	Control X	To Delay Y	xy	x^2	y^2
K	18	19	342	324	361
L	18	29	522	324	841
M	13	24	312	169	574
N	13	11	143	169	121
O	16	23	368	256	529
P	11	10	110	121	100
Q	6	16	96	36	256
R	15	16	240	225	256
S	7	8	56	9	64
T	13	24	312	69	576
n=10	$\Sigma X=130$	$\Sigma Y = 180$	$\Sigma xy = 2501$	$\Sigma x^2 = 1842$	$\Sigma y^2 = 3678$

This correlation, although not exceptionally high, does show a relationship between the two variables that is significant. Therefore, one might be able to anticipate that if greater emotional control were gained, a higher level of ability to delay gratification might also be found. (However, the reader is cautioned not to assign a cause-and-effect relationship on the basis of these data.)

Nonparametric Statistics

Nonparametric tests are also known as distribution-free tests because they are not based on the assumptions associated with the normal probability curve discussed earlier in this chapter. Suppose one of the variables to be analyzed is ordinal. Such data are not only not distributed in a normal curve (they are rectangular), but also they are nonquantitative; e.g., lane positions in a swimming meet or the rank order of finishes in the town tennis tournament, or the rank order of contributions made by citizens from census tracts, A, B, C, and D to the Senior Center which is located in tract C. There are also instances where the number of subjects being studied is very small (thus violating the assumption of normal distribution) when nonparametric statistics are used. Nonparametric tests are not as powerful as parametric tests.

The data collected in recreation evaluations quite often fall into the nonparametric category. Examples of these data are attendance data, number of people visiting a park, rank order of preferences of activities, participation frequency in a typical week, ranking worker performances, and the like. Therefore, for recreation professionals, it is important to present statistical techniques that can be used to deal not only with frequencies, but also with comparisons of differences between rankings of two groups or within a single group on a variable and the relationship between two rankings such as job performance and agreement with agency goals. These tests include the chi-square analysis, the Mann-Whitney U-test, the Wilcoxon matched-pairs signed-ranks test, and the Spearman rank-order correlation coefficient. Of these, the chi-square test and the Spearman's Rho are the ones recreation program evaluators are most likely to use.

Chi-Square Test
Chi-square is a statistic used to compare sets of frequency data to indicate whether there is a significant association between or among them. The data treated in this manner must be discrete and are nominal or ordinal in nature. These frequency data are arranged in what is called a contingency table, with one variable in the rows and another in the columns. A common configuration is 2 by 2, but more than two groups can be investigated, leading to other arrangements such as 3 by 2 or 3 by 3.

The chi-square test really tests whether two distributions of data are related. It does this by comparing the observed distribution of each variable with what the expected distributions would be if no relationship existed in the two sets of categories. Let us go through the procedure of computing a chi-square. The procedure for this and succeeding calculations are to (1) state the formula and define new terms, (2) complete all steps in computation up to the final value for a given set of data, (3) indicate how you determine whether the answer indicates that a significant relationship, association, or difference is there, and (4) present some examples of interpretation of the answer.

$$X^2 = \Sigma \left[\frac{(fo - fe)^2}{fe} \right]$$

where X^2 = chi square
         fo = observed frequencies
         fe = expected frequencies
         Σ = sum of

Figure 8.18

The data to be used in this example are shown in Table 8.5 and represents participation levels of senior citizens in center programs in relation to their income before retiring. Participation is broken down into three categories: high, medium, and low. The numbers in the contingency table represent the observed (fo) frequencies of those who were high, medium or low participators in each income category. For example, 26 low participators earned between 0 and 5,999 dollars.

Table 8.5
Contingency Table for Participant Level and Income

Income Categories	Levels of Participation			
	Low	Medium	High	Total
0-5,999	26	33	12	71
6,000-14,999	34	35	51	120
15,000+	5	3	9	17
Total	65	71	72	208

The steps in calculating chi-square are as follows:

1. The first step in computing a X^2 is to establish the expected frequencies (**fe**). This is done individually for each cell in the table by multiplying the marginal totals for each cell and dividing by the total N. For the cell containing 26, the total 71 would be multiplied by 65 and divided by 208. The expected frequency would be 22.19.

$$fe = \frac{(row\ total)(column\ total)}{total\ N}$$

Example for:
Low participation
0 - 5,999 inxome

$$\frac{(71)(65)}{208} = \frac{4615}{208} = 22.19$$

Figure 8.19   Calculation Formula for **fe**

For our example, the calculated expected frequencies for each cell are:

$$\frac{(71)(65)}{208} = \frac{4615}{208} = 22.19$$
$$\frac{(120)(65)}{208} = \frac{7800}{208} = 37.50$$
$$\frac{(17)(65)}{208} = \frac{1105}{208} = 5.31$$
$$\frac{(71)(71)}{208} = \frac{5041}{208} = 24.24$$
$$\frac{(120)(71)}{208} = \frac{8520}{208} = 40.96$$
$$\frac{(17)(71)}{208} = \frac{1207}{208} = 5.80$$
$$\frac{(71)(72)}{208} = \frac{5112}{208} = 24.58$$
$$\frac{(120)(72)}{208} = \frac{8640}{208} = 41.54$$
$$\frac{(17)(72)}{208} = \frac{1224}{208} = 5.88$$

Figure 8.20   Calculation for All Expected Frequencies (fe) Values

2. The next step is to complete the chi-square formula, using the observed frequencies and the expected frequencies computed above. The calculations appear below in Figure 8.21, and a summary of them appears in Table 8.6.

Step 1

$$\frac{(26-22.2)^2}{22.2} + \frac{(33-24.24)^2}{24.24} + \frac{(12-24.58)^2}{24.58} +$$

$$\frac{(34-37.5)^2}{37.5} + \frac{(35-40.96)^2}{40.96} + \frac{(51-41.54)^2}{41.54} +$$

$$\frac{(5-5.31)^2}{5.31} + \frac{(3-5.8)^2}{5.8} + \frac{(9-5.88)^2}{5.88} =$$

Step 2

$$\frac{(3.8)^2}{22.2} + \frac{(8.76)^2}{24.24} + \frac{(-12.58)2}{24.58} + \frac{(-3.5)^2}{37.5} + \frac{(-5.96)^2}{40.96} +$$

$$\frac{(9.46)^2}{41.54} + \frac{(-0.31)^2}{5.31} + \frac{(-2.8)^2}{5.8} + \frac{(3.12)^2}{5.88} =$$

Step 3

$$\frac{14.44}{22.2} + \frac{76.74}{24.24} + \frac{158.26}{24.58} + \frac{12.25}{37.5} + \frac{35.52}{40.96} + \frac{89.49}{41.54} + \frac{.096}{5.31} + \frac{7.84}{5.8} + \frac{9.73}{5.88} =$$

Step 4

$$0.65 + 3.17 + 6.44 + 0.327 + .867 + 2.15 + 0.018 + 1.35 + 1.65 =$$

Step 5

$$X^2 = 16.62$$

Figure 8.21 Total X^2 Calculation

Table 8.6
Chi-Square Summary Table

Observed Frequency (fo)	Expected Frequency (fe)	(fo-fe)	(fo-fe)^2	$\frac{(fo-fe)^2}{fe}$
26	22.19	3.8	14.44	0.65
34	37.50	- 3.5	12.25	0.327
5	5.31	- 0.31	0.096	0.018
33	24.24	8.76	76.74	3.17
35	40.96	- 5.96	35.52	0.867
3	5.80	- 2.8	7.84	1.35
12	24.58	- 12.58	158.26	6.44
51	41.54	9.46	89.49	2.15
9	5.88	3.12	9.73	1.65
			X^2	= 16.62*

*Significant at the 0.01 level of probability (df = 4).

3. In order to know whether this calculated X^2 indicates a significant relationship between participation level and income, we have to use a table of critical values of X^2. Table F.4 is in Appendix F. However, we cannot use the table properly unless we know one more thing and that is what the degrees of freedom (df) for this problem are. Degrees of freedom means "the number of values which are free to vary after we have placed certain restrictions on our data. To illustrate, if we had four numbers on which we placed the restriction that the sum must equal 115, it is clear that three numbers could take on any value (i.e., are free to vary) whereas the fourth would be fixed" (Runyon and Haber, 1971, p. 180). In chi-square the df is computed relative to the number of categories in the rows (r), multiplied by the number of categories in the columns (c); or

$$df = (r-1)(c-1)$$
$$df = (3-1)(3-1)$$
$$df = 2 \text{ times } 2$$
$$df = 4$$

This is true because the marginal total is fixed.

Now we are ready to look up our computed X^2 value (16.62) for df = 4 for the level of confidence that we set. What does this mean? It sets how much we are willing to risk in saying the difference we found is a real one and that we have not said there is a difference where one does not exist. For most of our purposes, we could set this at the 0.05 or the 5 percent level, or, put another way, we are willing to say that only five times in 100 would we say a difference existed when it did not. That is, we might be wrong five times out of 100.

Now let us look in the chi-square table for the value that our computed X^2 has to equal or exceed to show significance at the 0.05 level. Look down the df column and find 4. Moving over from df = 4, we find that the value under the p = 0.05 column is 9.488. Since $X^2 = 16.62$ in our sample and greater than 9.488, we can say that it is significant and indicates a statistical difference between groups. Inspection of the data indicates that the group having the highest percentage of participation had the highest income. We must be cautious with our conclusions, however, since the n in the highest income group is small.

Spearman's Rank Order Correlation
When it is necessary to determine relationships between scores, and the data you have are ordinal or rank-order data, the technique used is Spearman's rank-order correlation method. The formula used in this computation is:

$$r_s = 1 - \frac{6\Sigma D^2}{n(n^2 - 1)}$$

Figure 8.22

What are the steps in this computation? Let us use an example of test-retest self-concept scores of children in a creative dramatics program. These data were collected to give some estimate of the reliability of the test and are shown in Table 8.7.

Table 8.7

A Sample Table of Values for the Spearman's Rank-Order Correlation (r_s)

S	Test	Retest	Rank 1	Rank 2	D	D^2
A	111	111	2	2	0	0
B	114	117	1	1	0	0
C	93	84	6	7	-1	1
D	102	105	4	3	1	1
E	104	96	3	5	-2	4
F	90	93	7	6	1	1
G	99	102	5	4	1	1
H	78	75	8	8	0	0
I	66	63	9	10	-1	1
J	64	64	10	9	1	1
N=10					$\Sigma D = 0$	$\Sigma D^2 = 10$

Data from Fisher 1977.

The steps in the calculation are as follows:

1. Rank the scores on the test for each child for each time it was given.
2. Compute the difference between the ranks, enter it in a column headed D, and note the sign of the difference. **This column must equal 0.**
3. Square the D values and enter them into a column marked D^2.
4. Sum the D^2 column.
5. Solve for r_s using the formula given earlier.

$$rs = 1 - \frac{6\Sigma d^2}{n(n^2 - 1)}$$

Figure 8.23

6. Again, the final step is to match your calculated value for r_s in relation to the critical table values as provided in Table F.5 in Appendix F.

Referring back to the section on reliability, it could be interpreted that an r of 0.94 indicates a high relationship between the scores of the children on the self-concept test on consecutive days, thus indicating that the test demonstrates reliability or that the scores were stable over that period of time.

SUMMARY

Once the data are collected, it is incumbent upon the evaluator to do something meaningful with them, keeping in mind that the purpose of the analysis is to contribute to answering the evaluation questions and to indicate whether objectives have been met. The evaluator should see that the proper analysis is made. He or she does not have to conduct the analysis, but does have to understand what is being calculated and what the results of the calculations mean.

A review of the objectives will indicate whether you are looking for a description, a comparison, a relationship, a difference, or something else. Knowing this will lead you to the proper statistical technique. For example, if you want to know average age, you would compute a mean, but if you want to know if fitness is related to age, you would compute a correlation.

Some terminology and basic statistical concepts are important for the evaluator to learn and be able to apply. Included in these are measures of central tendency (mean, median, and mode); measure of variability (standard deviation, range and quartile deviation); and the normal curve and skewness. The definitions of these terms, how to compute their values, and where they apply, are included in this chapter.

It is necessary in deciding what statistical technique to use to know into what classification the data fall. The terms we are most concerned with here are discrete and continuous data; data that fall into one of the categories of nominal, ordinal, interval, or ratio; and data that are said to be parametric or nonparametric.

To be able to compare people with others on a known scale, it is beneficial to convert raw scores to some known standard scale. Standard scores commonly used are percentile ranks and z-scores.

Also of interest to the evaluator is the procedure used to draw the sample that will produce the data to be analyzed. The most well-known method is random sampling. Other ways addressed are stratified random sampling, simple random-cluster sampling and convenience sampling.

Selected basic approaches to the analysis of various kinds of data are presented. Included under nonparametric statistics is the technique of chi-square analysis. The parametric tests presented to show significance of differences or the relationships between variables are the independent and dependent t-tests and the Pearson product-moment correlation technique. To assist the beginning statistician in making correct choices in the selection of the appropriate statistical tool to use in analysis see Table 8.8, p. 296.

Table 8.8
Choice Table for Appropriate Statistical Tool

Variables		Statistic	Measures
Var$_1$	Var$_2$		
Intervally Scaled	Intervally Scaled	$r = \dfrac{n\Sigma xy - (\Sigma X)(\Sigma Y)}{\sqrt{\left[n\Sigma x^2 - (\Sigma X)^2\right]\left[n\Sigma y^2 - (\Sigma Y)^2\right]}}$	Relationship
Intervally Scaled	Nominally Scaled	$t = \dfrac{\overline{x}_1 - \overline{x}_2}{s_{\overline{x}_1 - \overline{x}_2}}$	Difference
Nominally Scaled	Nominally Scaled	$X^2 = \Sigma \dfrac{(fo - fe)^2}{fe}$	Association
Ordinally Scaled	Ordinally Scaled	$r_s = 1 - \dfrac{6\Sigma D^2}{n(n^2 - 1)}$	Relationship

BIBLIOGRAPHY

Anderson, S. B., Ball, S., Murphy, R. T., and Associates. (1976). *Encyclopedia of educational evaluation.* San Francisco, CA: Jossey-Bass Publisher.

Barrow, H. M. and McGee, R. A. (1979). *A practical approach to measurement in physical education* (3rd ed.). Philadelphia, PA: Lea and Febiger.

Bentkover, J.D., Corvello, V.T. and Mumpower, J.D. (1987). *Benefits assessment: The state of the art.* Dordecht, Holland: Reidel Publishing Co.

Carmines, E.G. and Zeller, R.A. (1979). Reliability and validity. Quantitative applications series in the social sciences (#17), Edited by John L. Sullivan, Newbury Park, CA: Sage Publications.

Ciarlo, J.A. (1981). *Utilizing evaluation: Concepts and measurement techniques.* Volume 6 in the Sage research progress series in evaluation, Newbury Park, CA: Sage Publications.

Farrell, P. and Lundegren, H. M. (1978). *The process of recreation programming: Theory and technique.* New York, NY: John Wiley & Sons.

Fisher, J. N. (1977). The effects of participation in a creative dramatics program on the self-concept of mentally retarded children in a six-week day camp. Master's thesis, the Pennsylvania State University, University Park, PA.

Hendon, W. S. (1981). *Evaluating employee performance.* Chicago, IL: Public Personnel Association

Lopez, F.M. (1986). *Evaluating employee performance.* Chicago, IL: Public Personnel Association.

Posavac, E.J. and Carey, R.G. (1985). *Program evaluation: Methods and case studies, 2nd Ed.* Englewood Cliffs, NJ: Prentice-Hall, Inc.

Rossi, P.H. and Freeman, H.E. (1989). *Evaluation: A systematic approach, 5th Ed.* Newbury Park, CA: Sage Publications.

Thomas, J.R. and Nelson, J.K. (1990). *Research methods in physical activity, 2nd Ed..* Champaign, IL: Human Kinetics Books.

EPILOGUE

You have now seen for yourselves that programming is, as we promised, hard work, that it is a process of planning that takes hours of time before the first participant ever steps into a facility, that it takes good leadership during the activity itself, and that following the activity, it takes time in evaluation and revision to make sure it will be a better program the second time it is offered. Let us take a final look at the programming process. Remember that this process progresses from assessment of participant needs, to writing objectives for program activities to meet these needs, to analysis of activities to satisfy the objectives, to the actual choice of the activity, presentation of the activity (the participant experience), and finally to evaluation of that experience to see whether or not the objectives were met and concurrently whether participant needs were satisfied. If the answer to these questions is an unqualified yes, you may find that you have to start over with assessing needs, or maybe you will find that you have done that well, but really need to look again at your objectives, or perhaps those two steps were fine and where you really need revision is in the activities you chose to meet those needs. In any case, you reenter the activity model wherever your evaluation results say there is need for revision.

Let us take a quick overview of what following these steps in the program process actually means. First, you have to find out something about your prospective participants, such as: (1) their backgrounds, age, income level, how much time they typically participate in leisure activities; (2) their activity interests and participation records; (3) their evaluation of past services from the agency; (4) something about the previous nonparticipant and why he or she did *not* come to programs; and (5) attitudes toward what you are thinking of offering for the program. In other words, you start by taking a survey or doing some interviewing of your constituency to find out where they are on this matter of programming.

Having done that, and with some good idea of what your perspective participants are like and think they want, you are ready to set some objectives for the program that, if they are met, will satisfy both participants' perceived needs and your knowledge of good program offerings. In other words, you set your objectives partially based on your expertise. Your objectives address both the overall broad goals of the program, such an enhancement of the quality of life, and specific objectives for an individual, such as to show positive gain in cardiovascular fitness, to play the saxophone in the community band, or to sing at the Christmas dinner with the recreation program-sponsored madrigal group.

Given such objectives, you now have to decide how to choose activities to meet these objectives. With the objectives cited here, one could establish a run-for-fun group, a band, and a madrigal group. A look at the program structure format says that these three activities come under the activity club format. This format suggests that the agency's role is to provide a facility within the master scheduling plan of the agency and give initial help to the club on formalizing itself, in selecting its leadership, and in establishing the financial base within the agency. The latter is very important and must be done carefully. The club's officers and members will be responsible for the various activities. You must be prepared to give a lot of time initially to help them get started, but after they are established, the leadership is their responsibility.

You must see that they have open tryout procedures and that guidelines for operation have been established. You may want to offer the club some start-up money, but make it clear that these dollars are only seed money and the club must become financially solid within x number of years.

You should plan to stay in touch with the club by meeting with its president, dropping in on its activities occasionally, and attending its special events, such as the madrigal Elizabethan dinner. The last step would be to evaluate the club and its activities. You might want to do some attitude assessment of audience responses to the specific performances, their quality, their program numbers, how much audience participation there was, and how much they cost. You might also want to query the group itself regarding these items and question them in regard to the amount and quality of agency help, the times they had the facility, and financial agreements. In other words, you might use a short attitude scale and brief questionnaire as your evaluation tools and simply calculate the percentages of the group questioned that were favorable in attitude as well as those who were not, and tally the responses to questions regarding satisfaction or dissatisfaction with the working relationship with the agency, and list the club members' suggestions for change. On the basis of these answers you can determine those things that can be changed, setting out to do so in conjunction with the club leaders, and for those things that cannot be changed, meeting with the club leaders to discuss the problems and hoping to help them understand why change is not possible.

Once again, the process is complete. Having selected your citizen program advisory board and administered interest inventories and applied need indices, you have decided on what to offer your clientele, your audience. You chose to program by objectives and to include the cognitive, affective and psychomotor domains while conducting some simple activity analysis to make sure various parts of the program were meeting perceived needs in these domains. The five-format structure model has been adapted to all program area groups and you can be accountable at a moment's notice for your leadership selection and the performance of those selected. You know the costs, scheduling needs, and facilities available, as well as special needs of each program area that you administer. Through in-service training you have taught your staff the technique of conducting formative evaluation. Using as a basis your questionnaires on all participants, your administration of leadership rating scales on each leader, your administration of a Likert-type attitude scale in a random sample of participants each season, as well as your leader's rating of you, you are ready to tie up the last details of your summative evaluation and submit your recommendations for future revisions in programming to your superior.

The program evaluation cube offers an opportunity to plot diversity and balance. A quick view of these data will present you with where your program is and where it might grow.

In the past twenty years the emphasis in the recreation and parks profession has been on acquiring land and developing it. At times this development took place without solid efforts at determining what the constituency's needs for recreation were. The priority was on getting land while the dollars were available. Program considerations were secondary.

In the last decade of the century, the horizon looks dim for a continuance of large land and water-based facility acquisition programs of funding. The time for the creative and innovative program administrator is at hand. It is obvious that, if the quality of life is to be improved, members of our society must learn how to enhance their own leisure life styles. Perhaps this means acquiring self-entertainment skills such as artistic talents, serious hobby interests, and low-cost camping and hiking skills. To believe that society can continue to keep up with the spiraling costs for expensive pleasures is unrealistic. The recreation programmer must assist others with finding those activities that enhance life and fit comfortably into a realistic framework. We think you are ready to do this. You are no longer "in-training"—you have mastered the process.

APPENDIX A

A.1.1
Sample Need Assessment Form

Participant Interest, Needs and Usage Survey

The following is a list of specific recreation activities. We are interested in knowing the levels of participation of the *adults* in your household for each of the activities. Place an "X" in the column labeled "Don't Participate" if you or other adults in your household do not participate in the activity, "Am Interested In Doing" if you do not currently participate, but would be interested in doing, etc.

Activity	Don't Participate	Am Interested In Doing	Periodically Participate	Participate Frequently
Visit friends/ family	_____	_____	_____	_____
Eat or drink out (restaurants)	_____	_____	_____	_____
Read	_____	_____	_____	_____
Swim (in season)	_____	_____	_____	_____
Play softball/ baseball (in season)	_____	_____	_____	_____
Play golf (in season)	_____	_____	_____	_____
Play tennis (in season)	_____	_____	_____	_____
Other sports; specify	_____	_____	_____	_____
_____	_____	_____	_____	_____
_____	_____	_____	_____	_____
Art (painting, drawing, etc.)	_____	_____	_____	_____
Photography	_____	_____	_____	_____
Play musical instrument	_____	_____	_____	_____
Crafts (woodworking, ceramics, needlework, etc.)	_____	_____	_____	_____
Dancing	_____	_____	_____	_____
Drama	_____	_____	_____	_____
"Nature-lovers'" programs	_____	_____	_____	_____

Source: Sample questions from Shippensburg Recreation Commission Questionnaire. Courtesy of Debra Tummins and Sandra Little.

A.1.2

Sample Need Assessment Form

How often do you:	Not At All	Periodically	Frequently
Work on lawn, garden, house	_____	_____	_____
Play games, cards, chess Monopoly, etc.	_____	_____	_____
Go shopping for pleasure	_____	_____	_____
Attend movies	_____	_____	_____
Go bowling	_____	_____	_____
Attend plays/concerts	_____	_____	_____
Attend art shows and museums	_____	_____	_____
Attend sporting events	_____	_____	_____
Attend adult-education classes for enjoyment	_____	_____	_____
Go fishing or hunting	_____	_____	_____
Go picnicking	_____	_____	_____
Go camping	_____	_____	_____
Bicycle for pleasure	_____	_____	_____
Jogging	_____	_____	_____
Skiing	_____	_____	_____
Boating	_____	_____	_____
Driving for pleasure	_____	_____	_____
Other: _____	_____	_____	_____
_____	_____	_____	_____
_____	_____	_____	_____

A.1.3

Sample Need Assessment Form

From the list below, place an "X" in the space beside those programs sponsored by the
Shippensburg Recreation and Park Commission that were participated in by you or other
household members.

_____	Fourth of July fireworks/celebration
_____	Kids' Halloween party
_____	Summer playground
_____	Pet show and peanut scramble at Shippensburg Fair
_____	Summer playground program at Memorial Park, Community Center, Nancy Grayson or James Burd Schools
_____	Tennis instruction at Memorial Park
_____	Shippensburg Tennis Tournament
_____	Swimming instruction at Shippensburg Area Senior High School
_____	Men's Winter Basketball Leagues
_____	Women's Winter Volleyball League
_____	Senior Citizen Center Programs
_____	Student dances
_____	Community Center student activities/game room
_____	Basketball instruction
_____	Karate instruction
_____	Other_____

A.1.4

We would like to know how you feel about your community, its Park and Recreation
System and other related items. Here are a few statements. For each statement, indicate
whether you strongly agree, agree, disagree, strongly disagree, or don't know.

	Strongly Agree	Agree	Strongly Disagree	Disagree	Don't Know
I am satisfied with the Park and Recreation facilities in Shippensburg.	_____	_____	_____	_____	_____
The quality of leadership provided by the Recreation and Park Commission is good.	_____	_____	_____	_____	_____
There are sufficient opportunities for children to use their free time constructively.	_____	_____	_____	_____	_____
The types of activities offered for teens are good.	_____	_____	_____	_____	_____
The quality of activities offered for teens is good.	_____	_____	_____	_____	_____

A.1.4 (Continued)

Sample Need Assessment Form

	Strongly Agree	Agree	Strongly Disagree	Disagree	Don't Know
Additional open space for Park and Recreation facilities is needed.	_____	_____	_____	_____	_____
The quality of maintenance of Borough Park and Recreation facilities is poor.	_____	_____	_____	_____	_____
The quality of maintenance of school or township Park and Recreation facilities is good.	_____	_____	_____	_____	_____
The Recreation and Park Commission should expand its services to meet needs of Shippensburg citizens.	_____	_____	_____	_____	_____
There are not enough activities for children under 12 years old.	_____	_____	_____	_____	_____
There are not enough activities for youth 12-18 years old.	_____	_____	_____	_____	_____
There are not enough activities for adults under 55 years old.	_____	_____	_____	_____	_____
There are not enough activities for adults 55 or over.	_____	_____	_____	_____	_____
Shippensburg has better Park and Recreation facilities than most other communities its size.	_____	_____	_____	_____	_____
I am properly informed about the activities offered by the Recreation and Park Commission.	_____	_____	_____	_____	_____
Public Park and Recreation programs/facilities are well worth their cost.	_____	_____	_____	_____	_____
The Recreation and Park Commission is spending its money wisely.	_____	_____	_____	_____	_____

APPENDIX B

TABLE B.1
Examples of General Instructional Objectives and Behavioral
Terms for the Cognitive Domain of the Taxonomy

Illustrative General Instructional Objectives	Illustrative Behavioral Terms for Stating Specific Learning Outcomes
Knows common terms Knows specific facts Knows methods and procedures Knows basic concepts Knows principles	Defines, describes, identifies, labels, lists, matches, names, outlines, reproduces, selects, states
Understands facts and principles Interprets verbal material Interprets charts and graphs Translates verbal material to mathematical formulas Estimates future consequences implied in data Justifies methods and procedures	Converts, defends, distinguishes estimates, explains, extends, generalizes, gives examples, infers, paraphrases, predicts, rewrites, summarizes
Applies concepts and principles to new situations Applies laws and theories to practical situations Solves mathematical problems Constructs charts and graphs Demonstrates correct usage of a method or procedure	Changes, computes, demonstrates, discovers, manipulates, modifies, operates, predicts, prepares, produces, relates, shows, solves, uses
Recognizes unstated assumptions Recognizes logical fallacies in reasoning Distinguishes between facts and inferences Evaluates the relevancy of data Analyzes the organizational structure of a work (art, music, writing)	Breaks down, diagrams, differentiates, discriminates, distinguishes, identifies, illustrates, infers, outlines, points out, relates, selects, separates, subdivides
Writes a well-organized theme Gives a well-organized speech Writes a creative short story (or poem, or music) Proposes a plan for an experiment Integrates learning from different areas into a plan for solving a problem Formulates a new scheme for classifying objects (or events, or ideas)	Categorizes, combines, compiles, composes, creates, devises, designs, explains, generates, modifies, organizes, plans, rearranges, reconstructs, relates, reorganizes, revises, rewrites, summarizes, tells, writes

TABLE B.1 (Continued)

Judges the logical consistency of written material	Appraises, compares, concludes, contrasts, criticizes, describes, discriminates, explains, justifies, interprets, relates, summarizes, supports
Judges the adequacy with which conclusions are supported by data	
Judges the value of a work (art, music, writing) by use of internal criteria	
Judges the value of a work (art, music, writing) by use of external standards of excellence	

Source: Gronlund, Norman. (1970). *Stating behavioral objectives for classroom instruction.* New York: The Macmillan Company. Used with permission.

TABLE B.2
Examples of General Instructional Objectives and Behavioral
Terms for the Affective Domain of the Taxonomy

Illustrative General Instructional Objectives	Illustrative Behavioral Terms for Stating Specific Learning Outcomes
Listens attentively Shows awareness of the importance of learning Shows sensitivity to human needs and social problems Accepts differences of race and culture Attends closely to the classroom activities	Asks, chooses, describes, follows, gives, holds, identifies, locates, names, points to, selects, sits erect, replies, uses
Completes assigned homework Obeys school rules Participates in class discussion Completes laboratory work Volunteers for special tasks Shows interest in subject Enjoys helping others	Answers, assists, complies, conforms, discusses, greets, helps, labels, performs, practices, presents, reads, recites, reports, selects, tells, writes
Demonstrates belief in the democratic process Appreciates good literature (art or music) Appreciates the role of science (or other subjects) in everyday life Shows concern for the welfare of others Demonstrates problem-solving attitude Demonstrates commitment to social improvement	Completes, describes, differentiates, explains, follows, forms, initiates, invites, joins, justifies, proposes, reads, reports, selects, shares, studies, works
Recognizes the need for balance between freedom and responsibility in a democracy Recognizes the role of systematic planning in solving problems Accepts responsibility for his or her own behavior Understands and accepts his or her own strengths and limitations Formulates a life plan in harmony with his or her abilities, interests, and beliefs	Adheres, alters, arranges, combines, compares, completes, defends, explains, generalizes, identifies, integrates, modifies, orders, organizes, prepares, relates, synthesizes
Displays safety consciousness Demonstrates self-reliance in working independently Practices cooperation in group activities Uses objective approach in problem-solving Demonstrates industry, punctuality and self-discipline Maintains good health habits	Acts, discriminates, displays, influences, listens, modifies, performs, practices, proposes, qualifies, questions, revises, serves, solves, uses, verifies

Source: Gronlund, Norman. (1970). *Stating behavioral objectives for classroom instruction* New York: The Macmillan Company. Used with permission.

TABLE B.3
Examples of General Instructional Objectives and Behavioral
Terms for the Psychomotor Domain of the Taxonomy

Taxonomy Categories	Illustrative General Instructional Objectives	Illustrative Behavioral Terms for Stating Specific Learning Outcomes
(Development of categories in this domain in still underway.)	Writes smoothly and legibly Draws accurate reproduction of a picture (or map, biology specimen, etc.) Sets up laboratory equipment quickly and correctly Types with speed and accuracy Operates a sewing machine skillfully Operates a power saw safely and skillfully Performs skillfully on the violin Performs a dance step correctly Demonstrates correct form in swimming Demonstrates skill in driving an automobile Repairs an electric motor quickly and effectively Creates new ways of performing (creative dance, etc.)	Assembles, builds, calibrates, changes, cleans, composes, connects, constructs, corrects, creates, designs, dismantles, drills, fastens, fixes, follows, grinds, grips, hammers, heats, hooks, identifies, locates, makes, manipulates, mends, mixes, nails, paints, sands, saws, sharpens, sets, sews, sketches, starts, stirs, uses, weighs, wraps

Source: Gronlund, Norman. (1970). *Stating behavioral objectives for classroom instruction.* New York: The Macmillan Company. Used with permission.

APPENDIX C

C.1 Sample 1

Sample Budget Forms

PROGRAM BUDGET
Work Sheets

Date prepared _____
Prepared by _____

_____
Program

Previously Held _____
            New _____

	Inc.	Dec.	N.C.
Fee	____	____	☐
Salary	____	____	☐
Length	____	____	☐
No. of Classes	____	____	☐

Class Limit _____
Length   Hr/wk _____
To be held _____
To begin _____ To end _____

ANTICIPATED REVENUE

1. Registration
   Fee _____ x _____ Participants x _____ No. classes_____
                                          % Registration last year_____
2. Reimbursements
   From _____ in the amount of _____

3. Sales
   Item sold _____ in the amount of _____

4. Contributions
   From whom _____ in the amount of _____

                    TOTAL Projected Revenue _____

C.1 Sample 1 (Continued)

ANTICIPATED EXPENDITURES

1. Personnel
   Salary_____ x No. hr/wk _____ x No. wk _____ x No classes = _____

2. Building, Rental
   Facility(ies) to be used _____
   Regular Rental _____ = _____
   　　　　　$/hr x No. hr x No. wk x No. classes
   Holiday Rental _____ = _____
   　　　　　$/hr x No. hr x No. wk x No. classes
   　　　　　　　　　　　　　　　　　　TOTAL _____

3. Supplies and Materials
   Expendable _____   _____
   　　　　　_____   _____
   　　　　　_____   _____
   　　　　　_____   _____
   Permanent _____   _____
   　　　　　_____   _____
   　　　　　　　　　　　　TOTAL _____ _____

4. Refunds
   _____@ _____ = _____

5. Miscellaneous 　　　　　TOTAL EXPENDITURES _____
   　　　　　　　　　　　　TOTAL REVENUES _____
   　　　　　　　　　　　　ACCOUNT BALANCE _____

C.2 Sample 2

Detail Sheet No._____

Budget Worksheet—Township Department of Parks and Recreation

SUBJECT: *Hayride and Hot Dog Roast for Fun Day Camp Children*	EXPENSE SUMMARY		INCOME SUMMARY	
Year: *1974*	Wages & Sal.	*$50.06*	Progm. Admis.	*$100.00*
Location: *Greenway Park and Boathouse*	Klted. Payroll		Sp. Ev. Admis.	
	Purch. Serv.	*$69.39*	Other	
Dates *October 20, 1982*	Actv. Suppl.			
By:_____	Furn. & Eq.			
	Total	*$119.45*	Total	

EXPENSES

1. Wages and Salaries: *Tractor driver 3 1/2 hrs x $6.24/hr x 1 1/2 overtime = $35.88* $50.06
Guard 3 1/2 Hrs x $4.05/hr = $14.18

2. Related Payroll: _____

3. Purchases Service Detail: _____

4. Activity Supply Detail:
Haywagon = $25.00
Hot Dogs (3 x 5-lb boxes—130 hot dogs) = $26.25 $69.39
Hot Dog Rolls (11 doz) = $10.34
Orange Drink (65 x 1/2 pt. cartons) = $7.80

5. Furniture and Equipment Detail:

6.   _____

7.   _____

INCOMES

1. Program Admissions $1.00/participant $100.00
2. Special Activity Admissions   _____
3. Other   _____
4.   _____

C.3 Sample 3

Subject

Location_____

PT Payroll	_____	
Purch. Serv.	_____	
Actv. Suppl.	_____	
Furn. and Eq.	_____	

Year_____ By_____

Dates_____ Detail Sheet No. _____   Total _____

1. PT PAYROLL DETAIL   _____

2. PURCHASED SERVICE DETAIL   _____

3. ACTIVITY SUPPLY DETAIL   _____

4. FURNITURE AND EQUIPMENT DETAIL   _____

5.   _____

6.   _____

7.   _____

INCOME _____
1. ADMISSIONS: _____
2. CONCERTS/LECTURES: _____
3. OTHER: _____

C.4 Sample 4

SUMMARY SHEET-BUDGET BY ACTIVITY

YEAR _____   By _____

ACTIVITY	Information from Detail Sheets		
	Sheet No.	Total Expense	Total Income

C.4 Sample 4 (Continued)

SUMMARY SHEET-BUDGET BY ACTIVITY (Continued)

YEAR _____   By _____

ACTIVITY	Information from Detail Sheets		
	Sheet No.	Total Expense	Total Income

APPENDIX D

D.1

Sample Volunteer Registration Form

Name   Ms
       Mrs._____   Phone _____
       Mr.

ADDRESS: _____

FAMILY COMPOSITION AT HOME: _____

_____

EDUCATION: **EMPLOYMENT HISTORY**

High School: _____   Title _____   Dates _____

College: _____

SPECIAL QUALIFICATIONS (eg., RN, Life Saving, EMS) _____

MEMBERSHIPS (Mention offices held) _____

VOLUNTEER EXPERIENCE (Mention training taken) _____

INTERESTS AND HOBBIES _____

TIME AVAILABLE and PREFERENCES _____

VOLUNTEER INTERESTS _____ **AGE GROUP PREFERRED** _____

(A list of opportunities should be included here)

Name _____

Training record (events, dates, hours)   Volunteer Assignments (dates)

_____

APPENDIX E

E.1

BIBLIOGRAPHY OF EVALUATION INSTRUMENTS

The following references were prepared from the perspective that they are easily interpretable and valid, but would not require high levels of expertise to utilize.

A.   Attitude Scales and References for Scale Construction

Kenyon Inventory for Determining Attitude Toward Physical Activity. (1976). Available as Document 9983 from ADI Auxiliary Publications Project, Photot duplication Service, Library of Congress, Washington, DC 20540.

The Martinek-Zaichkowsky Self-Concept Scale for Children. (1979). Available from Psychologists and Educators, Inc., Jacksonville, IL 62650.

B.   Personality and Related Constructs

Coopersmith, Stanley. *Coopersmith Self-Esteem Inventories.* Consulting Psychologists Press, Inc., P. O. Box 60070, Palo Alto, CA 94306.

Eysenck Personality Inventory. (1968). Available from Educational and Industrial Testing Service, San Diego, California. See also Eysenck, H. J. The Measurement of Personality. (1976). Baltimore, MD: University Park Press.

Fitts, William H. *Tennessee Self-Concept Scale.* Western Psychological Services, 12031 Wilshire Boulevard, Los Angeles, CA 90025.

Gough, Harrison G. *California Psychological Inventory.* Consulting Psychologists Press, Inc., P. O. Box 60070, Palo Alto, CA 94306.

Gough, Harrison G. and Heilburn, Alfred B., Jr. *The Adjective Check List.* Consulting Psychologists Press, Inc., P. O. Box 60070, Palo Alto, CA 94306.

Jackson, Douglas N. *Personality Research Form.* Western Psychological Services, 12031 Wilshire Boulevard, Los Angeles, CA 90025.

McKechnie, George E. *Environmental Response Inventory.* Consulting Psychologists Press, Inc., P. O. Box 60070, Palo Alto, CA 94306.

McKechnie, George E. *Leisure Activities Blank.* Consulting Psychologists Press Inc., P. O. Box 60070, Palo Alto, CA 94306.

Moor, Rudolf H. and Associates. *The Social Climate Scales.* Consulting Psychologists Press Inc., P. O. Box 60070, Palo Alto, CA 94306.

Piers, Ellen V. and Harris, Dale B. *Piers-Harris Children's Self-Concept Scale.* Western Psychological Service, 12031 Wilshire Boulevard, Los Angeles, CA 90025.

Schutz, Will. *The Firo Scales.* Consulting Psychologists Press Inc., P. O. Box 60070, Palo Alto, CA 94306.

Speilberger, Charles. *State-Trait Anxiety Inventory.* Consulting Psychologists Press Inc., P. O. Box 60070, Palo Alto, CA 94306.

C. Values

Study of Values (3rd ed.). 1970. (Allport, Vernon, Lindzey). Available from Houghton Mifflin Co., Boston, MA.

D. Behavior

Coopersmith Behavior Rating Form. (1975). Available from The Self-Esteem Institute, San Francisco, CA.

E. Leadership

Pfeiffer, J. W. T-P Leadership Questionnaire. (1974). and Jones, J. E. *A hand-book of structured experiences for human relations training,* Volume I. San Diego, CA: University Associates Inc.

Managerial Philosophies Scale. (1975). Available from Teleometrics International, P. O. Drawer 1850, Conroe, TX.

Management Transactions Audit. (1973). Available from Teleometrics International, P. O. Drawer 1850, Conroe, TX.

Blake, R. R. and Moriten, J. S. (1978). *The New Managerial Grid.* Houston, TX: Gulf Publishers.

F. Cognitive, Perceptual and Motor Skills

Ayres, A. Jean. *Sensory Integration and the Child.* Western Psychological Services, 12031 Wilshire Boulevard, Los Angeles, CA 90025.

Ayres, A. Jean. *Southern California Sensory Integration Test.* Western Psychological Services, 12031 Wilshire Boulevard, Los Angeles, CA 90025.

Bender Visual Motor Gestalt Test. Western Psychological Services, 12031 Wilshire Boulevard, Los Angeles, CA 90025.

Bruininks-Oseretsky Test of Motor Proficiency. (1978). Available from American Guidance Service, Inc., Circle Pines, MN.

Callier-Azusa Scale for Deaf-Blind Children. (1974). Selected subtests apply. Available from The Council for Exceptional Children, 1920 Association Drive, Reston, VA.

Cratty, B. J. (1974). *Cratty Six Category Motor Test.* (1967). *Motor Activity and the Education of Retardates* (2nd ed.). Philadelphia, PA: Lea & Febiger.

Frostig, Marianne. *Move-Grow-Learn Program.* Available from Consulting Psychologists Press, Inc., P.O. Box 60070, Palo Alto, CA 94306.

Eighth Mental Measurements Yearbook. (1985). Consulting Psychologists Press, Inc., P.O. Box 60070, Palo Alto, CA 94306.

Orpet, Russell E. *Frostig Movement Skills Test Battery.* (1972). Available from Consulting Psychologists Press, Inc., 577 College Avenue, Palo Alto, CA.

Fredericks, H. D. B., et al. (1980). *The Teaching Research Placement Test (Gross and Fine Motor for Moderately and Severely Retarded Children).* (1980) *The Teaching Research Curriculum for Moderately and Severely Handicapped.* Springfield, IL: Charles C. Thomas.

Werder, J. K. and Kalderan, L. H. (1985). *Assessment in Adapted Physical Education.* Minneapolis, MN: Burgess Publishing Co.

G. Activity Inventories

Mirenda Leisure Interest Finder. (1973). Available from Milwaukee Public Schools, Division of Municipal Recreation and Adult Education, P. O. Drawer 10-K, Milwaukee, WI 53201.

Witt, P. and Ellis, G. (1989). *The Leisure Diagnostic Battery: Researcher's Manual and Sample Forms.* Venture Publishing: State College, PA.

E. 2

Kite Festival Evaluation Form

Interviewer number _____

INTERVIEWER: ALL INSTRUCTIONS ARE IN CAPITAL LETTERS AND ENCLOSED IN A BOX. PLEASE READ TO YOURSELF ALL INSTRUCTIONS. READ THE FOLLOWING QUESTION TO EACH POTENTIAL INTERVIEWEE.

Have you taken part in our interview today to evaluate the Kite Festival?

IF SHE/HE RESPONDS, "YES," GO ON TO SOMEONE ELSE. IF THE RESPONSE IS "NO," CONTINUE WITH THE REMAINDER OF THE INTERVIEW.

Sex: Male _____ Female _____

FOR THE FOLLOWING QUESTION, READ ONLY THOSE RANGES THAT MAY APPLY TO THE RESPONDENT.

---

1. Of the age ranges I am going to read off, in which do you fall?
   - _____ 12 and under
   - _____ 13 - 17
   - _____ 18 - 23
   - _____ 24 - 40
   - _____ 41 - 60
   - _____ Over 60

FOR QUESTION 2: IF THE INTERVIEWEE DOES NOT KNOW THE NAME OF HIS/HER TOWNSHIP, BOROUGH, ETC., ASK FOR THE NAME OF THE NEIGHBORHOOD AND PUT NAME IN "OTHER" SPACE.

---

2. Where do you live?
   - _____ University Park
   - _____ Borough of State College
   - _____ College Township
   - _____ Ferguson Township
   - _____ Halfmoon Township
   - _____ Harris Township
   - _____ Patton Township
   - _____ Other (specify) _____

E. 2 (Continued)

3. How did you find out about this festival?
    _____ Newspaper
    _____ Radio
    _____ Television
    _____ Posters/flyers
    _____ From other person
    _____ At school
    _____ Other (specify) _____

5. Did you come:
    _____ Alone
    _____ With family members
    _____ With friends
    _____ Other (specify) _____

4. Why did you come to the Kite Festival?
    _____ To fly kites and compete in contests
    _____ To fly kites but not to compete
    _____ To watch others
    _____ Was already at the park and happened to find that more was going on
    _____ Other (specify) _____

6. What were the three things you liked best about the Kite Festival?
    _____
    _____
    _____

7. If you had been in charge of the Kite Festival, are there any things you would have done differently? Yes _____ No _____

    If Yes, what are they?
    _____
    _____
    _____

8. Did you enjoy the Kite Festival? Yes _____ No _____

9. If it is offered again next year, will you come? Yes _____ No _____

IF THE INTERVIEWEE IS 12 YEARS OF AGE OR YOUNGER, THE INTERVIEW IS COMPLETED. IF THE INTERVIEWEE IS OLDER THAN 12 YEARS OF AGE, CONTINUE.

E. 2 (Continued)

NOTE: IF THE INTERVIEWEE GIVES ANY OF THE FACTORS BELOW A RATING OF 2 OR 1 BE SURE AND ASK FOR AN EXPLANATION FOR THE RATING AND WRITE-IN THAT EXPLANATION IN THE SPACE PROVIDED TO THE RIGHT OF EACH FACTOR.

READ THE FOLLOWING TO THE INTERVIEWEE:

On a scale of 1 to 5, 1 being very poor and 5 being excellent, rate each factor below as it relates to the Kite Festival. You may use the numbers 1, 2, 3, 4, or 5. Do you understand the instructions and the values?

How would you rate:
_____ Choice of contests _____
_____ Number of contests _____
_____ Judging _____
_____ Display of kite flying by the participants _____
_____ Parking space _____
_____ Publicity prior to the event _____
_____ Organization _____
_____ Helpfulness of personnel _____
_____ Number of personnel _____
_____ Clowns _____
_____ Number of participants _____
_____ Chosen day of the week _____
_____ Time of the day _____
_____ Choice of location _____
_____ Display of kite flying by the demonstrators _____

| READ | Thank you very much for your cooperation.

E. 3

ARTS FESTIVAL SURVEY

PART ONE— PERSONAL DATA

1. Where do you live? _____ 2. Miles from State College?_____

3. Age?_____ 4. Sex?_____ Male_____ Female 5. Occupation? _____

6. Is this visit part of your vacation? ___ Yes ___ No 7. Write an "X" if unemployed___

PART TWO—ACTIVITIES

1. What was your main reason for coming to the Festival this year?_____

_____

2. If you had fun at the Festival this year, write down three words (or short phrases) that describe *why* it was fun.

a. _____ b. _____ c. _____

3. How big a group were you with when you visited the sidewalk art exhibits?
____ alone ____ 1 to 2 people ____ 3 to 4 people ____ 5 or more people

4. My three favorite sidewalk exhibits were: (circle only three)

Ceramics	Jewelry	Paintings	Prints	Wood
Fibers	Leather	Photographs	Stone	_____Other
Glass	Metal	Plants & Flowers	Wax	_____Other

GO ON TO OTHER SIDE FOR QUESTION NO. 5

E. 3 (Continued)

5. Check each activity visited. Then in the rank column, place a one (1) on the line of the event that you liked best: a two (2) on the line next to your second favorite, etc. Only rank those activities which you visited this summer.

Visited Rank Activity

____ ____ Pavilion (Bus Stop, Little Mary Sunshine)

____ ____ Shirt Sleeve Concert, Pa. Orch. and Colliery Band

____ ____ Museum of Art

____ ____ Playhouse (The Golden Apple, That Championship Season)

____ ____ Pennsylvania Ballet

____ ____ Movie Theaters

____ ____ Sidewalk Exhibits

____ ____ Other_____

____ ____ Other_____

Postage
Will be Paid by
Addressee

No
Postage Stamp
Necessary if
Mailed in the
United
States

BUSINESS REPLY CARD
First Class Permit No. 1. State College, Pa., 16801

LEISURE ACTIVITIES CENTER
c/o Recreation and Parks
Dr. P. Farrell
267 Recreation Building
University Park, PA 16802

227-11 (1001)

E.4

APPRAISAL OF EMPLOYEE FOR PROMOTION TO NONSUPERVISORY OR FIRST LEVEL SUPERVISORY POSITION

NAME OF EMPLOYEE	INSTRUCTIONS
PRESENT POSITION AND GRADE	An employee's performance in the present position or assignment will be rated only on those factors that are directly related to the requirements of the position to be filled. The rating factors checked below represent these requirements. Check the gradation that reflects the employee's performance in the identified factors and sign and date the form. Single appraisals must be reviewed by a higher level supervisor.
STATION NAME AND LOCATION	

RATING FACTOR	PERFORMANCE LEVEL					NOT OBSERVED
[ ] 1. Amount of work produced. (Consider the work produced in relation to requirements of the position.).	[ ] A. Work output is far below level expected.	[ ] B. Work output is slightly below level expected.	[ ] C. Work output meets requirements.	[ ] D. Work output exceeds requirements in most cases.	[ ] E. Work output consistently exceeds requirements .	[ ] F.
[ ] 2. Acceptability of work.	[ ] A. Work frequently has to be redone.	[ ] B. Work occasionally must be redone.	[ ] C. Work is generally acceptable.	[ ] D. Work is of high quality.	[ ] E. Work is of exceptional quality.	[ ] F.
[ ] 3. Application to the job and the extent of supervision and direction required.	[ ] A. Work habits are irregular. Requires considerable supervision.	[ ] B. Gets behind schedule unless closely supervised.	[ ] C. Completes work with normal supervision.	[ ] D. Completes work with minimal supervision.	[ ] E. Consistently completes assignments with minimal supervision and seeks out additional assignments.	[ ] F.
[ ] 4. Compliance with rules and approved procedures.	[ ] A. Disregards rules and procedures so frequently that disciplinary action is warranted.	[ ] B. Occasionally fails to comply and must be reminded of responsibilities.	[ ] C. Complies with clearly defined requirements.	[ ] D. Not only complies with requirements but makes an effort to follow their intent.	[ ] E. Follows full intent of rules and procedures and inspires others to do so.	[ ] F.

E. 4 (Continued)

APPRAISAL OF EMPLOYEE FOR PROMOTION TO NONSUPERVISORY OR FIRST LEVEL SUPERVISORY POSITION (Continued)

RATING FACTOR	PERFORMANCE LEVEL					NOT OBSERVED
[ ] 5. Ability to establish and maintain effective work relationships.	[ ] A. Gets along fairly well with some people but often antagonizes and irritates others.	[ ] B. Occasionally creates problems through lack of diplomacy.	[ ] C. Maintains satisfactory work relationships with most people.	[ ] D. Maintains effective work relationships with all types of people.	[ ] E. Is highly effective in dealing with all types of people, even in most difficult situations.	[ ] F.
[ ] 6. Effectiveness of skills and degree of job knowledge.	[ ] A. Exhibits deficiencies in essential job knowledge. Depends largely on others.	[ ] B. Demonstrates minimum knowledge of job. Rarely has ideas for improving work methods.	[ ] C. Has satisfactory knowledge of job. Recognizes need to improve work methods.	[ ] D. Has better than average knowledge of job. Looks for methods to improve work.	[ ] E. Has exceptional knowledge of job. Independently solves many of the problems presented by the job.	[ ] F.
[ ] 7. Acceptance of instructions and directions.	[ ] A. Often resists instructions or directions.	[ ] B. Occasionally resists instructions or directions and supervisory decisions.	[ ] C. Normally accepts and follows supervisory directions.	[ ] D. When requested, readily accepts and performs additional assignments. Works well as a team member.	[ ] E. Recognizes and assumes additional assignments without being told. Strongly supports supervisory authority.	[ ] F.
[ ] 8. Ability to present ideas logically, clearly, and consisely in writing.	[ ] A. Needs assistance to express thoughts and ideas.	[ ] B. Works slowly but eventually is able to express ideas fairly well.	[ ] C. Generally completes acceptable written products in a reasonable period of time.	[ ] D. Written communications reflects more than average ability.	[ ] E. Is able to communicate in writing exceptionally well.	[ ] F.
[ ] 9. Ability to present ideas clearly.	[ ] A. Has some difficulty with individuals and great difficulty with groups.	[ ] B. Expresses ideas fairly well with individuals but has some difficulty with groups.	[ ] C. Normally has little difficulty in presenting ideas orally and getting them across.	[ ] D. Displays more than average ability when talking with both individuals and groups.	[ ] E. Has exceptional ability to put ideas across with both individuals and groups.	[ ] F.

E. 4 (Continued)

APPRAISAL OF EMPLOYEE FOR PROMOTION TO NONSUPERVISORY OR FIRST LEVEL SUPERVISORY POSITION (Continued)

RATING FACTOR	PERFORMANCE LEVEL					NOT OBSERVED
[ ] 10. Ability to adjust to work changes and pressures.	[ ] A. Actively resists new or changing situations.	[ ] B. Has difficulty adjusting to new or changing situations.	[ ] C. Adjusts satisfactorily to new situations.	[ ] D. Adjusts quickly to new or changing situations.	[ ] E. Is extremely flexible in adjusting to sound proposals and inspires other to do the same.	[ ] F.
[ ] 11. Ability to make decisions.	[ ] A. Has difficulty in grasping important aspects of problems and frequently makes unsound decisions.	[ ] B. Struggles with problems for lack of ideas but usually comes up with sound solutions.	[ ] C. Generally is able to identify all essential facts and make sound decisions.	[ ] D. Makes sound decisions consistently and often anticipates developments.	[ ] E. Demonstrates exceptional ability to make sound decisions and anticipates developments.	[ ] F.
[ ] 12. Ability to think along original lines and to find new ways of doing things.	[ ] A. Shows little initiative and originality.	[ ] B. Follows established methods and procedures, but rarely proposes a change.	[ ] C. Questions established methods and procedures when difficulties arise and generally proposes acceptable solutions.	[ ] D. Often questions established methods and procedures and proposes workable solutions.	[ ] E. Is constantly alert to improving ways of doing things, and almost always develops better methods and procedures.	[ ] F.
[ ] 13. Observance of safe work habits.	[ ] A. Disregards safe working practices.	[ ] B. Must occasionally be warned about common hazards.	[ ] C. Works with reasonable care.	[ ] D. Anticipates and eliminates safety hazards.	[ ] E. Sets example and actively promotes safe practices.	[ ] F.
[ ] 14. Maintenance of materials, tools, and equipment.	[ ] A. Frequently does not exercise proper care.	[ ] B. Must be warned occasionally.	[ ] C. Exercises satisfactory care.	[ ] D. Exercises above average care.	[ ] E. Exercises exceptional care and practices good preventive maintenance.	[ ] F.
SIGNATURE AND TITLE OF APPRAISER						DATE
SIGNATURE AND TITLE OF REVIEWER						DATE
SIGNATURE AND TITLE OF EMPLOYEE (if applicable)						DATE

E. 5

NEW CASTLE COUNTY DEPARTMENT OF PARKS AND RECREATION
PART-TIME STAFF EVALUATION

Season(s)   Fall ___   Winter/Spring ___   Summer ___ Other _____
Name: _____   Position: _____
Site: _____   Program: _____
Resign with Notice: Yes ___ No ___   Termination Date: _____

Purpose of Employee Performance Evaluation—The primary purpose of employee evaluation is to inform employees how well they performed their duties and responsibilities and to offer suggestions, assistance and support in aiding employees in improving job performance.

Definition of Rating Categories

(5) - E = **Excellent**-The employee's performance is clearly superior in meeting work requirements. This rating is higher than the rating of "Good" since the employee consistently demonstrates exceptional desire and ability to exceed an acceptable level of performance.

(4) - G = **Good**-The employee's performance regularly meets and often exceeds the work requirements. This rating is higher than the level of "Fair" since the employee demonstrates a desire and ability to exceed an acceptable level of performance.

(3) - F = **Fair**-The employee's performance is reasonably adequate and he regularly meets work requirements. This rating is higher than the level of "Poor" since the employee usually demonstrates his willingness and ability to meet an acceptable level of performance.

(2) - P = **Poor**-The employee's performance often fails to meet work requirements. The employee has demonstrated some willingness or ability to improve performance but only on occasion. This rating indicates performance that is less than satisfactory and requires that steps must be taken to improve performance.

(1) - U = **Unsatisfactory**-The employee's performance clearly and consistently fails to meet work requirements. This rating indicates inadequate and unacceptable performance. The employee shows either an unwillingness or an inability to improve.

(0) - N/A= **Not Applicable**-Does not apply to this employee.

ABILITY	E	G	F	P	U	N/A
1. Makes best use of resources and facilities.	5	4	3	2	1	0
2. Stimulates creativity.	5	4	3	2	1	0
3. Plans and prepares activities well in advance.	5	4	3	2	1	0
4. Provides a balanced program for the age group served.	5	4	3	2	1	0
5. Encourages participation.	5	4	3	2	1	0
6. Knows his limitations and when to ask for help.	5	4	3	2	1	0
7. Gets along well with others: warm and personable.	5	4	3	2	1	0
8. Is sensitive to individual needs for affection, recognition, belonging and security.	5	4	3	2	1	0
9. Senses problems, disagreements, and apathy in individuals.	5	4	3	2	1	0
10. Stresses character building activities in his program (language, behavior, relationship with other participants, etc.).	5	4	3	2	1	0

E. 5 (Continued)

**NEW CASTLE COUNTY DEPARTMENT OF PARKS AND RECREATION
PART-TIME STAFF EVALUATION (Continued)**

CONDUCT	E	G	F	P	U	N/A
1. Wears proper uniform or identification.	5	4	3	2	1	0
2. Presents well-groomed appearance.	5	4	3	2	1	0
3. Accepts suggestions and constructive criticisms graciously.	5	4	3	2	1	0
4. Maintains positive attitude toward job responsibilities.	5	4	3	2	1	0
5. Displays unbiased judgments in maintaining order and discipline.	5	4	3	2	1	0

PERFORMANCE	E	G	F	P	U	N/A
1. Utilizes work time effectively.	5	4	3	2	1	0
2. Willing to accept additional responsibilities.	5	4	3	2	1	0
3. Prepares clear, concise, and accurate records and reports.	5	4	3	2	1	0
4. Meets deadlines as set by supervisor.	5	4	3	2	1	0
5. Adapts to unusual situations.	5	4	3	2	1	0
6. Uses effective means of demonstration.	5	4	3	2	1	0
7. Interprets Department's policies and program to public.	5	4	3	2	1	0
8. Involves parents and volunteers in program activities.	5	4	3	2	1	0
9. Makes follow-up contacts regarding participant accidents and problems.	5	4	3	2	1	0
10. Teaches care of equipment and safety awareness.	5	4	3	2	1	0
11. Takes prompt and decisive action to resolve potentially difficult situations.	5	4	3	2	1	0

ATTENDANCE	E	G	F	P	U	N/A
1. Rate of attendance.	5	4	3	2	1	0
2. Is punctual when reporting to work or whenever definite time schedule is to be met.	5	4	3	2	1	0
3. Reports for work before opening time and stays on the job after work.	5	4	3	2	1	0

ADDITIONAL COMMENTS:

Evaluated By:_____ Date_____

Reviewed By:_____ Date_____

E. 6

APPRAISAL OF EMPLOYEE FOR PROMOTION TO SUPERVISORY POSITION ABOVE FIRST LEVEL

INSTRUCTIONS

An employee's performance in his/her present position or assignment will be rated *only* on those factors that are directly related to the requirements of the position to be filled. The rating factors checked below represent these requirements. Check the gradation that reflects the employee's performance in the identified factors and sign and date the form. Single appraisals must be reviewed by a higher level supervisor. If possible, the employee's signature should be obtained if the appraisal is discussed with him/her.

NAME OF EMPLOYEE

PRESENT POSITION AND GRADE

STATION NAME AND LOCATION

(√)	Rating Factor	Performance Level					
		Fails to Meet Require-ments (A)	Needs some Im-prove-ment (B)	Meets Require-ments (C)	Exceeds Require-ments (D)	Excep-tional Perform-ance (E)	Not Ob-served (F)
	PERSONAL ATTRIBUTES— APPLICABLE TO ALL LEVELS						
	1. Judges employees objectively and fairly on their ability, and situations on the facts and circumstances.						
	2. Maintains poise and adjusts to change, work pressures, or difficult situations without undue stress.						
	3. Considers new ideas, the views of others, or divergent points of view.						
	4. Exhibits confidence, positive attitude, and firmness of position without an indication of inflexibility.						
	GENERALLY APPLICABLE TO LOWER ECHELON SUPERVISORS						
	5. Establishes rapport, gains respect and cooperation, inspires and motivates, and works effectively with subordinates who have a variety of backgrounds and training.						
	6. Accomplishes the quality and quantity of work expected, with adequate controls and within set limits of cost and time.						
	7. Plans and organizes work, defines assignments, and carries out assignments effectively.						
	8. Coordinates the work with that of other related activities.						
	9. Demonstrates skill in developing improvements in work methods or designing new procedures.						

VA FORM SEP 1976 **5-4668**   SUPERSEDES VA FORM 5-.4668, OCT 1971 WHICH WILL NOT BE USED.

E. 6 (Continued)

(√)	Rating Factor (Continued)	Performance Level					
		Fails to Meet Requirements (A)	Needs some Improvement (B)	Meets Requirements (C)	Exceeds Requirements (D)	Exceptional Performance (E)	Not Observed (F)

APPRAISAL OF EMPLOYEE FOR PROMOTION TO SUPERVISORY POSITION ABOVE FIRST LEVEL (Continued)

GENERALLY APPLICABLE TO HIGHER ECHELON SUPERVISORS

10. Establishes rapport, gains respect and cooperation, inspires and motivates, and deals effectively with individuals or groups representing widely divergent backgrounds, interests and points of view.

11. Adjusts work operations to meet emergent or changing requirements within available resources, maintaining proper controls, and with a minimum sacrifice in quantity or quality.

12. Establishes work objectives and standards, programs to accomplish objectives, and assesses progress.

13. Coordinates and integrates the work activities of several organizational segments or several different projects.

14. Absorbs new concepts analyzes organizational and operational problems and issues, and develops timely and economical solutions.

APPLICABLE TO ANY LEVEL BASED ON POSITION REQUIREMENTS

15. Communicates with others effectively both orally and in writing on matters related to the work.

16. Understands and applies the principles required to further management's goals in relation to normal work operations.

17. Represents the activity both within and outside the organization or agency and gains support for the agency's program goals.

18. Accepts responsibility, exercises practical judgments, and makes sound and effective decisions.

19. Gives clear directions to subordinates and delegates authority appropriate to program needs and the capacity of individuals.

E. 6 (Continued)

| APPRAISAL OF EMPLOYEE FOR PROMOTION TO SUPERVISORY POSITION ABOVE FIRST LEVEL (Continued) | | | | | | | |

(√)	Rating Factor (Continued)	Performance Level					
		Fails to Meet Require- ments (A)	Needs some Im- prove- ment (B)	Meets Require- ments (C)	Exceeds Require- ments (D)	Excep- tional Perform- ance (E)	Not Ob- served (F)
	APPLICABLE TO ANY LEVEL BASED ON POSITION REQUIREMENTS (Continued)						
	20. Maintains discipline, supports subordinates, and provides the basis for good morale without loss of effective-ness.						
	21. Resolves work-related employee problems and counsels employees.						
	22. Understands and applies sound personnel management practices which adhere to merit system principles and requirements.						
	23. Instructs, guides, and reviews the work of others, and provides necessary training.						
	24. Makes maximum utilization of employee skills, capabilities, and training.						
	25. Recognizes and appropriately implements public policy objectives in such areas as equal employment opportunity, employment of disabled veterans and other handicapped individuals, etc.						

REMARKS

SIGNATURE AND TITLE OF APPRAISER	DATE
SIGNATURE AND TITLE OF REVIEWER	DATE
SIGNATURE OF EMPLOYEE (*if applicable*)	DATE

APPENDIX F

Table F.1 Area Under the Normal Curve[a]

z	.00	.01	.02	.03	.04	.05	.06	.07	.08	.09
0.0	00.00	00.40	00.80	01.20	01.60	01.99	02.39	02.79	03.19	03.59
0.1	03.98	04.38	04.78	05.17	05.57	05.96	06.36	06.75	07.14	07.53
0.2	07.93	08.32	08.71	09.10	09.48	09.87	10.26	10.64	11.03	11.41
0.3	11.79	12.17	12.55	12.95	13.31	13.68	14.06	14.43	14.80	15.17
0.4	15.54	15.91	16.28	16.64	17.00	17.36	17.72	18.08	18.44	18.79
0.5	19.15	19.50	19.85	20.19	20.54	20.88	21.23	21.57	21.90	22.24
0.6	22.57	22.91	23.24	23.57	23.89	24.22	24.54	24.86	25.17	25.49
0.7	25.80	26.11	26.42	26.73	27.04	27.34	27.64	27.94	28.23	28.52
0.8	28.81	29.10	29.39	29.67	29.95	30.23	30.51	30.78	31.06	31.33
0.9	31.59	31.86	32.12	32.38	32.64	32.90	33.15	33.40	33.65	33.89
1.0	34.13	34.38	34.61	34.85	35.08	35.31	35.54	35.77	35.99	36.21
1.1	36.43	36.65	36.86	37.08	37.29	37.49	37.70	37.90	38.10	38.30
1.2	38.49	38.69	38.88	39.07	39.25	39.44	39.62	39.80	39.97	40.15
1.3	40.32	40.49	40.66	40.82	40.99	41.15	41.31	41.47	41.62	41.77
1.4	41.92	42.07	42.22	42.36	42.51	42.65	42.79	42.92	43.06	43.19
1.5	43.32	43.45	43.57	43.70	43.83	43.94	44.06	44.18	44.29	44.41
1.6	44.52	44.63	44.74	44.84	44.95	45.05	45.15	45.25	45.35	45.45
1.7	45.54	45.64	45.73	45.82	45.91	45.99	46.08	46.16	46.25	46.33
1.8	46.41	46.49	46.56	46.64	46.71	46.78	46.86	46.93	46.99	47.06
1.9	47.13	47.19	47.26	47.32	47.38	47.44	47.50	47.56	47.61	47.67
2.0	47.72	47.78	47.83	47.88	47.93	47.98	48.03	48.08	48.12	48.17
2.1	48.21	48.26	48.30	48.34	48.38	48.42	48.46	48.50	48.54	48.57
2.2	48.61	48.64	48.68	48.71	48.75	48.78	48.81	48.84	48.87	48.90
2.3	48.93	48.98	48.98	49.01	49.04	49.06	49.09	49.11	49.13	49.16
2.4	49.18	49.20	49.22	49.25	49.27	49.29	49.31	49.32	49.34	49.36
2.5	49.38	49.40	49.41	49.43	49.45	49.46	49.48	49.49	49.51	49.52
2.6	49.53	49.55	49.56	49.57	49.59	49.60	49.61	49.62	49.63	49.64
2.7	49.65	49.66	49.67	49.68	49.69	49.70	49.71	49.72	49.73	49.74
2.8	49.74	49.75	49.76	49.77	49.77	49.78	49.79	49.79	49.80	49.81
2.9	49.81	49.82	49.82	49.83	49.84	49.84	49.85	49.85	49.86	49.86
3.0	49.87									
3.5	49.98									
4.0	49.997									
5.0	49.99997									

[a] This table shows the percentage of total area under the normal curve between the mean and ordinate points at any given standard deviation distance from the mean. From: Linquist, E. F. (1942), A first course in statistics. Houghton Mifflin (by permission).

Table F.2 Critical Values of t

df	Level of significance for one-tailed test .05	.01	df	Level of significance for two-tailed test .05	.01
1	6.314	31.821	1	12.706	63.657
2	2.920	6.965	2	4.303	9.925
3	2.353	4.541	3	3.182	5.841
4	2.132	3.747	4	2.776	4.604
5	2.015	3.365	5	2.571	4.032
6	1.943	3.143	6	2.447	3.707
7	1.895	2.998	7	2.365	3.499
8	1.860	2.896	8	2.306	3.355
9	1.833	2.821	9	2.262	3.250
10	1.812	2.764	10	2.228	3.169
11	1.796	2.718	11	2.201	3.106
12	1.782	2.681	12	2.179	3.055
13	1.771	2.650	13	2.160	3.012
14	1.761	2.624	14	2.145	2.977
15	1.753	2.602	15	2.131	2.947
16	1.746	2.583	16	2.120	2.921
17	1.740	2.567	17	2.110	2.898
18	1.734	2.552	18	2.101	2.878
19	1.729	2.539	19	2.093	2.861
20	1.725	2.528	20	2.086	2.845
21	1.721	2.518	21	2.080	2.831
22	1.717	2.508	22	2.074	2.819
23	1.714	2.500	23	2.069	2.807
24	1.711	2.492	24	2.064	2.797
25	1.708	2.485	25	2.060	2.787
26	1.706	2.479	26	2.056	2.779
27	1.703	2.473	27	2.052	2.771
28	1.701	2.467	28	2.048	2.763
29	1.699	2.462	29	2.045	2.756
30	1.697	2.457	30	2.042	2.750
40	1.684	2.423	40	2.021	2.704
60	1.671	2.390	60	2.000	2.660
120	1.658	2.358	120	1.980	2.617
—	1.645	2.326	—	1.960	2.576

Source: Runyon, R.P. and Haber, A. (1972) *Fundamentals of behaviorial statistics.* Reading, MA: Addison-Wesley.
Used with permission of the authors. See text for full table values

Table F.3 Table of Critical Values for r

Degrees of Freedom (n-2)	Probability .05	.01
1	.997	1.000
2	.950	.990
3	.878	.959
4	.811	.917
5	.754	.874
6	.707	.834
7	.666	.798
8	.632	.765
9	.602	.735
10	.576	.708
11	.553	.684
12	.532	.661
13	.514	.641
14	.497	.623
15	.482	.606
16	.468	.590
17	.456	.575
18	.444	.561
19	.433	.549
20	.423	.537
21	.413	.526
22	.404	.515
23	.396	.505
24	.388	.496
25	.381	.487
26	.374	.478
27	.367	.470
28	.361	.463
29	.355	.456
30	.349	.449
35	.325	.418
40	.304	.393
45	.288	.372
50	.273	.354
60	.250	.325
70	.232	.302
80	.217	.283
90	.205	.267
100	.195	.254
125	.174	.228
150	.159	.208
200	.138	.181
300	.113	.148
400	.098	.128
500	.088	.115
1000	.062	.081

Table F.4 Critical Values of Chi-Square

df (r-1)(c-1)	Probability .05	.01
1	3.84	6.64
2	5.99	9.21
3	7.82	11.34
4	9.49	13.28
5	11.07	15.09
6	12.59	16.81
7	14.07	18.48
8	15.51	20.09
9	16.92	21.67
10	18.31	23.21
11	19.68	24.72
12	21.03	26.22
13	22.36	27.69
14	23.68	29.14
15	25.00	30.58
16	26.30	32.00
17	27.59	33.41
18	28.87	34.80
19	30.14	36.19
20	31.41	37.57
21	32.67	38.93
22	33.92	40.29
23	35.17	41.64
24	36.42	42.98
25	37.65	44.31
26	38.88	45.64
27	40.11	46.96
28	41.34	48.28
29	42.56	49.59
30	43.77	50.89

Source: Fisher, R.A. and Yates, F. (1963). *Statistical tables for biological, agricultural, and medical research*, (6th edition). New York: Hafner Publishing Co. Reprinted with permission.

Table F.5 Table of Critical Values for r_s Spearman's Rho

Degrees of Freedom (n-2)	Probability	
	.05	.01
3	1.000	——
4	.886	1.000
5	.750	.893
6	.714	.857
7	.666	.798
8	.632	.765
9	.602	.735
10	.576	.708
11	.553	.684
12	.532	.661
13	.514	.641
14	.497	.623
15	.482	.606
16	.468	.590
17	.456	.575
18	.444	.561
19	.433	.549
20	.423	.537
21	.413	.526
22	.404	.515
23	.396	.505
24	.388	.496
25	.381	.487
26	.374	.478
27	.367	.470
28	.361	.463
29	.355	.456
30	.349	.449
35	.325	.418
40	.304	.393
45	.288	.372
50	.273	.354
60	.250	.325
70	.232	.302
80	.217	.283
90	.205	.267
100	.195	.254

INDEX

C

M

Volunteers, 127
    administrative, 127
    assignment of, 127
    evaluation of orientation of, 130
    examples of, 130-133
    orientation, 129
    operational, 127
    placement of, 129
    recruitment of, 127
    training of, 129

W
Wolfensberger, W., 263
Woodcraft Rangers, 4
Writing instructional objectives, 53

Y
Yavorsky, D.K., 237
Young Men's Christian Association, 3
Young Women's Christian Association, 3

Z
z-scores, 280

OTHER BOOKS FROM VENTURE PUBLISHING

Acquiring Parks and Recreation Facilities through Mandatory Dedication: A Comprehensive Guide, by Ronald A. Kaiser and James D. Mertes

Adventure Education, edited by John C. Miles and Simon Priest

Amenity Resource Valuation: Integrating Economics with Other Disciplines, edited by George L. Peterson, B.L. Driver and Robin Gregory

Behavior Modification in Therapeutic Recreation: An Introductory Learning Manual, by John Dattilo and William D. Murphy

Beyond the Bake Sale—A Fund Raising Handbook for Public Agencies, by Bill Moskin

The Community Tourism Industry Imperative—The Necessity, The Opportunities, Its Potential, by Uel Blank

Doing More With Less in the Delivery of Recreation and Park Services: A Book of Case Studies, by John Crompton

Evaluation of Therapeutic Recreation Through Quality Assurance, edited by Bob Riley

The Evolution of Leisure: Historical and Philosophical Perspectives, by Thomas Goodale and Geoffrey Godbey

The Future of Leisure Services: Thriving on Change, by Geoffrey Godbey

Gifts to Share—A Gifts Catalogue How-To Manual for Public Agencies, by Lori Harder and Bill Moskin

International Directory of Academic Institutions in Leisure, Recreation and Related Fields, edited by Max D'Amours

Leadership and Administration of Outdoor Pursuits, by Phyllis Ford and James Blanchard

The Leisure Diagnostic Battery: Users Manual and Sample Forms, by Peter Witt and Gary Ellis

Leisure Diagnostic Battery Computer Software, by Gary Ellis and Peter Witt

Leisure Education: A Manual of Activities and Resources, by Norma J. Stumbo and Steven R. Thompson

Leisure Education: Program Materials for Persons with Developmental Disabilities, by Kenneth F. Joswiak

Leisure in Your Life: An Exploration, Third Edition, by Geoffrey Godbey

A Leisure of One's Own: A Feminist Perspective on Women's Leisure, by Karla Henderson, M. Deborah Bialeschki, Susan M. Shaw and Valeria J. Freysinger

Outdoor Recreation Management: Theory and Application, Revised and Enlarged, by Alan Jubenville, Ben Twight and Robert H. Becker

Planning Parks for People, by John Hultsman, Richard L. Cottrell and Wendy Hultsman

Playing, Living, Learning: A Worldwide Perspective on Children's Opportunities to Play, by Cor Westland and Jane Knight

Private and Commercial Recreation, edited by Arlin Epperson

Recreation and Leisure: An Introductory Handbook, edited by Alan Graefe and Stan Parker

Recreation and Leisure: Issues in an Era of Change, Third Edition, edited by Thomas Goodale and Peter A. Witt

Recreation Economic Decisions: Comparing Benefits and Costs, by Richard G. Walsh

Risk Management in Therapeutic Recreation: A Component of Quality Assurance, by Judy Voelkl

Schole: A Journal of Leisure Studies and Recreation Education

A Social History of Leisure Since 1600, by Gary Cross

Sports and Recreation for the Disabled—A Resource Manual, by Michael J. Paciorek and Jeffery A. Jones

A Study Guide for National Certification in Therapeutic Recreation, by Gerald O'Morrow and Ron Reynolds

Therapeutic Recreation Protocols for Treatment of Substance Addictions, by Rozanne W. Faulkner

Understanding Leisure and Recreation: Mapping the Past, Charting the Future, edited by Edgar L. Jackson and Thomas L. Burton

Wilderness in America: Personal Perspectives, edited by Daniel L. Dustin

Venture Publishing, Inc
1999 Cato Avenue
State College, PA 16801
814-234-4561